THINKING ABOUT FAITH

SPECULATIVE THEOLOGY

VOLUME ONE: LOVE

Thinking about Faith

Speculative Theology

Volume One: Love
Volume Two: Faith
Volume Three: Hope

Thinking about Faith

Speculative Theology

Volume One: Love

TIBOR HORVATH SJ

McGill-Queen's University Press
Montreal & Kingston · London · Ithaca

ISBN 13: 978-0-7735-3058-4 ISBN 10: 0-7735-3058-4

Legal deposit second quarter 2006
Bibliothèque nationale du Québec

Printed in Canada on acid-free paper that is 100% ancient forest free (100% post-consumer recycled), processed chlorine free

This book has been published with the help of a grant from the Canadian Federation for the Humanities and Social Sciences, through the Aid to Scholarly Publications Programme, using funds provided by the Social Sciences and Humanities Research Council of Canada.

McGill-Queen's University Press acknowledges the support of the Canada Council for the Arts for our publishing program. We also acknowledge the financial support of the Government of Canada through the Book Publishing Industry Development Program (BPIDP) for our publishing activities.

Library and Archives Canada Cataloguing in Publication

Horváth, Tibor, 1927 July 28–
Thinking about faith : speculative theology / Tibor Horvath.

Includes bibliographical references and index.
Contents: v. 1. Love.
ISBN-13: 978-0-7735-3058-4 (v. 1) ISBN-10: 0-7735-3058-4 (v. 1)

1. Sacraments – Catholic Church. 2. Love – Religious aspects – Catholic Church. 3. Faith. 4. Catholic Church – Doctrines. I. Title.

BX1751.3.H67 2006 264'.02 C2005–906942–2

Typeset in 10/12 Baskerville by True to Type

Contents

Preface

Thinking about Faith is a kind of *Summa*, generally a comprehensive work by a scholastic theologian-philosopher. The first volume is under the heading *Love*. It is expected to be followed by a second under the heading *Faith*. The third volume, on Eschatology, *Hope*, has been already published in 1993 by Wilfrid Laurier University Press as *Eternity and Eternal Life: Speculative Theology and Science in Discourse*.

Following the classic *Summa*, each chapter begins with a question "What is?" or "Is it?" in order to encourage the reader to begin to think along with the writer. The answer, given in the context of a recent problematic, is analyzed in terms of its eventual contribution to sacramental theology and to general systematic theology. Since we take a question as our point of departure, we find that question points to language and language to love as the ur-intentionality of being. Speculative theology is an effort to unify theology according to the various acts of human life, such as faith, hope, prudence, temperance, knowing, feeling, and willing, and we define our speculative theology as an effort to unify theology in the reality of love. The love that the early Christians had for Jesus Christ and was the origin of their faith, it will be argued, is a problem-solving and question-raising paradigm in the pre-gospel, pre-Pauline theologies, in the twenty-one Ecumenical Councils, and in the sacraments in their symbolic relation to their historical and systematic foundation, the Eucharist, symbol of love transcendental.

The work is a modest invitation to scholars to attempt in their own field a systematic presentation of a denominational, philosophical, or scientific system under the headings of *Love*, *Faith*, and *Hope*, our unifying triad in the present and common aspiration for the future.

Acknowledgments

My initial acknowledgment is to the authors whose names and works are listed in references and cited in the present book. Through their writings they opened my horizons, contributed to developing my ideas and joined me in my search for truth. Yet the author alone is responsible for the content of his book.

My next acknowledgment goes to my colleagues and students during my thirty-six years of teaching theology at Regis College, a federated college of the University of Toronto, and the Toronto School of Theology. We discussed together many ideas presented in this book. Their reflections, insights, and criticism were always inspirations for me. Without them the present work would be less lively.

My third acknowledgment is due to some of my earlier publishers for permission to include in revised, abbreviated, or expanded form some sections of my earlier writings – "Theology of a New Diaconate," *Revue de l'Université d'Ottawa*, vol 38 (1968); "Marriage: Contract? Covenant? Community? Sacrament of Sacraments? Fallible Symbol of an Infallible Love," *Sacraments* (Villanova University, 1976); *The Sacrificial Interpretation of Jesus' Achievement in the New Testament* (Philosophical Library, 1979); *Christ as Ultimate Reality and Meaning* (URAM Monographs, no. 2, 1994) – and to many scholarly periodicals for having published my essays as gradual steps in my search for the present *Summa*. At this point I acknowledge my indebtedness to *The New Oxford Annotated Bible*, edited by H.G. May and B.M. Metzger (New York: Oxford University Press, 1973). Its style and exactness gave me so much delight. I have to say as much also for *Decrees of the Ecumenical Councils*, edited by Norman P. Tanner, SJ (Georgetown

University Press, 1990). All references to the decrees of the ecumenical councils are taken from Tanner's two volumes.

My special acknowledgment must also go to John P. Perry, SJ, University of Manitoba; J. Patric Mohr, SJ, University of Scranton; Ladislas Örsy, SJ, Georgetown University; and the readers of the Canadian Federation for the Humanities and Social Sciences Aid to Scholarly Publications Programme, as well as to McGill-Queen's University Press, whose critical observations considerably improved the content and the style of my work and to Brother John P. Olney, SJ, for his technical help and hermeneutic talent in using the computer. I am particularly grateful to the Publications Committee of the Canadian Federation for the Humanities and Social Sciences for having found, after thorough examination, my manuscript to be worthy of CFHSS subvention. I am no less indebted to McGill-Queen's University Press for its skilful copy-editing and for publishing my book.

Finally, my thanks and acknowledgments go to all those who read the present book, especially non-Catholic, non-Christian, and secular readers who may be inspired to reflect on and perhaps write a systematic presentation of their own world view, religion, denomination, or philosophical and scientific system under the headings of love, faith, and hope.

THINKING ABOUT FAITH

SPECULATIVE THEOLOGY

VOLUME ONE: LOVE

Amo ut credam et intelligam
Amo ut intelligam et credam.

I love so that I may believe and understand
I love so that I may understand and believe.

1

Overture

1.1 THINKING

Thinking is asking and answering questions. We began to think when we addressed to our mother our first "why." The answer given was followed by a long range of questions, and the process will end with the last "why" at the end of our life.

Asking and answering questions is an intersubjective activity, and thanks to ever-growing communications, we are able to share our questions and answers with others and appropriate as ours the questions our listeners or readers have and the answers they propose. Our age may open a new chapter in the history of ideas and community living. The era of imposing answers on others has been replaced by a sharing of questions with others, so that with the help of our fellow human beings we may be able to answer our questions more correctly.

Thinking is inherent to any faith, and so are questions and answers. Questions may transcend any religion and faith. They may touch upon science, philosophy, history, psychology, sociology, ethics, arts, and so on, and they let us enter into universal human thinking and test our understanding of faith. We all need help from others in thinking and believing, yet no one else can think and believe for us. We all have to think for ourselves in the context we live in. As we meet more and more people, the context of our human existence widens, and the questions we have to answer become more universal and more personal at the same time. But the help others can provide will never provide a ready-made answer for us. Rather, it may be just a presentation of suppositions or earlier contexts which prompted questions and justified answers of other times.

As adult thinkers, we have to ask and answer the questions our lives are raising for us. Who I am? What do I think of others and of the world I live in? What am I doing with my life? What are my dreams and expectations? What do I believe in? Do I love anybody or anything? Do I believe that beyond endless space and time there is a God, an infinite person, who knows and loves me? How do I know that my faith is true? Have I ever thought about what *my idea of ultimate reality and meaning* is, that is, that to which I reduce or relate everything I know and which I do not relate or reduce to anything else I know? Have I ever given an account to myself of what *my final hermeneutic principle* is in light of which I understand whatever I understand and decide? Have I ever pondered what *my supreme value* is, for which I would sacrifice everything and which I would not lose for anything (cf. Horvath, 1978, 1, 3)? And if I have answered these questions for myself, do I have an answer ready if someone asks "why"? Are my ideas of ultimate reality and meaning, my last hermeneutic principle and supreme value, the same today as they were the day before? Does it or do they make sense in the world I live in? Does it or do they do any good for the world I live in? Should they make any difference for the world?

By looking for answers we look for coherence and consistency without excluding the principle of complementarity (Teller, 1969; Teller, Teller, and Talley, 1991, 129–43). The coherence and consistency we are looking for are judged not just by ourselves. They are challenged and measured by the intersubjective court set up by the language we speak and by our universal ability to speak languages. At the same time, our idea or faith itself challenges our coherence and consistency in a search for its own coherence and consistency. My idea, my faith, further summons my own thinking. It does so within the context of my complex experience of knowing, loving, feeling, acting, and sharing. My knowing, loving, feeling, acting, and sharing are interacting while my brain is trying to sort out the manifold data of my experience in the context of the world I know. The context of the world I know functions as light, truth, or value. It is "my ultimate." I accept it as real for me. I value it. It makes sense to me because I formed it in the light of my experiences. This context may be "here and now," like food, sex, play, family, or country. But whenever I know more, it may be something beyond my " here and now." It might become an ideology, a culture, the universe, a world view, faith, God, and so on.

1.2 LANGUAGE

Thinking as raising and answering questions is, then, a search for reference, coherence, and consistency between the world we know and the world we do not yet know. It is an effort to establish a communication between the " friendly home" and the "unknown, foreign world." And this communication takes place in language, through language. It seems that thinking and language are inseparable (Horvath, 1966, v–vii). When we speak, we say something to someone about something (Mohr, 1980, 319–20).We talk because we want to be understood. To be understood is to be accepted, affirmed by others in what we say and what we are. And this process is going on as long as we live and express ourselves by using words, gestures, and smiles or just by being what we are. Even without a single word being spoken, our being speaks for itself and communicates with others. For Thomas Aquinas, the fundamental intentionality of language, as well as of our being, is to be loved (intellect, go to, *hingehen*) and to love (will, give to, *hingeben*) (Horvath, 1966, 77–83). Any action streams out of love (ibid., 96–109). And this is so with any language, scientific language included. It is obvious when scientists during conferences present the result of their research to their colleagues. But it is also true when they test the physical world. Testing is another way of being accepted or affirmed, not by another human being, but by nature itself. Scientists are more ambitious in their search to be loved than their humanist colleagues. They want to be understood not just by another human being but by nature, by the cosmos, by the whole universe. Nature, their non-human partner, replies to the scientist not through words but by setting free a certain amount of energy, causing alterations that can be seen, measured and "understood." The amount of energy released indicates the degree of cooperation with which nature has been engaged with humans. The discovery of the atom bomb was a most "powerful dialogue" between the physical world and human beings. Humans and nature understood each other and affirmed each other (Horvath, 1980a, 157–8). Both the language of human beings and the language of the physical world may kill or exalt, but they are always an expression of reaching out and of being reached. Language is powerful. It can create heaven but hell as well. It is in language that we discover our time as sharing in the time of others and of the whole cosmos (Horvath, 1993, 56–60). Language serves as a key to open the door for us to science, to philosophy, to history, to psychology, to sociology, to ethics, to religion, and to faith, each with its own time and special language. In the interaction of these times and languages, we create our time and our "one word," by which after a lifelong trial, we finally express our identity once for all (Horvath, 1966, v). And our eternity begins.

Language has a human voice. Each human voice has its special melody and music. Our voice is like our DNA, which if we pay more attention to it, we find beautiful. Each human voice is beautiful. If for a while we prescind what the words mean and listen just to the sound by looking at the face of the speaker, we may discover there an "individual," another "I" created by and given to us by love. The human voice is an expression of love which moves created human beings on their way to reach eternity. Thus language is love and love is language because both are "a sort of way-making for our home, eternity" (Horvath, 1993, 59).

1.3 LOVE

The meaning of thinking is the meaning of language, and the meaning of both is to accept and be accepted, to love and be loved. Now, if love is the meaning of language, it has to be rational, just as language is rational. By analytic reflection, we may separate mind and heart, intelligence and affection, love and reason, but in life there is no understanding, no scientific research, no philosophy, no speculative theology without love. The reason why one can specialize in research, study nuclear physics or rhizopod protozo, is that we find in it a kind of love, because reason and love in life are not separable. "Love is in the reason" (*Caritas est in ratione*; Horvath, 1966). To understand a system, an ideology, a school, or any philosopher or scientist, a search for the love involved is not only helpful but indispensable. Departmentalizing knowing and loving is helpful and methodically necessary. But it may be dangerous and not only "uncharitable" but "untrue" if the separation is considered final. If we admit that love is in our reason, we may venture to say that " the reason is in love." The synthesis between the two is a common human task for all of us, moving back and forth from one to the other. Thomas Aquinas found a model for it in the Trinity (ibid., 42–5, 83–6, 109).

Thinking, asking and answering questions, using language – all are a search to be accepted by others and to accept others we live with, the society we are members of, the nature of which we are part, and the universe, all meant to be our home. And so is faith. It transcends all and tells us the same about God, whom "no one has ever seen" (Jn 1, 18) yet who is searching for being accepted by all of us and willing to accept all that exists. Faith tells us that God loves us and the world with the utmost love "that gave his only Son" (Jn 3, 16) for us and for the whole world. The compendium of such a faith is that somehow – notwithstanding that the world in which we live may look like chaos, a playground of human and cosmic dark forces where selfishness and hatred dominate and the fundamental verdict is *vae victis*, woe to the vanquished, to the poor and powerless, but "hail" to the fittest – God, the creator, is love (1 Jn 4, 16), and we have to love one another, our enemies included (Mt 5, 46), as "God loved us" (Jn 15, 12). Augustine just echoed Paul (1 Cor 13, 3) when a "lazy and tepid" baptized person asked him, "Why do you want to make me a Catholic when you are not going to give me anything more and admit that I have already received what you say you have?" and he replied, "Baptism without love profits nothing ... without love you are nothing" (Augustine, 1988, 142).

Love is the meaning of faith as well. It is the meeting ground where God and humans can meet. It is the final hermeneutic principle for faith and reason, the parameter of any answer given to any question proposed by both reason and faith. It is the highest court of coherence and consistency of the language we speak and our universal ability to communicate with another human being and with our environment.

Yet love is not just the end of questions; it is the beginning of new questions. Love is not the end of reason but the meeting place for reason, will, affection, and action, for interaction between God and humans; rather, it marks the beginning of a new life, creating a new kind of problem. Love has no simple definition because it is not a reality besides other realities. It is not an addition to a series of entities. It is not even just the most transcendental property of any being. Rather, it is the innermost reality of any being that makes being able to be, to be one, true, good, and active. It is the substance, the ur-being of any individual, as well as that of any people, the whole biosphere, of micro- and macrocosm, created and uncreated included.

But how can we say that love and not being (Thomas Aquinas), action and process (process philosophy), spirit (Hegel), matter (materialism), oneness (pantheism), the dualism of good and evil (Manichaeism), superman (Nietzsche), or nirvana (Buddhism) is the innermost reality of any being? If we take questions as our point of departure, we may find that they point to language and language to love as to the ur-intentionality of being. Language is the leading light, the *leitfaden*, the *fil conducteur*, to discover love as the mystery of being. The revelation of the Triune God by the Word revealing the Father as love in communion with the Holy Spirit does authenticate and confirm language and, in and through language, love as the innermost reality of the uncreated being as well. Being the meeting place for both reason and faith, love will be always a problem-solving as well as a problem-creating paradigm. All problems will be the problems of love, and all solutions have to be the solutions of love. But is it so?

There are many explicit and implicit questions that will be raised and answered in our speculative theology of "thinking about faith." But the fundamental question, the question of questions, is, Is love indeed the final problem-solving paradigm in Christian theology? Can we really say that Jesus Christ, his life and doctrine as well as the life and the doctrine of the Church and Christian people, is both the solution to all theological problems and contributor to the universal human question of what is love? To answer this question of questions is the task of the present work. We just hope that we will succeed in solving as well as raising the problem of how love is the meeting ground where God and humans as well as faith and reason, theology and science, systematic and "spiritual theology," Christians and non-Christians, believers and non-believers, in brief, the human mind and heart can meet as one in searching for the same.

The faith about which we are asking questions will be my Roman Catholic faith, but the questions we have are those that we as human beings, members of our family, our city, our company, our country, and the whole human race, Catholics, non-Catholics, Christians, non-Christians, believers, non-believers, may have. Faith as well as our intelligence has a question-raising power, and all those who ask questions and make contributions to answer them are our friends. Love involves faith and hope. So asking questions about the Roman Catholic faith involves questions about love, faith, and hope, a common aspiration of any human being.

We hope that the task we propose, the method we try to employ, and the way we try to proceed within Christian faith are a task, a method, and a way to proceed in speculating about any religion, any philosophy, any system. What we do here in the present work we hope will be done one day in other denominations, religions, and philosophical or scientific systems, always under the heading of love, faith, and hope. We all have the same common task, and all should be one in searching for love, which brings about faith and hope. We all are human beings, and love is our "innermost reality," our *ur*-being. This love is the subject matter of speculative theology.

1.4 SPECULATIVE THEOLOGY

Corresponding to the universal and complex nature of faith and to its different manifestations theology as understanding of faith may be scriptural (a written account of the early foundational faith), historical (faith developing in time), pastoral (self-communication of faith), dogmatic (the core tenets of faith), systematic (unifying all theological understandings from the point of view of one subject, such as Christ, the Church, or God, or concept, such as truth, participation; cf. Thomas Aquinas), or speculative.

Speculative theology is an effort to unify theology with all its branches and subjects, the various acts of faith, hope, prudence, justice, fortitude, temperance, and, in general, any act of knowing, feeling, willing, and doing in their relation to the act of love. According to the principal act that is fundamental to their creeds and rites, religions and organizations may be classified as religions of hope (eschatology), knowledge (gnosis), feeling (sentimentalism), justice (legalism), prudence (Aristotelian ethic), fortitude (asceticism), temperance (stoicism), faith (fideism), willing (voluntarism), or love. We argue that for Christianity, the love for Christ, God, and man, the love that includes all human beings (cf. Mt 25, 40.45), is the foundational and principal act which determines any act of faith, hope, prudence, justice, temperance, and any human act. It is the act of love that includes not only the acts of prudence, justice, fortitude, and temperance but also the act of faith and hope, any act of knowing, feeling, and willing. All these acts are the acts of love (cf. 1 Cor 13, 3). In the light of the Pauline axiom Thomas Aquinas could argue that love, as the "form," is the actualizing principle of all virtues. It is the foundation, the root that prompts, supports, and foments acts of hope, prudence, fortitude, willing, and feeling and prods the mind to know more (*Summa theol.*, 2, 2, q 23, a 8; 1948, 132).

In language, nouns and verbs, things and actions, mutually determine each other. So the two basic words are "is" and "doing." "Is" is doing, and "doing" is "somebody doing something." Static and dynamic world views, therefore, are complementary. Love includes all of them, because it always means that someone loves somebody else. It is for this reason that in faith the verb and action have priority (cf. Mt 7, 21–23; Rom 2, 13; Jas 1, 22), and Thomas Aquinas rightly interpreted being as an "act" and not a noun, not an idea or concept. Now, the theology that gives pre-eminence to the verb "love" we call speculative theology. The verb "speculate" includes question and action, both leading to the act of love as problem-solving and question-raising paradigm. As a challenge, speculative theology examines the method other disciplines raise questions and solve problems in order to theorize for their own disciplines. The axioms "I love so that I may believe and understand" and "I love so that I may understand and believe" make our description of speculative theology complete.

For our departure, we assume that our faith takes its origin in the love the first Christians had for Jesus Christ. They found Jesus lovable because he made God *available* and at the same time *hidden in himself* as a human being. This love prompted them to follow him, listen to him, write scripture, and celebrate him in the liturgy of the sacraments, which are the celebration of God's love for the faithful, every human being, and the world. Thus love, God's love, is the heading for the first volume of our speculative theology. As much as this love for Jesus Christ tries to be coherent and consistent with the rationality of human language, it formulates and expresses itself in dogmas, decrees, and ways of Christian life. So the heading for the second volume of our speculative theology will be "Faith" under the aegis of *Caritas est in ratione,* Love is in the reason. And finally, "Hope" is the title of the third volume, on Eschatology. Only those who love and have faith can hope.

1.5 A TEST CASE FOR AN ECUMENICAL PRESENTATION OF A CHURCH

In this volume we will think not about the subject matter of natural and human sciences but about faith, the subject matter of theology as an academic discipline. Faith is the subject matter of theology, asking questions about God, human beings, the world and eternal life, the Holy Scriptures, hierarchy, liturgy, devotion, worship, adoration, doing good, and acts such as loving, believing, and hoping. The acts of loving, believing, and hoping, as the "transcendentals" of believing and human existence, make up the three volumes of our *Summa.* As transcendentals, they are expected to serve as a test case for an ecumenical presentation of any church, denomination, or system. As a first test case, we take the Roman Catholic Church, not so much how it is but how it should be, and we ask Muslim, Jewish, Hindu, Buddhist, Orthodox, and Protestant believers and non-believers as well to help Catholics to become better Catholics, so that they may help Muslims to become better Muslims, Jews better Jews, Orthodox better Orthodox, and Protestants better Protestants and non-believer to love more, because being is to love.

In brief, union is God's making and not a human making. No one can force his or her own validation. Validation is a gift we can donate to each other in love. Fear of not receiving validation prompts wars.

Step by step, we moved from faith to love, which is the first volume of our *Summa*:

- by thinking about faith, we asked our first question, "What is faith?"
- reflecting on "What is faith?" we next asked " What is asking a question?"
- in asking, "What is asking a question?" we found that we use language;
- by asking, "What is language?" we concluded that language is a search for love, being accepted by others and being able to accept others as others;
- a reflection on love as the origin of Christian faith raised the question "What did the early Christians love?"
- as a further search for what the early Christians loved, we discovered that their love for Christ was the raison d'être of their Scripture, the councils, and the sacraments;
- when we asked what this love for Christ was, it became obvious that it

was a revelation that God loves human beings, friends and enemies alike;
- a concluding step was that Christians, loving Christ, are to love all human beings as individual persons, be they friend or enemy

Thus the title of the first volume is "Love." But the title of the trilogy is *Thinking about Faith.* Faith indicates that thinking in this book is not about philosophy or science, but about faith. Catholic faith is taken as a concrete example, inviting people to think about their own faith and ask questions about the same.

There are two ways of presenting a topic. One is to make a proposition and then argue that the proposition is true. The other is to ask questions, such as "What is the origin of faith?" "What is the raison d'être of the councils and the sacraments?" Then readers are invited to think and critically evaluate the answer the writer presents. It is the second way we will follow. We will introduce the topic of the various chapters in the form of a question. The questions are expected to put the mind of the reader in motion to discover the answer. Any statement was and still is the outcome of a certain discovery prompted by a challenging question. Faith too is and always will be a question to us and to the world. We should share our questions and all human questions in order to discover the real depth of all human questions and to search for answers in solidarity with all other human beings.

If we agree that no "holy" scripture can or should teach hatred, we hold that each faith (or system) is intrinsically ecumenical. This kind of ecumenical intentionality is to be developed from inside out. Ecumenism is therefore more than a dialogue. It is a fundamental human love for every human being and so a task for every human being. Not only Christians or Catholics love, believe, and hope. Every human being loves somebody or something, believes and hopes for something or someone. Is this not the real unity and the real difference in the authentic pluralism of the human race, unlike an abstract concept of a syncretist religion existing only in theological papers? Faith, love, and hope are not just religious categories; they are common human aspirations.

After Michael Polanyi's book *Personal Knowledge* (1958), more and more scientists have discovered subjective elements in their own thinking. Professor John C. Polkinghorne is one of them. In his books *Scientists as Theologians* (1996) and *Faith, Science, and Understanding* (2000), he listed scientists "who find in theology material for understanding" (1996, 19) and recognize that "the dialogue between science and theology that has been continuing for centuries ... is now world-wide and that it is increasingly drawing in all the great world faith traditions. Exciting times lie ahead for the international exploration of the relationship between the truth of science and the truth of God." (2000).

This is our overture, an "orchestral introduction" to our *Thinking about Faith.* Like any overture to an opera, it has presented the theme, the melody that is expected to resound throughout the work. It has disclosed love not only as a moving force for raising questions and a light for finding answers and the meaning of all that faith and theology have to say but also as a critical standard for evaluating any other problem-solving paradigm.

2

What Is the Origin of the Christian Faith?

2.1 INTRODUCTION

The first question about faith is Where does it come from? What is its origin? There are quite a few answers to this question. A sociologist would say that it comes from the society we live in. If we were born in a religious Shinto Japanese family, Shinto would probably be our religion and faith. So one's Catholic faith comes from the Catholic family one was born in. Yes, but not necessarily and not always. A psychologist would say, rather, that it comes from our special predisposition, our character. A historian could go further and lead us back to the origin of Christianity. A theologian might refer to the Church or to grace, Christ, God, or the Holy Spirit as the origin of the Christian faith. A philosopher would look for an answer in the mystery of our being. A biblical scholar would point to the Bible. And so on.

From what we have said earlier about the meaning of language and faith, it may be clear that for us speculative theologians, love would be the answer. Love is the origin of any faith. But what do we mean by that word " love"? The answers will be as many as the number of scholarly disciplines. There is a love of nature, a love of abstract forces, a love of human beings, a love of God, and so on. Even within one discipline one could say that there are as many answers as there are scholars. Love is universal and unique. It determines us as human beings and as individual persons. It is our humanizing and individualizing force. The kind of love we have constitutes the kind of person we are. If we reveal our love, we reveal ourselves, we give away ourselves. "For each person," Augustine said, "is such as one's love is. Do you love the earth? You will be earth. Do you love God? What shall I say? Will you be a god? I dare not say this on my own. Let us hear Scripture: 'I have said: "You are gods and Sons of the most High"' (Ps 82, 6)" (1995, 158).

Christians confess that they have faith in Christ, and their confession reveals both who Jesus Christ is for them and the kind of love they have for him. The first Christian confessions of faith are the books of the New Testament. They document the confessions of faith of the first Christians, who fell in love with Jesus Christ. Their love for him marks the beginning of the Christian life. This love was the inspiration for Paul and for all the authors of the New Testament to write books. From that time, through their books their love unceasingly enkindles a love for Jesus Christ from generation to generation until the end of the world. And beyond that because love is eternal life.

The love that Christ's followers had prompted their liturgical celebration, which preceded their creeds, their Christological and theological formulas. They " worshipped" Christ before they realized the theological implications of their love. It was a falling into a deep love with Jesus Christ and through him with every human being, their enemies included. They recognized Jesus of Nazareth as their great friend who shared with them everything he was and had. It was a kind of love that they never experienced before. Their worship was the outcome of the greatest love they could think of. Roman sources testify that they loved Jesus as their God. "The whole of their guilt, or their error, was," said Plinius Secundus Minor about them, "that they used to come together on a certain fixed day at dawn, when they sang a hymn in alternate verses to Christ, as to a god, *carmenque Christo quasi deo dicere*" (Horvath, 1975a, 128). Whether Plinius or an anonymous interpolator said this, the statement in any case is appropriate. It was not without reason that people called them simply "Christians" (Acts 11, 26), who loved "Jesus Christ with love undying" (Eph 6, 24; cf. Rom 8, 38).

The fascination of the first Christians with Jesus Christ is noteworthy. It is a novelty without which the origin of Christianity cannot be explained. We see here a group loving a human person, and in this love they discover the core of their own being. Love and concretely the love for a human being cannot be called myth except in the sense of expressing an otherworldly reality (the love of God) in terms of a this-worldly reality (the love for each other as human beings; cf. Bultmann, 1953, 10; Horvath, 1975a, 43–4). Unlike a mystical founder of a mystery religion, Jesus of Nazareth was a real historical person whose life and personality "fixed themselves in the hearts and minds of his followers, and he remained alive and vivid to them" (Hayes and Hanscom, 1983, 482). With him they could meet God, each human being as a "neighbour," and find heaven and earth as a home for everyone.

Karl Baus, scrutinizing the causes and consequences of the final victory of the Church, concluded that "the decisive reason which led to the victory of Christianity, the source from which all other factors ... received their force is the person of Jesus and the message proclaimed by him ... It is not difficult to perceive in the third century historical sources the unique fascination and the power appealing to all the capacities of the human heart that is exerted by the person of Christ (1965, 428).

The members of the post-paschal community had no "holy books" written by Jesus. They worshipped a human being whose life was a failure, ended by a shameful death and abandoned by God and men. The obvious question that comes to mind is this: as faithful monotheists, how could they do what they did? How could they worship a real human being without committing the sin of idolatry? It was not unknown to them that anyone who enticed a fellow man or fellow woman into the worship of another god should be purged as "evil" from their midst (Dt 12, 32–13, 18). They knew that they should not " bring their god in their hand" (Jb 12, 6) and magnify for ever a mortal king (Est 14, 10), because " the Lord gives his glory to no other" (Is 42, 8). Some of them, indeed, shortly tried to remove the ignominy of idolatry by denying Jesus' real humanity (1 Jn 4, 1–3; 2 Jn 7). Yet for most of them worshipping Jesus and loving God became synonyms. There is no worship without love. Worship is the utmost love.

Jesus' birth, narrated by Matthew and Luke, reaffirmed that Jesus of Nazareth was a real human being, but the presentation of Jesus' conception through the Holy Spirit pre-empted his idolatrous worship. The context of the infancy narratives in Matthew and Luke is obviously liturgical. The angels, the shepherds, and the Magi worship Mary's loving child, conceived by the Holy Spirit. Being conceived by the Holy Spirit, Jesus could be worshipped as God, since worship of him was serving the "only God." Matthew's "You shall worship the Lord your God and him only shall you serve" (4, 10) is an appeal to the great commandment of loving God "with all your heart, and with all your soul and with all your might" (Dt 6, 5).

The virginal birth of Christ, faith in his divinity, and his real presence in the Eucharist are cognate problem-solving and problem-creating paradigms for Christians worshipping their risen Lord. Denying one does not make it easier to accept the other two and any of the three would challenge the legitimacy of the liturgical, loving worship of Christ. The first Christians, indeed, were conscious that without loving Christ there can be no liturgical participation. For this reason, sharing in their celebration was reserved to those who loved Christ. Admittance to it was gradual and tested. Loving Christ was for them not a trifle. It was what sociologists and political scientists would call a context that changes meaning (Goertz, 1994, 4) and life. It had a rich variety of unexpected consequences for their faith, personal and community life, offices, and social organizations. It was for them like an "intellectual home" as well a " rational actor" emphasizing the future (see Elster, 1979) and operating not from "top-down" but from "bottom-up."

Love is one of the most effective "future-opening" models. It can be detected in the growth of Judaism, Mahayana Buddhism, Hinduism, and Islam and is a recommended paradigm for ecumenical interchange. For Christianity, one historical human being loved his followers and was successful in raising love for him in them. The question of the love-raising power of the historical Jesus will be discussed later. Now we would like first to present the way his followers expressed their love for him and how their love shaped their mind and life.

2.2 JOHANNINE THEOLOGY

The author of the fourth gospel reaffirms that the one who is worshipped is not only the son of the Father but the man also known as Jesus of Nazareth (Jn 1, 1–18). And then he presents him as a most lovable, attractive person who loves and wants to be loved. John writes his gospel for no other reason but that his readers may believe Jesus (Jn 20, 30), that is, accept him as the revelation of God's love (Jn 3, 16; 1 Jn 4, 9; Barrosse, 1957, 539). Such an acceptance (Jn 1, 11–12) is not possible without love. Faith is just a sort of "description" of love. It is an unconditional trust in Jesus that only love can guarantee. But again love requires an intellectual acceptance of certain facts about the trusted beloved one (Jn 16, 27; 20, 31), so much so that πιστεύω, believing, is γιγνώσκω, knowing, and knowing is believing (Jn 10, 38; and 11, 27 with 7, 26; 8, 24 with 8, 28; 17, 21 with 17, 23; 14, 12 with 14, 20; 20, 31 with 17, 3). All this is nothing less than communion with God (1, 13; 5, 38; 8, 47), having eternal life (3, 15; 5, 24; 6, 47; 11, 26; 20, 31). Christ is to be loved (21, 15–17; 9, 42) since God, who is love (1 Jn 4, 16), loves him (Jn 3, 35; Jn 10, 17). In turn, Christ loves his followers with the love with which God loves him (Jn 17, 23–26). Jesus' followers are asked to love another, "for love is of God and the one who loves is born of God and knows God, for God is love" (1 Jn 4, 7–8). In all those who confess that Jesus is the Son of God, "God abides in them and they in God" (1 Jn 4, 15), and "the one who abides in love, abides in God and God abides in him/her" (1 Jn 4, 16).

Verse 7 of the Second Letter of John is a scriptural example of *communicatio idiomatum*, a communication of properties, predicating human and divine properties of the same person and calling that person by a human and a divine name. Whereas in John 1, 14 we read that the "Word became flesh," in 2 John 7 we find that "Jesus Christ has come in flesh." The term ἐρχόμενον is a present participle and refers not to the Second Coming but to the Incarnation, preventing both a Docetist and an Arian interpretation. A Christian could say, therefore, not only "in the name of the Father, the Son, and the Holy Spirit" but also " in the name of the Father, Jesus Christ, and the Holy Spirit."

Verse 11b of the Third Letter of John offers the final development: "anyone who does good is from God" (Horvath,1974, 339–44). Faith, love, and doing good are parallel and synonyms. Each one is equally from God. One includes the others. This may sound simple and trivial, yet it can be considered the essence of Christianity.

All through the Johannine literature Jesus appears as a self-conscious leader who knows why he lives and what he has to do. He knows God and the scriptures as God's words. God's will is his life. He knows his people well. Though he knows human beings well and what is in them, he does not trust himself to them (Jn 2, 24–25); yet he gives his life for them (Jn 10, 15). His love is a free, selfless love which without waiting for love, creates love (Jn 15, 16; 1 Jn 4, 10, 19). He is master and lord, yet he washes the feet of his disciples. There cannot be any doubt that the author of the fourth gospel had a special love for Jesus, and the community he lived in had the same love. The communities of the synoptic gospels agreed with John, yet they differed in how they agreed with him.

2.3 THE WORLD OF THE SYNOPTIC GOSPELS

The writers of the synoptic gospels too witness to a sort of "blasphemous" worshipping love of the man Jesus. The most daring expression of this fascination we can find in the synoptic narratives of the Last Supper. The Passover celebration of Yahweh saving Israel has been changed into a remembrance of Jesus. Not Yahweh but Jesus is the centre of the new liturgy, which is a farewell (Lk 22, 18.22; Mk 14, 25) rather than the sacrificial thanksgiving of Passover. The Last Supper celebration was for Jesus not a celebration of salvation, as it was for the first-born of the Jews, but death, the fate of the first-born of the Egyptians (cf. Ex 12, 23). Remarkably, not the paschal lamb that was on the table but bread and wine were taken as symbols for both Jesus' imminent death and his eschatological banquet in the kingdom of God. The synoptic narratives, indeed, show a daring originality and creativity in reporting the Last Supper celebration (Horvath,1979a, 26–9). They suppose in Jesus' followers a burning, worshipping love of him that may rightly have been seen as a "blasphemous" celebration overshadowing God (Mt 26, 65; Jn

19, 7). Is this not a mystery, a mystery of a "foolish" love of a human being, "to be told, wherever the gospel is told" (cf. Mk 14, 3–9; Mt 26, 6–13)?

Like John, the other synoptic writers try to present Jesus as attractive. He is a successful debater (Mk 12, 28), a controversialist (Mk 8, 11) who silences his challengers (cf. Mt 19, 1–12; 21, 23–27; 22, 15–46). He masterfully bypasses their traps (Mk 12, 13–17; Mt 22, 15–22; Lk 20, 2–26) and in turn puzzles them with clever riddles (Mk 12, 35–37; Mt 22, 41–46; Lk 20, 21–44). He cures the sick, but he has the courage to say woe to the scribes and Pharisees, calling them hypocrites, serpents, a brood of vipers, whitewashed tombs (Mt 23, 1–39). He curses a tree for not producing fruit when it is not the season. This approach may have impressed his followers (Mk 11, 21; Horvath, 1975, 257), but it raises a problem for us. How is it compatible with the language's intentionality to love and to be loved and with the love of God, who cannot be angry and hate anyone?

If faith is presenting God as love and Jesus Christ is the revelation of God's love and the intentionality of his language is love and being loved, could not the early Christians see, as we do now, a contradiction between Jesus as the revelation of God's love for each human being he created and his curses and condemnations, with their threat of the eternal fire of hell for all those who do not accept him? Is such a love universal? Could not his first followers find Jesus to be a hate-monger? Was their love more fear than real love? Is Jesus' love really different from those people who are ready to kill all those who do not get along with them?

Like God's love in the Old Testament, Jesus' love was first a love of the oppressed, the poor, the sick, the humble. It was a generous and free love of justice and truth. He was a friend of the tax collector, the sinner, and the prostitute, but he could not love hate. He had to hate hatred and make a distinction between love and sin. Love is the being of God, and God cannot be identified with evil. He can forgive evil but cannot bless it. The incompatibility of God with sin is made manifest in Jesus' death. And this may be the meaning of the curses as well as of hell.

"Hell has Christological meaning which is expressed in the article of faith professing that there is no salvation without Jesus Christ" (Horvath, 1993, 70–1). Christ, as the forgiveness of the Father, is one of the most powerful arguments of the New Testament for loving Jesus Christ. He is forgiveness, yet without denying himself or giving up his mission of establishing the kingdom of God, which is not of this world. The tension between the will of the world and the will of the Father was the cause of his suffering and finally of his death. Faithful obedience to the will of the Father until death made Jesus' life atonement, "expiation," and forgiveness for the sin of the world. He could say at the end of his life, "It is finished." The work of redemption had been finished (Jn 19, 30). His followers grasped this and could not but love him. Since they loved, they believed and understood what the world could not understand, because those still in the world could not yet love. Yet he recommended to his followers that they love their enemies (Mt 6, 45; Lk 6, 35). Luke reported that at the end of his life Jesus prayed for all those who had rejected him (Lk 23, 34). And so the dialectic of love and hate ended with the victory of love. Love had a future; hate did not. Jesus' death revealed love as ultimately victorious, transcending time and space. It is universal yet not unconditional because it can never be defeated by hatred. It was not a love which people called by that name. Love became a revelation of what love is. It became a question.

The early Christians learned that they had to love Jesus and the world with the love with which Jesus loved them (Jn 16, 12). And that love was a sharing God's life (Rom 8, 15–17), which was not just *νεος*, that is, new only at the beginning, but *καινος*, always new, always beyond human conditions (Behm, 1985, 450–51). It was not called ἔρως, lust, or even φιλία, friendship, or στοργή, natural affection, but ἀγάπη, a love that humans by their own effort could not bring about. It was a gift of God (Mt 16, 17; 1 Cor 12, 3), a grace received by faith and in faith by a sharing in God's nature (2 Pet 1, 4). Such a love needed a special name and *agape* was chosen. Since the love for God they shared was not to be confused with ordinary love, a constant examination of their love for Jesus formed part of their celebration of the "breaking of the bread" (1 Cor 11, 28–29; Horvath, 1985a).

Before we examine the pre-gospel and pre-Pauline tradition of the Church's first love for Christ, let us recall three instances of how the Church tried throughout the history to remain faithful in worshipping Christ without falling into the sin of idolatry.

2.3.1 The Human Word as the Word of God

Unlike the prophets, Jesus did not appeal to God to give weight to his words and claim that what he said God indeed says. He simply said, "I tell you." Yet the community of Jesus accepted his saying "I say to you" not as the words of a man but as the word of God (1 Th 2, 13). At this moment the intentionality of human language to being loved and to love reached its ultimate goal. His followers felt that those human words convincingly communicated to them that God loved them and they were able to love God as Christ did. And this love let them reach and sense the innermost reality of Jesus' being as that of God. John is the most eloquent witness. The words that the evangelist learned as the words of the man Jesus were no longer the words of the man Jesus but the word of God (Jn 3, 34). The writings about Jesus became the books of God, and what Matthew, Mark,

Luke, John, and Paul said became what God said. With the books, through the books, they could worship the one who once had said what was written and believe that the one who said it, is saying it now, and will say it until the end of the world. And since Jesus accepted the books of the Old Testament, those books were his books as well. And thus what Isaiah, Jeremiah, or any Book of the Law and the Prophets said became what Jesus said and thus the books of God. Yet the reverence, the worship, was directed not to a bundle of pages but to the one who spoke through those pages.

The process was both a heuristic discovery and a loving praxis originated and prompted by the celebration of the "breaking of the bread." The Eucharistic words of Jesus brought about the recognition of the scriptures of the New Testament as the "word of God," which in turn allowed the "tradition" of the breaking of the bread. And so the circle of the celebration of the Eucharist and the celebration of the word of God was complete. It seems obvious that the first generation of Christians moved from the Eucharistic celebration to recognize their books as the word of God, whereas successive generations could turn from celebrating their scriptures as the word of God to celebrate the Eucharistic presence of their Lord.

2.3.2 Hypostatic Union

When Arianism challenged the legitimacy of worshipping a human being, the church went on to defend its liturgical celebration. It did so by declaring that Jesus is both real God and real man in one person. In Jesus' innermost being, the Church's love touched upon God, who was and is Jesus' ultimate personality. By removing in Jesus the inalienability of the human person and replacing it with the inalienability of God, the Church again succeeded in justifying its worshipping love of Christ without committing the pagan sin of idolatry.

2.3.3 Transubstantiation of the Eucharistic Bread and Wine

Again to justify the loving worship of Christ in the Eucharist, following the example of the Nicaea, Constantinople, and Chalcedon Councils, the Council of Trent found it necessary to say that by the consecration, the "substance" of the bread and wine had been removed and replaced by the "substance" of Jesus' body. Without transubstantiation, the adoration of the bread and wine would be idolatry. Thus by the word "transubstantiation" the Church defended its liturgy of worshipping Jesus' being present under the species of bread and wine truly (not just spiritually reminding us), really (not just figuratively), and substantially (not just virtually being there but substantially staying in heaven, but also here on earth, so that earth and heaven reached each other, earth becoming the space of heaven). The love the Christian Church had for Christ could not be satisfied with a heavenly distance since Jesus promised that he would remain with his faithful until the end of the world. This was again the "tradition" of the early Christians' love asking for the real presence of the beloved one. Without the word "transubstantiation," the worshipping of bread and wine would have been a pagan idolatry of material things. Love raised a problem and also solved it. Can love be mistaken? Can love be fallible?

Love has its own reason, yet it is rational too and has to answer reason. It did so by turning attention to the mystery of the Incarnation and calling for the legitimacy of symbolic knowledge. In combining analytic and synthetic knowledge with an understanding of the symbolic reality of the sacrament and in recognizing the *being* itself as symbolic (cf. Rahner, 1966), the Church gained a deeper understanding of Christ's gift of himself and a new dimension to love of him.

2.4 PAULINE TRADITION

The tradition of the first Christians' love for Jesus found in Paul new expression and articulation. It became a characteristic mark of Pauline theology. Paul attributed everything to Christ, keeping for himself as his own nothing except his weakness, in which alone he wanted to boast (2 Cor 11, 30). Whatever he gained he counted as refuse, as nothing. For Jesus' sake he suffered the loss of all things in order to gain him (Phil 3, 7–9). In an exuberant outburst of love of Christ he said that "...it is no longer I who live, but Christ who lives in me; and the life I now live in the flesh I live by faith in the Son of God, who loved me and gave himself for me" (Gal 2, 20–21).

Such a love was not a novelty, as if Paul were the first to experience it. After his meeting with Jesus on the way to Damascus, he went to the city, where he was with the disciples for several days and was told what he was to do (Acts 9, 9–19). He became an ardent believer and zealous with a specific mission for the Lord, yet he always acknowledged how much he owed to the community (Horvath, 1975a, 131, 222–3, 227–9). In the Christ-loving Christian communities under the leadership of the "super-apostles" (2 Cor 11, 5–13; 12, 11), he learned how much Jesus meant for them in their liturgical celebrations (1 Cor 11, 23–26). Though the members had an ardent love for Jesus, they called themselves merely faithful believers. As in our days, in those days also love had many meanings, and they found it more meaningful to call themselves "faithful." Yet that did not mean they were believers without being in love with Jesus. Rather, it meant that the love they had was a gift from God which they received in faith. Obviously, faith in Jesus Christ did mean not only an acceptance of a doctrine but also the acceptance of Jesus Christ in love as a living, loving person.

It is Paul's extraordinary love for Jesus Christ that explains his teaching on original sin. It also "justifies" his statements that all human beings are "under the power of sin" (Rom 3, 9), that all have sinned (Rom 5, 2), and that by one person's disobedience all were made sinners, so that no one can be an exception to Jesus' universal salvation. Paul, as it were, closed each human being in sin in order to make Christ, whom he loved above all, the saviour of all and, as such, to be loved by all. It was love for Jesus that raised the question for him about how could he let Jesus be loved by everyone in any age, and the same love gave him the answer. It was the same love for Christ that prompted him to see Christ as needed by anyone and to be needed in any time by anyone. Jesus is the only saviour, and there is no justification and eternal life for anyone without him. It was the same love that let Paul understand and proclaim Christ's salvific work as the work of his love for the world.

The motivation and the meaning of Paul's teaching on soteriology, reconciliation, justification, and glorification are his extraordinary love for Jesus Christ. In writing his anthropology and ecclesiology, he simply extended or applied his theology of Christ to all human beings. By doing so, he could say that Christ's life, death, resurrection, and glorification are the life, death, resurrection, and glorification of the faithful. They live in Christ, they die, and they are buried and rise with Christ. And even more, the life of the Roman and Colossian faithful, though hidden, is already with Christ, who sits at the right hand of God (Rom 6, 4; Col 3, 1–2).

The same love is the ground for Paul's theology of the Church as the mystical body of Christ. To be in Christ, to be with Christ, means a union greater than any social union. Paul called it "mystical" because it is close to the union of a body with its members. Yet unlike the members of a body, in the mystical body no one loses his or her personality, identity. The distinction of "I and you and him" will remain intact for ever.

Being in Christ, having Christ in us, is the foundation of the Pauline ethics (1 Cor 6, 15–20; 12, 27; Eph 3, 17; 5, 30). Paul sees and finds Christ in every human being, in nature, and in the whole cosmos. Yet precisely his great love for Jesus Christ saves him from pantheism. His love of God will be always a love for God in Jesus Christ. Since Jesus Christ is a historical human being, he cannot be altered or absorbed into Paul. Paul's love for Christ as "another" also saves his love for Christ from fading into a Pauline self-love. It will remain a love of "I and thou" and never a love of a transcendental ego. Paul made love his aim and asked the Corinthians to do the same (1 Cor 14, 1). Love is the "greatest," and without it they can gain nothing (1 Cor 13, 1–13). The Christological hymns that Paul inherited from pre-Pauline Christian communities are the hymns of his love. Yet they are the hymns of the pre-Pauline Christian communities as well.

2.5 PRE-PAULINE TRADITION

In the Pauline literature we find hymns that are from the early church in Palestine or in Antioch (Conzelmann, 1969, 170–2; Langkammer, 1970/71, 193–7; Wengst, 1972, 136–41; Schneider, 1992, 333–46). Paul incorporated them as previously composed literary units into his writings. Thus he was not the first to love Jesus Christ. Before him there were numerous communities that expressed their love for Jesus in liturgical hymns.

The focal point of these hymns is varied. It may be Jesus Christ's sharing in the creation of the world or his saving work of reconciliation or his exaltation and humiliation (Horvath, 1975a, 137–42). Yet in each there is an implicit affirmation of Jesus' pre-existence, of his being for ever. When we consider the love of those who used these hymns, this is not surprising. Love implies a certain sense of eternity (Horvath, 1979a, 155–62). It confers immortality on the beloved one. In all of these hymns we can sense a community in great love with a human being, Jesus Christ, whom members of the community knew as one who lived, died on the cross, and is risen to be next to God. And now all worship him. Being all one in this love, they tried to express together their love by borrowing biblical and non-Biblical vocabulary following their prevailing view of the world they lived in. This may have been gnostic redemptive mythology or stoic pantheism or pre-Christian biblical wisdom literature, yet each hymn is both an expression and justification of their worshipping love for Jesus. We find such formulas used for celebration in 1 Corinthians 8, 6, Philippeans 2, 6–11, Colossians 1, 15–20, Hebrews 1, 2b-4, and 1 Timothy 3, 16.

2.5.1 *1 Corinthians 8, 5–6*

Though "there may be so-called gods in heaven or on earth – as indeed there are many 'gods' and many 'lords'" for them (v. 5), we read,

> there is one God, the Father,
> from whom are all things and
> for whom we exist,
> and one Lord Jesus Christ,
> through whom are all things and
> through whom we exist.

The formula proclaims that Jesus Christ cooperates with God in the creation of all of us and of the whole world. By placing him as Lord next to the Father as God, the ancient formula acclaims that Jesus Christ is worshipped with the Father. The First Nicene Council and the First Council of Constantinople used the same distinctive words, "God the Father" and the "one Lord Jesus Christ" (Tanner, 1990, 5), to defend the Church's practice of worshipping Jesus Christ.

By comparing the twofold "from" and "for" formula to the "from," "through," and "to" threefold formula of Romans 11, 36, we can gather the liturgical meaning of 1 Corinthians 8, 5–6. There is one God, the Father, and one Christ, the Lord, and one is to be worshiped as the other. God the Father and Christ the Son are co-worshipped. One is therefore not less than the other (Schneider, 1992, 338). The leading idea is not directed to temporal pre-existence (as in Jn 17, 24; 1, 30; 8, 58; Col 1, 17). The focal point is that Jesus is being worshipped together with God the Father. The text is not philosophical but liturgical. It would be interesting to know who formulated this pre-Pauline creed for the first time. We do not know. What we do know is that such formulas were enthusiastically sung by a community (Kroll, 1968, 3–12; Sanders, 1971, 1–5) that felt glad and free to worship Jesus Christ, whom they loved above else. This enthusiastic joyful exultation is re-echoed in the *socia exultatione*, "in a jubilation shared with the angels of heaven," and in the "unending song of joy" of the later pre-faces introducing the Eucharistic prayers. "Pre-" literally meant "before" not a place but a person, that is, before God, who will be present in the celebration, and the congregation rejoices with the angels in loving praise.

2.5.2 *Philippians 2, 6–11*

Christ's pre-existence is supposed here with a descending and ascending schema of humiliation and glorification (Horvath, 1975a, 137–40):

6 Though he was in the form of God
he did not find incompatible with his equality with God,
7a but emptied himself
to assume the form of servant,
7b became like other humans.
And in external appearance he was found as a man;
8 he humbled himself
and became obedient unto death,
death on the cross;
9 therefore God had so exalted him,
and given him the name above all other names.

The crucial point is a justification that "at the name of Jesus every knee should bow, in heaven, and on earth and under the earth, and every tongue confess " since "Jesus Christ is Lord, to the Glory of God the Father." In other words, it is for the glorification of the Father that every knee bows in the name of Jesus. Therefore there are not two glories. God the Father and Jesus Christ the Lord are worshipped and glorified together. There is just one glory, the glory of the Father, in which the man Jesus is sharing.

2.5.3 *Colossians 1,15–20*

This is not a simple repetition of the previous formulas. There is a new insight. We read that Jesus Christ

> ... is the image of the invisible God,
> the first born of all creation.
> He is the head of the body
> the first born from the dead

There is no descent or ascent as in the previous formula. Jesus is simply the image of the invisible God. Christ's worship is therefore a must. His function is above all to reconcile all things in heaven and on earth. He can do so because he cooperates with God the Father in creating everything. He is the first of all creation and the first from the dead. The universality, the shortness, and the expressive force of the formula is amazing.

2.5.4 *Hebrews 1, 2b-4*

Here Christ is the heir of all things since through God he created the world (v. 2b). He is as much superior to angels as the name he has received is more excellent than theirs (v. 4). Verse 3 is the more precise confessional hymn. Christ

> ... reflects the glory of God
> and bears the very stamps of his nature,
> upholding the universe by his word of power.
> When he had made purification for sins,
> he sat down at the right of the Majesty on high.

The expressions "reflects the glory of God," "bears the very stamps of his nature," and "sat down at the right of the Majesty" suggest, not some kind of rabbinical instruction, but the liturgical celebration of joyful worshipping of the beloved saviour, Jesus of Nazareth, who is alive.

2.5.5 *1 Timothy 3, 16*

He was manifested in the flesh,
vindicated in the Spirit,
  seen by angels,
preached among the nations,
believed on in the world,
  taken up in glory.

This is probably a hymn of the Antioch church praising Jesus in his heavenly and earthly exaltation without mentioning his earthly ministry. In heaven he pre-existed but was manifested in the flesh, and vindicated in the Spirit, seen by angels, and taken up into glory, and on earth he became the Lord of the world since he is preached among the nations and believed in throughout the world. Antioch was the third and Alexandria the second city of the Roman Empire. Both were outside Palestine and very soon had followers of Christ, who expressed their adoration and love for Jesus in non-biblical Hellenistic language of a culture shunning the term "resurrection" (Stanley, 1958, 22–4).

2.6 SUMMING UP

These are some of the hymns of the various pre-Pauline Christian communities from AD 40, expressing their love for Jesus in different languages and cultures. Historians could consider them the history of Jesus' divinization, following the model of the divinization of Roman Caesars. Some, such as 1 Timothy 3, 16, may suggest a similar construction, but the language is original and supposes a creative mind. The hymns express faith in and love of a crucified human being without leaving behind a well-organized senate proclaiming the divinity of a defunct Caesar. The language of these hymns is much more sophisticated than that of the Roman Senate divinizing emperors. Unlike John 1, 1, Titus 2, 13, Romans 9, 5, Hebrews 1, 8–9, and 2 Peter 1, 1, these hymns do not call Jesus "God." Yet they refer to someone to whom the word "God" could be applied. For a person believing in one God to call someone else beside Yahweh God could have been misleading in certain times and places (Horvath, 1975a, 142–5).

Each hymn supposes an inventive "theological mind" that loves Jesus with the same love as the Father's. Obviously, no one should identify Jesus with God the Father, since Jesus was not the Father. Instead, the anonymous authors of these hymns transferred to Jesus more and more of those functions and attributes which, prior to Jesus, referred only to the God of Israel (Horvath, 1994, 11). Such a method proved more efficient in achieving what the hymns really intended, that is, to express and incite the love their community felt for Jesus. Their intention was not so much to proclaim a simple faith in the divinity of Jesus as to witness and share with others the love they felt for Jesus. And that love was a love "with all their heart, soul, mind and strength" (Mk 12, 30). These hymns were hymns of Eucharistic celebrations, and their roots went back to that occasion when the "Lord Jesus on the night when he was betrayed took bread, and when he had given thanks, he broke it and said, 'This is my body which is for you. Do this in remembrance of me.' In the same way also the cup, after supper, saying, 'This cup is the new covenant in my blood. Do this, as often you drink it, in remembrance of me. For often as you eat this bread and drink the cup, you proclaim the Lord's death until he comes'" (1 Cor 11, 23–26).

This "breaking of the bread" was the *Sitz im Leben* for the pre-Pauline hymns, celebrating the first Christians' love for Jesus Christ. We will return to this event dealing with the Eucharist as the historical foundation and hermeneutic principle of all the sacraments, which in turn are "symbols" of faith. But now we would like take a short survey of other texts of the Church, second only to the Holy Scriptures, the *Decrees of the Ecumenical Councils* (Tanner, 1990), and see how they reflect and echo the same love for Jesus Christ.

Any effort to argue that the first Christians loved Jesus Christ might seem unnecessary. Yet this simple fact we find foundational. The early Church by its nature is foundational, and as such, it determined the identity of the Christian Church for ever. It marked something essential without which the Church of today cannot claim authenticity. It resolved the kind of theology that the Church has to acknowledge as its own.

What a systematic theology takes as its point of departure is not without relevance. This can be an abstract notion of God, the monotheistic faith of Israel, the universal belief of the human race, Jesus Christ as the legate of God or as the Messiah of the Jewish people, or Christianity as a new religious movement, and so on. But we find the most experiential, verifiable, and characteristic element of the Christian faith to be the first Christians' falling in love with Jesus Christ and setting him above their highest joy (Ps 137, 6c). To return to this origin of our Church is to return to a faith that is identical with a love for Jesus Christ. It means that we interpret any dogma fundamentally as a safeguard of this love. And this may be the meaning of the re-evangelization and renewal of the Church at the dawn of the third millennium.

Therefore it is perhaps not trivial to document this love for Jesus Christ, which since the beginning has been a grace, a gift of God. Remembering

Jesus Christ has meant more than just a simple thinking of him again. It has meant rekindling the love the first Christians had for him. Thus a Christian theology will be not just a theology of ideas but a theology of life, a theology of a person who loves every human being who ever lived, now lives, or ever will live. This love is our protology and eschatology. It is the point of departure and the aim of our speculative theology. We think that such a proposition is really tenable and a worthy foundation for a pioneering theology.

3

What Is the Raison d'Être of the Ecumenical Councils?

3.1 INTRODUCTION

Ecumenical Councils are commonly seen as assemblies producing decrees and dogmas and excommunicating objectors and delivering them to Satan (1 Cor 5, 5). On the surface, they may appear to be a clash of conflicted interests, threats, and fears of irrational jealousy. Yet the councils were more than just that. They were celebrations with the Eucharist and prayers, mostly in a church, calling again and again upon the Holy Spirit. From the first council in the year of 325 to the last one in 1962–65, Christ remained " a model and guiding principle for solving problems" (Horvath, 1994, 51). In addition to a historical, secular, and religious interpretation, we propose a Christological one as a continuation of the early scriptural concern about how to safeguard the worshipping love for Jesus in spite of the challenges of passing time. The twenty-one Ecumenical Councils present a progressive formulation and realization of the first Christians' love for Christ and offer an appropriate journey to map the Church's intellectual and affective life. Since "conciliar," the adjectival form of the noun "council," might recall "conciliar theology," a theory that the council is above the pope, we will consistently use the word "counciliar" instead of conciliar.

The commandment "Love the Lord, your God with all your heart, and with all your soul, and with all your mind, and with all your strength" (Mk 12, 30) in Judeo-Christian faith meant that God is one, and "there is no other but he" (Mk 12, 32). To love God is to set him as ultimate, that is, as the one to whom the Church reduces or relates everything and the one to whom the Church does not relate or reduce to anything else. If the

Church reduces God to something or someone else, the something or the someone else would function as God, a danger the prophets and the councils always tried to avoid. But a real God must be not only ontologically but also epistemologically ultimate. God must be the last hermeneutic principle whom the Church does not interpret any further, yet in the light of whom it interprets anything else. Finally, the real God must be ultimate in an ethical sense as well. God has to be the supreme value for whom the faithful are expected to sacrifice everything and whom they would not lose for anything else. "There is no other but he" ontologically, epistemologically, and valuably as well. God is the "ultimate reality," the "ultimate meaning," and the "greatest treasure," in the words of the Psalmist, the " highest joy" (cf. Ps 137, 6c). Since God is one, God as ultimate reality, as ultimate meaning and ultimate value, must be the same one. Otherwise there is more than one ultimate, more than one god, and the system has ceased to be monotheistic.

In the Old Testament the love of God meant love for Yahweh. But as we have seen, in the New Testament this love of God became univocal with a worshipping love for Jesus of Nazareth. Faith in Yahweh gradually shifted to Jesus Christ. He became the ultimate reality and meaning, the last hermeneutic principle, and the supreme value for whom one was ready to sacrifice his or her life. The books of the New Testament attributed actions and functions of Yahweh more and more to him (Horvath, 1994, 11–12).

The worshipping love for Jesus Christ, on one hand, and the commandment to "love your one God," on the other, raised problems after the time of the New Testament as well and repeatedly required an answer. How can one justify the Church's worshipping love for Jesus with monotheistic faith in the God of Jesus? The question was fundamental. No less than the Church's worshipping love for Jesus and the legitimacy of the Eucharistic celebration were at stake again.

3.2 TWO PRIMARY COUNCILS: NICAEA I AND CONSTANTINOPLE I

The first two councils had significant consequences for the worshipping love of Jesus in relation to the others that followed. Though he was not the only one, said Arius (c.250–c.336), he was certainly the most pre-eminent among those who, by confessing monotheism, firmly believed that God is God and creatures are creatures and Jesus cannot be both. Jesus had to be just a man. Arius and the so-called Christian Monarchians loved Jesus and could, like Praxeas, even suffer for their faith in Jesus, but their culture or their faith in one God prevented them from being able to worship Jesus as God. For them, as for Arius, Jesus was not eternal. "There once was a time when he was not." He was not of the substance of the Father but made out of nothing. He was therefore a creature, yet not one of the creatures (Boularand, 1964; Wiles, 1962; Stead, 1964).

One does not have to agree with Gwathkin that Arianism was "unlovingness" (1990, 339). Arius too had a kind of love for Jesus, but it was not enough to support the worship of Jesus Christ already practised in the early Christian communities. The Christian Church therefore had to defend its liturgical celebrations. It had somehow to combine the Church's worshipping love of Jesus Christ with the monotheistic commandment of "Love your God with all your heart" (Mt 22, 37). This was the task the 318 participants of the First Council of Nicaea had to face, and the way they did it remained a model for doing theology in a changing world.

THE FIRST COUNCIL OF NICAEA, 381

The participants of this council did not write a new creed. Rather, they took one of the many used by various Christian communities, all expressing their own reasons for their liturgical celebrations and their way of living. One of the bishops present, Eusebius of Caesarea, had such a creed with him. So the participants took it and corrected it in the light of Arius's difficulties in order to safeguard their monotheistic faith with creative fidelity to their worshipping love for Jesus.

First, they crossed out some sentences of the Caesarean creed that seemed to them to support Arius's opinion. So they omitted expressions such as "first-born of all creatures" and "before all ages." Then they took some other expressions used by Arius and revised them by giving a correct meaning to them. So while Arius said that Jesus was "born from nothing," they said that Jesus was "born of the Father" and "from the substance of the Father." To underline that Jesus exists, as the Father does, they added as a proper insertion that Jesus is θεός ἐκ θεοῦ, θεός ἀληθινός, ἐκ θεοῦ ἀληθινοῦ, "God from God, ... true God from true God" (Tanner, 1990, 5). By saying that, they expressed their faith that Jesus Christ is a real God from a real God. The Greek word ἀλεθἰνός means true both in an ethical sense and in an actual ontological sense. To express the same faith in Arian terms, a third statement, parallel to the previous two – "of the substance of the Father" and "real God of real God" – the non-biblical term, *ὁμούσιος* of the same essence, was added. By using the term *ὁμούσιος* (*homoousios*), the Council of Nicaea expressed its biblical faith in the language of its time. Yet its meaning is to be understood, not in the sense of the classical dictionaries, but in the context of the previous statements and means nothing more and nothing less than that Jesus Christ is God in the same sense as the Father is, and whatever one would think or say of God, he or she should think and say the same of Jesus Christ as well.

By doing so the Council of Nicaea safeguarded the Church's Eucharistic celebration and its worshipping love for Jesus. Worshipping Jesus is not idolatry since he is the real God (Bright, 1882, 1–78; Burn, 1925; Grillmeier, 1989; Honigmann, 1936; Lonergan, 1976; Newman, 1833; Ortiz de Urbina, 1963, 15–36 ; Schroeder, 1937; Horvath, 1994, 14–21; Tanner, 1990, 1–19).

THE FIRST COUNCIL OF CONSTANTINOPLE, 381

This council achieved the same for the Holy Spirit, adding that love for Jesus Christ is a gift of the life-giving Holy Spirit. The celebration and the worshipping love for Jesus are not just a knowledge, a γνῶσις, but grace, love, a saving event. No one can say that Jesus is Lord except by the Holy Spirit (1 Cor 12, 3), who is constantly pointing to Jesus. Nicaea confessed that the Father is inseparable from Jesus, and Constantinople I acknowledged that the Spirit, ὁ παράκλητος of John's gospel, is inseparable from the Father and is worshipped with the Father and the Son together. The 150 Fathers of the First Council of Constantinople expressed their faith in the divinity of the Holy Spirit against the Pneumatomachi, who denied the divinity of the Holy Spirit, without using the terms "God" or *homoousios*. They did so in three steps.

First, they said that the Holy Spirit is "the lordly"(*τὸ κὐριον*, with a neutral article). The Spirit belongs to the category of lordships as Jesus Christ, ὁ κὐριος, does and not to the category of creatures. He is not created but proceeds from God the Father. Therefore he is not a servant of God but a lord. Furthermore, since he proceeds from the Father, he is to be worshipped and glorified as Jesus Christ and the Father are worshipped and glorified together. And finally, the Spirit is the giver of life, the life of faith, which is the life eternal (Tanner, 1990, 24). He is not sanctified but sanctifier, the giver of life. Thus the Holy Spirit has a divine name, a divine function, and a divine origin and is equal to the Father and to the Son. This is a remarkable theology, professing the Holy Spirit as God without using the term "God," yet giving a solid foundation for worshipping the Holy Spirit in the context of the Church's monotheistic faith (Bright, 1882, 79–108; Hanson, 1983; Kannengisser, 1981; King, 1957; Ortiz de Urbina, 1963, 139–242; Ritter, 1965; Zizioulas, 1983; Horvath, 1994, 22–3; Tanner, 1990, 21–35). The following four councils were confirmations of Nicaea and Constantinople.

3.3 FOUR CONSEQUENTIAL COUNCILS: EPHESUS, CHALCEDON, AND CONSTANTINOPLE II AND III

THE COUNCIL OF EPHESUS, 431

If the Word became flesh (Jn 1, 14), that is, a human being, argued the Council of Ephesus, it had to have a mother, and the mother of Jesus was the mother of the Word, who was God. If Jesus is real God, his mother is mother of God. Obviously, Cyril of Alexandria and the other participating bishops knew that God cannot have a mother and no woman can be *the* mother of God. Yet they felt it correct to subject concepts and words to the reality of Jesus and join two contradicting words, θεός and τόκος, into one word. Mary is mother of God because God is the ultimate subject of the divine and human properties. There is a communication of the divine and human properties, a *communicatio idiomatum,* and Jesus receives denominations from the divine and human nature. If Mary were not mother of God, it would mean that the man Jesus does not share the properties of divine nature. Such a conclusion would be against Nicaea and pre-empt the Church from the worshipping love for the Eucharistic Jesus. The proclamation of Mary as mother of God was therefore a confirmation of the Council of Nicaea and an introduction to the Council of Chalcedon.

The Ephesian proclamation presented the Christian love for Jesus more fully as a love for a human being, born into the human family. His love is also a love for all human beings and for their mothers. Just as Jesus' death, resurrection, and ascension are salvific, so is his birth, joining him as brother to anyone "born of a woman." This is so for Christian faith because the Word became man and a human being received a divine existence. Mary as a human being, a human person, becomes mother of God, and through her Son, she acquires a special relation to all human beings. For being the mother of Jesus Christ, the Christian tradition paid her a unique veneration, ὑπέρδουλεία, paying a homage higher than to any other creatures, including angels. Mariolatry of the Collydrians of the fourth century and the cult of Mary in the Eucharist in the eighteenth century were a sort of misunderstanding of Ephesus, and the Church censured both (Camelot, 1962; McEnerey, 1987; Scipioni, 1974; Horvath, 1994, 26; Tanner, 1990, 37–74), – declaring that Mary is θεοτόκος, mother of God (Tanner, 70).

THE COUNCIL OF CHALCEDON, 451

The logic of Ephesus worked also in the Council of Chalcedon. It combined Nicaea with Ephesus by emphasizing that Jesus Christ is really God and really man, consubstantial with the Father and with any human being without change and confusion (against the Monophysites) and without division and separation (against the Nestorians).

The Council of Chalcedon and all the other councils deductively "descend" from Nicaea, explicating the implications of that council. Any reversal of the Nicene Creed would mean the end of the Christian faith and could not be labelled "orthodox," that is, those moving ahead, but rather "unorthodox," that is, going back to pre-Nicaea, to the pre–New Testament era. The infallibility of each successive council depends on the infallibility of Nicaea. All the councils form an organic unity, a "collegiality," mutually and progressively completing each other. Their unity comes from Nicaea. The ecumenical union of Christian denominations is also founded on the Council of Nicaea's orthodox, "moving ahead" love for Jesus Christ.

What is particular to Chalcedon is that by stating that Jesus is really God and really man, it overruled the logical incompatibility of "God is God and not man" or "human is human and not God." Instead of the "either/or" the council used "and" and "and" as the basic problem-solving paradigm for subsequent councils and the expression of the internal dynamics of the universal catholicity of the Christian faith.

As a result, no human world view or system can be alien to a Christology, except one excluding others by their being "solely" or "no one else." There is no human language and culture in which Christology can not be expressed. Precisely because Jesus Christ is true God and true man, "every conceivable system in its positive aspect is not only open to God, but to Christ also" (Horvath, 1994, 28), who is both the foundation and the meaning of any system. The love for Jesus Christ has to be universal, including heaven and earth (Grillmeier, 1962; Sellers, 1953; Young, 1983; Tanner, 1990, 75–103).

THE SECOND COUNCIL OF CONSTANTINOPLE, 553

With its *Three Chapters*, the Second Council of Constantinople expressed the union of the two natures in Christ as a hypostatic union, a union in one person. This union is not just a union – by grace, by operation, by equality of honour or supreme authority, reference, or relationship, by affection or power, or simply on account of goodwill, a union of confusion, an accidental union by joining a fourth person to the Holy Trinity, or by adoption or the way a man and his wife become one, or even like being in the body as in a temple (Tanner, 1990, 114–22) – but a union according to hypostasis, which means that in Jesus there is only one personal grammatical subject of all propositions related to both the divine and human natures. All the properties of the two natures can and must be predicated on the one person of Jesus Christ. So the Council of Ephesus could state that Mary is mother of God because being born of a woman can and must be predicated of the one person, Jesus Christ, the Word of God. Because of this personal union a theologian can sense the close unity of Jesus' incarnation (into the human world), his resurrection (into eternity), and his procession from the Father (he was in the beginning with God). The invisible becomes visible, and the temporal eternal; the secular enters the divine, and the divine assumes the secular, yet without change and confusion, without division and separation (Moeller, 1951; Murphy, 1974; Tanner, 1990, 105–22).

THE THIRD COUNCIL OF CONSTANTINOPLE, 680–81

The participants in this council determined that in Christ, instead of one theandric will, which would be neither human nor divine, there are two wills, one divine and one human. And with that decree, the council expressed the view that Jesus Christ has a real divine and a real human love for the Father, for the world, and for the human race "without change and confusion, without division and separation." His real human love is a universal and eternal saving love. And his divine love is expressed in his human love, joining all human loves to his divine love. Because of the hypostatic union of Christ's divine and human love, Christians believe not only that the one who loves him or her loves God and will be loved by the Father, but that loving one of the least of the human race is loving Jesus Christ and in him God (Mt 25, 31–46; Percival, 1974; Horvath, 1993, 31); Tanner, 1990, 123–30). This union and distinction of the human and divine love in Christ is made explicit in the two next councils, the Second Council of Nicaea and the Fourth Council of Constantinople, laying the foundation for the following thirteen councils.

3.4 THE LAST TWO COUNCILS OF THE FIRST MILLENNIUM: NICAEA II AND CONSTANTINOPLE IV

THE SECOND COUNCIL OF NICAEA, 787

This council decided that Christ, being a real God and real man, could be represented in icons, and the pictures could be revered not by adoration, λατρεία, but with a relative love, πόδος, a yearning after or longing for the one who is represented there. Jesus as a real man therefore could be subjected to the standard of human arts, as he was to that of human language that spoke or wrote about him. The following councils discovered how Christ entered deeper into the realms of human endeavours (Alivastos, 1960; Bayes, 1951; Dumège, 1976; Jedin, 1960, 50–5; Martin, 1978; Ouspensky, 1976; Schönborn, 1976; Sendler, 1981; Tanner, 1990, 132–56; Horvath, 1994, 32).

THE FOURTH COUNCIL OF CONSTANTINOPLE, 869–70

The yearning love after Jesus, which extends to the arts and to other human disciplines to which Jesus is confined as man and not confined as God, was succinctly expressed also by the Fourth Council of Constantinople. It referred to the teaching of the Second Council of Nicaea when it professed "the one and same Christ as both invisible and visible lord, incomprehensible and comprehensible," *incircumscriptus,* not confined to a limited space, and *circumscriptum,* confined to a limited space, and *inscriptibilis* and *scriptibilis,* cannot be and can be inscribed in other human conditions (cf. Hussey, 1986; Stiernon, 1967; Tanner, 1990, 157–86; Horvath, 1994, 33).

Such a profession can be considered the culmination of the eastern Christological councils and at the same time opening the door for the western Christological councils beginning with Lateran I and temporarily ending with Vatican II. It is the foundation of a theology in search for how Christ can be found or represented in a given time, a given system or mindset, and experienced in them as πόδοζ, the yearning love after and for Christ confined and not confined there.

The Nicene-Constantinopolitan insight of "confined and not confined" is a spatial translation of the Nicene Creed of Jesus Christ as real man and real God. It may help the Church to discover the limits and the extent of Christ's presence in the world and to understand the position of Photius, who could not see that Christ, who is confined yet at the same time cannot be confined to Constantinople or by the same token to Rome. In a right perspective, one can look to Constantinople IV as an introduction to Vatican II in acknowledging that Christ can be and should be found and loved everywhere, yet cannot be imprisoned anywhere.

3.5 THE THIRTEEN COUNCILS OF THE SECOND MILLENNIUM

The councils of the second millennium experience Jesus as confined and not confined to the world (Horvath, 1994, 19–49).

THE FIRST LATERAN COUNCIL, 1112: INVESTITURE

Is the state above the Church or the Church is above the state was one of the questions of the investiture. Applying the Nicene-Constantinopolitan axiom that "Jesus confined and not confined," the council agreed that the bestowal of the regalia and sceptre, symbols of the power of the world over the subjects of the world, would be done by a king, the head of state, on a local leader of the Church. Thus it recognized that Christ, and consequently his Church, being in the world, is subject to worldly power. Otherwise neither Christ nor the Church would be really human. Yet at the same time Christ and consequently his Church are not confined to the world. They are not subject to the world. The bestowal of the ring, the seal of fidelity, and the pastoral staff, the sign of pastoral activity, has to be reserved to the pope as the Vicar of Christ (Tanner, 1990, 187, 190, 192; Foreville, 1965; Mollat, Tombeur, 1974a; Morrison, 1978).

THE SECOND LATERAN COUNCIL, 1139: SIMONY

This council was neither the first nor the last to consider the problem of money and the Church. Yet by this time the world and the Church dwelling in it had become increasingly affluent and this-worldly. Under Innocent III the Church reached the height of its this-worldly power. With wealth and power, the difficult choice was between loving Jesus for money or loving money for Jesus. The council presented Jesus Christ as confined (sustenance for the clergy) and not confined to the realm of money (Christ is not for sale).

On one hand, it censured the Monophysite spiritualist reform inspired by Arnold of Brescia as well as the followers of Henry of Lausanne, a precursor of the spiritualist movement of the Waldensians (Tanner, 1990, 196). On the other hand, it condemned simony in its first canon. The Church needs money because it has to live and build in this world, but above all in order to imitate God's generosity in helping the needy. But again no one should be able to buy Christ and his grace and debase him to slavery. The thirty canons of the council touched many more problems, and we assume that the "Christ confined and not confined" problem-solving paradigm may have enlightened each (Cheney, 1906; Poole, 1923; Tanner, 1990, 195–203; Horvath, 1994, 35).

THE THIRD LATERAN COUNCIL, 1179: WAR

That this council called faithful Christians to take up arms against "loathsome heresy" (Tanner, 1990, 224–5) was certainly a novelty (Vernet, 1925, 2649). Can a war be holy? Can a war be Christian? Can one defend the oppressed against the oppressor? I may be free to turn my left cheek to any one who strikes me on the right cheek (Mt 5, 39), but am I free also to let any one strike my neighbour?

We may recall that the Second Council of Lyons did not consider the Crusades a war for the propagation of faith but a self-defence or, more precisely, the defence of Jesus of Nazareth's right against unjust aggressors. The Crusades were considered in the same way by the Third Lateran Council when it addressed the fights against Cathars, Patarenes, Publicani, Brabanters, Aragonese, Navarrese, Basques, Coterelli, Triaverdini, and others who "practiced such cruelty upon Christians, that they respect, we read, neither churches or monasteries, and spare neither widows, orphans, old or young, or any age or sex, but like pagans destroy and lay everything waste." Therefore, the council said, the Church could grant faithful Christians who took up arms against them "remission of penance imposed on them" or "even greater indulgences" for defending the weak and defenceless. "The evidence of Christians in this matter, recommends the canon, is to be accepted" since, for example, the "Jews employ their own witnesses against Christians." But all are to be judged "on grounds of humanity alone" (canon 26, Tanner, 1990, 224–5).

It is known that all wars, or almost all wars, are proclaimed by both sides as self-defence against "unjust aggressors." And this attitude is understandable because war, defensive or offensive, is caused by loves misguided by fear and hatred, prompted by a sense of weakness, and with a deep inferiority complex. War is caused by fear of losing what one loves. Since what we love makes us what we are, war comes out of fear of losing ourselves.

There is no war unless one is afraid that the other is strong enough to take away what one has and loves. Thus fear makes us hate all that is strong enough to threaten us, and weakness makes us attack. Fear comes from hatred, and hatred from weakness. One-sided accusation without self-accusation is a sign of weakness. The admission of mutual guilt leads everyone to regain strength, liberates from fear, and brings about peace.

Is Jesus Christ too confined and not confined to physical force? The Third Lateran Council confessed that Jesus Christ could be violent. He cleansed the Temple, cursed the fig tree, and said that he came to bring a sword. The Second Vatican Council admitted that a "person in extreme necessity has the right to take from the riches of others what is necessary for personal sustenance" (*GS*, no. 69; Tanner, 1990, 1118). Yet Jesus was not confined to the realm of physical force. He recommended turning the other cheek to the person who struck one on the right cheek and giving a cloak to the person who took one's coat (Mt 5, 39–40; Lk 6, 29). He probably said this because he knew that war will not remove the causes of war, which are fear, hatred and weakness. He was to be "peace" by removing the " dividing wall between any differences" (Eph 2, 14) and reconciles any adversity by sharing his riches and thus liberates all from weakness, hatred, and fear. Liberation from all these three was believed to be the gift of the sacrament of forgiveness marked by the remission of penance and indulgences offered by the council (Kuttner, 1957; Longère, 1982; Vernet, 1925; Tanner, 1990, 205–25; Horvath, 1994, 36–7).

THE FOURTH LATERAN COUNCIL, 1215: TRANSUBSTANTIATION

The Church believed that Jesus Christ is confined (the bread and wine in the Eucharist) and not confined to the realm of the material world (the sacraments signify, point to, the Eucharistic Christ). Against the Cathari and the Albigenses, who shared the Manichaean doctrine expecting liberation from the body through redemption, the Fourth Lateran Council found it opportune to restate the mystery of Christ's confinement and non-confinement to the material world by saying that Christ's "body and blood are truly contained in the sacrament of the altar under the forms of bread and wine, the bread and wine having been changed in substance by God's power [*transubstantiatis pane in corpus et vino in sanguine potestate divina*]" (Tanner, 1990, 230). Just as Nicaea used the expression *homoousios*, of the same essence, so the Lateran Council again used a non-biblical word, "transubstantiation," to defend the Church's worship of the Eucharist. Without that word, it was felt that the worship of the Eucharist was " plain idolatry" and Jesus would be confined to "heaven." Yet by virtue of the Eucharist, the cosmic material world too may enter eternity as fulfillment of Christ's resurrection (Horvath, 1993, 148–54; Kuttner,

1957; Kuttner and Garcia y Garcia, 1964; Luchaire, 1980; Tanner, 1990, 227–71).

THE FIRST COUNCIL OF LYONS, 1245: THE FORMAL DEPOSITION OF FREDERICK II

The Christian mind had to realize that in following Christ, the Church is not confined to the world yet at the same time is confined to the power of the world (Lunt, 1918; Mollat, Tombeur, 1974b; Wolter and Holstein, 1966; Tanner, 1990, 273–301; Horvath, 1994, 39).

The success of Innocent III in enforcing his authority over kings and heads of states led to the understanding that since Christ is the priest-king, the Church shares his power over the world. So Innocent IV induced the council to depose Frederick II, who nonetheless remained emperor until his death. The power of the world prevailed. Christ as real man did not empty the world of its power. Though all authority in heaven and on earth has been given to Christ (Mt 28, 18–19), yet he did not intend to make the Church a superpower in the world. The divine nature of Christ had not overruled his human nature in order to let Jesus learn by the method of trial and discovery. The Church too had to learn the will of God by this method because Christ, the creator of the world, respects his world.

THE SECOND COUNCIL OF LYONS, 1274: THE CRUSADES

A further lesson was that Jesus Christ likewise was confined (*funiculus hereditatis*) and not confined to the Holy Land. For the Fourth Council of Lateran the Crusades were *negotium Christi,* Jesus Christ's business (Tanner, 1990, 268). The Second Council of Lyons considered the Holy Land to be the Lord's inheritance *funiculus hereditatis dominicae* (Tanner, 1990, 309), an expression found in Psalm 104, 4 and Psalm 77, 54. Since the Holy Land was Jesus Christ's heritage, a great injustice was committed against him when his land was lost to the Saracens. So the purpose of the Crusades was, according to the council, simply to regain the land for Christ.

But if Christ paid taxes to the administrators of his native land, and if as the risen Lord, he has the whole world as his own, in what sense is the Holy Land more his heritage than any other part of the world? Who is the "just" administrator of that land? Is Christ more confined to his native country than to any other country? If he is more present under the Eucharistic species in any sanctuary of his Church which is "truly, really and substantially" (Tanner, 1990, 697), one must say that he is not confined to the Holy Land.

In the Second Council of Lyons another motivation for the Crusades was the gratitude, love, and affection for Jesus Christ and for his homeland that Christians felt. Christ deserved the great love of those who were willing to leave their own home and give their lives to defend his cause, and for such a great sign of love and gratitude they deserved "the full pardon for their sin" (Tanner, 1990, 312). Love for Jesus Christ includes love of the Holy Land, but one can ask, Does it really matter who the worldly lord of that land is? The more so, since the Church believes that after the resurrection, Christ's homeland is the whole world, the symbol of which is the Holy Land (Emery, 1966; Geanakoplos, 1959; Tanner, 1990, 303–31; Horvath, 1994, 40–1).

THE COUNCIL OF VIENNE, 1311–12: THE STUDY OF LANGUAGES

Still mindful of the reconquest of the Holy Land, on the motion of Raymond Lull, this council promoted a new missionary method. Following Christ's example, "who wished that his apostles, going through the whole world to evangelize, should have a knowledge of every tongue" (decree 24; Tanner, 1990, 379), it prescribed that a great number of the faithful should learn many languages in order to be able to present the faith to those who did not know Christ yet. One could say that the most lasting heritage of the Council of Vienne was that Jesus Christ was confined and not confined to one language (Barber, 1978; Leclerq, 1964; Tanner, 1990, 333–401; Horvath, 1994, 42).

THE COUNCIL OF CONSTANCE, 1414–18: ENDING THE GREAT SCHISM OF THE THREE POPES

This council made manifest the dynamics of the interplay between the local church and the universal church and between the community of the bishops and the pope respectively. The Christological significance of the council was that Jesus Christ is confined and not confined either to the local church or to the universal church or even to the head of the universal church (Crowder, 1977; Gill, 1965; Jacob, 1943; Loomis, 1961; Spinka, 1965; Tanner, 1990, 403–51).

Because it is both local and universal – the Church of Christ, the real God and real man – the local church has an inner tendency to be the universal church and the universal church be the local church everywhere at any time. Thus the universal church tries to be present in the here and now of each local church, and the local church to be everywhere in the whole world. Consequently, the local bishop represents the unity of the universal church, appearing in the local church, and the episcopal college represents the universal church as the totality of the local churches. And the pope represents the unity of the universal church, appearing in the local church (Rahner, 1962, 20–30). Because of the presence of Christ in the Church, each local church has a tendency to become what the Roman Church is now: the symbol of the unity of all churches. Accordingly, each bishop has the "intentionality" of becoming pope, and the pope has the intentionality of being present in each diocese. Thus it is so that each church may consider itself a universal "Roman Church" and each bishop a "papal bishop."

This interplay came to the fore more visibly at the time of the Council of Constance, when three local bishops, three popes, and the community of local bishops were experientially tested as to how much Jesus Christ is confined and not confined to each one of them respectively and how the tendency toward unity was operating in their mutual diversity. There was a twofold tendency towards unity: the singular to universal and the universal to singular. Thus it seems that "a Church with episcopal and papal differentiation can be a more adequate expression of the unity of a Church endowed not with a single but with a twofold tendency towards unity" (Horvath, 1971a, 46).

THE COUNCIL OF BASEL-FERRARA-FLORENCE-ROME, 1431–45: UNIONS

The refreshing experience of this council was that Jesus Christ is confined and not confined to the rite of one geographic or linguistic area of the world (Gill, 1953, 1959, 1964; Hoffmann, 1959; Tanner, 1990, 453–9). Its main goal was union, a union of many churches. Union was established with the Greeks, Armenians, Copts, Syrians, Chaldeans, and Maronites, and the Armenian and Arabic languages were used for the first time. The lesson of the council is recalled ever since when the newly elected pope is told, "Do not be an acceptor of persons or of blood-ties or of homeland or of nation. All people are children of God and have been equally entrusted to your care." These are the words the first cardinal is expected to address to the newly elected pontiff "publicly in a loud voice" and every year on the anniversary of his election or coronation (*Form of Consent*; Tanner, 497, 496). And there is one more lesson that is not less significant: that "nobody shall in the future dare to call ... any individual among them, heretic(s)" (*Bull of Union with the Chaldeans and the Maronites of Cyprus*; Tanner, 591). And that will be truly "the Lord's doing" (*Bull of Union with the Armenians*; Tanner, 535).

We should note here that rite is not just a difference in language and geographical location. Rather, it is a "liturgical, spiritual and theological patrimony of living out one particular church's life of faith" (Žužek, 1989, 293) in Jesus Christ. The recognition of Greek, Armenian, Copt, Syrian, Chaldean, Maronite, and other rites was the recognition of a Christ not confined to one's own way of living out faith or to one's own rite. Each discovered that the others, too, loved the same Christ, lived out in each one's own liturgical, spiritual, and theological patrimony and life of faith. The Council of Florence could not change the world at once, but it could anticipate the future. Its fallibility and infallibility is not independent of the other councils. They are infallible in their close unity based on Nicaea, continuously building on each other (Horvath, 1994, 44).

THE FIFTH LATERAN COUNCIL, 1512–17: THE CULTURE OF AN AGE

The Church tried to emerge from the culture of its age, the new-Aristotelianism, and witness to Jesus Christ as confined and not confined to the culture of its age (the Renaissance). It felt it necessary to affirm that the soul is not one for all human beings, but one for each, and is immortal (Tanner, 1990, 605). Yet this is not a natural condition of the soul but a gift of Christ's grace. A similar detachment from the culture of the age is requested by the *Bull on Reform of the Curia,* which urges the cardinals "not to attract blame by display of splendor or superfluous equipment or in any other way" by having, for example, a great number of "personal attendants and horses" (Tanner, 618–19).

The same council supported the work of the Montes pietatis, a sort of charitable organization that lent money to the poor in great necessity. This was not usury; it made sure that Christ is confined and not confined to capitalism (Bilaniuk, 1973; Minnich, 1982; Schoeck, 1981).

THE COUNCIL OF TRENT, 1545–63: SYNTHESIS OF THE AUGUSTINIAN AND THOMISTIC THEOLOGIES

This was a council of theologians concerned with doctrines, rather than with individuals and abstract ideologies. It turned out to be a remarkable synthesis of the Augustinian, Jesuit, and Thomist theologies, presenting Jesus Christ as confined and not confined to one theological system. It led to a subsequent elaboration of the various theological notes, marking different degrees of evidence and certitude, shades of clarity that explain one's views and provide leeway for others. It was the Nicene "and" and "and" instead of the Arian "only" (*solus, sola, solum*). The message "was not just Augustinian, Franciscan, Suarezian, or Thomist, but the voice of a much larger universal Church expanding the mystery of the incarnated Christ in time and space" (Horvath, 1994, 46; *Concilium Tridentinum Nova Collectio,* 1901–38; Jedin, 1951, 1960, 1967; Kremnitz, 1971; Leclerq et al., 1981; Schroeder, 1967; Tanner, 1990, 657–799).

THE FIRST VATICAN COUNCIL, 1869–1970: INFALLIBILITY OF ONE INDIVIDUAL

In the light of the First Council of Nicaea, the First Vatican Council could extend the Nicene-Constantinople paradigm to the infallibility of the supernatural and reasonable faith. According to this supernatural and reasonable faith, Christ lives in the Church, his mystical body, which receives certain characteristics from its head. And one of them is Christ's infallibility, based on his being the perfect and definitive revelation of God (Mt 11, 27). Christ has a comprehensive knowledge of any word, expression, action, or being and their power to symbolize God. Being real God and real man, he is able to know God and the created world. He knows humans and their world precisely, in their deepest mystery, as being revelations of God.

Christ's infallible knowledge of the world and of his own being as the revelation of God is shared by the Church. The Church's infallibility, therefore, is not a surface knowledge of the world accessible to us by ability and studious effort. Rather, it is knowledge at a deeper level, where the Church is able to recognize certain words, expressions, and actions as the adequate and unambiguous symbols, firstly, of its own self as being a community of faith, love, and hope, and as such, the sacrament of Christ, and secondly, of the generosity of the Father, the integrity of the Son, and the authenticity of the Holy Spirit, the mystery of the Trinitarian God.

Now this infallible Christ is confined to the infallibility of the community of the Church and not confined to the same community as a totality of individuals. He is confined and not confined to the infallibility of the pope as one individual member of the community of individuals. Such an awareness of infallibility existed from the beginning. What Vatican I expressed about Christ's mystery of incarnation was that he is not confined to the community of the Church as a totality of individuals. What he is to the totality he can also be to one individual member of that community, who can share his infallibility, not independently of the community but truly as an individual. Papal infallibility is the revelation that Jesus can live not only in the Church as a community but in each member of it. The uniqueness of the pope is the symbol of the uniqueness of each of the faithful. There is a little pope in each of one of them. Christ abides not only in the community but in each individual, though not independently of the community (cf. Jn 15, 1–7).

The First Vatican Council perhaps laid the foundation for councils of the next millennium. They will be concerned with the mystery of how Christ dwells in each of the faithful and in each human being. It may be an experience of a love for Christ, who is confined and not confined to the church community as well as to the "spirit" of each member of the Church and of the human race. Each of the faithful has a direct relation to Christ, not through but in the community. Yet Christian life is a community life based on the inalienability of a person, which no community can take away or absorb. A Christian must always remain free to be confined and not confined to the world. Each one, the pope included, in all his or her activities is "bound to follow faithfully his/her own conscience and none ... must be forced to act against it" (*DH*, no. 3; Tanner, 1990, 1003). Precisely, this freedom is the great responsibility that each faithful and each human being has for the Church of Christ and for the whole world within the community of the Church and the human race (Aubert, 1967; Hasler, 1981; Pottmeyer, 1968; Tanner, 1990, 801–16. Horvath, 1994, 47–9).

THE SECOND VATICAN COUNCIL, 1962–65: WORLD AND TIME

It was an uplifting experience for the Church to find Jesus Christ confined and not confined to the visible, territorial Church. Expressed in a spatial language, this concept means that the world too can be a vehicle of the grace of the Church. Expressed in a temporal language, it means that Christ is confined and not confined to the past. He is in the future as well (Horvath, 1994, 49; Vorgrimler, 1967).

The world, though not independently of the Church, can be truly a vehicle of the grace which the Church has, but not on its own. The Church's grace is not only the grace of the Church but Christ's. As Christ's teaching was his own, yet not his but his who sent him (cf. Jn 7, 16), so the Church now knows that the grace which it has as its own is not its grace but his who sends it. This is why the Second Vatican Council could say that "some, and even most, of the significant elements and endowments which together go to build up and give life to the Church itself, can exist outside the visible boundaries of the catholic church" (*UR*, no. 3; Tanner, 1990, 910.). The Church is therefore not only a Church of a few, but the Church of all since in various ways all people are related to the Church, the people of God (*Dogmatic Constitution on the Church*, nos 6, 13–17; Tanner, 861, 859–62). Therefore non-Christian religions also belong to the Church and can become the vehicle of Christ's grace in the Church.

Christ was, is, and will be present in the Church, yet his presence is not confined to its boundaries, since he is the Creator, the Lord and Saviour of all peoples. The Christ of Vatican II is the risen Christ, who progressively and without any delay until the last day extends his kingdom in time and space by leading all peoples born in time to eternity. He is the eschatological Lord of the universal, eschatological Church existing in time yet already one with the Church in eternity. The tone of Vatican II, therefore, is not one of worries and complaints about evil in the world. It is a joyful reverberation of the Resurrection. Instead of looking back and around, it looks ahead. It has a vision of the future that is already a reality: Mary, the mother of Jesus Christ, in her bodily and spiritual glory as a sure sign and pledge of the Church's optimism. And this optimism is not limited to chapter 8 of the *Dogmatic Constitution on the Church*. It permeates all sixteen documents of Vatican II, recognizing Christ as confined and not confined to space or time. He is that real man and real God whom the First Council of Nicaea confessed as the ultimate reality and meaning of all.

3.6 ECUMENISM: "ORTHODOX" AND "UNORTHODOX" LOVE FOR CHRIST

Since for us love is not just the form of virtues but the foundation of any action and existence, we can argue that all Christians, orthodox and unorthodox, Catholic and non-Catholic, have a superlative love for Jesus Christ. All try to set him "above their highest joy," which is the "essence" of Christianity. Thus the twenty-one ecumenical councils of the Roman Catholic Church serve above all to safeguard such a love for Jesus Christ in the life of the Roman Catholic faithful. Therefore we conjecture that the councils could be understood and accepted by anyone as the expression and realization of the Roman Catholic Church's supreme love for Jesus Christ. And this is so even in the most disputed tenets that prevent the church from agreeing with other Christian confessions. Each church tries to express in its own tradition one and the same love for Jesus Christ.

Such an interpretation lets us see Jesus Christ as contained and not contained in one's own church, its confessions, and one's own being. It inspires any Christian to love and encourages any other church to foment the love its early members had for Jesus Christ. This common love for Jesus Christ is the foundation of the unity among all Christian churches. Yet the road to the realization of that unity is a long one. It takes some time before our mind and confessions are able to catch up with our love. The speed of reason is different from the speed of love. Mind and love both are in time and take time to enter each other and express their love in one confession.

Each of the churches has a vocation to foster such a unity between reason and love and to increase the common love for Jesus Christ. Until such a mission is accomplished, all Christians may try to achieve such a unity within themselves by incorporating the vocation and the mission of all Christians in their lives.

We are separated from one another because we are different, and the mystery of Christ for many reasons is not grasped the same way by all of us. This mystery challenges our being at its deepest reality, the love that is working in us by moving us to its full realization. It is the light and force of this love which let us discover that all Christians are occult Arians, Nestorians, Orthodox and Roman Catholics, Protestants, and so on. If a Catholic admits the problem-solving paradigm of "not only but" and instead of "either, or" and follow the Nicene and Chalcedonian "and" and "and" with the "contained and not contained" of Nicaea II and Constantinople IV, she or he will love his or her brothers and sisters and identify his or herself with their "going around doing good" and their "superlative love for Jesus Christ" in trying to set "Jesus Christ above their highest joy," yet deeply respect them for being different. There is much more in each of us than our negation and rejection of each other.

By doing so, one is far from becoming a neutral Christian without any existing church. Rather, I, a Roman Catholic, become a better Roman Catholic, a Protestant, a better Protestant or a better Salvation Army officer, and so on, who not only needs and welcomes other denominations but by loving them, as Augustine says, becomes one of them. It is by love that I become one of them and dare to say, "One can be Catholic, Protestant, or a member of the Salvation Army," and so on, even though, in respect and honesty, one is not going to participate in others' most characteristic celebrations, in order to respect others as they are and let each one celebrate his or her own identity and otherness so long as this has to be so. A universal participation in everything is a easy way out of facing the complex reality of being individual and God's given task to join the Church of Christ in the community of the whole human race. Love respects diversity and is strong in desire and hope. It is very much aware that "it is God's doing" (Council of Florence; Tanner, 1990, 535).

Such an internal unity of all churches prompts a Roman Catholic to discover and recognize the Reformation as a Catholic movement (Pelikan, 1959, 48) and admit that the "religious convictions of the reformers were animated by their fidelity to catholic ideals" (ibid., 51) and "to their love for Jesus Christ." And in turn, a Protestant may recognize the Catholic Church as a church which, by its nature, is a Protestant movement and keeps its identity and freedom by giving *soli Deo gloria*. It is an *ecclesia semper reformanda*. The twenty-one ecumenical councils aimed "at the reform of the church notwithstanding all the previous failures" (Horvath, 1994, 51).

The time for union is the time of Jesus Christ. And the road to that time is internal conversion to love for Jesus Christ, a love that forgives the sins of all the churches carrying his name. All have sinned, but by forgiving one another and mutually correcting and helping one another, the churches may confess and experience the mystery of the merciful Saviour Jesus Christ and pray with the Psalmist, "Your ways, Lord, make known to us; guide us in your truth, for you are God, our Savior" (Ps 24, 4–5).

To love God is to set him as ultimate. For the Christian churches, to love God and to set him as ultimate is to love and set Jesus Christ as ultimate because God is not found outside him. Jesus Christ is "God and Savior" (Gaines, 1966, 1106).

Yet ecumenism is more than denominational. It is human and universal with a task for everyone. It is universal love for every human being, to be achieved by each human being for each human being. It has a universal creed and a transcendental philosophy: *each human being is lovable.* To be lovable is something transcendental in any human experiential action in two senses of the word: it is a necessary category of any human action and it transcends the limits of space and time.

4

What Is the Raison d'Être of the Sacraments?

Scriptures and ecumenical councils witness to the love Christians had for Jesus. The celebration of that love preceded both. The love they experienced was more than spoken and written words could express. It reached down to the deepest level of their language ability, where their being broke through self-affirmation to affirm an "Other" as other yet one with them (Rahner, 1966). And this Other was Jesus Christ being with them, in them, and they in him. Their communion moved them to do something more than just talk. And this doing turned out be different from their ordinary words, speech, actions, and behaviour. It became more and more a kind of recalling, remembering, reinventing the words, speeches, actionss, and behaviour of the One they knew as Jesus Christ. It was a mysterious kerygmatic – the proclaimed one became the proclaimer (Horvath, 1993, 65) – experience of Christ, who was alive. He was the one, they knew, who died but now lived more than before in them, with them. It was the risen Christ being mysteriously, "sacramentally" – the eternal and heavenly in the here and now – present among them and imparting to them an "awesome" joy and happiness in a way that reminded them of theophanies. Yet these were not theophanies of the "old" but Christophanies bringing about a beatitude not of this world but of the kingdom of God (Horvath, 1975a, 242–72).

The source and the focus of this experience was the celebration of "the breaking of bread" in memory of their Lord (Acts 2, 46; 20, 7; 27, 35; Lk 24, 30; Mk 14, 22; Mt 26, 26; Lk 22, 19; 24, 23; Baus, 1964; Horvath, 1985b), a participation in the body of Christ (1 Cor 10, 16), later called the Eucharist. It prompted their Christology, the first Christian theology, which was an *expérience vécue*, a reflection on living their love for Christ expressed and sustained by the Eucharist. The outgrowth of this Eucharistic theology was the theology of the other sacraments with their special rites and their own theologies. We may say that the Eucharist and the sacramental life of the Church influenced and determined the nature of Sacramental theology as well as that of the fundamental and dogmatic, systematic theology of God, Creation, the Church, Christ, new life in Christ, moral theology, and eschatology. By celebrating the Eucharist and other sacraments, the Church discovered that all were symbols of the world, challenges to human existence, life functions of the Church, features of Christology, the revelation of the God of Jesus Christ, and hermeneutic principles for eschatology, pneumatology, and Mariology. They were celebration of the love the Church had for Jesus Christ.

4.1 WHAT IS THE SACRAMENT OF THE EUCHARIST?

4.1.1 The Eucharist: The Historical Foundation of Sacramental Theology

4.1.1.1 THE BREAKING OF BREAD: MIRACLE MOTIF AND CHRISTOPHANY

In Acts 2, 46 we find the "breaking of bread" used as a technical term to indicate one of the distinctive activities of the followers of Christ. We learn also that at Troas on the first day of the week the disciples gathered with Paul to "break bread" (Acts 20, 7, 11). Paul broke bread also across the Adriatic Sea on a ship in the presence of all, sailors and soldiers included (27, 35). We read in 1 Corinthians 10, 16 that the breaking of bread, τὸν ἄρτον, is a participation in the body of Christ," whereas "the cup of blessing is a participation in the blood of Christ." The breaking of bread and the cup of blessing are parallel, and there can hardly be any doubt that the breaking of bread was in the early days that what we call today a "Eucharistic celebration."

It is noteworthy that passages about the breaking of bread are always connected with a miracle motif. This may be the feeding of several thousand people with five loaves and two fishes (Mk 6, 41; Mt 14, 19; Lk 9, 16; Jn 6, 11) or seven loaves and a few small fishes (Mk 8, 6; Mt 15, 36). Jesus referred to that miraculous event by saying, "When I broke the five loaves" (Mk 8, 19). Exegetes agree that the passages dealing with the multiplication of bread were redacted in the light of Eucharistic celebrations. This is most obvious in John chapter 6. But we find a miracle motif in the resuscitation of Eutychus (Acts 20, 9–10), in the salvation of all who sailed with Paul (Acts 27, 44; Schneider, 1982, 397), and particularly in Christ's triumph over death following the Last Supper, when he broke the bread (Mk 14, 22; Mt 26, 26; Lk 24, 20; 1 Cor 11, 24). He did so again after his resurrection on the road to Emmaus (Lk 24, 30) in the miracle of recognition (Christophany), vanishing, and the joy and love of the burning hearts (Lk 24, 31) of the two disciples. The liturgical context is enhanced by the Christological interpretation of Moses and all the prophets (Lk 24, 27), as well as by the mission of the disciples in announcing the good news that Christ is alive.

There may be more than one reason, though, why the early Christians used the words "breaking of the bread" while later the word "Eucharist" would prevail. The term "breaking of the bread" made it clear that their celebration was no longer a Passover celebration and the feast of unleavened bread. It was the celebration of Jesus Christ, who broke bread and died but now was risen, as he foretold to them. It was a thanksgiving but a special one, unlike any other.

Breaking bread was not ἐσθίω, an ordinary eating, which occurs in the New Testament in about 147 passages. It was *κλάω, κατακλάω*, breaking, which occurs only 15 times and differs from *γεύομαι*, taste, as well as from *εὐχαριστέω*, giving thanks, with about 54 instances. The breaking of bread is not unknown in the Old Testament. It means not a regular meal but just fragments of bread (Ezek 13, 19) shared with the poor (Is 58, 7; Lam 4, 4; Ezek 18, 7–9) or with the distressed (Jer 16, 7; Schermann, 1910). It seems that there is no specific Hebrew expression for "breaking of bread." There is breaking the fast, which signifies the meal at the feast of Yom Kippur. There is also a custom on Friday night, when after the grace for bread, the father of family, instead of cutting the bread with a knife, breaks pieces with his hand and gives one piece to each person present. This custom, however, is not accepted by all Orthodox Jews (Horvath, 1985b, 604).

The expression of "the breaking of the bread" served the early Christians well. It reminded them of Jesus, the bread from heaven, broken and shared by all, and of his love and of his post-Resurrection Christophanies (Mt 28, 16–20; Lk 24, 13–50; Mk 16, 9–19; Jn 20, 11–23), with their miraculous salutary effects. Thinking of them, they experienced an uncommon love and joy shared with the community of the "poor" of Christ. In the early days, when memories were fresh, it was a good symbol charged with "grace." But later, because its ordinary meaning lacked any obvious reference to God it was replaced by the word "Eucharist," expressing God's greatest "mighty deed," Jesus Christ. In a non-Jewish world there was no need to distinguish it from a Passover celebration, and the Eucharist as praise and thanksgiving to God for Jesus Christ and his work was more expressive.

4.1.1.2 THE LAST SUPPER

4.1.1.2.1 The Marcan Tradition

THIS IS MY BODY AND BLOOD

According to the Marcan tradition, Jesus' special intervention in the celebration of the Passover took place during the meal. Mark does not say anything more about the meal. He informs us only that Jesus told his disciples that one of them would betray him. He was going to die, as it was written, and he felt sorry for the one who would betray him. After this introduction, Mark continues: "as they [he with the twelve, Mk 4, 17] were eating, he took bread, blessed and broke it, and gave it to them and said 'Take; this is my body.' And he took a cup, and when he had given thanks he gave it to them, and they all drank of it. And he said to them, 'This is my blood of the covenant, which is poured out for many. Truly I say this to you, I shall not drink it again of the fruit of the vine until the day when I drink it new in the kingdom of God.' And when they had sung a hymn, they went out the Mount of Olives" (14, 22–6).

Mark omits the "Do this in remembrance of me" but includes the astonishing statements: This *τοῦτό* is "my body" and this *τοῦτό* is "my blood." Whereas in all of his "I am" statements Jesus is the subject, here he is a "predicate" and "this" in its neutral form is the subject. He is the Good Shepherd, but the Good Shepherd is not he. He is the light, but the light is not he. Here is the difference. He takes the bread and he says, not "here is ...," but "this is my body." And he takes the cup and says, not "here is ...," but "this is my blood"; in other words, he says "this is me." We have here not just a comparison but a mysterious identification that means more than just a simple presence. By taking "this," that is, the bread and the cup, he expressed himself in something other than himself, that is, as the bread and wine, and then united that "other," the bread and wine, again with himself (this is "me"). By doing so, he made the bread and wine in his hand not just a "symbolic representation" of something else that is not itself, like a mathematical symbol or a sign pointing to outside itself. Rather, by the "this" he made the bread and wine a "symbolic reality" of his reality. Symbolic reality is not just a symbolic signification, or meaning. It is a reality in which the symbolized reality, Jesus Christ, is contained yet not contained – contained because Jesus was there and not contained because Jesus was not only there. He did not disappear by changing himself into bread and wine. He was there because he loved to be with his loved ones there and then. Yet he was not just there and then because he loved only those who were there and then but also the "many" whom he loved and for whom he also came. It was a real presence of a real love, which extended itself to an unlimited time and space. To distinguish this loving presence of the here and now from an empty sign or symbol of the "there far away," the Church found it necessary to use the word "mystery" and later the Latin "sacrament," indicating the sacredness of the symbolized.

Jesus' special intervention radically changed the nature and the intentionality of the traditional Passover celebration. From now on, the celebration was not oriented towards the past but towards the future. Its main feature was a farewell, rather than the sacrificial thanksgiving of the Passover. We have already noticed that, unlike the Passover for the Jews, the Last Supper for Jesus cannot be considered a thanksgiving for liberation from dying. Jesus was going to his death. For him, the Last Supper could not mean salvation as it did for the first-born of the Jews but, rather, death (cf. Ex 12, 23). Not the Paschal lamb lying on the table but bread and wine are taken up as the symbol of his imminent death as well as of his eschatological banquet in the kingdom of God. The unusual shifting symbolism of the Last Supper, moving from wine to the shedding of blood and then to a joyous festivity of happiness, supposes a daring creativity in composition.

But is this, one might ask, what Jesus had in mind when he said, "This is my body" and "This is my blood"? An attempt to discover whether the historical Jesus could have said that and, if he did, what he could have meant can be only based on an assumption about what a religious Jewish man of that time could have meant by making such statements. Such a study is legitimate and necessary (see below, 4.1.1.6). It is a question a historian has to ask. But we as historians will never be able to enter directly into the mind of the historical Jesus and find out what was going on there. We have only the words of the early Christians, who expressed what they had understood in faith through the words of Jesus and put it down in the books of the New Testament. If one can accept that these statements are biblical statements, then one can consider them "words of God" and as such, a revelation of what Jesus had in mind.

According to the concept of revelation, there can be no revelation on the part of God unless it is a received in faith by the faithful addressed. Otherwise, according to Isaiah 55, 11, the word of God would return to God empty without accomplishing the purpose for which it was sent. On account of the twofold aspect of the revelation–faith event, one has to consider what Jesus' followers understood of all that he told them. This is not just the only way but the only "objective reality" that a speculative theologian will scrutinize; the more so since it is valid for any human communication. If language is to tell someone something about something, the understanding of that something by the one who has been addressed is indispensable in any human communication and also in the theology of revelation. As there cannot be communication without mutual understanding, so there cannot be revelation without the mutual understanding between the revealer and the believer. And since we have more than one believing community celebrating Jesus' Last Supper, one interpretation of his mind can be scrutinized by another. Before we observe how the celebrating community of Matthew, Luke, Paul, and John understood Jesus' words, we would like to stay with Mark for a while.

THEY ALL DRANK OF IT

For what purpose? Mark does not only omit the "do it in remembrance of me" of Paul and Luke but also the pouring out "for the forgiveness of sins" of Matthew. Unlike Paul, Mark is very cautious about using sacrificial terms describing Jesus' achievement (Horvath, 1979, 6–19). Most of the sacrificial terms in his gospel refer to the sacrifices of the Old Testament. Mark is aware that Jesus' life was not just a "literal" fulfillment of the Old Testament sacrifices. It is interesting that he does not say here that the bread is "given for many." It seems that blood, the blood of the covenant, is the only straight sacrificial term for Mark. Yet even that oscillates between wine and blood and between the last cup and the next one at the eschatological banquet. The symbolism moves from the cup of "my blood" to the blood of the covenant – the blood of union thrown against the altar and upon the people (Ex 24, 18; Zech 9, 11; Heb 9, 15–22) – and back again to the fruit of the vine.

The presentation of wine as Jesus' blood must have seemed to any Jew an abominable rejection of Yahweh's prohibition (cf. Gen 9, 4, etc.). True, wine as a symbol of "the libation of the blood of the grape" in the time of Sirach (Sir 50, 15) was not unknown. But even as a symbol of blood, wine was to be poured out as a libation and not offered as a drink. The holocaust (Lev 23, 17–18; Ex 29, 38–42), as well as the sacrifices of *'ōlâ* and *zebah* (Num 15, 1–16), had to be followed by *minhâ*, an offering of flour mixed with oil and a libation of wine. No scholars, however, have so far tried to present the Last Supper as a sort of *minhâ* related to the holocaust of the cross. Interestingly enough, the term "holocaust," the sacrificial burnt offering, is never applied to Christ. All three instances refer to the holocausts of the Old Testament (Mk 12, 33; Heb 10, 6.8). This is surprising since Hebrews 13, 11–12 seems to suggest the idea. Nevertheless, Jesus is not called "holocaust." A reason one can think of for this omission is that the early Christians, when they celebrated the Eucharist, knew that by his death Jesus was not obliterated. He was alive and well (Horvath, 1979b, 11, 28).

One should also keep in mind that in the Jewish Passover wine did not play a central role. Exodus 12, 1–27 does not mention either wine or cup. In general, wine was not related to the cultic celebrations of the Old Testament. It was considered rather as a danger that might lead to sinful idolatry. Outside cultic celebrations, wine was a symbol of happiness and joy. According to Isaiah 25, 6–9, "the Lord of hosts will make for all people a feast of wine" on the mountain of Zion in the Messianic times. In the Marcan text, wine and bread as a symbol of happiness are used as symbols of the shedding of blood of a dying person looking forward to his eschatological banquet in the kingdom of God. Thus for Mark the Last Supper was not a commemoration of the Passover but, rather, the anticipation of the eschatological banquet where the body of Christ will be food giving eternal life (Jn 6, 51–58). Yet this did not mean that one who eats and drinks more now during the Eucharistic celebration will participate more fully in Christ's eternal life the way people do in pagan cultic celebrations (cf. 1 Cor 11, 19). Eating and drinking is symbolic. It represents communion with the Eucharistic Christ, who is now not only with them but in them too (Horvath, 1979b, 28–9).

Mark's reporting of the Eucharistic words in the midst of the meal is more significant than Paul's reporting them after the meal. For Mark, the Passover meal as meal was not important. It was just a time element, a mere occasion, indicating when Jesus' revolutionary intervention took place.

Therefore we find it difficult to agree with Marxsen that the meal played a special role in Mark or in the synoptic tradition in general. It seems that the opposite was the case. The meals in Mark appear as something rather incidental (see 1, 6; 3, 20; 5, 43; 7, 27). Even the meaning of the multiplication of bread was not cultic but, rather, an act of mercy (6, 34; 8, 2). Indeed, in Mark as well as in the Synoptics the tendency is rather to "secularize" the meal contrary to the ritual tradition of the Pharisees (cf. 2, 16.26; 7, 2–5). Mark's short ending does not recall apparitions to the eleven sitting at the table as does the longer ending (16, 14). His teachings, such as that of the Sermon on the Mount (3, 13–14, 33), his discourses with the Pharisees (8, 11–13; 12, 1–44), and his important eschatological speech (13, 3–37) are not table talk or table discussions like the one we find in Acts (20, 7–11) or in John (13, 1–17, 26). The meal at Bethany, in the house of Simon the leper, is again just an occasion for mentioning Jesus' anointing for his death (14, 8). From a merely statistical standpoint, the people of the Marcan tradition are portrayed as spending their time not so much in eating as in walking and going from place to place. Thus, for example, the term *'ἐρχομαι*, going, occurs in Mark 88 times, whereas *ἐσθίω*, eating, appears only 26 times. Indeed, according to the Synoptics and the Pauline and Johannine sources, Jesus' deed and what he offered to his followers and through them to the world – in one word, the Christ event – was not so much "eating" as the action of moving "from" and "to," from the present world to a new life in the eschatological future (Horvath, 1979, 2, 90–3). And this is the meaning also of that all drank of the cup.

THE BLOOD OF THE COVENANT POURED OUT FOR MANY

We know that the blood of the covenant was to establish union between God and his people (Ex 24, 5–8; Gen 15, 7–21). In the Acts of the Apostles we read that the blood by which the Church has been brought into being is Jesus' blood (20, 28). Now, blood of every creature belongs to God (Gen 9, 4–6; Lev 3, 17) but none as much as the blood of Jesus Christ, the servant of God (Acts 3, 18.26), which can rightly be called "the blood of God." Matthew combines Exodus 24, 5–8 with Exodus 30, 10 and Leviticus 14, 4–7 and 16, 1–34 and calls Jesus' blood expiatory, having the power of purifying and of forgiving sins (26, 8). For Mark it is clear that Jesus' blood brought about a new covenant, and no more animal blood would be necessary. The wine of the cup and the blood of Calvary are identified with each other. They are one and establish a union between God and his people that lasts for ever. It is a covenant of God with many, not limited to the covenant of Moses (Ex 24, 5–8) or to that of Abraham (Gen 15, 7–21).

I SHALL NOT DRINK AGAIN OF THE FRUIT OF THE VINE UNTIL THE DAY WHEN I DRINK IT NEW IN THE KINGDOM OF GOD

The "drink" of the Marcan Last Supper did not mean just a commemoration of a past but also that of the future banquet (14, 15), which within a day became past yet remained future for ever as well. The kingdom of God with Christ became both present and everlasting future (Horvath, 1975a, 145–55). Thus it is understandable that, unlike Paul and Luke, Mark did not feel it necessary to report Jesus' commandment "Do this in memory of me." The living Christ with his community is the guarantee that the Eucharistic celebration will go on. Jesus' life, death, and resurrection, together with his community, interpret the Eucharistic commemoration. Thus the Marcan presentation of the Last Supper is not complete without the commemoration of the Marcan Jesus and of his followers. It is a celebration of Jesus' body together with his mystical body, as Paul expressed it.

THE MARCAN JESUS' LIFE AND DEATH

After we have read the prophets, it is surprising that in Mark's gospel God displays no signs of anger as he did in the days of the prophets. Rather, God is well pleased (1, 1, 11; 9, 8). Nor does Jesus in Mark manifest any intention of appeasing God's wrath by offering a sacrifice for that purpose. Mark's purpose was to show that this man, Jesus, who is known to be risen, is the Son of God, who does what the Father wants him to do and that there is a loving relation between the two. He is obedient in accepting death because that is the will of his Father. He does not ask, "Why?" Surely dying was not his will, yet it became his will because it was the will of the Father.

According to Mark, Jesus foretold his death to his disciples (9, 31–32; 10, 33–34) but gave no other reason except the Scripture (14, 21), which for him meant the will of his Father. Why death? The emerging answer in Mark, as well in the other gospels, is the great commandment "You shall love the Lord your God with all your heart, and with all your soul, and with all your mind, and with all you strength" (Mk 12, 30), at any cost, even of death. Death reveals the depth of love, and so the death of Jesus reveals his love for his Father. Being the obedient Son of God, he lived up to the great commandment. This love is the most fundamental reason for and the light in which one may discover the meaning of the dogmatic and theological explanations of expiation, atonement, "paying the price" for reconciliation and forgiveness of sins. All dogmatic and theological disputes can find their final answer in that love (Lyonnet, 1957–60).

For Mark, Jesus came to inaugurate the kingdom of God by preaching and working miracles. His life was a life for others. In chapter 10, verse 45 it was called a ransom for many and not just for a select few. The *λύτρον* of verse 45 is connected with unselfish service, like that of that of a slave mentioned in the context (10, 41–45). Jesus was a ransom because he became a servant to others in order to free them. He cured and restored to health (1, 22–34; 3, 4; 5, 23–34; 6, 56; 7, 37; 8, 35; 13, 10; 15, 30–31). He asked for repentance and forgave sin, which only God could do (2, 5–12; 3, 28). Jesus did this and could do this because he had that perfect love of God which wipes out sins. Thus it is not unexpected that, according to Mark, neither the chief priests with their whole assembly nor Pilate could find just cause for putting Jesus to death. Pilate decreed his death solely to satisfy the request of the former. Yet reading his gospel, one can sense that Mark knew the reason. It was Jesus' own way of life (Horvath, 1979b, 20–9, 96).

According to Mark, there was a growing and dramatic tension between Jesus and the world around him. It started when, for the first time, he rejected the old, "man-made," selfish traditions and way of life, which, in his view, rendered God's word null and void. In Mark 2, 15–17 we read that Jesus rejected the traditional separation of the holy and unholy, the clean and unclean, the Pharisaic distinction between justice and sinfulness. He refused to fast (2, 18–20) because he did not want to sew a patch of new cloth onto the old. He did not observe the Sabbath (2, 23–26) or the ritual washing of hands before eating or any other purification tradition of the Pharisees. He was against the *qorbān,* or gift dedication to God, because it supplanted God's commandment of doing one's duty to one's parents.

According to Ephesians 2, 14–16, Jesus came to break down the dividing wall of hostility by abolishing in his flesh the law of commandments and ordinances. Mark in his Gospel pointedly describes this hostility. He attaches great importance to the opposition aroused by Jesus. In chapter 2 we learn that Jesus' failure to observe the Sabbath scandalized the Pharisees so much that they held counsel with the Herodians as to how to destroy him. Later, Jesus in his turn called them hypocrites (7, 6–9). Even Peter is charged with being deceived by Satan for staying on the side of humans and not on the side of God (8, 33). It seems that for Jesus there was an utter incompatibility between the kingdom of God and the adulterous and sinful generation of his time (8, 34–38; 7, 21–22; 10, 19–22). That is why he declared unforgivable any challenge to his integrity that linked him with the unclean spirit (3, 29). He was extremely sensitive to the accusation made by the scribes that he was possessed by Beelzebub (3, 22–30). Likewise he silenced the unclean spirits that acknowledged him as Son of God (5, 18–19). According to Mark 12, 12 ,the chief priests, the scribes, and the elders (cf. 11, 27) tried to arrest him because they perceived that the parable that he had recounted had been directed against them. His condemnation of the blasphemy that he was or claimed to be the Christ (14, 22), as well as the charge that he intended to destroy the Temple (14, 58; 15, 29), indicates how unwilling Jesus was to conform to the established value system.

Thus it seems that the Marcan reason why Jesus had to die is to be found in his uncompromising integrity of being faithful to his love of God. He died rather than, for the sake of the "human way," give up the mission his Father had given him. Nothing, not even death, could prevent him from being on the side of God instead of the world (7, 9; 8, 13). And at the moment of his greatest temptation when dying on the cross, he was challenged by the taunt "Let the Christ, the King of Israel, come down now from the cross, that we may see and believe" (15, 32; Horvath, 1969), which prompted his crying out, "My God, why hast thou forsaken me?" (15, 34). Yet his love for his Father triumphed. He gave his last testimony that he loved God the Father more than himself. His dying on the cross became the revelation of his most perfect, unconditional, unselfish love for his Father. He knew that to God, to his Father, all things were possible, and he appealed to his Father's love for him to save him from death (14, 36ab). Yet without waiting for an answer, he offered his unconditional love: "not what I will, but what you will." His Father's will prevailed. Being abandoned by world and God, seemingly defeated in his effort to save the world, he could say yes to the incomprehensibility of the love he had for God. It looked like a foolish love, a stumbling block to many (1 Cor 1, 18, 23–24), but Jesus remained loyal to such a foolish love, which could accept the incomprehensibility of God's power hidden in weakness. Incomprehensibility, solidarity with each human being, good or bad, in sorrow and guilt, made up Jesus Christ's unconditional love for God in dying on the cross. He suffered the "hellish pain" of being forsaken by God. This act was the consummation of his obedience "and the deep love of the heart," a heart that could say, "Father to this God who still stands before him as the consuming fire of judgment," a heart "that could surrender its poor life into His hands" (Rahner, 1966a, 240). From this moment on, his cross became the touchstone and criterion of Christ's love celebrated in the Eucharist and shared by each participant. It served the model for St Paul describing Christian love in 1 Corinthians 13, 4–8.

All this may not correspond to the common notion of sacrifice in religious studies. But it conveys a great love for God that wipes out every sin. And this is the notion of sacrifice that the Council of Trent wanted to save for both the sacrifice at Calvary and the sacrifice of mass (Council of Trent, session 22, chapter 1, canon 1, 2; Tanner, 1990, 732–3, 735). Jesus Christ, being the same one "who offers himself by the ministry of his priest" (ibid., 733), is actively present at the Eucharistic celebration and has the same perfect love of God that he witnessed at Calvary "once for all." In virtue of this presence, he is adored by the worship of adoration, due to the true

God (Council of Trent, session 13, canon 6 with chapter 5; Tanner, 698, 695) and shares his perfect love with his faithful by elevating their imperfect love to the perfect love of God. He does so either by the grace of contrition made perfect by love or by the grace of imperfect love made perfect in the sacrament of penance (Council of Trent, session 14, chapter 4; Tanner, 705), absolving "even enormous offences and sins" (session 22, chapter 3; Tanner, 733).

Love can indeed forgive sin because from its beginning, sin is the denial of the reality of an essentially unselfish love. If the Eucharist is the sacrament of Jesus' unselfish love, each grace is the grace of love, the grace of the Eucharistic Jesus' love. There is no forgiveness without the sacrament of the Eucharist together with the sacrament of penance, the expression and realization of the Eucharistic Jesus' unlimited, forgiving love. If the words "This is my body" and "This is my blood" mean a real presence of the author of all graces, Jesus Christ, here and now in the world, any grace given in any time and place is not a direct grace from heaven but a Eucharistic grace of the here and now. Moreover, since those words are the efficacious words of Jesus Christ, the Eucharist represents and brings about each sacrament as an encounter with the risen Christ, who died and rose for every human being. It is in this sense that the sacraments are sacraments. They are sacraments of love by virtue of the Eucharist.

The recognition of the sacramental nature of any sacrament, therefore, seems to be related to the recognition of Jesus' real presence in the Eucharist. The Eucharist, as the sacrament of Christ's unselfish love for the human race, is the meaning and the foundation of the other sacraments. It is the first and last, the alpha and omega of the other sacraments and the hermeneutic principle for sacramental theology. It is the historical foundation of the sacramental theology because it is the presence of the eschatological kingdom of God in time.

To express the peculiar nature and value of Jesus' redeeming and sin-forgiving love, biblical authors and theologians have used various models. All know that this was not a love in the ordinary sense of the word. It had a weight, depth, and effect exceeding any human measure. Interpreting the "ransom" of Romans 3, 25 and the "precious blood" of 1 Peter 1, 18–19 in the slave-owning world of the time, Origen thought that Jesus by his death had to make a heavy payment to redeem sinners from Satan, who because of sin had acquired rights over them. Anselm of Canterbury proposed the idea of satisfaction which Jesus made to God the Father offended by sins. Being an offence against the infinite God, sin required an infinite satisfaction, which only Jesus as God-man could offer. The Reformers understood that Jesus accepted death as a punishment for our sins and made "at-one-ment " by "reconciling God with human beings." Peter Abelard saw in Christ's dying for the sinner just an example of love prompting love in return by sinners. Athanasius, in his book *On Incarnation*, argued that Jesus shared human nature so that the human race might share God's nature. As a substitute, he was the representative of each human being, example and granter of a share in his life.

In the final analysis, these are all various interpretations of Jesus' unique love for his Father and of his sin-forgiving love for the world. The validity of each interpretation hinges on its ability to touch the innermost reality not only of Calvary but of the Eucharist as the presence of the ever-loving risen Christ.

Since love is the threshold of time and eternity (Horvath, 1979a, 159–60), the Eucharist touches upon the eschatological and cosmic dimension of the reality of the Resurrection. Through his resurrection, the God-loving, sin-forgiving Christ conquered time and space and related them to eternity. His unselfish forgiving love, manifested in a definitive time and space, was made present to every human being as well as to the cosmic universe. Thus the Eucharist became the sacrament of eternity and made eternity the meaning of time. It became the sacrament of time and made time an expression of eternity (Horvath, 1993, 116–17). Since space and time are correlative terms, the Eucharistic real presence required a new concept of time that in general is a determining notion for theology (ibid., 27–42).

THE LIFE AND DEATH OF THE MARCAN JESUS' FOLLOWERS

In Mark's account the sacrificial meaning of the life and death of Jesus' followers does not differ much from that of Jesus' own life and death. But there is only one difference. For his followers to follow the way of God is now to follow Christ. If one wants to be one of his followers, says Mark, he or she has to take up his or her cross and lose his or her life for Jesus' sake, for this the individual may be hated and put to death, just as Jesus was for being faithful to his Father and to his kingdom (13, 9–13). Everything that is old, even one's eye or foot (9, 42–48), must be given up for the new (10, 17–27), because the old and the new are incompatible (4, 10–32). Thus it is not surprising that, unlike in Assyrian worship and in that of the Old Testament (Lev 2, 13), not the meal but Jesus' followers are to be salted (9, 49–50). They are the ones who purify the old and preserve what is new (cf. Lev 2, 13; Ezek 16, 4: 2 Kgs 2, 2), and as new leaven, they bring about Jesus' eschatological kingdom established by his death and resurrection. And that kingdom is sharing Jesus' unrestricted love for his Father and for every human being.

Jesus' life, death, and resurrection and the life, death, and resurrection of his followers relate to the Eucharist and the Eucharist to them. One cannot be fully understood without the other because one is an interpretation of the other. The transformation of the bread and wine is a symbol of the transformation of the faithful transcending the present, which in the light of the Eucharist appears as relative, "old," and peremptory. The Eucharist is not a thing but a person, the person of Jesus Christ and the persons of his Church. The Eucharist makes the past – the Last Supper, Calvary, and Emmaus – present, and it brings eternity in the time. It joins Christology with ecclesiology, anthropology, and eschatology (Horvath, 1993, 68–82). All this seems to be coherent and consistent with a realistic understanding of the statements "This is my body" and "This is my blood," confirmed by the following more extensive theologies of the Eucharist.

4.1.1.2.2 The Matthean Tradition

"Now as they were eating, Jesus took bread, and blessed, and broke it, and gave it to the disciples and said, 'Take, eat; this is my body.' And he took a cup, and when he had given thanks he gave it to them, saying, 'Drink of it, all of you; for this is my blood of the covenant, which is poured out for many for the forgiveness of sins. I tell you I shall not drink again of this fruit of vine until that day when I drink it new with you in my Father's kingdom'" (Mt 26, 26–29). This description is almost identical with the one presented by Mark. The eschatological orientation is confirmed with the additional words "with you." The glorified Christ will not be alone in his Father's kingdom. He will drink again of "this" fruit of the vine together with his followers. Eternal life in heaven is promised to his followers in virtue of their sharing with him his Eucharistic celebration. In an exclusive sense, the same account can be found in John, extending to any one who lived, lives, and will live, when he says "unless" one eats the flesh of the Son of man and drinks his blood, he or she will have no life (Jn 6, 53–56).

The sacramental presence of "This is my body" and "This is my blood of the covenant" is restated with the additional words of "forgiveness of sins," exclusive to Matthew yet consistent with the Marcan Jesus' love for his Father. The forgiveness of sin is central in the lives of Jesus and of his followers.

THE LIFE AND DEATH OF THE MATTHEAN JESUS AND OF HIS FOLLOWERS

The Marcan tradition concerning the meaning of Jesus' life and death was known to Matthew. Jesus had to come and perform his task (1, 21–23; 2, 5.13–17; 3, 3; 4, 4–7.10–14; 8, 17; 11, 10; 12, 17; 13,.14. 35; 15, 7; 21, 4.16.42) and to suffer (26, 4.54.56). It was so written, and he fulfilled the will of the Father (26, 39.42) when the hour came (26, 45). The "had to" (δεῖ; 16, 21) was for Jesus an obligation "imposed" on him by his love for his Father in the same way as we have seen in Mark. But Matthew makes it explicit that this love for his Father includes his love for sinful human beings and brings to them the forgiveness of sins (1, 21; 9, 6; 26, 28).

Sin, for Matthew, is not some kind of ceremonial negligence (15, 1–2)) that angers God. It is injustice committed against people (cf 15, 19; 18, 15.21; 27, 4). It is refusing the way of Jesus, who preferred to die rather than to kill (26, 52–53). Even the sin against the Holy Spirit is a sin against Jesus and his way. It is a refusal to accept the Holy Spirit's witness to him (16, 31).There is no neutrality in regard to Jesus (12, 30; Horvath, 1971b, 385–6). Once faith is demanded not in God alone but in Jesus, sin acquires a new meaning. It means a wrong and unjust attitude to any human being. It is a refusal of Jesus' love for human beings, for whom he poured out his blood.

As for Mark, so for Matthew too, it was Jesus' incompatibility with the leaders of his people that resulted in his death (15, 1–12; 26, 61–64; 27, 12). This incompatibility, however, is formulated by Matthew as an inward quality of mercy, as opposed to concern for external regulations. When Jesus is criticized for eating with sinners and tax collectors, Matthew points out that Jesus wants mercy rather than sacrifice (9, 13; 12, 7). If, therefore, one wanted to apply the term "sacrifice" to the life and death of the Matthean Jesus, it would mean a life of mercy and forgiveness even at the price of death. So too for the life and death of Jesus' followers (Horvath, 1979b, 37–40).

The fundamental idea of the Sermon on the Mount, which was expected to form the pattern of the life of Jesus' followers, is that the internal must come first and the external must flow out of the internal (Mt 5, 17–48; 15, 10–20). The authentic life of the disciples, like a house built on rock, is unshakable. The Matthean Jesus also demands from his followers mercy and forgiveness of the sins committed against them. Reconciliation with a brother or sister should precede any gift to the altar (5, 23–24). Coming to terms with one's opponent is also recommended (5, 25). After the Lord's Prayer, Matthew makes it emphatically clear that if the disciples do not forgive others, God will not forgive them the wrongs they have done (6, 14–15). Everyone has to forgive the other from his or her heart (18, 35). The verses of Luke concerning forgiveness (17, 3–4) are considerably extended by Matthew (cf. 18, 15–22). Entering the heavenly banquet depends on what one has done to one's fellow human beings (25, 32–46). Thus the Eucharistic words of "pouring out ... for the forgiveness of sins" covers as well as discloses the meaning of the live and death not only of Jesus but of his followers too (Horvath, 1979b, 37–40) and underlines the great love of the Eucharistic Jesus precisely in forgiving sins.

4.1.1.2.3 The Lucan Tradition

"'I have earnestly desired to eat this Passover with you before I suffer: I tell you I shall not eat it until it is fulfilled in the kingdom of God.' And he took a cup, and when he had given thanks he said: 'Take this, and divide it among yourselves; for I tell you that from now on I shall not drink of the fruit of the vine, until the kingdom of God comes' (Lk 22, 15–18). 'And he took bread and when he had given thanks he broke it and gave it to them saying, 'This is my body which is given for you. Do this in remembrance of me.' And likewise the cup after supper, saying, 'This cup which is poured out for you is the new covenant in my blood'" (22, 19–20).

Both the bread and the cup are given or poured out "for you." Luke does not mention the Matthean "for the forgiveness of sins," but he knows about the Pauline "Do this in remembrance of me." The double giving of the cup combines Marcan and Matthean eschatological with the Pauline commemorative moment of the Last Supper celebration. The use of the two cups may indicate more clearly the difference between the Jewish Passover and the Last Supper as *the* Last Supper. The eschatological expectation is probably connected with the first cup, which according to Mishnah ritual, has been followed by the recital of part of the Hallel blessing (see Ps 112, 1–113, 8). After this, according to Luke, Jesus introduced a new significance to the celebration.

At the moment when the head of the family is supposed to give an explanation of the Passover, Jesus turns the whole celebration into a memorial of himself. Immediately after the bread is distributed, he admonishes those present: "Do this in memory of me" (22, 19). In Paul this admonition is repeated twice (1 Cor 11, 24–25). In Luke the emphasis is achieved by the shock of Jesus' revelation that one of them sitting with him at the table will be his betrayer (22, 21–23). The bewilderment and questioning that follow work in two ways: they make the traditional meaning of the Passover sink into oblivion, and at the same time they impress on the minds of those present the tragic significance of what is about to happen. The Eucharistic celebration now points towards the death of Jesus. It becomes the symbol and the words expressing the meaning of his death with an eschatological hope. The death on the cross is to be understood in the words of the Last Supper, which signify proleptically the messianic banquet, and this in turn is to be reinterpreted by the event of the cross (Horvath, 1979, 35–7). The "giving" of the bread and the "likewise" of the wine in communion is a most intimate form of being-in-one-another, Jesus in his disciples and the disciples in Jesus. This being-in-one-another is the intentionality of all three: neither the cross (he dies) nor the Last Supper celebration (he will live for ever) with his followers (together) can be excised from the life of Jesus: "This is my body" and

"This is my blood" mean the presence of Jesus and his life in union with his followers.

4.1.1.2.3 The Life and Death of the Lucan Jesus and His Followers

In many respects, the Lucan Jesus' life and death is similar to that in Mark. Like Mark, Luke does not feel that God the Father is to be appeased and reconciled by Jesus' life and death. The Lucan God is not angry. Rather, from the first, he is well pleased (1, 30–33; 2, 40; 3, 22; 4, 34; 9, 35). Jesus' time is a time of God's favour and joy for all the people (2, 2). It is true that, unlike Mark, Luke agrees with Matthew that John the Baptist presented the day of the Messiah as a day of anger, retribution, and judgment. Nevertheless, the purpose of Jesus' life, as well as the reason for his death, is not explicitly appeasing God. He forgives sins apart from his own suffering and death (5, 17–25). He is convinced that people without repentance might perish like the Galileans killed by Pilate (11, 1–5). Yet when he talks about the purpose of his life, he does not express it in the terms used by John the Baptist. In Nazareth he discloses the meaning of his life by quoting Isaiah 61, 1–2, that is, to give liberty to captives, sight to the blind, freedom to the oppressed, and good news to the poor (4, 18–22; 7, 18–22). In brief, the purpose of his life is to live for others by helping people and saving them from all their miseries.

To the question Why did Jesus have to die? Luke again, following Mark, has a double answer. First, Jesus had to die because he did not follow the way and the patterns of his contemporaries, and secondly, he had to die because it was so written. Already, the twelve-year-old Jesus did not follow his parents' way of thinking because he had to be busy with his Father's affairs and followed his own way (2, 29). Later he antagonized his own townsfolk by not performing the marvellous deeds they asked for. They were so enraged that they wanted to kill him (4, 20–30). Again, he rejected the devil's temptations because the suggestions of his tempter were against the way of his Father, as recorded for him in the Scriptures (4, 4.8.12). Like the Marcan, the Lucan Jesus too was extremely careful to avoid any suspicion that he has any kind of communion with the devil (4, 41). For this reason he did not let the man from whom devils had been cast out (8, 38–39) remain in his company.

He did not fast, did not keep the Sabbath, and ate with sinners (5, 29–36, 11; 13, 10–17). After seeing all this, says Luke, the leaders of the people started to dispute among themselves about what they could do with Jesus (6, 11). Jesus felt that the reason why he was rejected by others as a glutton and drunkard was that they did not recognize God's plan. He was rejected, and in turn he rejected all who did not welcome and esteem God's work and his plan (7, 30–35). Uncompromisingly, the Lucan Jesus assailed anyone who opposed God's plan. He attacked the Pharisees because they were scandalized that he did not wash his hands before dinner (11, 37–54). He condemned them because they liked taking the seats of honour, and because they seized the property of widows. He called them fools, for, while outwardly clean, inwardly they were filled with extortion and wickedness, overlooking and neglecting the justice and love of God. And when some of the lawyers protested that they too felt insulted by Jesus' words, he condemned them as well. They had taken away the key of knowledge. They did not enter and had prevented others from entering the kingdom. After this denunciation, the scribes and Pharisees set many traps to catch Jesus out in something he might say.

On the same grounds, the Lucan Jesus also blamed the crowds. They could interpret the face of earth and sky, but they could not interpret their own times (12, 56). According to Luke, Jesus came to cast fire on the earth and bring division instead of peace: division of house against house, division of father against son, and so on (12, 49–53). It is not surprising that before Pilate Jesus was accused of inciting people to revolt (23, 5). And Pilate, without finding any other reason, delivered him up to the demands of the people (23, 34). In condemning Jesus, the Sanhedrin followed the same line. Yet he dared to confess that he was the Christ, the Son of Man, to be seated hereafter at the right hand of the Father (22, 66–70).

Thus Jesus met death because he would not abandon the way of God for the human way. Having accepted God's plan, he strove to realize it in spite of all opposition. If one calls the life of such a man a sacrifice, then sacrifice would mean nothing else than the acceptance of God's plan, whereas the refusal of sacrifice would be equivalent to the thwarting or rejecting of God's plan and the following instead of the ways of other human beings. As the Marcan, so the Lucan Jesus was dedicated to his Father's will, as expressed in his last words at the cross: "Father, into your hands I commend my Spirit" (23, 46). The loud cry of desperation in Mark turns out in Luke to be the expression of Jesus' whole life: a loving dedication to his Father's way.

The fact that the Last Supper and the Crucifixion occurred at the time of unleavened bread and the Passover feast suggests that Jesus was recognized as the paschal lamb, as he, indeed, is so presented by Paul and John. Yet it is clear that the faithful of the Marcan, Matthean, and Lucan traditions did not conceive Jesus' life in terms of a Passover victim. His life and death were seen much more as a definitive dedication to follow God's way in forgiving others and doing good to them, rather than to follow human ways, and this even at the price of life. We find that this is the meaning reflected in the life of Jesus' followers and in the Eucharistic ceremony described in Luke (Horvath, 1979b, 29–37).

The love for Christ presented in the Synoptics may be still a way of life for today and for tomorrow. It remains a criterion of true love because love is essentially unselfish and the opposite of sin, which is self-centred. This is also the central message of Paul's Eucharistic celebration, with its own clarity and riddles.

4.1.1.2.4 Paul: The Lord's Supper and Their Own Meals

The first letter of Paul to the Corinthians, where we find his description of the Last Supper (1 Cor 11, 20–21) was written before the synoptic gospels were put down in writing. It is earlier in time yet more comprehensive than any of them. The recurrence of the essential words of "This is my body" and "This is my blood" confirms that the Eucharistic celebration was the foundation of each Christian community. No writer could ignore it (cf. Jn 6, 35–71). Each had to employ it in presenting Jesus' life, as the Synoptics did, or in the life of a Christian community, as Paul had. To overcome social differences experienced during Eucharistic celebrations, Paul reminded the community of what he had earlier told them about the Last Supper. He claimed that, unlike the tradition about Jesus' resurrection (1 Cor 15, 3), he had received the account directly from the Lord (1 Cor 11, 23).

This reception "from the Lord" can be interpreted in three ways. One would be that Paul had recognized any early tradition of the Church as a direct tradition from Christ. This interpretation is unlikely, since he made distinctions and more than once appealed to his vision on the road to Damascus for his own authority and advantage (Gal 1, 11–12; 1 Cor 1, 17; Horvath, 1975a, 226–9). Another way could be that the words "This is my body" and "This is my blood," being so consistent in each tradition, were considered by Paul as well by others as what theologians would call today *ipsissima verba Christi* and recognized as being received from Christ. This interpretation is not impossible, but it is unlikely since different versions of the Eucharistic institution existed, all equally accepted as the authentic words of Christ.

The most probable interpretation is the third one. Paul had received the account directly from the Lord in the revelation granted to him on the way to Damascus in the words "Saul, Saul, why do you persecute me?" (Acts, 9, 4; 22, 8; 26, 14). In Jesus' identifying himself with his followers, Paul recognized that Christ is alive and is present in the midst of his followers' celebrating him in the breaking of bread. His understanding of the mystical body of Christ and of the Eucharistic presence was so closely related that for him one was the foundation of the other and neither one could be believed without the other. It is noteworthy that Paul begins his presentation of the Last Supper with words of his first encounter with the "Lord" Jesus (Acts 9, 5; 22, 8; 26, 15) and he writes like an eye witness. "The Lord Jesus on the night when he was betrayed took bread, and when he had given thanks, he broke it and said, 'This is my body which is for you. Do this in remembrance of me.' In the same way also the cup, after supper, saying, 'This cup is the new covenant in my blood. Do this, as often you drink it, in remembrance of me. For as often you eat this bread and drink the cup, you proclaim the Lord's death until he comes'" (1 Cor 11, 23–26). The text is considered the earliest, yet theologically the most complete, testimony about the Last Supper.

THE REAL PRESENCE AND THE MYSTICAL BODY

"This is my body" and "This cup is the new covenant in my blood" (1 Cor 11, 24–25) mean for Paul first of all an encounter and union with Christ identifying himself with his followers. It is a participation in the body of Christ and communion in the blood of Christ by all, who though they are many, yet are "one body" since they "all partake of the one bread" and have "a communion in the blood of Christ" (1 Cor 10, 16–17).

FOR YOU ... IN MY BLOOD

BLOOD UNITES

The "new covenant" is new because it is in the real blood of Christ. Since it is a covenant, all that is known about the Sinaitic covenant and the prophetic messianic age (see Jer 31, 31–34) is helpful. Yet for Paul the meaning of the new covenant is Christ. The new covenant is the mystical body of Christ in his blood. Jesus' blood, as the blood of the covenant, binds all the faithful together. The cup of the Lord and Jesus' blood are inseparable. No one can share in the cup of blessing without sharing in the blood of Christ (1 Cor 10, 16). The union between the bread and the cup, on the one side, and the body and blood of Christ, on the other, is such that by unworthily eating and drinking, one profanes nothing less than the body and blood of Christ (1 Cor 11, 27). Anyone who does not distinguish, διακρίνω, the bread and the cup of the Lord from any other bread and cup will be charged, κρίμα, and set apart by the same bread and cup of the Lord (1 Cor 11, 28–29). Paul seems convinced that such a failure to discern the body and blood of Christ from an ordinary meal, whether at home (1 Cor 11, 34) or at fraternal gatherings (1 Cor 6, 7), is the reason why many of the Corinthians "are weak, and ill, and some have died" (1 Cor 11, 30). Furthermore, he carefully distinguishes the Lord's Supper (κυριακὸν *δεῖπον*; 1 Cor 11, 20) from the private meals of the participants (*'ἴδιον δεῖπον*; 1 Cor 11, 21). The latter are to satisfy hunger and should not be the reason for coming together in the assembly of the faithful. The meaning of the Lord's meal is not to satisfy hunger but to proclaim the death of the Lord until he comes (Horvath, 1979b, 65–6).

BLOOD IS REDEMPTIVE AND EXPIATORY

It is remarkable that in his record of the Lord's Supper, Paul does not mention "the forgiveness of sins," though sin and expiation play a central role in his explanation of why Jesus had to die (Horvath, 1979b, 47–58). Yet for Paul, Jesus' blood operating in the Eucharist, in addition to its uniting power, has a redemptive and expiatory one as well. The role of Jesus' blood is like that of faith. Just as by faith justification (Rom 3, 28.30; Gal 2, 16; 3, 8.24) by the blood of Jesus is given, so also is redemption (ἀπολύτρωσις). Redemption is to be received by faith in the blood of Christ (Rom 3, 24–25), for all who are justified by (ἐν) his blood now (Rom 5, 9) shall be all saved from the wrath of God (Rom 5, 9). And those who are reconciled by the death of the Son shall be saved also by his life (Rom 5, 9). It seems that in the the letter to the Romans Paul "brings forward explicitly the idea that the reason of Jesus' death was the propitiation of an angry God by the blood of his innocent Son" (Horvath, 1979b, 54–5).

Many New Testament scholars have been puzzled by seeing the reappearance of the wrath of God in Pauline writings (ibid., 97–8). Yet one should remember that just as with any grace, so also Paul's grace of conversion too progressively penetrated his human mind and let him grasp the impact that Christ's revelation made on his notion of God. As a former Pharisee (Acts 23, 6), he knew the Old Testament well, and the wrath of God was not just an anthropomorphic note. Rather, it meant a living, loving person with feelings unlike the idols of the pagans, who do not see, hear, or know (Dan 5, 23).

In his earliest writing, the first letter to the Thessalonians, Paul says that Jesus raised from the dead will come from heaven to save all from the anger (1 Th 1, 10) which will come upon all who displease God (1 Th 2, 15–16). Through Jesus Christ, who died for them, the believers are destined not for wrath but for salvation (1 Th 5, 9). Here is the first instance where Jesus' death has been connected with the idea of salvation from the wrath of God. The Thessalonians are told that they should please (ἀρέσκειν; 1 Th 4, 1) God and not disregard him, for God is an avenger (ἔκδικος; 1 Th 4, 6). Unlike the God of the Synoptics, who does not appear to be angry, Paul's God is an angry avenger who punishes all who disregard him. On the basis of such a notion, it is easy to understand that for Paul the notion of expiation will be of great importance.

The idea of a punishing and revenging God, so familiar from the Old Testament, is further stressed in the second letter to the Thessalonians. Jesus himself will inflict vengeance and eternal punishment upon those who do not acknowledge God and refuse to accept the gospel (2 Th 1, 8–9). Those who are chosen from the beginning to be saved will endure persecution and suffering in order to manifest that the judgment of God is just. Nevertheless, all those who afflict the elected of God will be repaid (ἀνταποδίδωμι) through their own affliction (2 Th 1, 6). It seems that suffering is inflicted to satisfy the righteousness of God. Since God restricts vengeance to himself (2 Th 1, 5), the faithful should themselves refrain from repaying evil with evil (1 Th 5, 14).

God's justice as the reason for Christ's suffering and death returns in the letter to the Galatians. The reason for Christ's death is justification. If justification had been possible through the law, says Paul, then Christ would have died for no purpose (Gal 2, 21). He gave himself up for sinners to deliver them from the present evil age (1, 4). But precisely the death of Jesus, who gave himself up for Paul, revealed the love of the Son of God (Gal 2, 20). Thus justice, love, and death are systematically connected in Paul. In order to justify Paul, Jesus died for him because he loved him.

This personal experience of Jesus' love for him let Paul understand love as the universal, final reason for Jesus' death. Since Jesus wanted to redeem all who were under the law, he had to be born subject to the law (Gal 4, 5). Now since the law curses everyone who does not persevere in everything that is written in the law (cf. Dt 27, 26), Jesus himself had to become a curse (*κατάρα*; Gal 3, 10, cf. *ἁμαρτία* of 2 Cor 5, 21 with *ἐν ὁμοιώματι σαρκος ἁμαρτίας* of Rom 8, 3) and made himself responsible for the curse. And since the Scripture says that the cursed must hang on the tree (Gal 3, 13; cf. Dt 21, 13), Christ had to die on the tree of the cross to expiate the curse of the law. He had to suffer and die because he had identified himself with the human race condemned by the law to death. This mysterious identification of Jesus with the human race, on the one hand, and that of the human race with Christ, on the other, are the outcome of Paul's vision on the road to Damascus and the foundation of his theology. From this it follows also that all those who belong to Christ must be crucified to the flesh, with its passion and desires (Gal 5, 24).

The judgment known from the letters to the Thessalonians is found also in the first letter to the Corinthians. But there is a difference. Christ will not judge in the proper sense of the word. He just discloses the work of each one by the test of fire (1 Cor 3, 13–15; 4, 5). The why of Christ's suffering is the revelation that the apparent weakness of God is stronger than human strength and wisdom (1 Cor 1, 13–31; 2, 7–8). It seems to be some sort of ransom by which the faithful are bought by Christ. They are joined closely to Christ like a slave to his or her Lord, therefore free of anyone else (1 Cor 6, 20; 7, 23). Suffering is the measure of love uniting the believers closely to Christ as members of his mystical identity (body). By now sin is more than something that deserves punishment and an evil fate. It brings an enmity that must be reconciled.

In the second letter to the Corinthians (5, 18–21) it is not God who is to be reconciled. Rather, he is the one who reconciles the world to God in

Christ and through Christ. It is God, and not the faithful, who provides the sin offering, *ἁμαρτία,* by making Christ a sin-expiatory sacrifice so that all may become in Christ the justice of God (2 Cor 5, 21). God gave us Christ in order that, by his obedient love for God, God may be reconciled with the world. By sharing Jesus' love, the faithful become the justice of God, and thus love has been revealed by justice and has forgiven sins. On account of this sharing, Paul, as the ambassador of Christ, beseeches his followers to be reconciled to God, who now has reconciled the world with God's self. Thus the difficult verses of 2 Corinthians 5, 16–21 find their meaning in the short Augustinian saying cited by Trent: "God loves us so much that he wanted his own gifts (Christ included) to be our merits" (session 6, chapter 16; Tanner, 1990, 678).

Christ died for all because he loved all, and Christ's love (*ἀγάπη* τοῦ Χριστοῦ; 2 Cor 5, 14) is connected with God's holiness and justice. This is still more forcefully presented in the letter to the Romans. The ultimate reason for Jesus' suffering and death was to manifest God's universal merciful love towards the human race (Rom 5, 7–8; 8, 32). The main thesis of the letter – that God's salvation is absolutely free and no one, neither Jew nor pagan, can claim that he or she does not need the mercy of God (Rom 1, 16–3, 31) is an axiom for ecumenism and reconciliation.

In order to put everyone under the power of grace, Paul places everyone under the law of sin (cf. Rom 11, 32). He finds that the more universally and more deeply he can show to his readers the universal wrath of God, the more he can demonstrate the universal gratuity of God's mercy (1, 18–32). The judgment rightly falls upon everyone, since all, as the Scripture says, have turned away from God and all have done wrong (3, 12). Now, in order to manifest not only his righteousness but his grace as well, God ordered redemption (ἀπολύτρωις) in Jesus, who was put forward through God as expiation (ἱλαστήριον) by his blood, to be accepted by the faithful in faith (3, 21–26). The expiation is needed on account of God's justice (3, 21), and reconciliation was demanded because of God's wrath, and all were received by Jesus' blood (5, 11).

There may be some hypothetical historical explanation of why Paul brought forward the idea of the propitiation of an angry God through the blood of his innocent Son (Horvath, 1979b, 54–5). In reading his letter, no one can doubt that it served the purpose mentioned earlier: it was a way of arguing for the manifestation of God's gratuitous and infinite love towards every member of the human race, sinner and enemies included (5, 12–21). For Paul, the love of God is not a cheap, empty word. It is a love that is strong enough to sacrifice everything just to reveal its power and might. It reveals a God who sacrifices (Horvath, 1975b, 370). The sacrifice of Christ is the revelation of God's great love for the human race.

BLOOD AS REVELATION

For Paul, in addition to its uniting, purificatory, and expiatory function, the blood of the new covenant has a revelatory function as well. It reveals not only God's wrath, righteousness, and forbearance (Rom 3, 25–26; 5, 9) but also his love for us, for it was in Christ's own blood that he justified the believers (Rom 5, 8–9; Horvath, 1979b, 17; 1975b, 370).

The sacrificial term *θυσία is* applied to Christ once in verbal form (1 Cor 10, 19–22) and once as a noun (Eph 5, 2). It is connected with "giving up," *παραδίδωμι*, as its epexegesis and substitutional synonym (Rom 4, 52; 8, 23; Gal 1, 4; 2, 20; 1 Tim 2, 6; Tit 2, 14). Not only did the Son give himself up, but the Father also gave up his Son (Rom 4, 25; 8, 32) for the sins of all (Gal 1, 10; 1 Tim 2, 6; Tit 2, 14). In this sense of *παραδίδωμι*, they are not the faithful to God, but rather God is the one who is "sacrificing" to them. Sacrifice (*θυσία*), giving up (*παραδίδωμι*), and redemption (*λυτρόω*) are correlated terms in Paul. *θυσία* is used when the action moves towards God, and *παραδίδωμι* when it moves from God to the world. Here Paul's theology of sacrifice reaches from the symbolic (my sacrifice) and intersubjective (my sacrifice with that of the people of God) to the theological one recognizing God who sacrifices in Christ and in his people (Horvath, 1975b, 369–70). On this level, a God who sacrifices will not seem absurd, since here sacrifice is understood as an epiphany, that is, a moment when God and the faithful mutually disclose themselves in virtue of their common and mutual self-communication (ibid., 350–70). So great was the love of God for the world that he wanted his own sacrifice to be the sacrifice of the human race in "a mutual self-communication." God gave the faithful his love that the faithful might love him with a love that is his gift. And this is the mystery of the Pauline Eucharist.

IN REMEMBRANCE OF ME

The commemorative motif "Do this in remembrance of me" is repeated twice by Paul, and it underlines the eschatological nature of the remembrance: "Do this" (present) " in remembrance," proclaiming the Lord's "death" (past) "until he comes" (future). It is not only a remembrance of the past of Christ, who died, but a "remembrance" of the presence of Christ, in whose body they share as well, as of the future of Christ, who will come. Eucharistic celebration is a celebration of the past, present, and future because it is not a remembrance of a Passover but of Jesus Christ, who is past, present, and future (Heb 13, 8). By eating "this bread" and drinking "the cup," one does not proclaim a banquet but the "Lord's death until he comes" (1 Cor 11, 26).

The death of Christ meant the end of life according to the flesh (κατὰ σάρκα) and the beginning of the new life according to the spirit (κατὰ *πνεῦμα*, Rom 8, 5) His death seemed to be necessary in order to reveal the irreducible newness and independence of the new from the old. In Jesus' death God revealed his willingness to establish a new order that was opposed to the old world of futility, decay, and death. The new life was not an endless continuation of human life. It was a *καινὸς*, a new life, the eternal life of God, into which Jesus took up human nature and with it the whole world. Thus Jesus' death has further shown God's gracious retribution and the wealth of his mercy (Rom 9, 22–3).

It is noteworthy that not in 1 Corinthians 11, 19–22 but in 1 Corinthians 5, 1–9 did Paul apply the term *θυσία* to Christ's death. In the latter passage he asked the Corinthians to expel from their midst a man who had committed incest. The reason was that because of Christ's pascal immolation, they were the unleavened bread of sincerity and should not associate with immoral men (1 Cor 5, 9). So it was not the sacrifices to idols and the breaking of bread of 1 Corinthians 10, 19–22 that reminded Paul that Christ had been sacrificed as the Passover victim but the need to cast out an evildoer from the community. It was not the liturgical connection between the feast of unleavened bread and the feast of the Passover that turned Paul's mind to the idea of Christ's immolation, but rather the incompatibility between the old and new leaven (Horvath, 1979b, 7–9). The old must be rooted out (αἴρω, ἐκκαθαίρω, *ἐξαίρω*; 1 Cor 5, 2.7.13; Horvath, 1979b, 8) since the new Passover had begun. This idea is confirmed in the letter to the Romans (12, 2), who are asked to give up the old by changing themselves into the new. The living sacrifice of the Romans is nothing else than giving up hatred in order to be transformed into the love of Christ.

THE PAULINE INTERPRETATION OF THE LIFE OF JESUS' FOLLOWERS

The noun *θυσία* is applied three times to the lives of Christ's followers (Rom 12, 1; Phil 2, 17; 4, 18). For Paul, the style and the way of life of Jesus' followers is very similar to that of Jesus as described by the Synoptics. We can assume that when Paul applies to such a life the term "sacrifice," it means, firstly, to be faithful to God and, secondly, to live a life of the spirit opposed to a life of the flesh. The way of the spirit and the way of the flesh are utterly incompatible. The fruits of the spirit are love, joy, peace, patience, kindness, goodness, faithfulness, gentleness, and self-control, which are diametrically opposed to the works of the flesh, immorality, impurity, idolatry, enmity, selfishness, anger, sectarian spirit, and so on (Gal 5, 16–25; 1 Cor 6, 9–10; 2 Cor 6, 4–10; Rom 1, 29–31; Eph 4, 17–20; 2 Tim 3, 11–12; Tit 2, 1–5; Horvath, 1979b, 58–65). The new way, a life of faith, love, and hope (1 Th 1, 3), is a way of eternal life. In brief, for Paul the Eucharistic life is a "sacrifice" of passing from this life through death into eternal life (Horvath, 1979b, 58–63).

4.1.1.2.5 Johannine Tradition

John's first Eucharistic narrative follows the multiplication of wine (2, 1–11) and the multiplication of bread (6, 1–15). We read that the real life, the eternal life, is to eat Jesus' flesh and drink his blood (6, 53–56). All who eat him will have life because of him (6, 57), for he is the bread of God come down from heaven to give life to the world (6, 33–35.48–51.57–58). To eat Jesus' flesh and drink his blood is to have eternal life, because it means the presence of Jesus and his Father (6, 56–57), from whom Jesus draws his own life.

The language is straightforward and could very well appear intolerable (cf. 6, 60). The identification of Jesus with the bread and wine is so close that the properties of the one are predicated on the other. Once the life of Jesus is understood as a self-giving to the Father and to God's people, it is possible to see the revelational relationship between Jesus as the life of the world and the bread and wine given at the Last Supper as a memorial of himself. This self-giving love is the obvious milieu of the Last Supper in the Johannine tradition. Jesus showed them that his love had no limit (13, 1: *εἰς τέλος*; 13, 2–16; cf. 13, 34–35; 14, 2–3.18–21.31; 15, 1–17; 16, 20–33; 17, 1–26).

The synoptic presentation of the institution, as well as the Johannine Eucharistic discourse of 6, 1–71, would not be complete without John's recount of the oration Jesus gave during the Last Supper (13, 1–17, 26). It is a sort of homily given during the celebration of the Last Supper and replacing the reading of Exodus (4, 1–15.27). This was Jesus' exodus "out of this world to the Father" (13, 1) when his "captivity" was coming to an end. The time of his liberation was at hand for him and for all who loved him. A self-examination was in order once more to help his friends celebrate his memory on their way to follow him in the new exodus out of this world to the Father, where he was preparing a place for them (14, 1–7).

The farewell homily is well structured. There are five themes repeated again and again to underline their importance and to impress them on the minds of the listeners. The five sayings about the Eucharist are the following. Firstly, there are the sayings about the loving union between the Father and the Son (13, 3 with 16, 10.28 and 17, 8; 13, 32; 14, 6–11.20.24.31; 15, 9–10; 16, 32; 17, 1–7.22–24.26). Secondly, we find sayings about Christ's love for all, with the insistence to "love one another" as he loved them (13, 1.4–17.20.26.34–35; 14, 2–5.20–24 with 16, 33; 15, 1–17; 16, 2.17; 17, 9.11–22.26). Thirdly, we can detect the sayings of giving whatever they ask for in his name (14, 12–14; 15, 7.16; 16, 23–24.26). Fourthly, there are the sayings of the promise of the Holy Spirit, the counsellor, the Spirit of truth (14, 16–17.25; 15, 26; 16, 7–15). And fifthly, the rejection sayings reiterate that acceptance of Christ is free

(13, 18.21.27; 14, 24.27.30; 15, 18–24; 16, 1–4.16–22.29–33; 17, 7b.10.12). These sayings are not just ordinary homiletic words. They are words of revelation pointing to the Eucharist as their realization.

THE LIFE AND DEATH OF THE JOHANNINE JESUS

Like the Synoptics, John is convinced that Jesus met his death because he was faithful to his divine vocation and would not conform to his surrounding human world. The opposition between Jesus and the leaders of his people led necessarily to the point at which he had to witness to the truth by his blood (2, 13–21; 5, 10–18.42–47; 6, 64–66; 7, 20–24.45–52; 8, 44–59; 10, 36–39; 12, 42–43; 15, 18–27; 16, 5–11; 18, 14.28–37; 19, 7–16; Horvath, 1969; 1975a, 188–98). The new element in John is that Jesus has come to give witness to what he has seen in heaven (3, 31–32; 7, 14; 8, 40; 16, 28), and to communicate it to the disciples as God's own word (3, 34; 5, 31–36; 7, 16). Jesus' witnessing by his blood is expressed also in 1 John 5, 6–12, where together with the witness by water and that of the Holy Spirit, it is called the witness of God for the Son (1 Jn 5, 9).

The intrigues and annoyance existing between Jesus and his opponents receives in John a deeply theological significance. The actual historical reason for Jesus' death and its theological meaning are not separated any longer. The external, visible historical human sign conveys a transcendental, divine meaning perceived in faith. For John, Jesus' intransigent, uncompromising attitude toward the world, which caused his death, is at the same time the pledge of God's limitless love for the world.

The Johannine literature presents God's love as a boundless self-giving to the Beloved. Just as because of the Father's love for his Son, the Father gives everything (3, 55) and shows everything (5, 20.26–27; 6, 27; 10, 17–18) to the Son, so because of his love, the Son in turn gives himself to the Father. The meaning of Jesus' life and death was to fulfill the Scriptures (2, 22; 5, 39–40; 19, 28.36–37, etc.). The meaning of the Scriptures for Jesus, however, is not some written law but his Father's will (4, 34), the commands given him by the Father (10, 18). Obedience to the Father (cf. 8, 28–29.40; 12, 48–50; 14, 31; 15, 9–11) is his *food*. His life is said to be consummated (19, 30), when he has accomplished the work the Father gave him (17, 4). For the same reason, he lays down his life. This is his vocation, given by the Father, and the Father loves him for that same reason (10, 15.18; 12, 49).

Love as an unlimited giving of oneself to the Father includes the power of withdrawing oneself from everything else in order to give oneself completely to God. Thus self-giving has a semblance of death (cf. 12, 24–25). Since love is an unlimited self-giving to another, death almost becomes the necessary condition for the realization of the greatest love (cf. 15, 13; Horvath, 1980b). It manifests who a human being is (cf. 7, 28) and the power that his or her love has (12, 31–2; Horvath, 1979b, 74–5).

Besides these two elements, unlimited self-giving and completely free self-possession, a third feature of God's love is revealed in Jesus' life and death. A love that is unlimited and absolutely free is now revealed as essentially oriented to human beings. The unlimited free self-giving to God is realized in a self-giving to humans. God has manifested his love by giving his Son for human beings that they may have life (3, 16; cf. 1, 12–13; 2, 21; 5, 29; 6, 39–54; 10, 10–11; 11, 25–26; 15, 1–17) and that they may really understand in what love consists – in laying down one's life for other human beings (1 Jn 3, 16). God's love had been disclosed by sending the Logos into the world to bring life and to be the expiation (ἱλασμος) for the sin (1 Jn 4, 9–19) of the whole world (1 Jn 2, 2; Horvath, 1979b, 76).

Since life and the remission of sin are connected, Jesus is introduced at the beginning of the gospel as the Lamb of God who takes away the sin of the world. He is a sacrificial, expiatory victim for sin (1, 29.36). The Lamb is a significant symbol for John and includes three ideas: the idea of the servant of Isaiah 53, who takes on himself the sins of people; that of the expiation of Leviticus 14; and that of the Passover of Exodus 12, 1 (cf. Jn 19, 36).

In such a context it is not surprising that, unlike the Synoptics, John's gospel speaks of the anger of God, as did Paul. Unlike in Paul, however, in John the divine anger appears mysterious and unapproachable. It falls upon those who will not believe (3, 36). While Jesus takes away the sin of disbelief, he does not make it impossible; rather, he reveals its real nature (cf. 3, 18–21.36; 10, 22–29; 11, 45–47; 12, 42–43.48; 15, 18–27; 16, 5–11). These two worlds – one the world of blood, flesh, and the human will (1, 13), the world without love, and the other, coming from above, the world of the Spirit and of love (1, 13; 3, 3–8; 8, 23) – are incompatible. For this reason, as in the Letter to the Hebrews, 1 John doubts that the propitiation offered by Jesus is without limit. There is one sin that is deadly, for which John suggests no prayer (5, 16–17). The reason for it is freedom, an indispensable precondition for love. Jesus came to save the world, not to condemn it (12, 46–47), but those who do not want to believe are condemned already by themselves (3, 18).

For the same reason, the victory of the Lamb of the Book of Revelation does not entail the impossibility of his being rejected. The Lamb, as the Lord of history, opens the seals of the different epochs (5, 6; 22, 9). He has freed the world from sin by his blood and has made a kingdom of priests of God, a new covenant with the world (1, 5). By his blood he has ransomed for God people from every tribe and nation (5, 9) and made manifest his love for them (1, 5). Yet his love knows wrath for his enemies (6, 16; cf. 15, 7.14; 16, 1; 19, 15), who claim that love can be ignored (22, 12; Horvath, 1979b, 74–7).

But love cannot be ignored. It is universal and does not admit exception. The condemnation of non-belief is the reaffirmation of the universality of love. There is no alternative to love. Death is the realization of the inevitability of unselfish love (Horvath, 1993, 102–4). The rejection of those who do not accept love means that there is no exception whatsoever to the belief that Jesus Christ, being the revelation and sacrament of the supreme love for God and for every human being, is the only saviour. There is no salvation without him, because there is no salvation without the love he made a reality. Thus hell is a Christological event, which as such does not pre-empt the real possibility and/or the actuality of eternal damnation (ibid., 133–4). Eternal damnation is a witness to the universality of love. Love cannot force and does not take away the freedom of its negation.

THE LIFE AND DEATH OF JESUS' FOLLOWERS IN JOHANNINE WRITINGS

The followers of Jesus are born, not from blood, nor from human will, but from God (1, 13). Their good deeds in helping others manifest that they are born of God, even though they may not know God and Christ (1 Jn 3, 11b; Horvath, 1974). Like Jesus, they may lose their life in order to keep it (12, 29) by loving each other and giving up their lives for others, the sign of the greatest love (15, 12). Since the love of God is essentially also of "human beings," the double commandment of Mark and Matthew (12, 29–31; 22, 37–39) is summed up in Johannine theology in one commandment: love one another (1 Jn 2, 7–10; 3, 11.16–17; Horvath, 1979b, 77–8).

In the Johannine writings the real presence, sacrifice, sacramental signs, and eschatology are all related. They are all the revelation and the realization of love, the raison d'être of the Eucharist with the other sacrifices and sacraments. After the victory of the Lamb in the Book of Revelation, the faithful are invited as brides (22, 17) to the marriage supper prepared by the Lamb (19, 9), where the glory of God is the light and the Lamb is the lamp. The infinite love, proleptically presented at the Last Supper, will be eschatologically realized at the marriage banquet of the Lamb as a symbol of gentleness and power (Horvath, 1979b, 77–8).

4.1.1.3 THE EUCHARIST AND THE HOLY SPIRIT: THE EPICLESIS

The Epiclesis, a prayer invoking the descent of the Holy Spirit upon the bread and wine, is found around the year 215 in the *Apostolic Tradition* of St Hippolytus and in a more consecratory form in the Liturgy of St Basil. St Cyril of Alexandria has a commentary on it in his *Catechetical Lectures* (c. 350). The bread and wine is "the body of Christ" and "the blood of Christ" "by the coming of the Holy Spirit," we read in Theodore of Mopsuestia's

Catechetical Commentary on the Eucharist (1933, 113). From the fourth century it became universal in Eastern liturgies, and since the Second Vatican Council the second, third, and fourth Eucharistic prayers of the Roman eucharistic Prayers have a double invocation of the Holy Spirit, one before and one after the consecration. The one before asks God "to let his Spirit come upon the gift, so that they may become the body and blood of Jesus Christ," and the one after the consecration prays to let the Spirit come upon the mystical body, the faithful, so that they may be united by the same Holy Spirit (Congar, 1983, 3, 228–49).

The Epiclesis reminds us of the mystery of the Incarnation. It was by the power of the Holy Spirit that Jesus Christ entered the world and became the centre of human life; so now by the same Holy Spirit he takes bread and wine and makes them become his body and blood, not surprisingly, because, according to the gospels, the Holy Spirit was not only the gift but the agent of Jesus Christ. The action of the Spirit was always to point to Jesus and to witness that he is Lord (1 Cor 12, 3). Being conceived of the Holy Spirit, Jesus could be worshipped, and his worshipping was a worship to God. So now by the power of the same Spirit, the Eucharistic Jesus Christ can be worshipped, and worship of him is service of the one God. The Epiclesis confirms that the transformation is real, since it is effected by God, and Christ being present brings about salvation and deserves adoration. The "accept the offering" of the Roman canon in its form of petition is also the affirmation and the expression of the consecratory action. It calls to mind that no one else but God was doing what happened just now, and being present, the faithful can address God in prayers and worship God.

To specify the action of the Holy Spirit for the Eucharist as well as for the mystical body, we have to turn to the notion of the Spirit in biblical sources as well as in the history of the human notion of what the Spirit is. Summarizing both biblical and anthropological-philosophical sources, we can say that the Spirit is a force attracting to self-transcendence (ecstatic element) from our present time into a new life in the future and thus constitutes the identity of the faithful in relation to themselves as well as in relation to the community they live in. Likewise, it was the same Spirit who moved Christ into his future destiny, which determined his identity for himself as well in relation to his mystical body. Again, it is the spirit of each human being, which lets one transcend the past and the present for a future which he or she projects and which will give identity as well as a role that one is going to play in his or her community.

Finally, we can say that it is the role of the Holy Spirit, as well as the meaning of the Epiclesis prayers over the Eucharist, to prod the Eucharistic church into the future of the new eschatological life. Corresponding to the role of God's individualizing love for us, it is the role of the Holy Spirit to make the Eucharist an individualizing and personal grace as well as a force to build the Church and serve the human race. It is not just in the Eucharistic invitation but also in the communion that the believer may discover the Holy Spirit providing special individual gifts for creating and determining one's personal eschatological future and role in the Church and in the world.

4.1.1.4 ANAMNESIS

The Old Testament recalls and reflects on the Exodus as an important foundational and historical event. The Eucharistic Jesus operates in a similar way in the New Testament. Anamnesis in Greek corresponds to the *Unde et Memores* of the Latin canon. It means "memorial," the remembrance of Jesus' life, passion, death, and resurrection (cf. 1 Cor 11, 24; Lk 22, 19). It is not just a subjective remembrance of Jesus in the believers' consciousness. Rather, it is recognition of the Eucharistic Lord as the same Jesus of Nazareth (cf. Lk 24, 25–31), who by his death and resurrection saved and saves now and here.

The Eucharistic presence is an objective, effective presence of Jesus performing his salvific work here and now. And because this is the action of the eternal person of the Logos, it has a perennial quality, being contemporaneous to any instance of space and time. It is a memorial of the past of Jesus, who is alive and takes and presents his mystical body to share in his resurrection. The form is a meal, but the purpose is not to satisfy a hunger of body but a hunger for Christ. It is not a Hellenistic or Jewish festival meal. In the form of a meal, it represents and, by the power of the Holy Spirit, realizes the most intimate form of being-in-one-another. Christ is in his faithful and his faithful are in him. It makes clear that there is no love without sacrifice and no sacrifice without love. Love is the origin and the end of sacrifice remembered in the anamnesis.

Moreover, the anamnesis indicates that Jesus' sacrifice is historical. It is the one that took place in history. It is therefore different from the cultic celebration of winter and spring of nature religions. *Unde et memores ... offerimus* emphasizes that God's holy people, together with his ministers, remember the passion and resurrection of Jesus Christ and offer to God his gift, "the pure, holy and immaculate sacrifice." It is unfortunate that the English translation of the Roman canon's "Father, we celebrate the memory of Christ your Son" misses the word *Unde* of the original Latin text. *Unde* means "therefore" and closely unites the anamnesis, the memorial prayer of the "recalling to mind," with the "Do this in memory of me" of the consecration. The "pre-face," being in the presence of God, and the anamnesis are to be understood as one. The offer and the offering person are the same, and the prayer of the Epiclesis, the "look with favour," and the "accept the offering" that is the resurrection and glorification of Jesus are part of the same sacrifice (Jungmann, 1956).

4.1.1.5 THE EUCHARIST

The word *εὐχαριστέω* (Mk 14, 23; Mt 26, 27; Lk 22, 17. 19; 1 Cor 11, 24) means offering a gift as an expression of thanks. The Hebrew notion of "blessing" was a recalling of God's mighty deeds, the *magnalia*, the wonders of God. In the New Testament the reality of Christ himself, with his being and works, is God's mighty deed, the *magnalia*, the wonder of God. Thus we can say that the Eucharist is the actualization of the saving reality, the presence of Jesus Christ through the words of thanksgiving uttered over the bread and wine. It is not a supper excised, removed, from the life of Jesus but the presence of him and all of his life. It is not a meal that symbolizes Jesus' life; rather, Jesus' life and work are symbolized in taking bread and wine as God's abiding in us. "Do this in remembrance of me," and not in remembrance of the Passover unless the Passover is a remembrance of him.

The Council of Trent stated this concept by saying that the Eucharistic Christ is truly, really, and substantially present (session 13, canon 1, chapter 1; Tanner, 1990, 697, 693): truly, that is, not spiritually in the sense of being just a similitude of the body of Christ; really, that is, not figuratively, expressing one thing in terms normally denoting another that may be regarded as analogous; and substantially, that is, not only dynamically sharing merely the power of the body of Christ being present only in heaven. Therefore the Eucharist is worthy of adoration until it is consumed in communion or the elements became organically altered. Otherwise the taking, the "eating," would make the consecration and not the word of consecration with the Epiclesis. Once more, it is not the words that explain Christ, but it is Christ, with his life together with the life of his followers, who gives meaning to the various Eucharistic expressions. Christ with his people, his mystical body, belong to the Eucharist, and the Eucharist cannot be fully interpreted without them.

4.1.1.6 THE HISTORICAL JESUS AND THE INSTITUTION OF THE EUCHARIST

The institution and celebration of the Eucharist, as we have seen, supposes an innovative, creative mind. Since the historical Jesus was an authentic Jew, one can ask whether he could have said, "This is my body" and "This is my blood." Some, such as the proponents of the Hellenistic interpretation, suggest that Jesus, who never left his country and remained a Jew until he died on the cross, could not and did not celebrate his Last Supper the way it is recorded by the New Testament writers. His Last Supper was just a simple farewell Passover meal. In remembrance of the meal and of Jesus' bloody death, some of his Greek followers began to feel themselves to be "the body of Christ" and linked Jesus' invisible presence materially to the rite of a visible meal.

Now as we have already suggested, there is much data that make such an assumption doubtful and, at the same time, support the faith of the Church that the historical Jesus was the one who commissioned what his followers began to do after his death. First of all, the history of both the traditions and the redactions indicates that neither the evangelists nor Paul invented the Eucharistic celebration. Prior to their writing, it already existed in various communities with its own particular, yet essentially identical, formulas. It had been accepted by both Greek and Hebrew communities based on an authority that no one except the historical Jesus could have granted. The innovation was so radical that no one could have introduced it and remained nameless and anonymous. Without the historical Jesus, it is difficult if not impossible to explain the authority of the institution of "This is my body" and "This is my blood," the more so since the institution was new, on one hand, and yet, on the other, was coherent and consistent not just with the life of Jesus but also with the Judaism of the prophets.

The words " This is my body" and "This is my blood" are not only coherent and consistent with the multiplication of the bread and with Jesus' proclaiming that the kingdom of God, the final eschatological superlative presence of God in the world, was at hand (Horvath, 1975a, 145–55). They are also consistent with Yahweh's feeding Israel and his ever-increasing presence in the midst of Israel (Dt 4, 7). Through the history of the Jewish people God was getting closer and closer to God's people. At the beginning it was in the pillar of cloud and in that of fire that the Lord used to go in front of Israel in the desert (Ex 13, 21–22). Later, on Mount Sinai, the glory of God rested in a cloud, the *šekînāh* (Ex 24, 16). The glory of God was a perceptible phenomenon (cf. Dt 5, 22–23) manifesting the presence of the holy God. The same glory of God filled the meeting tent (Ex 40, 34–35) and later Solomon's temple. In the time of the prophets it was God in their words who announced the eschatological time (Horvath, 1975a, 109–24), when God would dwell in Jerusalem (Ps 135, 21) in a way that would supersede all its preceding modes, so that nations may come to adore Yahweh in Jerusalem (Is 2, 2; Jer 60, 1, 66, 18–20; Mic 4, 1–3; Hag 2, 7; Zech 2, 7; 8, 20–23; cf. Gen 18, 16; Tob 13, 13–14).

Moreover, the words "This is my body and "This is my blood" are coherent and consistent with the "kingdom of God is within you" (Lk 17, 21) and with the prophets' teaching that external, formal religion was to be replaced (Hos 6, 6; Jer 31, 34; 32, 19; Ezek 18, 31; 36, 26) by a new covenant, with its law written upon the new heart (Jer 31, 33) given by God (Ezek 36, 2). There was to be a new union of God with God's people in their heart.

Furthermore, the bread of presence was not unknown in Jewish tradition. Literally, it was called the bread of face, since it was placed on a special table (Ex 25, 23–30) before Yahweh on behalf of the people as a covenant for ever and for the priests as a memorial portion (Lev 24, 5–9). Only the priests could eat it, and Jesus was well aware of that restriction (Mt 12, 4; Lk 6, 3–4). The tradition was very old and reflected a nomadic life when food was offered as nourishment to divinities. Even though the bread of presence was not considered sacrifice, it was a Jewish tradition. One does not have to go to the Hellenistic tradition for such a symbol. The bread of presence may have prompted the mind of the historical Jesus to think of a Eucharistic event; the more so if we think of another historical event.

In our presentation we find that the historical Jesus was an authentic Jew who loved God with all his heart, soul, and mind and with all his might at any cost and communicated his God's love to his people to a supreme degree, so much so that loving him, his followers felt so close to God that they felt loving him was loving God. Such a man facing his imminent death may have had a wish to stay with his followers, whom he loved and wanted to serve as he had done all his life. The bread of presentation, which he had already secularized (Mt 12, 4; Lk 6, 3–4), could remind him of being present before God on behalf of his disciples, and he could see it as a means of ensuring a new covenant (Lev 24, 5–9) and of the eschatological happiness foreseen by the prophets. He could and perhaps only he could sense it in the challenges of his own time.

By announcing that the "kingdom of God" had arrived with his time (see Horvath, 1975a, 151–5), he could understand his time from the side of eternity and express his great desire to drink "of the fruit of vine in the kingdom of God" (Mk 14, 25; cf. Lk 23, 43). It was in the mystery of death and resurrection (Ez 37, 12–14) that he could consider his time to be the meaning of all times as well as the end of all times. And if we can assume the distinction between our philosophical "I" and our theological "I" (Horvath, 1993, 76–8, 89, 112–16), it is possible that he could consider his life to be a kind of union of time and eternity (ibid., 65–78) and his destiny to open the way to the eternity with God as the fulfillment of the prophetic promises. Thus he may have thought of himself as the bread of the presence of eternal life.

In any case, the words "This is my body" and "This my blood for you" are the mysterious and kerygmatic expressions of the promised inner union of God with the faithful. They are mysterious since they "present" the eschatological banquet of there and then as here and now. They are kerygmatic since they let the word of love proclaimed bring about the subject who loves, that is, Jesus Christ present by the consecration. And so perhaps it is not impossible to see Jesus emerging as an authentic Jew par excellence and realizing the essence of the Judaism proclaimed by the prophets of Israel, yet in an unexpected way transcending any expectations. In the Eucharist, it seems, Jesus was able to realize this new union by giving his body and blood to his faithful. In communion he was personally able to enter into the hearts of his followers so that he might abide in them and they in him (Jn 6, 56; 17, 26).

4.1.1.7 THE EUCHARIST AND ECUMENISM

THE EUCHARISTIC PRESENCE

The Eucharistic words are forever a challenge to the human mind. It was "a hard saying; who can listen to it" at the beginning (Jn 7, 6), and it is so today and will remain so. How can Jesus give us his flesh to eat (Jn 7, 52)? Since we do not like eating human flesh, some explanation is needed.

In the beginning the question was not so much about the way Christ is present in the Eucharist (see Justin, *Apology*, 1, 66; Iraeneus, 1867, 5, 2, 2) but about the name that would intimate what the Eucharist is. We have already discussed the breaking of the bread of the Last Supper, anamnesis, and the Eucharist. By the end of the first century the word "Eucharist" was more or less universal. St Cyprian, Theodore of Mopsuestia, and St Augustine called the Eucharist a sacrifice, and St Ambrose *oblatio.* The community aspect that people come together for the Eucharist was expressed by the term *collecta* or *processio.* The Greeks preferred the word *leiturgia,* liturgy. It means work or service performed to God on behalf and with the people. The Latin word *officium,* service, stresses the divine aspect of the same. In the *Acts of Martyrs* the Eucharist was referred to as *dominicum,* the Lord's celebration, Lord's doing, or just "Holy things" (*res*) *dominica,* "belonging to the Lord," just as the day of celebration was *dies dominica,* the day of the Lord. In the Celtic church, "offering" was general. "Mass," from the Latin *mittere, missa,* dismissal, meant the final dismissal of the people with a blessing. St Ambrose already applied it to the Eucharist.

The question about the way the Eucharistic Jesus is present (Powers, 1967) was raised first by Paschasius Radbertus (790–859), who said that by the consecration the same body which Jesus received from Mary was multiplied and his suffering repeated as many times as the words of consecration were pronounced. Ratramnus (d. 868), of the same monastery as Paschasius, argued that the suffering and death of Christ cannot be repeated. They can be only represented by the bread and wine, which are not changed by the consecration. They remain images, *figurae,* of the body and blood of Christ. Therefore the body of Christ is not really, *in veritate,* present but only in image and power. Ratramnus's book *The Body and Blood of Christ* was first condemned by the Synod of Vercelli in 1050 and put on the Index first in 1559 but removed from there in 1900. It is noteworthy that even the Reformers could not agree on whether or not his doctrine supported their view of the Eucharist. It seems now that Ratramnus did not want to defend a pure symbolism.

Berengar of Tours (1010–88) wanted to explain Christ's presence by using the terminology and logic of the emerging scholasticism, which was at that time more Platonic than Aristotelian. He could not believe that the glorified body of Christ in heaven, the only real, spiritual "substance," would come down to earth before the end of the world. The external appearances of bread and wine on earth were just images, "accidents" sustained by the spiritual reality of Christ in heaven. It sounded as if a concept of the Platonic otherworldly spiritual reality that may have prevented Berengar from recognizing the validity of the material "substance" and from accepting that not only in heaven but also here on earth, in the Eucharist, Christ can be adored.

Lanfranc (1010–89), one of the early Scholastics, first an itinerant scholar and later Abbot of the Abbey of Bec, studied and wrote a book entitled *Grammar, Logic and Rhetoric.* His skill in this subject appears in his commentaries on St Paul and the Psalms as well. He saw correctly that the presence of Christ cannot refer only to his spiritual substance in heaven but also to the earthly substance of bread and wine, which through the consecratory words of Christ, the Redeemer, are substantially changed into the body and blood of Christ. Therefore Christ is present not only in the sign and power of the sacrament *per signum et virtutem* but *in proprietate naturae et veritate substantiae,* in true nature and substance of his body and blood; born of the Virgin Mary, he suffered, died, rose again, and is now sitting at the right hand of the Father. The change brought about by God was a transubstantiation, even though he did not use the term. It would not be correct to say that Lanfranc denied or weakened the symbolic function of the Eucharist. Rather, like the later, classic Scholastics, he strengthened the symbolism by affirming that bread and wine are not empty symbols but symbolic realities containing the symbolized reality; that is, the body and blood of the Redeemer, who as God, performed the "change." Orlando Bandinelli was the first to name this change *transsubstantiatio.* He was followed later by Thomas Aquinas and the Councils of Florence and Trent.

Like Lanfranc, the classical Scholastic theologians did not deny Christ's presence in sign and in power. They rightly stressed the "not only," because the "This is my body and my blood," as revertible statements of Jesus' "I am" statements, for them meant much more than a sign or power. For their faith in the Incarnation, their minds could find a welcome support in Aristotelian "materialism." They were able to take matter seriously, as well as material elements and recognize the revelational nature of matter and the material word. Thus they could apply the Aristotelian concept of matter and form in their Sacramental theology and cast an anchor for their theology in the visible, tangible, concrete world surrounding them.

The matter, the visible element and action used in the sacraments, and the form, the pronounced words, the dynamic intentional language event, together made up the first level, which only signify, and are called, therefore, *sacramentum tantum.* The first level points to the second level – that of the invisible created power, the grace, which further signifies and points beyond itself and is therefore called *res et sacramentum.* The third level is where the faithful meet the author of grace, the Redeemer, Jesus Christ, who being uncreated by any human mental creativity, is simply called *res tantum.*

Lexiografically, *res* meant what Kant called "Ding an sich," a reality independent of human knowing, and referred to God as being as real as the cosmos in which we live. *Res* in itself has a crude material implication, but it is unscholarly to say that the Scholastics made out of Christ a thing, an object. The word in that context meant that Christ is more than a human idea, meaning or sense. He is real and gives meaning and purpose to all other realities and meaning. Thanks to Christ's real presence, the Eucharist reveals a new meaning and new purpose. We will see its transfinalizing and trans-significative power in each sacraments as a challenge to the world.

The three levels of the scholastic sacramental theology served as a framework, presenting the close connection between the visible material world and the invisible power of grace, both participating in the life of Christ, the real God and real man, and thus both revealing him. It was a framework that allocated various degrees of symbolic understanding and symbolic reality, somewhat like surface level, deep level, and basic level in a structural understanding. A considerable advantage of the framework is that it can incorporate views such as those of John Wycliffe, Martin Luther, Ulrich Zwingli, and John Calvin and appreciate their contributions by mitigating their exclusiveness. On the first level, the Eucharist is indeed a real memorial rite (Ulrich Zwingli); on the second level, it is the power and virtue of Christ having spiritual and moral impact on the faithful (Wycliffe and Calvin); and on the third level, the Lord is present in the Eucharist as Luther thought, yet not just side by side with the substance of bread and wine.

Extolling interiorness at the expense of exteriorness, subjectivity versus objectivity, and bringing heaven down to earth or lifting up the world to heaven are the extremities we all experience as a result of the precision with which we form our concepts, and we find it difficult to bring our love into our minds. It is the law of the mind that "this is only this and not that."

The law of love is that "this is this and also that as well." Our love presents a challenge to our reason, and our reason to our love. Our life task, which might be the key to a successful life, is to bring our reason to terms with our love, but not at the expense of our reason, and to bring our love to terms with our reason, but not at the expense of our love. Cannot we ask, therefore, "Is it impossible to change the following sentence?"

We Catholics believe that

> If anyone denies that in the most holy sacrament of the Eucharist there are contained truly, really and substantially, the body and blood of our lord Jesus Christ together with the soul and divinity, and therefore the whole Christ, but says that he is present in it only as in a sign or figure or by his power: let the one be anathema. (Council of Trent, session 13, canon 1; Tanner, 1990, 697)

and change it to a sentence such as

We Catholics and Protestants believe that

> If anyone denies that the body and blood of our lord Jesus Christ in the most holy sacrament of the Eucharist there contained truly, really and substantially, together with the soul and divinity "only and not also" in a sign or figure, let one be anathema.

and agree on that?

Likewise

We Catholics believe that

> If anyone says that in the venerable sacrament of the eucharist the substance of the bread and wine remains together with the body and blood of our Lord Jesus Christ, and denies that marvellous and unique change of the whole substance of the bread into the body, and of the whole substance of the wine into blood, while only the appearances of bread and wine remains, a change which the catholic church most aptly calls transubstantiation: let the one be anathema. (Council of Trent, session 13, canon 2; Tanner, 1990, 697)

and change it to the sentence

We Catholics and Protestants believe that

> If anyone says that in the venerable sacrament of the Eucharist the substance of the bread and wine remains together with the body and blood of our Lord Jesus Christ

unless "one admits" that marvelous and unique change of the whole substance of the bread into the body, and of the whole substance of the wine into blood, while only the appearances of the bread and wine remain, a change which the Catholic Church most aptly calls transubstantiation: let the one be not anathema.

and agree to that?

This may sound very involved. But so is love in "trying to use all the means proper to save the proposition of the beloved one" (Ignatius of Loyola, 1963, 21).

The "not only" grammatical formula is simple, yet it was powerful enough to express the common understanding of justification between the Catholic and Lutheran committees on 31 October 1999. After praying together, they were able to see that "not only" the Catholic but also the Lutheran understanding of justification was absolutely wrong or incomplete without the other. There was a mutual "understanding" then, which was not there before. The representatives of the Roman Catholic Church tried to find the principles and doctrines of the Reformers in their own principles and doctrines, and the representatives of the Lutheran Church tried to find the principles and doctrines of the Roman Catholic Church in their own principles and doctrines. It was an effort to apply the "principle of 'not only'" to their own principles and doctrines (Horvath, 1993, 20–1, 46). For one instance, we can admit that Luther's belief that the Lord is present side by side with the substance of bread and wine may be a welcome corrective to the scholastic framework. Since the "unique change" of the consecration can take place only through Christ, Christ is to be recognized as really present at the first level of the framework side by side with the matter of bread and wine and with the form, the priest's words of consecration. In our description of the Eucharist, on the first level we begin by saying that "the Eucharist is a sacrament in which Christ, with a successor of his apostles, the minister of his Church, and the Church, come together," and to get closer to them, Christ breaks down the mediating wall of the substance of bread and wine. He transcends the juxtaposition of substances and takes bread and wine up in his life and offers an immediate personal encounter to his friends to share with them all of his life and let them abide in him and he in them. Because of his immediacy, which his friends feel so much so that they can adore him and worship him without any sin of idolatry, he can share with them here and now the fruit of his sacrifice. It is very simple. It is just the way of God's love. So is the Eucharist the sacrament of love, revealing both what is love and how only God can love fully.

EUCHARISTIC SACRIFICE

If Jesus Christ is personally present in the Eucharist to share the fruits of his redemption and salvation, it may be difficult but not impossible to change the sentence

If anyone says that a true and proper sacrifice is not offered to God in the mass, or that the offering is nothing but the giving of Christ to us to eat: let the one be anathema. (Council of Trent, Session 22, canon 1; Tanner, 1990, 735)

to the sentence

If anyone says that a true and proper sacrifice is offered to God in the mass, or that the offering is not nothing but the giving of Christ to us to eat: let the one be not anathema.

or the sentence

We Catholics believe

If anyone says that the sacrifice of the mass is only one of praise and thanksgiving, or that it is a mere commemoration of the sacrifice enacted on the cross, and not itself appeasing; or that it avails only he one who receives and should not be offered for the living and the dead, for their sins, penalties, satisfactions and other needs: let the one be anathema. (Council of Trent, session 22, canon 3; Tanner, 1990, 735)

and change it to

We Catholics and Protestants believe

If anyone says that the sacrifice of the mass is *not* only one of praise and thanksgiving, or that it is not a mere commemoration of the sacrifice enacted on the cross, and not only itself appeasing; or that it avails not only the one who receives and may be offered for the living and the dead, for their sins, penalties, satisfactions and other needs: let the one be not anathema.

We can just try to transform "*I* believe" and "*you* believe" into "*we* believe" if not for other reasons but that Christ permits us to share his supreme love of God.

It may take time, but with the grace of Christ, perhaps it is possible and helpful to transform the "*I* believe" and "*you* believe" into "*we* believe" through the dialogue of ecumenical love with the following steps:

1 You believe what God wants you to believe.
  I believe what God wants me to believe.
2 I can believe what God wants you to believe.
  You can believe what God wants me to believe.

3 We can believe what God wants us to believe.
4 We do believe what God wants us to believe.

No. 2 is the touchstone for a far-reaching ecumenism. It may be easier if we begin with "you do what *you* want to do, and *I* do what *I* want to do" in order to reach "*we* can and do what *we* want to do" (Horvath, 1975a, 1–3).

The pattern again is similar to the one we find in the Joint Declaration on the Doctrine of Justification, subscribed to by Lutheran churches and the Roman Catholic Church on 31 October 1999 at Augsburg. It took place about four hundred years after Luther fixed his ninety-five theses to the door of the Schlosskirche at Wittenberg. The churches did not take the earlier condemnations lightly, but came "to new insights" and to see condemnations "in a new light" (no. 7).

This new insight and light may have been prompted by a more complex notion of time, which is the basis of theological differences. We have seen that Christ's Eucharistic presence is a real immediate objective and effective presence to his salvific work. His words "This is my body for you ... do this in remembrance of me" have the power to bring about this salvific work. And since this is the action of the eternal person of the Logos, it has a perennial quality, being contemporaneous to any instance of space and time (Horvath, 1993, 65–80). It is a memorial but a memorial of the past of Jesus, who is alive and present and leads his mystical body to share in his resurrection.

4.1.1.8 THE EUCHARIST: SPECULATIVE THEOLOGY AND SCIENCE IN DISCOURSE

Speculative theology and science in discourse is not speculative theology and science in dialogue. Theology and science in dialogue is an exchange of ideas between theologians and scientists, each within his or her own field, using the methods and hermeneutics of their own disciplines. Discourse means a penetrating scholarly expression of thought on a subject – in our case, the Eucharist. Speculative theology is a discourse of learning from the way that other sciences go about solving the anomalies discovered in their system and testing its viability in solving theological problems. Theology, therefore, remains within its own parameters, trying to achieve a most penetrating understanding of the Eucharist by analogy with what we know from human sciences (cf. First Vatican Council, chapter 4; Tanner, 1990, 808).

Thomas Aquinas gives an example of this process when in the Questions 75–8 of the third part of his *Summa theologiae* he tries to answer various questions about how the bread and wine become the body and blood of Christ. He faces questions about the way Christ is present in the Eucharist, the quantity and visible dimensions of the bread and of the body of Christ, the role of language in such a conversion, and so on. He scrutinizes these questions by studying the science of his day, Aristotle, whose works were available to him in timely translations.

Aristotle solved many of his philosophical problems with the notions of substance, quantity, and spatial dimensions. With the help of these notions, Thomas found his way out of the problems the Eucharist presented to his mind. It is remarkable that in presenting the sacrament of the Eucharist, Thomas spoke more about *conversio,* conversion, changing into, than transubstantiation. The consecration, he said, resembles a natural change, yet because it is a special conversion into, it may properly be called transubstantiation (*Summa theol.*, 3, q 76, a 7). His usual term "conversion," resembling natural changes, suggests that Thomas's thinking about the Eucharist was a kind of discourse with natural sciences of his time.

As to the question of why we cannot see the body of Christ with our eyes after the consecration he found an easy answer. The substance of any being, material substance included, cannot be seen by our ordinary eyes, but by our spiritual eye, which is our intellect. The substance, that is, the real essence of that what really is, *quod quid est,* can be grasped only by our intellect *(Summa theol.*, 3, q 76, a 7).

The conversion of the bread into Christ's body, he found, has a certain resemblance to creation and to natural changes, yet at the same time it differs from both. All three have in common that one extreme is after the other. In creation, being is after not-being; in natural changes, for example, fire follows the air; and in the sacrament of the Eucharist, the body of Christ is after the substance of bread. Yet consecration is not creation, because it is not out of nothing. Rather, it is like a natural change. In both there is something that remains. In the natural changes it is the subject. It is the same subject that loses one substantial form and receives another. It is true that in the Eucharist the substance of the bread and wine do not remain. But there is something that remains, the appearance of the bread and wine. The consecration, therefore, is not a creation but, rather, a conversion because the appearance of the bread and wine remains, and by synecdoche, that is, naming the part for the whole, we can say that the bread and wine become the body and blood of Jesus Christ. The body of Christ is contained under the same appearance under which the substance of bread and wine appeared before (*Summa theol.*, 3, q 76, a 8).

Since the substance is not a place, Christ being substantially present in the sacrament does not mean that he is present in the sacrament as in a place (*Summa theol.*, 3, q 76, a 5). He is present purely in the way the substance is contained by the dimensions of the bread and wine. But this does not mean that the body of Christ is not present with its quantitative dimensions. Both the bread and the body of Christ are present, each with its own quantitative dimensions. There are, therefore, two quantitative dimensions in the sacrament.

One is the way that the quantitative dimension of the appearance of the bread is present. This quantitative dimension is there by its own commensurability. In other words, it can be measured by a common unit numbered by an integral number of times, just as any surrounding object can be measured. This way of the presence of the quantitative dimension is the standard for dimension: the whole in the whole and each part in each part (*totum in toto et singulae partes in singulis partibus*). In such a way the whole Christ would be in the whole sacrament, and the parts of Christ in the parts of the sacraments. But this is not the way his quantitative dimension is present in the Eucharist.

The other way the quantitative dimension can be present is by way of substance, that is, the whole in the whole and the whole in every part (*tota [substantia] in toto, tota [substantia] in qualibet parte*). In the Eucharist the whole Christ is present in the whole sacrament, and the same whole Christ is in any part of the sacrament. Just as before the consecration the substance of the bread was present in the whole bread as well in any part of the bread, so after the consecration the whole Christ is in the whole sacrament and in any part of the sacrament. Substantial presence does not mean that the substance of the body of Christ is present without its non-substantial parts. It means that the whole substance of the body of Christ, with its shape and form, is present in the way of substance, that is, being in the whole as well as in each part of the Eucharist (*Summa theol.*, 3, q 76, a 4, ad 1). Christ's body is, therefore, not despoiled of its non-substantial accidents or of its dimensions. It is expanded, but not in space, as the appearance of the bread and wine. The body of the risen Christ is not measured in space and in time by its own quantitative dimension (*secundum commensurationem propriae quantitatis*) but by way of the dimension of the appearance of bread and wine (*Summa theol.*, 3, q 76, a 5, ad 1).

The presence of his body is measured by the measurement of the here and now of the bread and wine. When the sacramental appearances of the bread and wine cease to be, the body of Christ ceases to be under them. This can happen because the Eucharistic presence of his body is not measured by his own quantitative dimension the way it is in heaven, but by the appearances which are not his own, that of the bread and wine limited by their own appearances. Christ is circumscribed yet not circumscribed, defined and not defined, contained and not contained, in the sacrament of the Eucharist. The one Christ, with his own quantitative dimension, can be present in any consecrated bread and wine without being divided into many Christs. He is in space and he is not in space (*circumscriptive et non circumscriptive*) (*Summa theol.*, 3, q 76, a 5 ad 1; cf. Second Council of Nicaea and the Fourth Council of Constantinople; Tanner, 1990, 137, 162). Therefore Christ's body is not in the sacrament in the sense of being restricted to it. If this were so, it could be only on the altar. But Christ is always in heaven with his own proper appearances, and his body is on the altar under its sacramental appearances (*Summa theol.*, 3, q 76, a 5, ad 1).

We find that conversion and commensuration are the key words for Thomas in explaining the Eucharist. Extension is not identical with measurement. Time and space for Thomas are not identical with measurement. Yet some measurement is necessary for being in space and in time.

It is remarkable that the analysis of Thomas Aquinas and of Luther are not as different as one would expect. Luther speaks of two substances, and Thomas talks about two quantitative dimensions measured in time and space by one measurement. The dimension of the bread is in the normal way, that is, harmonized with the dimensions of containing place, and the dimension of the body of Christ is in the way that is normal for a substance except that its measurement is only one, that of the bread, which is supported not by the substance of the bread but by the substance of the body of Christ. Both agree that Christ is by his own appearances (species) in heaven, yet Thomas is able to link that to a real space and real time by the time and space of the appearances of the bread and wine.

The role of the appearances of the bread and wine is to make Christ circumscribed and "definitive," being here and now (*Summa theol.*, 3, q 75, a 5, ad 1). Such a role is limited yet symbolically expressive. It still has the meaning of nourishment, sustenance. But it is not a nourishment indispensable for one's survival. It is not done in the ordinary way, that is, by filling up an empty stomach and sustaining us in life. This time it is indispensable, not for an earthly life, but for the new life in Christ. Thus the symbolism of nourishment is for the Christian life. It expresses the necessity of Christ for Christian life. Christ is as necessary in new life as the bread and wine are for the sustenance of corporeal existence.

By taking up bread and wine and by identifying them with his body and blood, Christ was successful not only in expressing his love for human beings by his desire of staying with them as near on earth as possible without ceasing to be in eternity; he made himself for them absolutely necessary, without whom they can do nothing. And this is another token of love, linking one to the other and the other to the one.

Finally, by the words "Do this in remembrance of me," he let human language share the love-creating power of his words and raised human language to its highest potentiality. We said that the intentionality of language is love and the words of the priest, in union with those of Christ, share a certain instrumental creative power which brings about the sacramental change (*Summa theol.*, 3, q 78, a 4). The language not only signifies what comes to our mind from impact and encounter with reality but actually brings love into being (*habet vim factivam*; *Summa theol.*, 3, q 78, a 5). It is the mysterious power and dignity of human words that they can not only reveal but create love.

The notion of substance, which is just the object of the intellect, is foreign to the modern natural sciences. So is the hylomorphism of Aristotle, who thought that matter and form make up the physical reality. The twentieth century brought about unprecedented advances in the knowledge of physical matter. The special and general theories of relativity, the uncertainty principle, quantum mechanics, electromagnetic theory, and wave-particle dualism solved some problems and raised new ones about the reality we call by the common word "matter." What is matter? Certainly, much more than what we have thought until now. It has endless surprises. The surprises that matter may yet deliver are close to infinite (Teller, Teller, and Talley, 1991, 220). Though Edward Teller was acclaimed as the giant of the golden age in physics (Blumberg and Panos, 1990), he could say that he felt that we now know as much "about matter as a person would know about mathematics if he had just discovered how to count" (Teller, Teller, and Talley, 1991, 220).

Like matter, life has endless surprises. We have learned more not only about matter but about monocellular and polycellular beings, viruses and retroviruses, ribonucleic acid (RNA) and deoxyribonucleic acid (DNA), and so on, discovering more and more surprises. What is life? The more we know, the more we know how little we know about life. Yet perhaps we have learned that life and matter, organic and inorganic worlds are interrelated. Knowing one is knowing a little of the other as well. By now we have biophysics, molecular biology, geophysics, physical chemistry, material science, physiology, and other frontier sciences. It is in this vein that Teller could conclude his book *Conversations on the Dark Secrets of Physics* by saying, "To me one challenge in the inorganic world remains: to explore the frontiers between it and the living world. To arrive at those frontiers may take millennia, but it seems to me that the growth of science has become exponential" (Teller, Teller, and Talley, 1991, 221). The question we can ask now is, Is there any way that a speculative theologian is able to achieve "a most penetrating understanding" of the Eucharist "by analogy from what" we will know by the human sciences of the twenty-first century (cf. First Vatican Council, chapter 4; Tanner, 1990, 808)?

The Eucharist has been and remains a challenge to an inquiring mind. It shares not only the mystery of the Incarnation but the mystery of the organic and inorganic worlds as well. It would be too easy to say it is a mystery being beyond the realm of reason or simply deny it by reducing it to a pure symbol or religious myth. A believing Catholic intellectual or just a curious human mind interested in contradictions (Teller, Teller, and Talley, 1991, 129–70) may ask whether matter has a sort of ability to become plants, animals, human beings, or even the Eucharist?

And if human nature can be considered as being to open to the Incarnation so that Jesus Christ as true man and true God is the realization par excellence and fulfillment of the human potentiality of sharing in the nature of God and his eternity, can the Eucharist be considered as the realization par excellence and fulfillment of the groaning and "eager longing of the whole creation," matter and life, to reveal (Rom 8, 18–22) the whole cosmos entering into eternity (Horvath, 1993, 148–50) as the expression of Christ's unique love for each of us (ibid., 150–3)? Thus the Eucharist is the pledge not only of the eternal life of each of us but of the new earth and new heaven, the new world, as well (Rev 21, 1; Is 65, 17; 66, 22), which already became a reality with the resurrection of Jesus Christ and the assumption of Mary, mother of God.

The science of the nineteenth century visualized the evolutionary changes from the beginning of time, not by receiving new forms of a Platonic world of ideas, but by a sort of "self-organization" of the matter, the cells, the molecules, and so on into the complexity of human life, and one would venture to say into the complexity and simplicity of the risen body of Jesus Christ. The new heaven has already become a reality, and the Eucharist is its sacrament on earth. This is consistent and coherent with John's gospel when he says that "all things were made through him and without him was not anything made that was made" (Jn 1, 2–3), echoing what we can read in the Letter to the Colossians: "For in him all things were created, in heaven and on earth, visible and invisible ... He is before all things and in him all things hold together" (Col 1, 15–17).

If a body can be described as "a unified field of energy which, by balancing a multiplicity of biological times, creates its own time, its own individual biological time" (Horvath, 1993, 76), we can say that spatialization of time functions as a secondary element in time. It provides reversible changes for measuring the irreversibility of time – concretely, the irreversibility of biological time. Biological time is understood as the synchronization of a number of cellular clocks probably regulated by a rhythmic centre (master clock) not independent of cosmic time, which follows a linear direction "commended by a 'run-down' flowing from a maximum level of energy to a maximum level of entropy according to the laws of thermodynamics" (ibid.).

In the Eucharist, when the body of Christ replaces the "body " of bread and wine, this may mean that the field of energy of the bread and wine has been replaced by the field of energy of Christ's body united with his soul and divinity, which begins to turn the direction of the "run-down" of death and mortality into his time, eternity, by letting it share his own love of God and life. Thus we can understand that the Eucharist is not only the pledge of eternal life but the instrumental power of Jesus Christ, the eschatological unity of time and eternity, raising us mortal beings up, and with us the cosmic world in which we as mortal beings are embedded (ibid., 124–53).

4.1.2 *The Eucharist Is the Eucharistic Christ*

Summing up we would like to offer the following description of the sacrament of the Eucharist. The sacrament of Eucharist is a sacrament in which

1 Christ, his minister, as a successor of his apostles, and his Church, taking bread and wine as sacramental signs for commemorating Christ's redemptive event, announcing his coming through the history of his people, his farewell supper, his death and resurrection, and his ascension, and sending his Holy Spirit, come together to bring about by the power of his Holy Spirit (surface level of the sacrament: *sacramentum tantum*)

2.1 Christ's immediate somatic personal encounter with his people to reconcile them and the world by giving them a share in his life, death, resurrection, and final destiny through the communion (during the celebration or later, whenever he is received, a mass is not completely finished until all the consecrated hosts are received) and so, in virtue of

2.2 the Eucharistic Christ, there is an "organic" unity among all the masses, and

2.3 the most intimate form of being-in-one-another, he in one and all the believers with the world and the world with all and the individual believer in him, is formed (deep level of the sacrament: *res et sacramentum*); and thus

3 Christ is bodily present there in the world and remains with his loved ones, because he is pleased to be with human beings and shares his eternity with them (basic level of the sacrament: *res tantum*).

In brief, the Eucharist is an abbreviation for the Eucharistic Jesus. One can say the Eucharistic bread, but the real meaning is the Eucharistic Christ. Saying "This is my body" and "This is my blood" is, simply, "This is me." The believer does not worship a thing there but the person Jesus Christ, the Saviour, who is there together with his mystical body, the Church.

4.1.3 *The Eucharist: The Systematic Foundation of Sacramental Theology*

4.1.3.1 METHOD IN SACRAMENTAL THEOLOGY: THE EUCHARIST IS THE SACRAMENT OF SACRAMENTS

Sacramental theology traditionally begins with an introduction to a theology of the sacraments in general, followed by a presentation of baptism, confirmation, the Eucharist, reconciliation, anointing of the sick, order, and marriage (Vorgrimler, 1992). The sacraments of initiation are followed by the sacraments of healing and service for others. Yet the priority and preeminence of the Eucharist is recognized by anyone because in it Jesus Christ, the author of the sacraments, is personally present. The Eucharist is therefore the source and end of all other sacraments. All are ordered to the Eucharist and culminate in it. It is the most efficient of all the sacraments (*Summa theol.*, 3, q 65, a 3; Thomas Aquinas, 1948, 3: 406–7).

We consider the Eucharist the sacrament of the sacraments and take it as the model for sacramental theology. Our assumption is that Christian sacramental theology is not founded on and not dependent on religious mysteries and rituals. Rather, it is the celebration of the Eucharist that gives meaning to all rituals and religious mysteries the Church may share with other religious beliefs and human institutions. Without denying their real meaning, it is the Eucharistic Christ event that will always remain the last hermeneutic principle to re- and trans-interpret each and all of them. We can say that Christian sacramental theology is the recapitulation of the theology of the Eucharist.

The summary of our presentation of the Eucharist will form the different sections of our sacramental theology. As the Eucharist does, so each sacrament means a personal encounter with Christ, a union with Christ and with him with all the believers and through them with the whole world by the virtue of the Holy Spirit, a participation in Christ's life and his work of salvation, and a sacrifice reconciling the world with God.

4.1.3.2 SACRAMENTS ARE PERSONAL ENCOUNTERS WITH CHRIST

As in the Eucharist Christ is the one who by his words "This is my body" and "This is my blood" brings about the conversion of the bread and wine into his body and blood, so he is the one who baptizes, confirms, forgives sins, comforts the sick, ordains one of his faithful to be his minister, and in marriage joins the love of a marrying woman and man to make it a sacramental sign of God's love for them, the Church, and the human race. In a word, all sacraments are personal encounters with Christ, because it is always Christ who is the one who confects the sacrament. Whenever a priest pronounces, "This is my body," "I absolve you," the "I" is the "I" of Jesus Christ, who brings about each and all the sacraments. And this was, and still it is, the meaning of the theological expressions *ex opere operato.*

Ex opere operato is simply a short form for *ex opere operato Christi,* of the work of Christ. It means that it is not the priest or the sacramental action that brings about grace but the activity of the risen Christ, who does what no created being could perform. A Christian sacrament is not a human or magical force, but a work done by Christ. It is by virtue of the Eucharistic

Christ that we can say that "the sacraments are not things, but one's encounter here on earth with the glorified Christ in heaven," who is present here on earth "in visible form not directly through his own body, but by the sacramental signs extending among us on earth in visible form the functions of his bodily reality which is in heaven." "The sacraments are the prolongation of the Incarnation," the "earthly extension of the 'body of the Lord,'" "the gesture of Christ and through them Christ is the absolute contemporary to all generations, an encounter with Christ in his Paschal mystery of his death, resurrection-pentecost" (Schillebeeckx, 1963, 44, 63, 118). We can therefore say that sacraments are not only for us, *propter homines,* but also for the incarnated and glorified Christ, *propter Christum incarnatum et glorificatum,* the Saviour of the world. When Christ baptizes, forgives sins, or alleviates the sick, he is not acting from a distance from heaven but from and through his Eucharistic presence here on earth. The efficacy of a sacrament comes, therefore, not from the rite as such, but from the free will of the present Christ. The prayers to the Eucharistic Christ are always vital.

The Eucharistic presence is, further, the guarantee that Christ can be encountered in other sacraments. It was the Eucharistic experience that made possible the recognition of a foundational rite as sacrament. So long as such an experience of the presence of the Eucharistic Christ was not discovered in a rite, the rite remained just a rite, for example, washing, eating, and walking. In the Eucharist too it was not the rite of eating and drinking that made the Eucharist a sacrament. Rather, the Eucharistic encounter with Christ, with the paschal mystery of his death and resurrection-Pentecost in the commemorative meal of the Last Supper, made the Eucharistic rite a sacrament. The time element involved in such an experience may be the reason that it took the Church about fifteen hundred years to finalize the number of its sacraments. In such a recognition process, theological understanding may have been instrumental. The presence of the Eucharistic Christ in a sacrament is also the explanation why a sacrament must be instituted by no one less than Christ himself. It could not be up to the Church but only to Christ to decide when and in what circumstances he wanted to be present and encounter his people. This is one more indication that sacraments cannot have magical powers. The Church never has had nor ever will have the power to force Christ to do what the Church wants him to do.

4.1.3.3 SACRAMENTS ARE UNION WITH CHRIST AND IN HIM WITH BELIEVERS AND THROUGH THEM WITH THE WHOLE WORLD BY THE HOLY SPIRIT

In his vision on the way to Damascus, Paul understood that a mystical union existed between Christ and his followers, whom he had persecuted. He recognized that the historical Jesus was alive and became the "mystical" risen Christ, who from that time on would never be present in a sacrament without his mystical body, the Church. The Eucharistic celebration was by its nature not the celebration of a ghostly, mystical figure but the celebration of Jesus, who had lived, worked, preached, and helped people to be free from their miseries without distinction. He was doing all this together with his apostles and disciples, whose lives were closely connected to his life, death, and resurrection. He commissioned them to do what he was doing and promised to be with them in the world until the end of the world.

The sacramental Christ, therefore, cannot be separated from the people and the world he loved. Whenever he is encountered acting in any sacrament, he is encountered with his believers and through them with the whole world. By his incarnation, Christ became brother to each human being, baptized and not-baptized, and consequently all human beings became brothers or sisters to one another. Living and dead, believers and non-believers, heretics and orthodox, good and bad, all became "neighbours," who should love one another as brothers and sisters. *Sive adhuc pagani ... sive divisi a nobis ... velint, nolint, fratres nostri sunt,* "non-believers, or anyone separated from us, willy-nilly, without choice, they are our brothers and sisters," Augustine interpreted Psalm 32 (33), verse 28 (1956, 272).

The sacraments are all real social sacraments. They are not just for the recipients, but in and through them, they have universal dimension and impact. The universal and social impact of each sacrament is the result of the Epiclesis of the Eucharist shared by all sacraments. By means of the sacraments, it is the Holy Spirit who sanctifies and guides the people of God by distributing special gifts for the building up of the Church (*Dogmatic Constitution on the Church,* no 12; Tanner, 1990, 858). In the spirit of Pentecost, it is the Holy Spirit who moves the Church into the future, progressively transcending the limits of space and time.

4.1.3.4 SACRAMENTS ARE PARTICIPATION IN CHRIST'S LIFE AND HIS WORK OF SALVATION

A person is not just his or her being but her or his doing as well. Union with a person, love of a person, means a sharing in his or her life, works, and above all destiny. Christ is alive today and continues his works and "his dream," the salvation of the whole world. The sacraments are the means and realization of Christ's dreams, as well as calls to share his dream and his love for every human being. His motto is "I love every human being without distinction," and he looks with loving eyes at every human being through his sacraments. He saves people from their fears and provides them with the freedom of "children" of God, who experience that they are loved and are strong enough to love and to sacrifice. It is this energy that is felt by the silent worshippers of the Eucharistic Christ and makes the faithful sure that it is Christ and not just bread present.

4.1.3.5 SACRAMENTS ARE SACRIFICES RECONCILING THE WORLD WITH GOD

According to the threefold level of reflection upon the reality of sacrifice, the theology of sacrifice can be divided into objective, intersubjective, and revelational dimensions. The objective dimension is concerned with the vast field of sacrifice, in the Christian, non-Christian religious, and secular contexts of the past and present age. Because of the Incarnation, the sacrifice of the Eucharistic Christ is expected to be the redemptive fulfillment of not only the Hebrew but of all the sacrifices and sufferings endured and offered by any human being during the history of the human race. This level of reflection upon the reality of sacrifice might be called "symbolic" in the original sense of the word συμβαλω, to bring together all the sacrifices. It also includes the intersubjective dimension of the sacrifice, recognizing all the sacrifices of the human race as our and my sacrifice, and the revelation dimension of sacrifice, recognizing our sacrifices as an epiphany, that is, a moment when God and human beings mutually disclose themselves in virtue of their common and mutual self-communication through Jesus Christ (Horvath, 1975b, 367–70).

4.1.3.5.1 The Objective Dimension of the Theology of the Eucharistic Sacrifice

We can here only suggest in a few lines the universal reality of the sacrifice in time and space together with the history of theology of the Eucharistic sacrifice. Sacrifice is a common human reality, and so is the term "sacrifice" in the Christian, non-Christian, and secular world. The actual meaning of the term is more often "offering" (*jajña,* Sanskrit; *fórn,* Icelandic), yet it means also to "give" a present (*wotata,* Koko-ya-o, Eastern Australian Aboriginal), "being slaughtered" (*dhabiha,* Arabic), "burning" (K*konu,* Buin, New Guinea*),*"renunciation, loss of" (*'zhertva,* Bulgarian*),*"to give up, offer" (*hsi-sheng,* Chinese), "worship with prayers and hymns" (*yasna,* Avesta, Iranian), "undergoing of pain spontaneously" (*pagpapakasákit,* Tagalog, the national language of the Philippines), and so on. The English term "sacrifice" comes from the Latin, "making sacred."

Since there is no general term, the Hebrew sacrifices are called by their specific names. So *'ōlâ* (holocaust), *zebah* (communion sacrifice), *tôdâh* (praise), *n'dābâ* (devotional sacrifice), *neder* (votive offering), *hattā't* (expiatory sin-offering), *'āsām* (sacrifice of reparation), *minhâ* (gift, vegetable offering), *lehem happânîm* (the bread of the Presence), *q'tōret* (offering of incense), *kipper* (purifying sacrifice), *qorbān* (vow offering), Passover, law concerning the first-born son, blood rites, circumcision, human sacrifice, and so on.

Concerning the origin and meaning of sacrifice in the history of humankind, there are many theories. They can be classified in six groups: the meal theory (Smith, 1962); gift theories (Tylor, 1958), such as refreshment-gift theory (Spencer, 1885) or *do ut des,* or commercial gift theory (van der Leeuw, 1920–21); homage theory (Schmidt, 1922); totemism, exogamy (Frazer, 1910); magic (Codrigton, 1891; Uppsala School, cosmogonic vitalism); and expiatory-reconciliation (Thomson, 1963). The last is a theological question.

The question of the relationship between the Last Supper, the cross, the body and blood of Christ, the Eucharist, and the Christian life appeared early at the beginning of Christianity. We already find it in the writings of early Christian writers, such as Ignatius of Antioch, Justin, and Irenaeus. For them the presence of the body and blood of Christ was the central mystery and the Eucharist and the Christian life were seen as ἀντίτῦπος, the authentic representations of it (Solano, 1952, 721–4). Thus the early theology already raised the problem of "re-presentation." In Greek theology, the Alexandrian theology saw in the Eucharist as sacrifice, a transformation (μεταποιέω), representing not just the bread and wine but those who take the bread and wine (Gregory of Nyssa, *Oratio catechetica,* 37; PG, 45, 93–7). For Theodore of Mopsuestia, of the Antiochene School, what the priest was doing on earth was the image, τῦπος, of the heavenly sacrifice that Christ was offering in heaven. The Eucharist was, no doubt, a memorial sacrifice offering the body of Christ broken and his blood poured for all, but it was also an image representing the likeness of the service of heaven (Theodore of Mopsuestia, 1933, 79).

In Latin theology Augustine gave a description of the sacrifice that underscored the sacrifice of the Church, the mystical body of Christ. Sacrifice is, he said, every work that unites us in holy communion with God, every work that is directed to that final good in which alone we find true happiness (*De Civitate Dei,* 10, 6; PL, 41, 263). Christ is the offering and the offerer, but the Church has to offer itself too. The external sacrifice is just a sign of the internal self-giving.

Alger of Liège (died c.1132), in his book *The Sacraments of the Lord's Body and Blood* (PL, 180, 739–972), developed the idea of sacrifice as immolation, and since Trent defined the mass as real sacrifice, theologians have tried to apply the notion of immolation to the mass, somewhat independent of the presence of the Eucharistic Christ (cf. *continetur,* Council of Trent, session 22, chapter 2, Tanner, 1990, 733) as the one who offers himself and forgives sins. Some interpreted the sacrificial immolation in the mass as a mere offering (for J. Maldonado, see Amann, 1927, col. 1772–6), an oblation made by Christ in heaven (Lepin, 1926) or an oblation made by the Church offering Christ (de la Taille, 1921). According to others, the immolation is real but in a sublime sense of perfection. So according to Suarez, the profane bread and wine becomes the body and blood of Christ (Schepens, 1924) by a transformation more adequately expressing Christ's resurrection and his hypostatic union than his death on the cross (Scheeben, 1946, 439). For John de Lugo, Carl R. Billuart, and Johann Baptist Franzelin, for example, the immolation was not formal but "virtual." Christ was placed in a less-perfect status, being deprived of the normal actions of human bodily life.

There were others who proposed that the sacrifice in the mass is only a figurative immolation. The mystic Christ's immolation is sacramentally shown under the separated species of bread and wine, according to Alphonso Salmeron (Dudon, 1939; Billot, 1896). Immolation is real, some such as Leonard Lessius, Salmanticenses (Cuervo, 1948), and Alphonsus Ligouri proposed, in the sense of a sort of destruction affecting Christ himself, who is presented in the state of food and drink by the consecration and consumed at least in regard to his sacramental existence during the communion. According to G. Vazquez (Shea, 1923), the destruction occurs only in the species. Others suggested that that the words of consecration tend to the physical separation of the blood of Christ from his body, though the separation does not occur by virtue of the concomitant presence of the blood.

The long list of proposals, lasting over almost five hundred years (Michel, 1928, cols 1246–316), underlines the theological importance of the Eucharist as sacrifice. What all said made sense, yet they failed sufficiently to stress the presence of the Eucharistic Christ. In summarizing the dispute, Pius XII pointed in that direction when he said that the substance of bread and wine separated by the words of the consecration represents Christ's death at Calvary, who offers himself in the mass to his Father (*Mediator Dei*, 1947, 543).

The questions that preoccupied theologians in the twentieth century concerning the Eucharist were better directed. They could be summarized as follows. In what sense can the mass be a sacrifice? Is the sacrifice of the mass specifically and numerically distinct from the sacrifice of the cross and from the Last Supper? What is the sacrificial action in the mass? How does the sacramental action make the sacrifice of the cross present? Is there one sacrifice and many masses?

To answer these questions, let us see what the Council of Trent and the Second Vatican Council said. According to the Council of Trent, the mass is a "truly propitiatory sacrifice" (session 22, chapter 2; Tanner, 1990, 733). In this statement we can detect two assumptions. One is that

Christ's sacrifice in the mass is real because it forgives sins. A real sacrifice is, therefore, one that forgives sins. And the other is that the Eucharistic Christ in the mass really forgives sins, "even enormous offences" (Tanner, 733). The mass, therefore, cannot but be a real sacrifice because Christ's death cannot be separated from the life of the risen Christ. The Eucharistic Christ who offers and absolves sins in the mass is the same who forgives sins in the sacrament of forgiveness. Thus the sacraments are all the sacraments of the Eucharistic Christ. The Eucharistic Christ is rightly the foundation of the organic unity of the seven sacraments. We should also keep in mind that in the spirit of the Second Vatican Council Christ's resurrection is an essential element of the paschal mystery and so is that of Christ's sacrifice. John's gospel already presented the death-resurrection bias. Christ's glorification is his lifting up on the cross, and Jesus' redemptive work is attributed not only to his death but to his glorification as well. The sacrifice-resurrection synthesis is the foundation of the sacraments as sacrifice (Sabourin, 1961; Stanley, 1961; Lécuyer, 1962; Tillard, 1967).

We can see that the problems presented ask for a close union of the Eucharistic presence with the Eucharist as sacrifice. Only the real presence of Christ in the Eucharist will answer the question raised by the early Christian writers not long after Pentecost. And this was the road we followed when we described Jesus' great sacrifice. For Jesus, sacrifice was, we have found, to love his father with all his might, mind, and heart at any price, even at the price of his life and love for God's people as well. The Eucharist is, therefore, the sacrament of this love, and any sacrifice is a participation in the Eucharistic sacrifice with its horizontal and vertical dimensions (Horvath, 1979b, 80–2). The Last Supper, Calvary, Jesus' life and death, and that of his followers, together with the life and death of every human being, are not to be separated from the Eucharistic celebrations because none can be separated from the risen Christ, who stays in the world by virtue of his Holy Spirit. Each one mutually clarifies the mystery of the other. The God-and-world-loving Jesus is determined to bring to completion the salvation of the world that he initiated.

4.1.3.5.2 The Intersubjective Dimension of the Theology of Sacrifice

The intersubjective theology of sacrifice calls for experiencing the sacrifice of Christ as one's own sacrifice, as the sacrifice of the Church, the people of God, and the whole human race. And the sacrifices of the whole humankind are looked upon as one's own sacrifices, and the Church's utterances concerning Christ's sacrifice as utterances about the life of every human being. The Council of Trent already recognized this interpretation when it said that the many images of sacrifice in the history of human race, with the values they signify, are all embraced and find their fulfillment and consummation in Christ's sacrifice (Council of Trent, session 22, chapter 1; Tanner, 1990, 733).

Jesus was and is an authentic human being, an image of anyone who had dreams and shattered hopes, suffered much, and died an ignominious death. To a historian he may look like a dreamer in his time and in any time. And Jesus was and is indeed a "dreamer," a courageous one. He dared to dream an "impossible" dream for which he sacrificed everything, his life included. His plan was and still is to conquer hate and violence by love, to bring peace and life by his death. It is this unique sacrificial love of Jesus Christ to which his Church, the people of God, joins its own sacrificial love for offering to God (*LG*, no. 11, Tanner, 1990, 857).

There are two possible attitudes towards a courageous dreamer who is willing to sacrifice everything for his mission and love for his Father. One is the attitude of the critical mind that points out the mistakes the dreamer makes and advises: "Do not get involved in a hopeless adventure. Leave the dreamer alone." The other is the attitude of a critical yet loving mind that advises: "Since you are a dreamer too, encourage your 'fellow travelers' by telling them, 'Be reasonable but do not give up your dreams. Just wait for the time when God, who is at work in you, both *to dream and to work for it* (Phil 2, 13), will let you do it.'" It is the Eucharist that does not let one give up at Gethsemane. Death is never the end. Rather, it is the beginning of the dream come true. One who stays at the foot of the cross of the greatest dreamer, nailed to his cross because of his dreams, will experience the energy radiating from the body, the "unified field of energy"(Horvath, 1993, 78) of the Eucharistic Christ reconciling the world with God. So did Francis of Assisi, who experienced this energy emanating from sharing in Christ's dream for peace and formulated it in a prayer: "Lord, make me an instrument of your peace, where there is hatred, let me show love" (Appleton, 1985, 75). This can be the meaning of Jesus' and of his followers' sacrificial life and death, bringing about peace and the forgiveness of sins. The prayer of St Ignatius of Loyola echoes it: "Lord, teach me to be generous ... to give and not to count the cost ... to labor and not to seek reward, save that of knowing that I do thy will" (ibid., 86).

4.1.3.5.3 The Revelational Dimension of the Theology of Sacrifice

Finally, the revelational dimension of the theology of sacrifice is the experience and recognition of one's sacrifice, together with the sacrifice of the Church and the human race, as the sacrifice of God in Christ. On this level the theologian realizes that the believer is not sacrificing only with the people of God. There is a third person present who acts with, in, and through them. The action of sacrificing originates from God. God is not only the subject to whom the sacrifice is offered but also the subject who sacrifices in Christ and in every human being. God discloses God in the sacrifice, and the sacrifice becomes an epiphany, a revelation of God, a moment when God and the human being mutually disclose themselves in virtue of their common and mutual self-communication through Jesus Christ.

The philosophical foundation of this new reality is the analogy of being. This analogy is not just an analogy of concept. It means a turning to reality to discover a unity of the beings as the outcome of the unity of their first principle (Montagnes, 1963, 168). It means a "radical and irreducible reference of the conditional to the absolute" as its first term. It is the foundational structure of the being, according to which any conditional with all not-self-sufficient beings is referred to the unconditional cooperating with the created being (Hayen, 1957, 92). There is a universal "absolute identity-in-difference" (Splett and Puntel, 1968, 22), a universal relation to the first term apart from which the finite can do nothing (Jn 15, 5).

There is a relationship between God and the world that cannot be placed in parentheses without its having forgotten or ignored "being." Ideas as images can be abstractions, but ideas as reality can hardly be. No one can sacrifice unless God sacrifices with her or him, because love is the foundation of being. The "I am who I am" of Exodus (3, 14) was revealed by the Johannine theology as God is love (1 Jn 4, 8). The affirmation that God is love confirms that "I am who I am" is love. It means at once that being is love and that love is an "I," a person, and not just an abstract notion or feeling. Revelation made love the foundation of being and the metaphysics of the theology of love.

Thus we can understand that it is God who reconciles Oneself with the world and gives us the ministry of reconciliation, διακονία τῆς καταλλαγῆς (2 Cor 5, 18). Sacrifice is forgiveness and forgiveness is sacrifice. By forgiving, all share in Jesus' work of reconciling God with the world and the world with God (2 Cor 5, 20).

4.1.3.6 ORGANIC UNITY

Since Christ is *Urbild,* prototype and ideal, as well as *Ursache,* creator of the unity of grace (Horvath, 1966, 279–83), his presence makes the Eucharist the foundation of the organic unity of all the sacraments. Each individual sacrament receives its grace from the Eucharist and is therefore Eucharistic grace. Each one cannot be but an actualization of the Eucharist, which in turn is the actualization of each sacrament. Thus we can speak of a "collegiality" of the sacraments in the sense that no sacrament can exist or be rightly understood without another. By a sort of "self-organization," each sacrament enters into the organic unity of all sacraments by virtue of Jesus Christ being present in the Eucharist. And so by virtue of the Eucharist, each sacrament, without sublating the others, convenes all others. By placing one sacrament in the context of the other sacraments as well as of other theological treatises, we situate each sacrament in the proper *Sitz im Leben,* in its own "ecology," giving to each an opportunity for it to manifest, to reveal, itself the way it is in its own "home."

Thus we may say that the method of sacramental theology is unique and not unique at the same time. It is not unique because it can be used in other theological treatises (Horvath, 1975a, 91), yet it is unique because the Eucharist, along with the other sacraments, has a critical role in the sacramental hermeneutics. Its history (Powers, 1967) is a beacon for the history of the other sacraments and of sacramental theology in general (Vorgrimler, 1992).

4.1.3.7 THE WORD OF CHRIST

Since the sacraments not only help the faithful in their needs and are the life function of the Church but are also the revelation of Jesus Christ and in him the epiphanies, or revelations of God, it follows that the Church cannot have power over the sacraments. Like any human being, so God too, as a real person, can freely reveal God's mind and feelings to another person only in symbols. As free human persons, we do not have to be open to another person unless we want to be so. We cannot be forced to reveal ourselves to someone else. We are free to choose and to create a symbol in which and through which we let someone else enter into our inner life. This freedom to select symbols is, however, limited. We are free to select and chose a sign, but only at the beginning of our self-revelation. Since each symbol is a realization and determination of the symbolized person, once a symbol is selected, it cannot be revoked without causing some confusion in the other person. If we change the symbols that we previously offered to someone to let him or her enter into the innermost part of our personality, we may cause disappointment, suspicion, or deception.

We may have three reasons for changing our self-revealing symbols. One is the recognition that the symbol we have chosen is not an adequate symbol of ourselves. Another is recognition of the instability of our personality. We realize that we have changed, and the old symbol no longer corresponds to our altered personality. We need new symbols. Finally, there may be another reason for changing our self-revealing symbols. We feel a sudden unwillingness to reveal ourselves to another. We do not want to be known any longer. We replace the right symbol by deceptive symbols which, instead of helping, will hinder the recognition of who we are.

Now, since Christ, the supreme revealer of the Father, instituted the sacraments as symbols of God, they are meant to be symbols manifesting the real nature of the unseen God. Like any human being, Christ too was free to choose and designate a sign in and through which he could and wanted to reveal God and God's feelings towards us. But once he did so, he could not change it without causing disappointment or suspicion of his inability or of God's instability. One conceivable reason for changing the sacraments as God's self-revealing gestures would be God's adaptation to each generation. According to the disposition and character of each generation and of each individual in it, God could change symbols over and over again in order to help each generation to approach him in its own way. But such an attitude on God's part would make it difficult to recognize the one and the same God revealed to the whole human race. Such a God would a tribal god but not a universal one. The one and the same God of all should be one who is able to manifest God as the same to everyone, having the same divine feelings for everyone any time.

If, then, the God of the whole human race selects and freely chooses symbols, these symbols should be not only unambiguous to every generation but also adequately powerful to manifest God as reliable and faithful forever (1 Pet 1, 25). For this reason, one may appreciate why Jesus as the definitive final revelation and the eternal sacrament of God, is expected to be forever as he is. God freely elected a way, the incarnation in Jesus, to reveal the Trinitarian God. But having once given Jesus and his sacrament to the Church, God cannot put him aside.

This is the reason why the Church, which never pretended to have power over Jesus, God's definitive sacrament, has never claimed power over the sacraments either. It faithfully keeps them and has never tried to introduce new ones that would be some new, God-symbolizing gestures. It is true that the sacraments are to serve human beings (*sacramenta sunt propter homines*). This is an anthropological description of the sacraments, considering them as medicine for people. But if the sacraments are conceived as manifesting words and gestures of the revealing God who addresses human beings as persons, it cannot more rightly and certainly be said that the sacraments are for people than it can be said that God is *propter homines* and we have magic power over God, a concept that has always been rejected in the Judeo-Christian tradition (Horvath, 1970, 396–7).

That the sacraments are words of God signifies more than that the words uttered over a symbolic action are not just human words. It means that the sacraments are instituted by Christ, who, as real God and real man, created the sacraments by his words. It is up to the Church to recognize them and interpret them but not to create them. The way of recognizing and interpreting them is not unlike the way that the Church has recognized and interpreted the Bible. Like the canon of the Bible, the canon of the sacraments resulted from experience and from eliminating choice.

Like the gospels for the other books of the New Testament (*DV*, no. 18; Tanner, 1990, 978), the Eucharist also has a special pre-eminence for recognizing a symbolic action as a sacrament. By reading the gospels more and more, a community experiences their special power to bring about the presence of the risen Christ in words and saving actions. So too more and more communities have experienced the grace and power of the Eucharistic Christ in certain symbolic actions and recognized their close connection with the Eucharist. Such an experience is not infallible. It was up to the universal Church to make an infallible judgment and separate infallibly sacramental actions from purely symbolic actions. It is not insignificant that the number of the sacraments was definitively defined at the same time as the number of the inspired books. It is by virtue of the close connection between the Eucharist and the Scriptures, on the one hand, and the sacraments, on the other, that like Christ's words (Lk 22, 33), they will not pass away.

Since for the Church Jesus Christ is the revelation of God, his determination of a sacrament is God's mind concerning a sacramental symbol. Therefore a careful consideration of the apostolic age's understanding of the sacrament is indispensable. If the apostolic time were not the *norma normata* for all the coming generations, human understanding could replace God's understanding of the sacraments. When, therefore, the Church determines the words and actions to be used in the sacraments, it is not creating something that did not exist before. It is only trying to translate God's gift and its divine meaning into the language of the present age. The work cannot be creative but only hermeneutic in order to understand Christ's mind expressed in the context in which this has been disclosed. The sacraments are historical symbols of God, who is revealed by Christ in a historical context in which the symbols and their meaning were disclosed.

As for different hermeneutics, so for the sacramental hermeneutics too; a certain set of rules has been worked out through history under the following headings: accidental rites, essence, and the substance of the sacrament. Accidental rites are those that translate the meaning of a sacrament into the language of the people in a certain age. They are not required for the validity of a sacrament. Their aim is pedagogical in order to make the sacrament more solemn and attractive to the faithful of a linguistically different local church. The essence of a sacrament implies that specific symbols (matter) and words (form) are required for validity at a given time in the Church. It presupposes the active role of the universal Church of a certain age. It is distinguished from the substance of the sacraments. The substance of a sacrament is made up by those actions and words which, according to the sources of the divine revelation, Christ himself determined to be kept in the sacrament. It implies both the determination of the meaning, that is, what kind of sanctification is signed by it, and the determination of the symbol, the sensible reality chosen to express a symbolized reality.

The determination of the meaning and of the visible symbolizing reality can be achieved in two ways. Christ determined the meaning and the word by which the meaning is expressed (cf. Eucharistic consecration) or left it to the Church to determine the words without changing the meaning (cf. baptizing "in the name of Christ" or "in the name of the Trinity"), or he determined the symbol in general and further determination was left to the Church to conserve the fundamental meaning. The substance of the sacrament of order, for example, is the external bestowal of ministerial sharing in the mission of Christ. The bestowal is determined by Christ, but how the bestowal is divided – such as twofold, episcopal and diaconal, or threefold, episcopal, presbyterial, and diaconal ministry, and expressed either by function, such as handing over the instruments or by following the praxis of the apostolic times by the imposition of hands – can be further determined by the Church (cf. Pius XII, 1948).

4.1.3.8 THE CHURCH AS MINISTER

Since a sacrament is an encounter with Christ, the real God and man, he is the one who brings about the sacraments in each case. The role of the Church in the sacraments is serving Christ and the people of God, the mystical body of Christ. The Church exercises this ministry in its ministers, the priests, and in the faithful. The priests by the sacrament of order represent the apostles, and the faithful by the sacrament of baptism represent the early Christians. The two sacraments, baptism (which could be called the sacrament of the faithful) and order (which could be called the sacrament of the apostles in the sense of the New Testament), determine the basic structure of the Church united in the sacrament of the Eucharist.

The presence of Christ and of the Church with the apostles and faithful is required in each sacrament. The actual presence of God is guaranteed by Christ's infallible word instituting the sacramental symbols. By the institution of the sacrament, Christ expressed his willingness to meet people and reveal God whenever people want to meet him freely in the sacramental event of the Church. The sacrament is therefore the absolutely faithful word of God, guaranteeing that whenever the Church and the faithful concur in these symbols, God will never fail to be present. The so-called *ex opere operato* doctrine, based upon the promise of the infallibly faithful God, means nothing more than the guarantee that the sacrament is an epiphany of God. God is present there not by virtue of the action but by virtue of his promise. His promise is expressed, for example, in the sacrament of order when Christ reveals that wherever this person is, he is always available to do what he promised to do in building his Church.

The presence of the Church, as the mystical body of Christ, is expressed by the jurisdictional or canonical mission given to the priest and by the conditions laid down for the valid reception of the sacraments. The intention ensures the freedom of both the minister and the recipient of the sacrament acting as the member of the mystical body of Christ in deed or in desire.

The presence of the mystical body is not restricted to sacramental celebrations. It extends to prayers, to ecumenical services, to assemblies, to indulgences, and to non-sacramental symbolic actions, known as "sacramentals," used to help others or the person performing them. They may be prayers, anointing, grace at meals, giving alms, blessing ashes, litanies, saying the rosary, stations of the cross, and so on. They convey their effect by the intercession of the mystical body of Christ and try to communicate the love the Church has for God. Any grace offered and received through these actions is related in its origin and purpose to one of the sacraments and finally to the Eucharist. We may believe that all graces originally and finally derive from the Eucharist. They are Eucharistic and salvific.

4.1.4 The Eucharist and Systematic Theology

The Eucharist does not only serve as a model for sacramental theology. In its close union with each sacrament, it raises issues for any treatise of systematic theology. It gives directions for solving problems and may provide some further understanding of the mysteries of the Christian faith through their connection with the mystery of the Eucharist (Vatican 1, *Dogmatic Constitution on the Catholic Faith,* chapter 4; Tanner, 1990, 808).

Choosing a symbol for oneself, one's family, country, business, or entertainment is more than selecting a means or sign to achieve something. It expresses a view, a world view that one has of him or herself, of family, people, work, purposes, dreams, or expectations, of philosophy and belief, the God one worships, in one word, the love one has. So we can assume that choosing and instituting sacraments directly or indirectly was for Jesus also more than just electing an action to achieve an end. It expressed what he thought of the world he incarnated, of what human existence is all about, the kind of church he had in mind, the way he saw himself, what he wanted us to know about his Father, the way he visualized eternity, what he expected from the Holy Spirit, and what he thought about his mother.

Each sacrament is a kind of message, which we will discuss briefly, hoping that our readers, prompted by the idea, will reflect on, correct, and deepen the insights presented here. In any case, the discussion will reflect our speculative theology of the world, human existence, the Church, Christology, God, Eschatology, the Holy Spirit and Mary, mother of God.

4.1.4.1 THE EUCHARIST IS A SYMBOL FOR THE WORLD: THE WORLD IS PRESENCE

THE EUCHARISTIC PRESENCE AS A SYMBOL OF THE WORLD

Signs and Symbols The Eucharist turned systematic theology towards semiotics, a theological and philosophical discipline of signs and symbols. The Eucharistic words "This is my body" and "This is my blood" are not simple analytic or synthetic statements. Neither a simple analysis of the concepts of natural language nor pragmatic experience would justify them. Pointing to concrete and visible elements such as bread and wine, they can be understood as signs which by their definitions point beyond themselves. Signs turn the human mind to something other than what they are. A sign to a place moves the traffic towards another location. A picture or a card from someone calls to mind a person who is more than the picture or the card. A sign as sign opens itself up and turns its own meaning, its obvious signification and plain finality, to something that transcends itself. Its transitive function can be rightly called *trans*-signification, *trans*-figuration, or *trans*-finalization (Schillebeeckx, 1982).

The Eucharistic bread and wine are signs; however, they are more than just signs. Signs that are only signs can be replaced by other signs which are better signs, since they signify as well or even better the signified reality. Signs that are irreplaceable in leading us to a reality which cannot be reached without them are called symbols. So, for example, our body is the symbol of our personality, which cannot be reached and encountered without our body. As we have seen, in the Eucharist bread and wine are signs in which the body and blood of Jesus Christ as a living person are recognized and worshipped. They are, therefore, not only signs but symbols of the living Christ. As our body is an exclusive symbol for meeting us, so the bread and wine are for the presence of the body and blood of Christ, expressed by the word of "unless." The words of John 6, 53–56 express both the real presence and the intimate nature of the union of Christ with his people.

Because of their comprehensiveness, the Eucharistic words "This bread is my body" and "This wine is my blood" have not one but a twofold symbolism: one is the insertion of their symbolism into the world, and the other is the assumption of the bread with wine by the words "this is" to up there where the body of Christ belongs. The Eucharist thus becomes both the descent of the divine into the human-cosmic world and the elevation of the human-cosmic world into the life of God. So the theologians were able to unfold a double symbolism of the Eucharist: incarnation and assumption.

Created World as Symbol of Christ By taking bread and wine as his body and blood, Christ opened up the natural meaning, the obvious significations, and the direct finality of the biosphere to which bread and wine belong and made them transcend their natural meaning, signification, and finality. They assumed the meaning, signification, and finality of the world where Christ's own body and blood belong. By doing this, Christ deepened his incarnation into the world of the biosphere, reaffirmed its anthropic finality and that of the whole cosmic world, and initiated their assumption into eternity (Horvath, 1993, 140–53). He did so not to overrule but, rather, to elevate and fulfill the finality of the created world and, in it, of every human being to God.

Human beings, and with them the whole world, were created by God in his own image, as we read in Genesis (1, 26–27). Image is more than a vestige, a track or trace. Human beings are the image of God, so that looking at them, one can recognize God as an intelligent and loving person. Encountering human beings, one can encounter God. One who loves a human person finds that God too has to be a person. And one who believes in God as a person finds human persons beautiful, no matter how they look. But we may encounter in nature and in the whole visible world special instances when and where God's presence is not rarely felt with God's personal message to us. The burning bush, the *šekînāh*-temple, and the still, small voice that Elijah heard (1 Kgs 19,12–13) are examples par excellence from the Old Testament. Not only the God-created world but signs made by human beings, particularly the signs of love, such as marriage, non-Christian marriage included, may be symbols of loving God and considered a natural "sacrament" (Leo XIII, 1879–80, 392).

This kind of ability of the created world to welcome Christ and his destiny was not unknown in the early Church. Justin (*Apology*, 1, 46) and Irenaeus (*Against Heretics* 3, 18: 4, 6, 7) called it *semina verbi*, the seeds of the Word, the "actions of the Logos, who always stands by the human race and illuminates everyone coming into this world" (Irenaeus, ibid.). Scholastic theology knew about the *potentia obedientialis*, and Vatican II recognized that "the Word of God before becoming flesh was already in the world as true light that enlightens everyone" (GS, no. 57; Tanner, 1990, 1108). From the beginning of human history, the history of salvation was a preparation for both the Old and New Testaments (Horvath, 1981, 312).

If geology, biology, and anthropology act together in a synergetic operation, the total effect is more than the sum of the effects taken independently. Anthropology becomes geo-anthropology and geology anthropo-geology, because both share origin, time (action), and destiny. Each discovery is a dialectic of hypothesis with experiment (geology) and theory and praxis (anthropology). Initiated by a mutual misunderstanding (anomalies in observation and a search for their explanation by experiment and praxis), they end up in a mutual understanding and communication through language (anthropology) and in release of energy (geology). There is something personal in the earth and something geo-logic in humans. The earth has a kind of geo-humanism, and humans have a kind of geo-logism. Humans have a cosmo-logism, and the cosmos has a geo-logic humanism. The strong anthropic principle expresses this link by saying that the universe is made so that it may support the existence of human beings and that a mutual "understanding" between the two is possible (weak anthropic principle).

That a human being, a "morsel" of the universe, is able to understand the universe is an indication that everything which exists, humans and the cosmos included, is made through the Logos (Jn 1, 1–5), and everything that exists is a symbol of the Logos made flesh, dwelling among us (Jn 1, 14). The Eucharist is the outcome of the Incarnation. The Ascension cannot mean that Christ left the world. The Eucharist is the sure sign and guarantee that his presence in the world is more than just a memory of the past. After his death and resurrection, Christ's presence took a new form not limited any more to the space and time of his earthly life. He is in the world as the one who is saving the world, and as such, he reveals himself in the world. His being in the world is, above all, being with each one of us personally. This mysterious being with all of us is the continuation of his incarnation and might be called the mystery of in-hominization. Jesus is revealed as incarnated and now he is going to be revealed progressively more and more as "in-hominized." His revelation of who he is in himself was made once for all in his incarnation. His revelation of who he is for, in, and with the human race is an ongoing process (Horvath, 1976, 449).

Any sign, any symbol of God, takes its symbolizing power from Christ's Eucharistic presence in the world. He may be present to anyone in any way, but it is by virtue of his Eucharistic presence that his presence is active and salvific. He approaches and calls any human being and wants to be one with him or her. But his presence in individuals cannot be complete unless he unites himself with them as geo- and cosmo-logical human beings. In them and with them, he leads the world to its transformation in the new earth and new heaven. His in-hominization is an in-hominization of the earth and of the cosmos. It is a revelation of how much Jesus Christ, as real God and man, can love each of us individually, in a way that he never loved anyone before us and never will again. We are unique. The uniqueness of his love for each of us is the foundation of the uniqueness of each of us (Horvath, 1993, 153).

At this point the Eucharist has surpassed symbols as just a symbolic presence. By now it is an active revealing and redeeming presence and the foundation of any power symbolizing God in the world. It is a sacramental presence that causes certain symbols to be symbols, sacraments to be sacraments and sacramentals. The Eucharistic bread and wine mean more than the words that signs and symbols could cover. The two words had to be further qualified and given the new name "sacrament" since in them Christ was acting as real man and real God, revealing and prompting his love as God's love in human hearts and making his gifts the human race's gifts. He accomplishes this in justification, in forgiving sins, the fruit of his sacrifice, and he invites everyone to go and work with him in moving the world to be kingdom of God in eternal life.

By virtue of the Incarnation, there may be no distinction between the sacred and profane, but there remains always a Christian distinction between God and human beings. I will never be God and God never will be me. "At no point," we read in the Chalcedon Definition of the Faith, "was the difference between the two natures taken away" (Council of Chalcedon; Tanner, 1990, 86). No Monophysitism, no Monothelitism, no Docetism, and no Arianism, just a simple Nicene Johannine faith.

Theology of Symbols It is because of the Incarnation that the philosophy of symbols calls for a theology of symbols. Karl Rahner, in his article "Theology of Symbols" (1966), skilfully demonstrated that being is essentially symbolic. He was able to do so because his theology was his philosophy. It was the mystery of the Trinity that determined and revealed his notion of being having not three but four transcendental necessary conditions. Being, for Rahner, is not only one, true and good, as scholastic philosophy taught, but also symbolic. The symbolic nature belongs to the perfection of being. All beings are by their nature symbolic, because they necessarily express themselves in order to attain their own fulfillment in their nature. Being is, of itself, independent of any comparison with anything else, is plural in its unity. For its fulfillment, being merges into a plurality, of which the supreme model is the Trinity. One, plurality, and expression are the three momenta of the dynamism of being as such. Each being forms, in its own way, more or less perfectly according to its degree of being, something distinct from itself yet one with itself because being expressive, it is derivatively in agreement with itself

Symbolic reality, according to Rahner, is much more than symbolic presentation. Symbolic reality, symbol strictly speaking, means the tendency to make oneself present in another. Being is symbolic reality because "it must realize itself through a plurality in unity, the condition of possessing itself in knowledge and in love" (Rahner, 1996b, 230). Each being gives itself away from itself into the "other," and there it finds itself in knowledge and love. It is not difficult to recognize in this statement a precise description of God's Trinitarian life.

The symbolic nature of being therefore transcends the visible dimension of being. Not only is the incarnate Jesus Christ the symbol of the invisible Logos, the second person in the Trinity, but the invisible Logos, the divine person, is the symbol of the Father. Thus the Trinitarian life prior to the creation and incarnation is symbolic reality in so far as the Father realizes himself in the Son, the "other," who in agreement with the Father is expressive in the unity of the person of the Holy Spirit.

Here we discover an inner love relationship between the sacraments as the sacraments of the Church, the Church as the sacrament of the Son, and the Son as the sacrament of the Father. The being of the Father expresses itself in the second person of the Trinity, who, expressing their unity in the Holy Spirit, does the same in the humanity of Jesus. In turn, Jesus Christ expresses himself in the Church as his sacrament, which in turn is the symbolic reality of the sacraments. And the sacraments, as revelations of God in Jesus Christ, are the sacraments of the world and for the world. An account of this close love relationship should make obvious the fact that only Jesus Christ, the real God and real man, could institute the sacraments as symbolic reality enclosing in itself the symbolized reality. Since the sacraments are the visible gestures and the language of Jesus Christ, in whom everything was created, the sacraments tell us something of the world.

THE EUCHARISTIC PRESENCE AS A SYMBOL FOR THE WORLD

Independent of its religious context, the Eucharist makes sense in a secular world as well. It is a common good and makes a contribution to the world as presence, a presence to be achieved. Being of the world, the Eucharist is not only a symbol of the world but also a symbol for the world, representing what the world is and projecting what the world is going to be. The Eucharist as presence is both awareness and a program for the world.

Presence is always a presence to somebody or to something else. It means difference. And we know that creation brought about the most radical difference: the difference between and the presence of the creator to the creatures, the difference between and the presence of the eternal to the temporal, the difference between and the presence of the infinite to the finite. The ongoing creation and evolution further extends, dilates, and differentiates the world by moving instances and places further away from each other. Creation, evolution, is not a simple multiplication by cloning. Each creature is new and different. And because they are new and different, they extend and take up more space. Yet in spite of the ever-growing expansion and moving of the constituent elements further away from each other, at the same time, they are all tending more and more to be present to one another. The presence means both distance and distance from where. And the "from where" makes the "distanced" and the "distanced from" face each other, encounter each other. It seems that in the world of the universe, as well as that of human relationships, distance is a necessary condition of being present to something and to somebody. It is the distance that makes one exist as well as be present in the other.

Scientific discoveries make us aware that the world, with its past, present, and future, is a presence and try to make the universe more and more present to itself. Communication media, international agencies, travel, and conferences promote, never without self-interest, a universal presence by making distances, differences, present to one another. And this can be achieved because the world is fundamentally a presence.

The world as presence is a given, but it is also a task. It is a task to break down the dividing wall of hostility (Eph 2, 14) and to prompt the presence of each in the other as other. The world as presence challenges the solitary narcissism of any absolute power that denies the presence of the other, be it a world power, a single state, or an arrogant individual. The one who kills another and the one who kills millions, the one who does injustice to another and the one who does injustice to millions, the one who abuses another and the one who abuses millions – each denies and tries to destroy the world as a presence. Each one tries to hide him or herself from the presence of the world, ignoring the fact that sooner or later everyone has to "face" the world (cf. Mt 10, 26; Lk 12, 3).

The Eucharist is both the symbol and the underlying force of the world as presence. It is in the Eucharistic body of Christ as a unified field of energies in which God and human beings of the past, present, and future are not standing side by side but face each other, belonging to each other. The Eucharistic presence is not a prison closed up from the other. It is an encounter of people of far away who yet face each other and create each other, affirming the other as a real other, who precisely as other belongs to each. It is not a confrontation of two competing extremes pushed into the neighbourhood of another foreign "body." Rather, it is a loving invitation to create and affirm the other as other in the hope that one cannot die until the other is alive. Thus the Eucharist, as the pledge of eternal life, means that Christ is present to the past, the present, and the future and that in him past is present to the present and the future to both. The past is not absent from the present, and the future is present to the now and to the past.

The Eucharistic prayers are different in form, yet one in that they reflect this universal presence. It is a universal prayer that knows no limit. The whole world with its past, present, and future, all its people living and dead, together with those who are to be born – all are present there. Heaven and earth pray together *in socia exultatione.* It is in this sense that the mass is a commemoration, yet not of something or someone past who had been but is no more. It is a com-memoration, "passing time together," since we are all present to each other with the one and in the one in whom past and future are present. The mass is a real microcosm of the macrocosm. It is the centre, the model, the sacrament for the world as presence. The prayers of the faithful reflect that. It is a prayer with the power of forgiving sin and enabling them not to sin any more.

The sharing in the body, the unified field of energy of Christ, is a sharing in his power to undo injustice by removing distances between the poor and rich not just by distributing millions to the poor. Instead of our denying their existence by closing our eyes and moving away from them in order to overcome our anger or shame at being unable to help the "miserable" (Horvath, 1975a, 271–2), it calls to recognize them as equal. By the energy of the Eucharistic presence, one is able to face the poor, to look in their eyes, and to give them what we all should have, a friendly face (Acts 3, 4–6), by discovering ourselves in the poor, feeling one with the poor. One can give what perhaps the poor need most: dignity and courage to face the world as it is and find a place in it. The Eucharistic presence is a powerful presence of doing good in the world (Acts 10, 38).

It is by virtue of the Eucharist that Christ is always present (Mt 28, 20) and can be found everywhere and whenever, not only when two or three are gathered in his name to pray but also in doing good everywhere and whenever (Mt 18, 20). The Eucharist is, and through and in it, all the other sacraments are, *propter mundum universum,* for the whole world, as well as *propter hominem,* for any human person. It is this power of the Eucharistic presence that is further qualified and strengthened by the other sacraments.

The sacrament of marriage as sacrament of love is both a symbol of the world and a symbol for the world by manifesting that the pattern of differences is a universal pattern for the world. The sacrament of order as the sacrament of a call is a symbol for the world. It asserts the primacy of call over force in the world and for the world. The sacrament of conversion is a further symbol of, and for the world, ensuring that mercy is always a possibility. The sacrament of the anointing of the sick is a symbol of the world and for the world by reminding everyone that the world is always more than what we know about it. The sacrament of baptism reminds the world that our name is real; it means us and asks for respect. The revelation of it is an invitation to friendship and love. And finally, the sacrament of confirmation, as a symbol of the world and for the world, proclaims that language is the way to success in building a world of forgiveness and peace.

THE EUCHARISTIC PRESENCE AS SACRIFICE

The Eucharistic presence is not static. It is the presence of Jesus Christ, the Saviour of the world who is never idle. Like the Father, he is still working (Jn 5, 17). One can be physically present yet absent if one does not pay any attention to one's neighbours and to the surrounding world. The Eucharistic presence is a saving presence for the world. Thus the separation or even the distinction between Eucharistic presence and Eucharistic sacrifice can be only mental. Jesus cannot be separated from his life, from his works and merits. Without Christ's presence in the Eucharist, the mass is not a sacrifice and cannot forgive sin. It is the presence of the Eucharistic Christ who forgives sins, and his presence is a sacrificial one. The mass is a sacrifice and forgives sins because Christ is doing so in the mass (Council of Trent, *Teaching and Canons on the Most Holy Sacrifice of the Mass*, session 22, chapter 2; Tanner, 1990, 733). The Eucharist is a real sacrifice in virtue of the presence of the Eucharistic Christ, whose intention is to share with every human being his perfect love for the Father and the human race in a mutual exchange of lives, sacrifices, and merits.

4.1.4.2 THE EUCHARIST IS A SYMBOL FOR HUMAN EXISTENCE, A CHALLENGE TO LOVE AND TRUST

The classic definition of a sacrament, a visible and efficacious sign of grace, concerns itself primarily with the manifold human needs and underlines the anthropological function of the sacraments. That the sacraments are for human beings is the leading principle for a sacramental theology which primarily considers human need and the way the sacraments respond to that need. The sacraments strengthen us, feed us, forgive us, and heal us. Indeed, the Eucharist is a marvellous grace of sharing in God's life in a communion of being in God and God in us.

But because of the peculiarity of the Eucharistic gifts, the Eucharist and all the other six sacraments are also a challenge to human existence. They are a summons to a journey to move from the ordinary, controlled life of the here and now to a promised but unknown future. It is a challenging invitation to a journey to move from the present to the eschatological future, from human existence to God's life. Christian life is a moving from slavery, darkness, selfishness, fear, and anxiety to freedom, to a life of courage, to a share of the eternal happiness of God (Horvath, 1979b, 90–3). The Eucharist and the other sacraments are the symbols of this passage.

In addition to its contribution to the Christian life, the Eucharist makes sense even in a purely secular world. As a challenge, it makes a contribution to human life as experienced by any human being. It challenges love and trust. It is an invitation to face the unknown, the unbelievable, and to have courage and boldness to go forward yet remain faithful to the loved ones until death and even after (cf. Jn 13, 1). No matter the extent to which our life may have been fortunate, enriched, and sophisticated or, on the contrary, less fortunate, impoverished, and simple, we have to remember that there have always been people who loved us and the love they once had for us cannot pass away. They are all present to us in the one who is present to anyone. Later, some may have abandoned us or even betrayed us, as Peter did his master (Jn 13, 38; 18, 25–27; 21, 15–19), and hated us. They may have changed, aged, become sick and poor, useless for our purposes, and unable to recognize us. Yet the Eucharist calls us not to forget but to forgive and remain faithful, even though others have become unfaithful. Love has a future; hate does not. The future will conquer present and past. By the grace of the Eucharist, the present world becomes a proleptic anticipation of the world to come, even for those who have never experienced love in their life. Being a sacrament of God's daring love for all human beings, the Eucharist is a challenge to every human being. A *new* commandment, a *new* challenge – new in the sense of *kainos,* that is, exceeding in kind all other challenges. It is a love that is more than the love one has for oneself. It is a love such as Jesus has for any human beings (Jn 13, 34).

The Eucharistic challenge to remain in love and in trust is strengthened and qualified by the other sacraments. The sacrament of marriage, as a sacrament of love, is a challenge to our human existence to always respect the other as "other" and to cooperate with the other as "other." The sacrament of order, as sacrament of a call, is a challenge to our human life for never-ending initiative. The sacrament of forgiveness is a challenge to us human beings to have the strength and power to confess our failures and to have mercy. The sacrament of the anointing of the sick is a challenge to people to never give up. The sacrament of baptism is a challenge to transcendence, to live up to our Christian name. And finally, the sacrament of confirmation is a challenge to our human existence to create clarity out of confusion and unity out of babel.

EXPOSITION OF THE EUCHARIST

Shortly after the paschal event, the early Christians learned that sharing the Lord's Supper had a special power to make Christ, sitting at the right of the Father, present and let them burst into thanksgiving and adoration of God. The breaking of bread was interrupted for a short time to pay homage to God the Father in the company of the angelic choirs and saints through prayers of adoration, invocation, and petition. The early liturgical prayers of the Eucharist witness to that. It was this special healing and attracting power that prompted the early Christians to take the Eucharistic bread to the sick. The attractive power of the Eucharist, backed by contemporary Platonic philosophy, inflamed in them a desire for heaven and let them interpret both Christ's descent into the world and the Eucharist as just a transitory step in their journey towards heaven.

It was only after almost a thousand years that, thanks to the prevailing Aristotelian philosophy, Christ's descent into the world was interpreted as also a dwelling in the world, and sacramental theology took on a new dimension. Christ's Eucharistic presence was welcomed as his staying with us in this passing world. The communion could be postponed for a longer period, and Eucharistic adoration became current. Congregations were founded for perpetual adoration of the Eucharist.

And this practice continued even in a time when congregations of perpetual adoration, for lack of vocations, had to close their doors. The laity took over their role and organized adoration lasting twenty-four hours a day with the exposition of the sacrament in various churches. The Eucharist still has its attracting and challenging power for our earthly existence. Without any organized prayers or spoken words and visions, in the silence of intimate dialogue of "Thou and I," we sense the presence of Christ listening to us and answering us by releasing the human and divine energies of his risen body. And this energy is an invitation and mission to take up our personal responsibility and remain faithful in love and trust to serve the salvation of the world through his Church according to our individual vocations and gifts.

THE SUNDAY EUCHARIST AS THE REDISCOVERY AND REKINDLING OF THE FIRST CHRISTIANS' LOVE FOR JESUS CHRIST

Since the time of the apostles, Christians have celebrated the first day of the week, the Lord's Day (Rev 1, 10), *dies dominica*, commemorating Jesus' resurrection from the dead. It was a day of joy and hope that kept the community together. Everyone came freely and with great sacrifice. Some gave their lives for it. Love for Jesus Christ was still burning in their hearts, and this common love for Jesus was expressed, rekindled, and strengthened by meeting and seeing all those who loved and worshipped the same person. In commemorating him, everyone felt his presence again in the Eucharistic breaking of the bread. There was no need to urge people to come. It was for all of them "the day" they were waiting for with a cheerful expectation. This cheerful expectation even today resounds in the closing prayer of the Divine Office of Saturday: "Come and stay with us, Lord, this night that by your help we may rise tomorrow to rejoice in the resurrection of Christ, your son." Real and unselfish love is a sharing in the happiness of the loved one. One is happy because the loved one is happy (Thomas Aquinas, *Summa theol.*, 2, 2, q 23, a 1; Horvath, 1966, 229–55). The first

Christians were overjoyed that Christ is risen. His happiness was their happiness. They were glad to celebrate the Lord's Day, eagerly hoping to see him again and very soon. That was a time of early fervour and love when a great number of Christians met their death for Christ with Eucharistic enthusiasm. But it was also a time of denial and forgiveness.

This was more so as time passed and the distance between the first news of the resurrection and the present grew. The number of Christians increased more and more, and they felt the joy of the risen Christ less and less. The Lord's Day celebration became a burden for many and an obligation for everyone. Though the same grace of faith was communicated to each of them through baptism, yet becoming a glowing ember, it had to be rekindled week after week. And the rekindling became more and more difficult in a changing world. Most Christians were like Martha, anxious and troubled about many things but failing in the most-needed thing (Lk 10, 41–42), loving Jesus Christ. Attendance at Sunday mass became the hallmark of a healthy Christian community, and its decline a lasting concern. There were a few ways to remedy it.

The first was the easiest, a commandment and a treat. If anyone missed one mass on any Sunday or day of obligation, he or she committed a mortal sin and became worthy of eternal damnation. We can find this interpretation recently in the *Catechism of Catholic Church* (1994), no. 2181: "Those who deliberately fail in this obligation commit grave sin." Whereas according to article 5, on the Fifth Commandment, murderers commit "a sin that cries out to heaven for vengeance" (no. 2268), abortion is a moral evil (no. 2271), and euthanasia is morally unacceptable (no. 2277) and according to article 6, on the Sixth Commandment, fornication is seriously contrary to the dignity of human persons and their sexuality (no. 2353), we find that only those who deliberately fail in their Sunday obligation "sin gravely." There is supposed to be a special danger in missing Sunday mass.

The *Constitution on Sacred Liturgy* exhorted that Sunday be presented as a fundamental feast day for the religious observance of believers (SC, no. 106; Tanner, 1990, 838). The *New Code of Canon Law*, published in 1983, changed the obligation to hear holy mass of the 1917 code to the prescription that the faithful are " bound" to participate in the mass (canon 1247). John Paul II, in his Apostolic Letter *Dies Domini*, of 13 July 1998, recalls the requirement that "faithful are bound to attend" Sunday mass by adding the words "entailing a grave obligation," which according to the pope is the teaching of the *Catechism of the Catholic Church.*

Is there some justifiable foundation for such a traditional concern and rigour? According to the gravity of the object, the *Catechism* recognizes the traditional distinction between two kinds of sin, mortal and venial. The gravity of sins admits different degrees. Murder is, for example, more serious than theft (no. 1858). Yet it seems that murder, adultery, theft, and deliberately missing one mass on Sunday, though in different degree, are all equally grave matters, and the person who commits any of them, "if it is not redeemed by repentance and God's forgiveness ... merits the eternal death of hell" (no. 1861) because, the *Catechism* says, all attack "the vital principle within us – charity" (no. 1856). A passage from Thomas Aquinas clarifies this: "When the will decides on something opposed *per se* to the love that orders it to its ultimate end, then the sin by its very object has to be mortal ... whether it contradicts the love of God, e.g., blasphemy, perjury, or the love of neighbor, e.g., homicide or adultery ... But when the sinner's will decides on something containing itself a disorder but not opposed to the love of God and neighbor ... such sins are venial" (no. 1856; *Summa theol.*, 1, 2, q 88, a 2).

In the sense of this definition, the missing of one mass is not a sin "whose object is grave matter" (*Catechism*, no. 1857), because then no one would be allowed to ever miss a mass, just as no one is allowed to commit adultery. Missing a mass on Sunday is a "grave sin," according to the reference to Thomas's *Summa*, if one does it as an expression of one's "contradicting the love of God, or the love of neighbor." But if one does not miss a mass on Sunday as an opposition to the love of God and one's neighbours, it seems, then one would not "sin gravely," though one would certainly miss an occasion par excellence to rekindle the ember of love for Jesus Christ and for human beings. But this is precisely the Eucharistic mass. It is the most efficient way to activate, conserve, and cultivate love for Jesus Christ and love for any human being. According to the Christian faith, the Eucharistic mass is the most faithful observance of the first commandment – "You shall love the Lord your God" – granting strength and meaning for observances of all the commandments of the Christian faith.

Thus missing mass on Sunday may be looked upon as disobedience to the first commandment, "You shall love the Lord your God and your neighbors" (no. 2083), and there we could find some justification for the seriousness of failing one's Sunday obligation by missing mass (John Paul II, 1998, no. 47). Prolonged failing to attend mass may easily lead, indeed, to the extinction of one's love for God, given in baptism and the sacrament of forgiveness. It is a serious negligence to let vanish one's most vital principle within, namely, charity, the promotion of which is anyone's responsibility and mission.

Another, more obvious way of remedying the decline in attendance at Sunday mass seems to be to make it a more interesting, more entertaining "show." This can be done by more active participation of the faithful and by making each time during the mass something different, something unexpected. This approach may be helpful. But no matter how ingenious one may be, sooner or later everything becomes déjà vu. Any kind of effort of this type is praiseworthy and to be encouraged. It shows effort on the part of the priests and of the community to serve the One who is celebrated by the mass and their love for him and his people. These are the people who come freely, because their love for Jesus inspires them, as it did the first Christians. And here we touch upon the best way of remedying the decline in attendance at Sunday mass. We propose it in a form of questions.

At the beginning of the third millennium, is it possible that the Christians may experience again the same burning love in their heart as the first Christians? Are the priests able to rekindle the same love for Christ in the heart of the faithful, so that they will come eagerly and freely? Is there any way that faithful Christians can experience their love for Jesus Christ which brings them to come and express itself in the liturgy of the mass and to meet all those who have the same love and joy that keeps their community together? Is there any way that during the mass they can feel that their love for Jesus is rekindled and strengthened by meeting and seeing all those who love and worship the same person? In commemorating him, do they feel his presence again in the Eucharistic breaking of bread? Is it possible that for them too *dies dominica*, the Lord's Day, will be *the* day they are waiting for with a cheerful expectation? Might they share the happiness of the risen Lord as their own happiness? Or is this just a gift for a few, a mystical grace for monks and some solitary friends of Jesus Christ? Can we, as John Paul II encouraged us to, rediscover the joy of Sunday and rekindle the first Christians' love for Jesus Christ? Is it possible to love Jesus Christ as our brethren and sisters did two thousand years ago and were able to give their lives for their love for him?

In order to answer these questions affirmatively, we have to say that the love for Jesus Christ enticed by Sunday mass is not necessarily a charismatic or mystic love voiced in mysterious languages, in fainting, or in the ecstatic dancing of some distinct groups. Rather, it is the simple quiet, deep Eucharistic love for the crucified and risen Jesus Christ expressed and formulated in the liturgical prayers of the mass and given to any baptized. It is already there and felt when one decides to attend mass to be rekindled and strengthened more fully during the mass. Listening and paying attention to these words heard so many times, one may find that those prayers express more powerfully the love one senses in his or her heart than some "big" new ideas. Those are the words of Christ-loving Christians joined together over two thousand years in a never-ending love for Jesus Christ and for all people of God.

The Sunday celebration is "the fundamental feast day," "the basis and centre of the whole liturgical year," as we read in the *Constitution on the Sacred Liturgy* of Vatican II (*SC*, no. 106; Tanner, 1990, 838), because love is the centre and foundation of Christian celebrations. It is a love that is much more than just a smile, shaking hands, or talking loudly to one another. It is a love that is an ember in our heart, and we may enkindle it in silence. And when love is burning we find that the world around us is beautiful. We love people. We love everybody in the world, as God does, and we are ready to help the poor, the needy. This is the time when we find that God's love is the foundation of any love we may experience: love for sport, love for entertainment, love for work, the love of oneself, even the love of the cross I have to carry. It is the foundation and fulfillment of my love for sport, for my dog, for my friends, and much more for my parents – in a word, of any kind of human love. Love for God is the source and the end of a happy human life. It is the great gift we should ask for in a prayer such as this: "God, let me love you more and more, and may the reward for my love for you be that I may love you even more." Such a prayer is one that is certainly answered. God just cannot refuse it, because God cannot deny God.

There is one more way to increase Sunday mass attendance. Really, it is not different from the previous one. Rather, it is the outcome of it. It is to search and find how to make attractive and lovable the person of Jesus Christ so that, as for the first Christians, he "is fixed on our hearts and minds and remains alive and vivid to us" (Hayes and Hanscom, 1983, 482). And this is precisely the vocation and mission of any ordained priest. The fundamental task and duty of the priest was, is, and always will be to help people in their greatest need of and search for God. It is his role to help human beings to encounter God (Horvath, 1968, 253). Through ordination the priest becomes Christ's active invitation calling others into a dialogue of love with God (Horvath, 1971a, 51). A priest may be good or bad, but by virtue of his ordination and priestly character, he has a special power of witnessing to Christ as the one who loves a human person more than anyone else ever did or ever will. It is the experience of this great love of Christ celebrated in the Eucharist which makes Christ lovable and attractive.

Weekday Eucharistic celebrations are extensions of the Sunday mass celebration. They are in a certain sense the "octave" of the previous Sunday celebration of the resurrection of Jesus Christ. Each morning is a resurrection day. Its celebration is a pledge of one's burning love for Jesus Christ. To make Christ attractive and lovable is a challenge. It is the challenge of the Eucharist to all human beings. It is a challenge to reach the depth of love (Eph 3, 18–19), the "vital principle within us." It is a challenge to the Church of Christ in the world. It is a love of faith, a love that is "in our reason."

4.1.4.3 THE EUCHARIST IS A SYMBOL FOR THE CHURCH: BEING WITH PEOPLE IN THE WORLD

The Eucharist has a message not only to the world and to any human being but to the Church. It is more than just a verbal message. It is a mission, a life for the Church. The Eucharist and the other sacraments are not only for the world or for human beings but also for the Church. The sacraments are for the Church. They are life functions of the Church in which its life is actualized and expressed. Just as human beings through the exercise of their life functions, such as understanding, will, procreative powers, and so on, can develop their personality, so the Church by the sacraments actuates its very being (Rahner, 1963). Even more – the Church itself is a sacrament. The Church is a sacrament, we read in *Dogmatic Constitution on the Church* LG, no. 1), "or instrumental sign of intimate union with God and of the unity of all humanity" (Tanner, 1990, 849). It is through sacraments that the sacred character and the organic structure of the Church are brought into effect. It is in the Eucharist, "the source and culmination of all Christian life," that the people of God offer Christ and, with him, themselves and show forth their unity, symbolized and brought about in this "most noble sacrament" (*LG*, no. 11; Tanner, 1990, 857).

It is by the Eucharist that the Church is effected. It is a reminder for the Church that, in spite of its eschatological nature and being one with the Church in heaven, yet it is a sacrament of the unity of all humanity here on earth. Its place still is in the world, and there is nothing human that should be alien to it. There is no human being who by his or her own call would not be part of the Church as the people of God. With the loving presence of the Eucharistic Christ, the Church, like Mother Teresa in India, has to be present to the whole world and to every human being by caring, uplifting, saving, and witnessing. This is the mission to preach the gospel everywhere (Mk 14, 15, 20) in season and out of season (2 Tim 2, 4), laity and priests together.

The Church's being in the world is strengthened and confirmed by the other sacraments. The sacrament of marriage, as sacrament of love, is a life function of the Church in its self-giving without any restriction to God and to the human race. The sacrament of order, as the sacrament of a call, is a life function of the Church in its constant dependence on the historical risen Christ as its leader. The sacrament of forgiveness is a life function of the Church in its mission to repent and to forgive. The sacrament of the anointing of the sick is a life function of the Church in its loving of the sick and the poor. The sacrament of baptism is a life function of the Church in its ever-growing in the world until the end of the world. Finally, the sacrament of confirmation is a life function of the Church in being the sacrament of the unity of all peoples.

4.1.4.4 THE EUCHARIST IS A SYMBOL FOR CHRISTOLOGY: CHRIST IS IN THE WORLD

Christology is the knowledge of Christ, the real God and man, the second person of the Trinity and the Saviour of the world. Presenting Christology first and the Eucharist afterward, a theologian may give the impression that Christ is alive in heaven and the Eucharist is only a sacrament of community celebration. One may prefer "Christology from above," presenting Christ coming down from heaven, and another "Christology from below," seeing Christ as our brother leading us to our Father in heaven.

But if we begin with Eucharist, we may find a more balanced Christology. Heaven and earth are close together and we do not have to go up or come down. The Eucharist is not really a "thing" but the living person of Jesus Christ, whose presence is marked by the space and time of the bread and wine, yet he is not imprisoned there. He is there because he could not just leave the world liberated from the shackles of time and space and go up to heaven. He is there, yet he is not just there. He is here redeeming the world. He is here because he loves to be with us and could not leave us. He loves to be in the world to bring heaven close to earth.

The Eucharist makes a valuable contribution to our Christology. It is a Christology of the historical Jesus and the Christ of faith. It is not so much that Christology reveals the Eucharist but, rather, that the Eucharist discloses the kind of Christology one has. The sacraments are for Christ as the crucified and glorified one, *propter Jesum Christum crucifixum and glorificatum.* The Eucharist specifies: *propter Christum crucifixum and glorificatum in mundo,* for the Christ crucified and glorified in the world. So do the other sacraments.

The sacrament of marriage, as the sacrament of love, is a feature of Christology by presenting Christ in his unrestricted self-giving to God and to the human race in the love of one woman and one man. The sacrament of order, as the sacrament of a call, is a feature of Christology by displaying Christ's sharing of his call with us in this world. The sacrament of the forgiveness is a feature of Christology by conferring forgiveness as sacrifice. The sacrament of the anointing of the sick is a feature of Christology by culminating in Christ as Saviour of the sick, the poor sinners of the present world. The sacrament of baptism is a feature of Christology as the one who strengthens his presence in the world by each baptized. And finally, the sacrament of confirmation is a feature of Christology by making explicit implicit Christologies.

4.1.4.5 THE EUCHARIST IS A SYMBOL FOR THE REVELATION OF THE TRIUNE GOD: A GOD PLEASED TO BE WITH THE HUMAN RACE

Since Jesus Christ is the revelation of the Triune God, we may discover in each of the sacraments the inner life of God. Each sacrament shows us what kind of God our God is. Thus in addition to the universal, anthropological, ecclesiological, and Christological descriptions, we should add one more which we would like to call the revelational or theological description of the sacraments. Accordingly, a sacrament considered in relation to the Triune God can be seen as a symbol of God's Trinitarian life. The fundamental principle of such a sacramental theology is that the sacraments are revelations of the Triune God, *sacramenta sunt revelationes Dei trini* (Horvath, 1970, 1971a, 1988, 1989).

The revelation of the Triune God takes place in each sacrament, but there is a different emphasis in each. The Eucharist reveals a God who is pleased to be with us as a human being in the world. God's incomprehensibility notwithstanding, he is "Emmanuel," God is with us. The sacrament of marriage, as a sacrament of love, portrays God's infallible love in the fallible love of a woman and a man chosen by God to be a sacrament of God's love. The sacrament of order, as the sacrament of a call, is God's revelation that wherever this minister is, God is available. The sacrament of forgiveness discloses the forgiving God as free and independent of the worthiness of the sinners. The sacrament of the anointing of the sick reveals the incomprehensibility of God's love for us. The sacrament of baptism presents God's infinite generosity (Father), integrity (Son), and authenticity (Holy Spirit). Finally, the sacrament of confirmation proclaims love, faith, and hope as the Triune God's gift to us.

4.1.4.6 THE EUCHARIST IS A SYMBOL FOR ESCHATOLOGY: ETERNAL LIFE IS PRESENT IN THE KERYGMA

The kerygma is the power of the proclamation that the future of God appeared in the present overpowered by the "past" of the historical Jesus' life, death, and resurrection. The sacraments – and first of all, the Eucharist, the sacrament par excellence – are the expression and actualization of the kerygma (Horvath, 1993, 71–2). The reality of eternal life is present in the kerygma. The proclamation about Jesus becomes his own proclamation of himself and of all those who are with him (Lk 23, 43; Jn 14, 3; Horvath, 1993, 65–6).

The threefold orientation of the sacraments – commemorative sign of the past, demonstrative sign of the present, and prognostic sign of the eschatological future (Thomas Aquinas, *Summa theol.*, 3, q 60, a 3) – directs our attention to the Eucharistic Jesus Christ, whom we may discover as the eschatological union of time and eternity. Having united in himself time and eternity, he can save his Church together with peoples and societies, the cosmic world included, from the power of sin and death and lead them on their way to enter into eternity (Horvath, 1993, 124–53).

The connection between the Eucharist and eternal life seems to be definitive and exclusive (Jn 6, 53). Since everything is mortal except God (1 Tim 6, 15) eternity is not some unlimited space or time. It is a person, God. God is eternity and eternity is God (Thomas Aquinas, *Summa theol.*,

1, q 10, a 2; Horvath, 1993, 31–2) and only Jesus Christ as real God and real man can bridge the gap between God (eternity) and human beings (time). The Eucharist and eternal life are inseparable, because eternity is above all an encounter with Jesus Christ, the only one who is able to let a person share God's life, that is, eternity. Thus we can say that there is no grace that is not eschatological since each grace is a sharing in God's life. The sacraments are, therefore, the eschatological realizations of Christ's redemption. Thus it also follows that if each grace is eschatological, it must be also Eucharistic. This does not mean that only the Eucharist gives grace or that without sacraments, no grace is given at all. Rather, it means that no grace is given without the Church, which is effected and supported by the Eucharist. It means, further, that if Christians and non-Christians receive grace, the grace is always communicated to them through the sacraments of the Church received by the faithful.

Any grace given is through the mediation of one of the sacraments of the Church. Moreover any grace given to us is a grace not just to us as individuals but to us as members of the Church and of the whole human race. Thus a grace given to non-sacramental marriages of non-Christians may be communicated through the sacramental marriages of Christians and therefore is a sacramental grace. By virtue of the Eucharist, there is an organic unity, a "collegiality," not only among the sacraments but among any grace given to anyone whenever or wherever. This is so because the Eucharistic Christ is the eschatological union of time and eternity.

The sacrament of marriage, as a sacrament of love, is a symbol of eschatology by announcing that love has a future, that hate does not, and that the future is stronger than the past and the present. The sacrament of order is a symbol of eschatology by confirming Christian eschatology as irrevocable once and for all. The sacrament of forgiveness is a symbol of eschatology by foretelling that the merciful shall obtain mercy. The sacrament of the anointing of the sick is a symbol of eschatology by ratifying that time is the revelation of eternity. The sacrament of baptism is a symbol of eschatology by revealing that the Trinitarian life is eternity. Finally, the sacrament of confirmation is a symbol of eschatology by announcing the unity of all languages in Christ, who is the language of all languages.

4.1.4.7 THE EUCHARIST IS A SYMBOL FOR PNEUMATOLOGY: A CHURCH-BUILDING HOLY SPIRIT

Word and Spirit, Logos and Pneuma, Christ and the Holy Spirit are a dyad that implies difference, a certain dualism. Past and future, old and new, institution and persons, static conservatism, dynamic pluralism, ascetics and mystics, hierarchic and charismatic communities, and down-to-earth realism and up-to-heaven spirituality are respectively associated concepts.

One may think of pneumatological Christology (Congar, 1983, 3, 228–49) or of Christological pneumatology (Berkhof, 1964). According to the first, Christ is the principal agent. He sends and gives the Spirit. Following the second, the Spirit has priority and leads Jesus. The Spirit is Lord and creates a new world independent of the old, he illuminates, testifies, and organizes. Christological pneumatology is for reform and is an agent of the spiritualist movement as a reaction to the non-spiritual, sacramental, hierarchic, and Eucharistic. Pneumatologic Christology is focused on Christ, moved and helped by the holy Spirit.

The hermeneutic principle justifying the differences is whether Christ, the Spirit, or the Father is considered the ultimate reality and meaning in the light of whom the other two divine persons are interpreted. The choice depends on personal experiences of various kinds. One may find more sense in understanding the Son in the light of the Spirit, rather than the Spirit in the light of the Logos or both in light of the Father. There may be some who see all three in the light of an abstract notion of godhead.

For a speculative theology having its point of departure in the love that the Church has for Jesus Christ as celebrated in the Eucharist, Eucharistic pneumatology is the favoured term. Eucharistic pneumatology understands the Holy Spirit as Paraclete, the advocate of Jesus, and relates the Eucharist closely to as pneumatology. In a certain sense, the two are interchangeable: the Eucharist is pneumatology and pneumatology is the Eucharist. Whereas the Eucharist as pneumatology suggests that the Holy Spirit is to be met in the Eucharist, pneumatology as the Eucharist means that the Holy Spirit is building the Church.

THE EUCHARIST IS PNEUMATOLOGY

Following John 14, 9–11, classical theology rightly stressed that the divine persons' actions *ad extra*, in relation to the world, are common and one. The Holy Spirit does nothing without the Father and the Son, and the same is true of the Son and the Father. This does not mean that the Father, the Son, and the Spirit do not act in the world as Father, Son and Holy Spirit. It means, rather, that none of them do anything alone. The Father is always working together with the Son and the Holy Spirit, and so is the Son and the Holy Spirit. The Eucharist is, therefore, a meeting with the Son as well as a meeting with the Holy Spirit. The Eucharist is not just a fraternal gathering with Christ, our brother, around a table but a real, yet mysterious, transcending presence of God. The presence is not only a purely "physical" one. It is a spiritual presence since Jesus Christ is contained and not contained in the Eucharist. Jesus Christ is present in the Eucharist in his body yet not visible and measured by the spatial and temporal dimension of the bread and wine. He is present there as God together with the Father and the Holy Spirit, as well as all the saints and departed faithful. In the Eucharist with Christ the Church appears as "a people made one by the unity of the Father and the Son and the holy Spirit" (*LG*, no. 4; Tanner, 1990, 851).

PNEUMATOLOGY IS THE EUCHARIST

The Holy Spirit as Paraclete is the advocate of Jesus Christ (Jn 14, 26; 16, 12–15). The action of the Spirit points to Jesus Christ and builds up his Church (Acts 2, 1–47). Being self-effacing, the Spirit does not build up a Church of the Spirit but a Church of Jesus Christ. In a Church built by the Spirit, the Spirit, as the spirit of unselfish love for Jesus Christ, strengthens his followers to proclaim their love for Jesus boldly and without fear. The Holy Spirit is the Spirit of Jesus Christ and, as such, is present wherever Jesus Christ is present. A spirit that is not Eucharistic is not the Spirit of Jesus Christ and therefore cannot be the third divine person of the Trinity. The Spirit of Jesus Christ is the one who makes Christ the language of the languages (Horvath, 1993, 142–3) and his Church one and universal.

The sacrament of marriage, as a sacrament of love, is a symbol of the Holy Spirit building up the Church of Jesus Christ. The sacrament of order is a symbol of the Holy Spirit asserting the freedom of Christ's call. The sacrament of the forgiveness is a symbol of the Holy Spirit forgiving sins on earth and in heaven as well. The sacrament of the anointing of the sick is a symbol of the Holy Spirit raising mortals into immortality. The sacrament of baptism is the symbol of the Holy Spirit descending upon the baptized and making them the beloved sons and daughters of the Father. Finally the sacrament of confirmation is a symbol of the Holy Spirit, the Spirit of hope, boldness, and the courage of wisdom.

4.1.4.8 THE EUCHARIST IS A SYMBOL FOR MARIOLOGY: EUCHARISTIC GRACE IS UNIVERSAL; MARY IS THE MEDIATRIX OF ALL GRACES

The Second Vatican Council saw Mary as the model of redeemed human beings. The mystery of the Eucharist helps us to savour the mystery of Mary. It presents her as the pre-eminent paradigm of the overwhelming gifts of the Eucharist to the human race. Since grace is both Eucharistic and eschatological, so the grace that Mary received ahead of time was a sharing in God's life. Furthermore, as Christ's Eucharistic presence is both personal and universal, so Mary's grace is personal and universal as well. What is given to Mary is shared by each faithful receiving grace through the sacraments for him or herself and for others as well as praying for every human being and the whole universe. Thus we may say that any grace and its power given to us is not limited to us but made accessible to others. We all share, though in a lesser degree, the grace given to Mary as the mediatrix of all graces. Jesus Christ's loving and saving presence is the mystery of her motherhood and that of God's indwelling in us through the sanctifying grace.

Mary is, indeed, the model of the redeemed human being. It is in her that the Church recognized that grace must have a universal oneness, as do all the sacraments in virtue of the sacrament of the Eucharist. Each grace is a grace of love for Jesus Christ, and the love Mary has for Jesus Christ is the foundation of the love the believers have for her. By replacing the words "devotion to Mary" or "veneration of Mary" with the "love for Mary" that believers have, we may better understand the origin and taste the merit of the Marian devotion and cult the Church has had for Mary since apostolic times.

4.2 WHAT IS THE SACRAMENT OF MARRIAGE?

4.2.1 The Pre-eminence of the Sacrament of Marriage

Thomas Aquinas, in his *Summa theologiae* (3, q 65, a 3), asked whether the Eucharist was a more pre-eminent (*potissimum*) sacrament than the other sacraments. In his response to the last of the objections, he replied that each sacrament has its own special pre-eminence. And so does the sacrament of marriage. Its pre-eminence (*excellentia*) comes from its symbolic meaning of signifying the union between Christ and his Church. The same union between Christ and his Church that is symbolized (*figuratur*) through the sacrament of the Eucharist is expressed visibly by the sacrament of marriage. Since the sacrament of marriage, like any sacrament, is related to the Eucharist, marriage signifies the union of Christ with his Church but not independently of the Eucharist. Thus the sacrament of marriage signifies the Eucharist, and in its signification it involves (*attingit*) the Eucharist too. For Thomas there is a difference between the *significatio* of marriage and the *figuratio* of the Eucharist. Whereas marriage manifests the conjunction of Christ with the Church, the Eucharist is the *unio*, the unity of the two (ibid.). Marriage, like the other sacraments, is a sacrament by virtue of the Eucharist.

Marriage as human experience is an intentionally "never-ending" mutual love between one man and one woman. This love is the outward sign of the sacrament of marriage and the foundation of its pre-eminence among all the other sacraments. Since love is the meaning of all the other sacraments, the sacrament of marriage can be considered the sacrament of sacraments. Love being the "subject matter" and the problem-solving paradigm for our speculative theology, the sacrament of marriage has pre-eminence in our sacramental theology. In affirming this with Thomas Aquinas, we rely on Ephesians 5, 32. We assume that the Pauline passage does not speak only of Christian sacramental marriage but of any marriage as a human experience of love between man and woman. The great mystery in Ephesians 5, 32 refers to the relation existing between the union of Christ with his Church, on the one hand, and the union of a man with his wife, on the other. The relation between the two was hidden in the past but made known to Paul (see Eph 1, 9–10; 3, 3–6), and it finds some understanding in the love existing in the marrying couple. On account of this love one leaves father and mother in order that the two become one flesh (Eph 5, 31). The verse is a reference to Genesis 2, 18–24, where the inspired author tries to explain that mysterious powerful force which attracts man and woman to each other. This mysterious force is called love.

4.2.2 The Human Mystery of the Sacrament of Marriage

The sacrament of marriage is the only sacrament in which not a special ritual but a universal human reality, existing long before Christ, is taken up as a sacrament. This may be one of the reasons why it took so long before the Church could finally list marriage as one of its sacraments. It is in this sacrament that the Christ event enters directly into a human reality created by God before Christ's entering in the world, and this characteristic makes Christianity not only a transcendental, otherworldly realm but a reality deeply rooted in this world. Any attempt that would reduce the sacrament of marriage to a ritual ceremony after marriage would deprive Christianity of its roots and anchor in this world. It would deny the sacramental value of human love and remove it from being a bridge joining human life and the world of faith together. It is understandable that the Church cannot agree with that.

Edward Schillebeeckx entitled his book, first published in 1963, *Marriage: Human Reality and Saving Mystery*. But it may be the other way around: marriage is human mystery and saving reality – human mystery, because it is far from being easy to tell what marriagc is; saving reality, because it is the most common human event in which and through which Christ's grace may reach a great number of human beings.

Marriage is a complex reality. It is a topic for politicians, economists, lawyers, biologists, doctors, sociologists, psychologists, priests, and theologians. The more common and basic a human experience is, the more difficult it is to express and explain. Such is the case with marriage. It has many names and a diversified history. It is not enough simply to say that marriage is a contract, a covenant, a community, a business, sex, or love (Horvath, 1979b), because the next question will be to ask what kind of contract, covenant, community, and so on it is. Marriage is a universal human reality, yet it is personal, unique, and the most fundamental social event in our life, touching upon the mystery of life and time, creature and creator. We try to name it, yet each word raises more questions than the explanations provided.

The enigma of marriage is indicated by the great variety of words and expressions we find in various languages. The English word "marriage" has in its root the Latin *mas,* male, meaning a woman getting (*maritare,* give or get) a man as husband. The word "husband" comes from the Old Norse or ancient Scandinavian word *husbonde,* householder. Whereas the word "marriage" implies the role of man, the word "matrimony" intimates woman becoming mother. Greek, too, had many terms to express marriage: *γάμος,* marriage feast, *γâμέω,* take a wife, *έπιγâμία* alliance, *συβîοώ,* common life, *συνοικία,* living together. The *γάμος* was a religious ceremony. Before leaving the house of her parents, the bride offered sacrifices to the gods of her family. The Latin *nuptiae* meant a religious celebration when a woman was covered by a veil. *Coniugium* suggests sharing a common yoke. *Consortium* reminds us of the common destiny, the common fate of wife and husband. The Hindu word *kanyadana* means the handing over of the bride to the bridegroom and the joining of their right hands together with the recitation of some marriage hymn about the prototype of all marriages, the wedding of Soma, the moon, with Surya, the daughter of the sun (De Sales, 1963). The Hungarian word *házasság* could be rendered by the expression "acquiring a house."

4.2.2.1 A CONTRACT? WHAT KIND?

Peoples of earlier times already considered marriage as the acquisition of property, a position of wealth and prestige. Among the old Teutons, after the husband paid the dowry, ownership over the bride passed from her parents to him. The Anglo-Saxon *beweddung* was not binding until payment was made. In many Germanic groups the transfer of authoritative ownership was the original form of marriage. Even later in medieval times, when the amount was of no importance, if nothing had been given, the presumption was against the marriage. So long as payment had any importance, the woman had not too much to say in marriage.

As among other peoples, so among the African peoples too, marriage was a complex affair with its economic, social, and religious aspects (Mbiti, 1975, 133). It was a duty, a requirement imposed by society to participate in the rhythm of life. It was an attempt through procreation to regain immortality by producing someone who would remember one, keep him or her from oblivion, and let one be a member of the "living dead." It is true that some attempts were made to remove any aspect of commercial motivation, yet it is true also that the date for marriage was never fixed until the parents agreed on the amount of payment to be given to the girl's family, usually three or four cows or the equivalent in money or goods. If the father of the bridegroom had no money, he was willing to became a servant or slave in order that his son might obtain a wife and he might stay alive through his grandsons and daughters. The plea of one father, cited by John S. Mbiti, is moving: "I have come to be born in this house, to be a son, to be a servant if you like, to take cattle to the river to drink, to buy you clothes, to help alleviate your needs. I am prepared to do all these things and many more, if you give me a wife for my son" (ibid., 138).

This was the custom of ancient times, and the Hebrews were no exceptions. Hosea, for example, paid fifteen shekels of silver and a homer and a lethech of barley (Hos 3, 2) for a woman, who from that time was exclusively his own, belonging to no other man (Hos 3, 3). The Deuteronomist (22, 28–29) saw fifty shekels as a fair price. But Jacob had to serve seven years for Leah and seven years for Rachel (Gen 29, 18–30; see also Gen 34,

11–12). Instead of payment, Saul asked David for a hundred Philistine foreskins for Michal (1 Sam 18, 27).

Roland de Vaux has suggested that for the Hebrews the sum of money was not a real purchasing amount and that the woman was not considered a sort of merchandise but, rather, the seal of a genuine contract (de Vaux, 1961, 26–9). This may be true, yet it seems that precisely a genuine contract implied the idea of the real ownership which a man had over his wife, who was not one of the contracting partners. The woman became his property. The man was *ba'al,* the owner, and she his *be'ilah,* the owned one (see Dt 22, 22; Hos 2, 16). The man could divorce her or keep her as long as he wanted, but the woman was never free to go. It is true that there were children who rebelled against parents (Gen 26, 34–45) and that parents sometimes accepted the choice of their children (see Gen 24, 8.58; Jgs 14, 2), but fundamentally the parents gave their consent to the marriage, and marriage was seen a union between families.

In the beginning the people of the Bible were just like any other people of the ancient world, and it took a long time for God to teach them through the prophets to see marriage more as an image of the union and love between Yahweh and Israel. The idea already appears in Hosea, chapter 2, where the point is that Yahweh's enduring love is stronger than Israel's infidelity. This view is repeated and echoed over and over again from this time on (see Is 54, 4–8; 62, 4; Jer 2, 2; 3, 20). In late Jewish rabbinical literature, "betrothal" meant a covenant that later was also associated with sanctification and dedication to the holy (Neubauer, 1920, 195–8).Yet marriage as a form of personal relationship was not well known in the ancient Near East. It was not a mutual agreement between the partners but a contract between the fathers of the families (Gen 24, 2–67; 38, 6; Dt 7, 3; Jgs 14, 2–4). Love did not make a marriage. It was expected to follow it.

Whereas the idea of marriage as a contract was linked among the ancient peoples with the idea of acquisition, in the Roman world, where the equality of man and woman was more respected, marriage meant, first of all, the free consent of the partners. According to the Romans, the essential element in marriage was the consent of the partners and of the persons under whose authority the partners were. Consensus, not sexual intercourse, made the Roman marriage: *Nuptias non concubitus, sed consensus facit,* we read in the Latin *Digest* (30, 1, 17; 2, 33, 2). Though the Roman jurists did not speak explicitly of marriage as a contract, the contractual aspect was prominent. The reading of the tablets, *recitatio tabularum,* signed consequently by the parties and the other witnesses, was essential to marriage ceremonies. In later times, when the Church began to speak explicitly of marriage as a contract, it wanted to underline precisely the idea of the freedom of the parties. Not blessing but the consent of the contracting parties was the essence of a valid marriage (Nicholas I, 1963, 214).

The idea of a contract as a free agreement between two equal parties is considered to be essential to the notion of marriage, especially in our age, when human rights of both sexes are respected. It is particularly operative in some trends when marriage is considered a job or an occupation instead of a "romantic love affair." In 1977 the Ontario Status of Women Council of the Ontario Secretariat for Social Development published a study entitled *About Face: Towards a Positive Image of Housewives.* It recommended that marriage contracts should negotiate and agree on points such as housework, child care, and financial sharing. Among the nineteen suggestions, the full disclosure of individual assets by each person is included and the agreement that these should continue to be owned separately by each person. Women were to take responsibility for birth control and reserve the right to end an unwanted pregnancy. Both parties could continue to pursue individual careers, and should one partner have to relocate for business purposes, the other was under no obligation to follow. If child care was not shared equally, then the employed spouse would contribute a certain sum every year to a savings account or pension fund in the stay-at-home partner's name. If both worked, half of each income was the property of both during the marriage. At any time either partner could initiate a review and revision of this contract as the relationship grew and changed. Finally, each partner could take two weeks' vacation a year, alone if desired (Ontario Status of Women Council, 1977, 24–39). Such a contract is evidently not one of buying a wife. It is a business contract with equal sharing and rejects the concept of marriage as a contract that obliges the husband to support his wife, who contractually obliges herself to remain sexually faithful to him. Sexual faithfulness as a bargaining element of the marriage contract, the study continues, sees marriage as a remedy against concupiscence by having a sexual partner easily and permanently available.

From what we have said so far, it should be clear that the notion of marriage as a contract is ambiguous, and we cannot simply say without further qualification that marriage is a contract. This is all the more so since marriage considered merely as a contract does not make it indissoluble, as the sacrament of marriage is believed to do. It is well known that after some hesitation between Roman law (marriage is a contract) and German custom (marriage is sexual intercourse) in the time of Pope Alexander III (1159–81), the Church found a synthesis by saying that the expression of mutual consent makes a marriage a true marriage, *matrimonium verum,* and all subsequent marriages null. Yet such a marriage without sexual intercourse would not be absolutely, from every point of view, indissoluble (Alexander III, 1963, 240–1).

The papal response to the bishop of Brescia and the archbishop of Salern (year uncertain; DS, nos 754–5) allowed a married woman to enter a religious order before her marriage was consummated in conjugal union. Permission was based on a canonical distinction between objective and subjective and internal and external dissolubility of marriage. Objective dissolubility means that the objective reality of the marriage dissolves by itself – "marriage dies." Subjective dissolubility could be internal or external. Subjective internal dissolubility of a contract would take place by the consent of partners involved: in the case of marriage, the wife and husband. Subjective external dissolubility of the marriage meant that marriage was dissoluble by an external authority, civil or ecclesiastical. The Old Testament recognized subjective internal dissolubility of marriage. So did Paul for a mixed marriage between a Christian and a non-Christian. If the unbelieving partner desires to separate, Paul said, so be it (1 Cor 7, 15). The church of the New Testament believed that marriage as a natural institution was internally indissoluble. It reserved the right of dissolving non-sacramental marriages but denied a similar right for sacramental marriage until Alexander III. The pope introduced two kinds of true sacramental marriage: one dissoluble by ecclesiastical authority and one indissoluble by any external authority, papal authority included.

This innovation was of no little importance. The sacramentality and indissolubility of the sacramental marriage were separated. Indissolubility became conditioned by the event of sexual intercourse within marriage. To answer the question In what sense was the conjugal act part of the sacramental sign? some theologians appealed to the mystery of the Incarnation as an image of two becoming one in the flesh (Thomas Aquinas, *Summa theol., Suppl.*, q 61, a 2, ad 1); some, such as Leo XIII, to the mystical union between Christ and his Church (1879–80, 392); and some to the consummation of the institution of the Church on the day of Pentecost.

Marriage as a contract raises another question. How can one by contract transfer the right over one's body for sexual pleasure, which one does not have, to someone else? Is the sacrament of marriage a sort of contract through which the Church gives permission to both parties to have sexual pleasure with each other without committing sin? Thus, whereas the contractual aspect of marriage in ancient societies seemed to be related to regulations for the acquisition of goods and wealth, marriage as a contract in the modern sense seems to relate to regulations for sexual activities between a free man and a free woman. The concept of marriage as a contractual regulation of sexual activities seems be the underlying principle of the present praxis, which sees grave sin, not in the breaking up of the marital life and in abandoning the other, canonically called *separatio a thoro et a mensa*, but in remarriage and the resumption of sexual activities with another person. Divorce as separation is permitted without grave sin, but remarriage is not. In this case human sexuality seems not fully integrated into the mystery of what true marriage is all about.

In brief, we cannot simply say that marriage is a contract unless we want to underline the freedom of the two parties involved. But a contract is not enough unless we consider the mystery of human love. We just do not know what the visible sign of the sacrament of marriage means in the way we understand, for example, what bread and wine or water and oil mean as the symbols of the Eucharist, baptism, or the anointing of the sick. Marriage is mystery, and we do not know what it is.

4.2.2.2 A COVENANT?

Since marriage is a much deeper mystery than any concept of a secular contract can express, some other concepts have been offered in light of the prophetic insights of the Old Testament. It has been suggested that marriage is not a contract but a covenant, like the one Yahweh had with Israel. But again, in applying the concept of a covenant to the human mystery of marriage, we will find more than one difficulty (Horvath, 1979a).

The first difficulty is that the biblical notion of a covenant does not imply equality of the two who enter the covenant relationship. A covenant, *berith*, is a treaty or contract between unequals. The more powerful one promises to protect the poor, the weak one, and in return the weak one promises to serve the stronger. As in vassalage, there are conditions laid down by the lord, who binds himself to fulfill the conditions, not by reason of justice or equality, but out of his own free generosity. The parties can pledge themselves by oath, sanctioned by a sort of curse or imprecation accompanied by a ritual: for example, by cutting an animal in two (see Gen 15, 7–11.17–18; 17, 7–14; Jer 34, 12; Gal 3, 10–13). The practice of circumcision also had something to do with keeping the covenant. It was a sign in the flesh of God's everlasting covenant (Gen 17, 13; Rom 4, 11; Acts 7, 8). Like a planted tree or a stone set up (see Gen 21, 33; 31, 48–30), it signified that the circumcised man belonged to God (Gen 17, 9–14).

Now, in the Old Testament the inequality of the partners of the covenant, that is, God and Israel, fittingly paralleled the inequality existing between men and women at that time. The superiority of the man and the inferiority of the woman on the social plane served as an example of the superiority of God and the submission of Israel to God. But we have to admit that the covenant between God and Israel is not the best paradigm for understanding marriage as a relationship between two equal but sexually differentiated human beings. If we ask Does the biblical presentation of the covenant between God and Israel illuminate the image of marriage, or rather, does the image of marriage illuminate the covenant? we must opt for the latter. At that time precisely the inferior status of women may have been helpful in understanding the status of Israel in regard to the free generosity of Yahweh. Marriage was understood then as the typical Hebrew marriage and not as a universal human experience. To understand what the sacrament of marriage is, we have to ask whether Hebrew marriage or marriage in general is the "sacramental sign" of the seventh sacrament of the Church. Following the discernment of the Jerusalem Assembly (Acts 15, 1–35), we should again opt for the latter.

We do so because we believe that a covenant is more than a marriage as a human experience. A covenant is not just a human reality. It is God's given saving symbol of the Church as a community striving to realize its union with God and imitate God's love manifest in the covenant. The covenant as union between God and God's people is the symbolized reality of the sacramental sign which we believe the human experience of an intentionally "never-ending" love between one man and one woman is. Love is personal, "person-creating." The loved one becomes not just somebody but a unique individual. The covenant is more than human love. It is the end of the sacramental marriage. It opens up and turns the meaning of human love and directs its finality to the love that God has for God's Church.

Such a meaning is expressed by biblical terms. One is the covenant in blood. About the meaning of the covenant in blood, we learn something from Exodus 24, 6 and following, when Moses poured some of the blood on the altar, the symbol of God, and with the rest he sprinkled the people to mark the lasting union between God and Israel. Here blood means an enduring union between God and Israel as well as its strength. But blood also means life, pledge, responsibility, expiation, forgiveness, redemption, and particularly in the New Testament, the blood of Jesus Christ, the revelation of the love God has for us. Some other concepts almost synonymous with covenant confirm this. We outline three here.

The first is *hesed* (Dt 7, 2–9; 1 Kgs 18, 23; Neh 1, 5; 9, 32; Ps 50, 2; Ex 20, 5, etc.). It means a feeling of the mercy and tender love of God (see Is 63, 7; Joel 2, 13; Mic 7, 18; Ps 5, 7; Jer 3, 12; Mal 2, 14; Ezek 16, 8; Prov 2, 17; Hos 2, 18ff), which remains constant even though it evokes no response from Israel (see Ex 34, 7; Is 43, 7; Jer 32, 18; Ps 106, 4–5; 145, 8).

The second is *'emet,* loving faithfulness, and it means the amen the lover says to the beloved (see Dt 7, 9; Is 49, 7; Jer 4, 2; Hos 11, 12), like the yes the Church says to Jesus (2 Cor 1, 19–22). A covenant relationship includes lifelong fidelity. This, however, was not true of Hebrew marriage, since Jewish legislation did not consider marriage as indissoluble and subsequent unions as adultery.

The third term for a covenant is *quin e' ah,* the jealous and exclusive love of a rival (see Ex 16, 23–25. 38–42). For Ezekiel, Yahweh's love was just such a jealous marital love (Ezek 16, 163). Here again, the covenant is more than the image that marriage can suggest. Therefore one cannot simply say that marriage is a covenant. Marriage is, rather, an image to show what a covenant is not. A covenant is an image of God's love.

The image of marriage, like other images such as king and subject, master and slave, was used to underline the inequality existing between the faithful God and unfaithful Israel. The existing marriage was a way to express what the covenant with God was and not the other way around. By the covenant Israel became like a wife (Mal 2, 10–16) who bore children (Hos 2, 4–7), but for her there was no way of getting a divorce because Yahweh loved her unshakeably and would never give her dismissal letters.

4.2.2.3 A COMMUNITY?

The idea of inequality inherent in the notion of covenant can perhaps be obliterated if we say that marriage is a community. Indeed, marriage is a community of two sexually differentiated human beings for the sake of human solidarity and human survival. Considering marriage as community solves some problems, but at the same time it raises new ones. It is not enough to say that marriage is a community without stipulating what kind of community we have in mind. Are the children, for example, indispensable or not indispensable members of the marriage community? If not, what kind of community of two adult persons are we thinking of?

The most obvious answer is a community based on sexual interaction between two sexually differentiated persons. Now, by saying this we have not yet solved the mystery of marriage. As it was in the preliterate age, so even today sex is a mystery. In our day more than one scientific research project has been conducted to discover the meaning of human sexuality. We cannot assume that sex is basically the same as a genetically determined natural function, such as breathing or moving the bowels, which everyone begins to exercise immediately after birth (Calderon, 1974, 88). In this sense evidently we cannot take sex as a determining element of community. Sex is not just a natural function like breathing, for instance, on which no special community has to be based. It is not just a biological function performed with someone else. Human sexuality is not just a performance, a thing to do; rather, it is a way to be. It is more than, for example, eating together or sleeping together. It pervades and absorbs the whole human being and thus is to be researched by more disciplines than biology alone.

Sex is not just a topic for the doctor, like the respiratory function, but for the sociologist as well. On this level of research, sex might appear to be a real factor in changing society. Earlier studies, such as *The Naked Ape* (Morris, 1976) or *Territorial Imperative* (Ardrey, 1966), suggested that human sexuality is an evolutionary product of nature whose purpose is to keep man and woman longer together, since the child needs longer care than other animal offspring. This is why, one may think, that human sexuality is not limited to a certain season or period of time, as is the case with other animals. Rather, it is operative the whole year around for many years, holding the male and female together until the offspring becomes viable on his or her own. In such a conception, sex undoubtedly has community as its origin as well its binding function. It is, therefore, understandable that sex should not come under the aegis of doctors only but also under the control of society.

Furthermore, sex pervades the whole human personality. Human sexuality is also the responsibility of each individual, and its actualization belongs to each person's freedom. Therefore it shares the mystery of a relationship existing between individuals and society as well as the mystery of personhood. At this point we may find some help in psychology.

Moreover, since according to Catholic faith, marriage is a sacrament, human sexuality has been brought into the event of God's salvation. Its function is, therefore, not only to keep man and woman together in order to ensure the survival of the human race but also to ascertain a way of salvation and to function as a sacramental encounter between God and the faithful. Thus, as a symbol of God's love, sex enters into the realm of the Saviour of the world. Unlike other natural human functions, human sexuality shares the different levels of the mystery of human existence and the salvation of the world. True, sex and religion have always been found to be somehow related, even in the preliterate stage and some modern religious practice, but the way sexuality enters into the Christ event is very different from the way it entered and enters without him. The Jews had already tried to secularize marriage and keep sexuality out of the covenant relationship. This antagonism between the covenant and sex was providential. It suggested that when marriage becomes a sacrament of the Church, the sex that enters into the salvation event of Christ will not remain on the surface level of the sexual encounter. It will be a moving force on the level of human friendship towards the fulfillment of a never-ending love in the kingdom of Christ. For this reason the human reality of marriage is a mystery for theology as well.

Thus we can say that marriage as community is one of the most complex communities we know. It is biological and social, private and public, personal and communitarian, profane and religious, natural and supernatural. It belongs to the realm of the secular world as well as to the realm of the Church of Christ.

4.2.2.4 "NEVER-ENDING" LOVE BETWEEN ONE MAN AND ONE WOMAN GIVING LIFE AND TIME TO A NEW HUMAN BEING

So far we have seen that each term we have studied has its own ambiguity and is problematic. What should we now say about marriage as the outward sign of the seventh sacrament of the Church? The Pauline passage of Ephesians 5, 32 had a decisive influence on the Church in recognizing marriage as a sacrament. The great mystery there is not only the union of man and woman becoming one flesh. It is not even just the union of Christ with his Church. The great, μέγα, mystery is the relation of the first union to the second one, in the εἰς Χριστὸν καὶ ἐις τὴν ἐκλησίαν, in reference to Christ and the Church.

According to the text, the relation of the marriage as a human experience has to the relation between Christ and his Church is not a contract, covenant, or community, but the reality of love, ἀγάπη, which makes man and woman one, so that they are no longer two but one flesh (cf. Mt 4, 5; Gen 2, 24) and Christ's giving himself up for his Church (v. 25). Human love becoming the sign of the love of the Eucharistic Christ is the great mystery that gives pre-eminence to the sacrament of marriage as the sacrament of sacraments, joining time to eternity.

To describe this relation, the inspired author uses, on the side of man, the term *agapé*, love (see Eph 5, 25, 28a–b, 33) and, on the side of woman, *ὑποτασσομαι*, a respectful courtesy (cf. Eph 5, 22), and *φοβέομαι*, admiration (v. 31), which all believers owe to each other in Christ (Eph 5, 21). The text follows very closely the terminology of the Old Testament, where, except in 1 Kings 18, 28, we do not find that woman loves man. In Ephesians 5, 32 the word "love" is not used, but neither is *ὑπακούετε*, obedience, which servants and children owe to their masters or parents.

But the meaning of those words does not come from the Greek but rather from the love Jesus has for his Church (Eph 5, 32). The two loves, that of the man and the woman, on one hand, and of Christ and his Church, on the other, are joined together by the εἰς Χριστὸν for being both members of Christ's body (vv. 30.32). They are one flesh (v. 31), meaning one human being; a man, who has his life and his time with another human being, a woman, who has her own life and time, together are able to bring about another human being with a new life existing in time, yet called by Christ to eternal life. Moreover, these two human beings are able to communicate the same creative power to their sons and daughters, who are expected to become one flesh with other sons and daughters to communicate to others the same creative power. And thus love becomes never-ending.

The great mystery of the union with Christ obviously involves the mystery of human beings created and invested with similar powers to God's. The reference to Genesis recalls Creation, when God out of unselfish love created man and woman, giving them life and time to live and a share in God's creative power (Gen 1, 28), with a pleasure which echoes God's joy in saying, "Behold, it was very good"(Gen 1, 31). Out of unselfish love, God created sons and daughters by giving life that God had so far without beginning and without end, now given to them with a beginning and with an end, which Christ, the new Adam, and Mary, the new Eve, transformed into a life without end.

Life- and time-creating power is always divine because it is the unselfish creative love, the *agape,* that Christ had for the Church, revealing God's being as unselfish communication in the joy of life. Marriage is the sign of this love when one man and one woman experience a love as never-ending in the sense of being able to live together forever. And that love becomes never-ending in their children and also in their married life without divorce. By virtue of the sacrament, such a love of two fallible human beings is elevated to be the visible sign of God as love and the sacrament of marriage as salvation for the human race.

We should remark that the love to which the author of Ephesians 5, 32 refers is not a spiritual love but a love in which sexual union is considered the ultimate in communication between woman and man. Precisely this love, embodied in sex and actualized in sexual relations, is that mysterious human experience which, as a visible and efficacious sign of grace, is ordained to the sanctification and salvation of the human race. It is this love "which has sprung from the divine fountain of love" (*GS*, no. 48; Tanner, 1990, 1101).

The Ephesian insight, therefore, does not consider marriage *in fieri* and *in facto* as two separate entities. On account of Ephesians 5, 32, we think that the sacramental symbol, called the matter and form of the sacrament of marriage, is not just a reciprocal, contractual consent of offering and accepting each other as husband and wife but the never-ending love of man and woman toward each other expressed in those words. The words, therefore, must be taken, not in the contractual sense of an instantaneous promise of a mutual agreement, but as true expressions of that never-ending love which man and woman experience for each other in their creative ability to bring a human being into this life and with God into eternal life.

Therefore we can conclude that for Ephesians 5, 21–33 the love between man and woman is the symbolic sign revealing the relation existing between Christ and the world and between Christ and his Church. And this love is a mystery since, on the one hand, it includes a tendency of never-ending transcendence and, on the other, at the same time it shares in the fragility of two ever-changing historical human existences destined to become sooner or later a life without end. Such a mystery is consistent with the mystery of faith but nevertheless surprising. It is a revolutionary twist that turns around the generally supposed principles of sacramental theology.

4.2.2.5 THE FALLIBLE SYMBOL OF INFALLIBLE LOVE

Whereas in the other sacraments the visible-tangible elements of the material world, as water in baptism, bread and wine in the Eucharist, and oil in confirmation and in the anointing of the sick, are taken up and made the visible and efficacious signs, in the sacrament of marriage two free human persons' experience is made the symbol of all that the sacrament of marriage signifies and brings about – the saving love of God. And this makes the sacrament of marriage different from all other sacraments. The symbols of the other sacraments – water, bread and wine, and oil – being complete in themselves, are integral symbols, incapable of being further developed in their symbolic value. But human persons as historical beings change, sometimes for the better, sometimes for the worse. They advance by passing through a process of fuller integration of their human potentialities or by retrogressing through a process of deterioration to a complete disintegration.

It is true that in the sacrament of forgiveness too, two human persons are involved, one by judging and absolving and the other by repenting and confessing. Yet their actions are completed and brought to an end in the sacrament of confession. The sacramental symbol of marriage, however, is not just a passing action but, rather, a progressive realization of itself. This difference will be especially clear when we consider the sacrament of marriage not just in its anthropological, ecclesiological, or Christological function but also in its God-revealing theological function.

The sacrament of marriage does not just help human beings to overcome human weakness and achieve perfection and sanctification. It is also for the Church insofar as in the love of husband and wife the Church exercises, develops, and fulfills its nature, actuates its very being (Horvath, 1970, 388–9). For it is through marriage and in marriage that the Church becomes a salvation milieu wherein the union between the Church and its Saviour, Jesus Christ, is achieved. This ecclesiological function of the sacrament of marriage draws its validity from its Christological function insofar as the love of two human beings becomes a sort of earthly extension of Jesus' risen body and, as such, the visible manifestation of the risen Christ's beatifying presence among human beings.

Furthermore, the sacrament of marriage has a revelational function, disclosing the kind of God that Christians believe in and the kind of love God has for human beings. At this point the general principles of sacramental theology are somewhat turned around. For in the sacrament of marriage, the symbolized reality, God's love, is the most evident and most certain element of which we have clear knowledge, whereas the symbolizing reality, the love of two human persons, is ambiguous and far from being a sure and certain factor. From the revelation of Jesus Christ, we know more clearly what God's love is than what human love is. If we consider the nature of the symbol and the nature of the sacramentally symbolized reality, the discrepancy is shocking and confusing.

God's love is described in the Bible as an everlasting, faithful, gracious, compassionate love (Jer 31, 3; Is 54, 8), slow to anger and always forgiving

(Ezek 16, 56–63). These qualities are constant attributes of God's love (Ex 34, 6–7; Num 14, 18; Neh 9, 17; Ps 103, 8–12; 145, 8; Jer 32, 18; Jon 4, 2). The term *hen*, gracious, occurs thirteen times as an exclusive adjective of God. *Rahamim*, merciful, is repeated over a hundred times, stressing that, in spite of our sins, God always deals mercifully with us (Ex 34, 6; Is 49, 13; Ps 25, 6; Hos 2, 16; Ezra 9, 9). God's love, furthermore, is not only gracious but ever-faithful since it is based on God's personality and remains so even though Israel breaks the covenant (Is 54, 10). According to Jeremiah 3, 6–14, God gave a decree of divorce to Israel, but he would take her back anytime. Thus Israel is never really divorced, just punished for a time (Hos 2, 14–23).

This is much more so in the New Testament, where God, the God of love (2 Cor 13, 11), is simply identified with love (1 Jn 4, 8. 16). God's love is gracious, since God gave God's own son for us while we were sinners (Rom 5, 8). Jesus is the manifestation of God's merciful, faithful, true love (Rom 3, 4; Eph 2, 4; Rev 19, 11). He made it clear that where sin increased, grace abounded all the more (Rom 3, 20). Unlike us, who love what is lovable, God's love creates our love. We love because God first loved us (1 Jn 4, 19).

We can, therefore, ask how this eternal, never-ending love of God can be symbolized in the sacrament of marriage through the love of two human beings, a love so different from the love of God we learned about through revelation. Human love can be gracious but certainly not without end or limit. By nature it is changeable, mortal, and mutually dependent. Decrease of one's love brings about a decrease in the love of the other. Though it has an implicit intentionality to last forever, yet by reason of its historicalness, of its being embedded in time, love will end. Sometimes its end is tragically precipitated by its own efforts at survival. In order to nurture itself, it often challenges and tests the love of the other. And then love can destroy itself either by demanding too much or by demanding too little. The first occurs when the beloved gets tired of having to prove him or herself without end and refuses the challenge; the second, when the beloved interprets the lack of testing as a lack of care and further interest. Yet love, being dynamic, cannot be stagnant. If it does not grow, it decreases. But again, in growing, it may grow in the lovers on a separate scale, and the difference will make its survival difficult. Changing values can create differences that cannot be ironed out even with the best will of each partner. And love may vanish as mysteriously as it sprang up. Human love is a wonderful, powerful, yet very precarious event. A person who knows her or himself well enough will be reluctant to believe that her or his love can last forever, yet this is what one experiences in being in love. Human love is a mystery in its origin, in its survival, and in its termination.

The love between a man and a woman is a very ambiguous symbol of God's love for us. We may, therefore, find it surprising that Jesus Christ, by instituting the sacrament of marriage, joined this ambiguous human mystery and the unambiguously sure reality of God's saving love together and made one sacrament out of the two. In so doing, he may appear to us either as a romantically poor observer of human reality or as a young systematic theologian ignorant of revealed realities, or perhaps as an imprudent moral theologian who fails to realize that as a consequence of his or her action he or she may be responsible for taking non-existing realities for sacramental signs and thus exposing the sacrament of marriage to empty ceremonies, something every minister of a sacrament is expected to avoid under grave sin.

To feel the seriousness of the matter, we should think of the gravity of the declaration of a marriage as non-existent and null. This may occur knowingly, if the partners never loved each other, or unknowingly, if in spite of the initial love which the partners experienced and which may have lasted for many years, they now are told that they were never married and that in spite of their best conviction, they have lived in concubinage and their children are illegitimate. And it may happen if love is not taken seriously and if it, as a precious gift, is not appreciated and cultivated. Otherwise, after some years it may vanish and husband or wife or both begin think of divorce and feel fortunate if their marriage is declared null and their love labelled just a mirage.

It looks, indeed, as if the Lord founded the sacrament of marriage on very shaky ground. And we cannot help but remember his own words about the foolish man who built his house upon sand and when the rains came and the wind blew and beat against it, it fell (see Mt 7, 26–27). The foundation of marriage is not as solid and sure as that of the water or the bread and wine, which are what they are as long as they exist, unlike human beings, who may kill their love, the foundation of their marriage.

But it is also true that "the foolishness of God is wiser than men and women" (1 Cor 1, 25), and building the sacrament of marriage on the fallible love of human beings reveals the power and the wisdom of God. God could and did risk founding the seventh sacrament on the very shaky and capricious love of two human beings. By doing so, God gave the sacrament of marriage its pre-eminence in expressing God's own love and mercy. And thus the sacrament of marriage can appear as the sacrament of sacraments, the symbolization of all the sacraments, the actualization of God's love and mercy, notwithstanding human sinfulness. If we take a little more time to think about this concept, we can see that, indeed, the infallibility of God's love as such cannot be revealed more successfully than precisely through the fallibility of human love. The strength of the first will be manifest in the weakness of the second.

4.2.2.6 LOVE AS THE THRESHOLD OF HISTORY AND SALVATION

By saying that marriage as a human experience is not so much a contract, covenant, or community as it is above all love between a man and a woman, we restate our opening argument: marriage is a human mystery. It is a mystery because love is a mystery. It is much more difficult to say what love is than to describe what a contract, covenant, or community is. If we have found these concepts wanting, it is precisely because they fail to express the uniqueness of the mystery of the sacrament of marriage and its unequaled position in history and redemption (Horvath, 1979a, 159–63).

In analyzing what love is, we find that one of its most salient features is its abstraction from time and limits. It is a common experience that when two people really fall in love with each other, they feel that they could live together forever. This "being able to live together forever" seems to be the distinguishing mark of real love. A survey (Horvath, 1979a, 173–4) indicated that the interviewees who responded to our request agreed that they did fall in love with someone with whom they thought they could live together forever. They agreed, too, that the feeling of lasting forever is part of true love. Quite a few experienced this kind of love more than once in their life, but they admitted, too, that the first real love somehow always survived at least in memory. Some acknowledged not only that there was a relationship between their first love and the rest, but also that they were somehow always looking for their first love whenever they fell in love again. This "never-ending" intentionality makes the termination of love rather intriguing. Love just does not want to die; rather, it does, as it were, confer immortality on that which is truly loved (Armstrong, 1969, 104). It is extremely hard, if not impossible, to know whether the first love has really ended or just lies in a "coma" and may come back to life. The mystery of true love is much more intriguing than we think. We might try to ignore it and declare it non-existent. Yet it reappears in the most curious forms of disguise, such as flirtation or pretended indifference, cynicism or overactivity, depression or hatred, even murder. The real history of the human race is the history of love and its struggle against its own termination. Because of its never-ending intentionality, love is an instance in history when time transcends itself and enters eternity (Horvath, 1993, 58–64).

Now, since human sexuality is related to love, it assumes the characteristics of both love and human nature. It shares the never-ending aspect of love as well as the precariousness of human nature. Sex at its deepest level reflects the transcendental, immortal aspect of love through its constantly recurring demand as well as through its all-embracing ecstatic force. Human sexuality is "reaching out to the source of life by giving oneself completely to another. It is a con-creativity, a creative release of new reality" (Pannenberg, 1969, 64–7), which is linked to the power of the future. It grants new existence in spite of the "self-assertive arrogance" of the here and now (ibid., 65). As a power of the future overcoming present and past, love is the synthesis of time and eternity, of past, present, and future.

The knowledge of love as the creative release of new reality, affirming the power of the future over the present and the past, has its origin or at least its pre-eminent instance in the Redemption, which revealed that the love of God is the origin of all reality, of creation as well as of redemption. From the beginning, God's love was the cause of life, transcending all limits. It is unbounded and absolute. This unlimited and unrestricted nature of love is expressed in Mark 12, 30 (see also Mt 22, 37; Lk 10, 27), which, following Deuteronomy 6, 5, mentions heart, soul, mind, and strength, repeating "all" each time, that is, wholly, without boundary of any kind. It refers to a totality of power determining the whole personality in loving service of God and other human beings (Stauffer, 1969, 29). The Greek ὅλος, like the Hebrew *kl*, is the relevant word of the great commandment. Its meaning is expressed in God the Father's giving God's Son for us (Rom 8, 32; 5, 8; Eph 3, 1–2; see also Mt 3, 17; Mk 1, 11; Lk 3, 22; Jn 3, 16; 1 Jn 4, 9). This unlimited and unrestricted "all" reflects the Trinitarian life of God as the total and unrestricted giving of oneself to another, so that the Son can be the complete and perfect image of the Father, and the Holy Spirit fully equal to the Son and to the Father, and therefore really God.

At the same time, because of its unlimited and unconditional intentionality, only love can forgive with no condition attached to it. The unlimited creative power of love does not just stop or surrender to the power of sin. Love is the ultimate motive both of God's creative activity and of God's unconditionally full forgiveness. God's love is the only really limitless love. Therefore, it is the only real love that is at once the source of love and the source of redemption. Because of its unlimited creative and redemptive intentionality, love is that instance of history wherein history transcends itself and enters into redemption. It is that point toward which time and eternity, cosmos and history, creation and redemption, God and humans, Christ and the faithful, converge.

Now, if we consider marriage as human experience to be an intentionally "never-ending" love between man and woman, we find it to be the universal salvation milieu where man and woman can meet their Saviour. By taking up the most human experience into a sacramental sign of his Church, "the instrumental sign of intimate union with God and of the unity of all humanity" (*LG*, no. 1; Tanner, 1990, 849), Christ drew marriage as a human experience into the salvation milieu, thereby transforming the creation relationship of human love into the fullness of a creation-salvation relationship. He incorporated his redemption into the history of human love and thus into the most universal human experience. This experience could become the most universal saving reality of God's redemptive love in Jesus Christ.

By doing this, Jesus radically changed all marriages, since as a result of his action, each marriage, as a human experience, becomes implicitly or explicitly the symbol of God's love for all in Jesus Christ and, as such, a means of salvation. If there is no marriage that is not love, then there is no marriage that is not a sacrament either, in the sense that all non-Christian marriages have an internal dynamic tendency toward Christian sacramental marriage as their full objective as well as their definitive meaning. By drawing the human mystery of marriage into the salvation milieu, Christ transformed the initial dynamism of human love. *Agape* has been incorporated into *eros*, which will merge progressively as the old, yet at the same time completely new. An old human event assumes the characteristics of God's love in Christ's death and resurrection. A human event manifests the characteristics of the invisible symbolized realities as the potentialities of the old. After the Christ event, the love of the husband and the wife will never be the same, since they symbolize not only the human within but God's within and God's feelings for human beings.

Because of this internal transformation of the mystery of human love, the marriage sacrament of the baptized may become the sacrament of non-Christian marriages. The latter receive sacramental grace through Christian marriages in a similar manner as extra-sacramental forgiveness is channelled through the sacrament of forgiveness of the Church to anyone who receives the grace of reconciliation outside confession. Thus there is no marriage grace that is not sacramental grace, since the Christian spouses, through their sacraments, provide grace not only for themselves but also for all non-Christian spouses in order to allow them to realize progressively their salvation and that of the whole world, to which they are invited and initiated precisely through their marriages.

Thus by making the human experience of marriage one of the seven sacraments of his Church, Jesus Christ indeed proved himself as an extremely successful systematic theologian. He nailed his salvation into the roots of human existence and anchored his sacrament in the marital love of two human beings. Some recent tendencies that seek to separate the sacrament of marriage from the marital experience miss this wisdom of the founder of the sacrament and renew the old mistake of Melchior Cano, who considered the sacrament of marriage to be a sort of priestly blessing. Such a consideration conceals the concern of a moral theologian for increasing the number of the non-absolutely indissoluble marriages, rather than that of a systematic theologian. The separation of the sacrament of marriage from marital love is inadmissible since it would deprive Christ's redemption of its incorporation into the history of human love, which is the most universal human experience. What Christ made into his sacrament is not a priestly blessing but human experience that is rooted in the historicalness of human existence. For this reason precisely, it would be a mistake to consider the sacrament of marriage *in fieri* and *in facto*, the promise and the realization, as two completely separate realities.

Precisely because the sacramental symbol of marriage is not a commercial contract or any eventual ecclesial-religious ceremony but real marital love between husband and wife, we have to admit that the sacrament of marriage is not an instantaneous moment but an event which shares the historical nature of human existence as well as that of the Church. The sacrament of marriage is a progressive self-realization, moving from fragmentary sacramental symbolism to perfect sacramental symbolism. Though the symbolized reality, the love of God, is one and indivisible, its sacramental expression, the love of a woman and a man, necessarily reflects the fragmentariness of human existence and its ability for self-creation or for self-destruction. Consequently, the sacramentality of marriage in this sense is the responsibility of the couple. They are, however, not left alone in the progressive realization of the sacramental sign since the grace of the sacrament brings about its own full realization. As in the sacrament of forgiveness, where according to St Thomas, the movement of free will (called *paenitentia interior*) is both caused and signified by the sacrament (personal acts of the penitent with the absolution of the minister; Horvath, 1979a, 178; Thomas Aquinas, *Summa theol.*, 1, 2, q 113, a 8; Poschmann, 1964, 169–74), so too in the sacrament of marriage the progressive love is both produced and signified by the initial love as human experience. The divine force of the sacrament prepares and transforms the yet imperfect symbol and lets it develop to became a perfect symbol for God's infinite faithfulness in love. When we consider the greatness of the symbolized reality and the weakness of the symbol itself, the sacrament of marriage is the perfect configuration of the indefectibility of God's love and the defectibility of human love, while it reveals God as both a God of love and a God of mercy.

Since the symbolized reality modifies the symbol, the sacramental nature of marriage will never mean anything like a prototype of the wedding of divinities. Human love has its real meaning by opening up to the symbolized reality. In the case of the sacrament of marriage, this ability is neither beside nor beyond, but is present in the symbol itself. It becomes more and more transparent by progressively transforming it so that the human mystery will be not only the symbol of something else but in a true sense the reality of the symbolized reality (see Col 2, 18). Therefore the progressive development of the symbolism of marriage does not mean the transportation of sexuality into the divine sphere. It becomes, rather, the entry of God's love into the sphere of human sexuality by conferring eternal life therein, without any further marrying (Mt 22, 30). The sons and daughters of the Resurrection (Lk 20, 36) live the life of God, who is neither woman nor man but the fullness of complete self-giving.

Eternal life, however, does not enter at once into human life. Experience confirms that reception of the sacrament of marriage does not transform man and woman at once into the indefectible symbol of God's love. A woman and a man who love each other can destroy their love, can divorce each other; then the question arises, What happens then to the sacrament of marriage?

4.2.2.7 THE SIN OF DIVORCE

If marriage as a human experience is considered to be only a contract, annulment is the most logical possibility after the event of divorce. With such an assumption, some matrimonial jurisprudence rightly looks for contractual incapacities. But if marriage as human experience is considered a never-ending love between a man and woman, after the event of divorce, logically the first questions are about the existence or non-existence of such a never-ending love, about its possible termination and the eventual sinfulness involved. Now according to prevailing practice, it seems that we are more willing to say that love never existed than to say that real love did exist but has been destroyed and is now dead. It may be logical to assume that love never existed and the lovers were incapable of making a marital contract. In such a case, love was mistakenly believed to be real and divorce is a blessing.

But all this will not be so obvious if we accept the assertion that not just a contract but love as a human experience is the sacramental sign of marriage, and the Church's teaching and practice about the indissolubility of marriage is rooted not so much in the fact of consummation or non-consummation as in the never-ending intentionality of love. This is even more the case since love may be killed but it never dies of "old age." Such a consideration could and should make it clear both how great a sin is the sin of divorce and how the sacrament of marriage is the pre-eminent sacrament of love and of mercy.

Once we consider the sacramental sign of marriage to be not reciprocal contractual consent alone but the never-ending love experienced by a man and a woman toward each other, divorce is a sin, a serious sin against God, against the Church, against the partner, and against one's self. The sin of divorce is a sin of injustice, of infidelity and selfishness. It is an outgrowth of the sin of injustice, since the lovers failed to help each other to find fulfillment on the different levels of need, whether physical, intellectual, emotional, or religious, and to develop their own human dignity. The reason for this failure may be the fact that marriage, like life in general, is penetrated by the mystery of fear and selfishness. Fear and selfishness can lead one to a dream of utopia, generating disillusionment and bitterness instead of helping a person to accept a cross with redemptive forgiveness and realize that no one can carry one's own cross unless someone else carries it with him or her in the hope of salvation, success, and happiness.

Moreover, the sin of divorce is a sacrilege because it profanes and desacralizes a sacrament by destroying human love, the outward sign, the "species" of the sacrament of God. When parties divorce, they sin by going back on their word to accept the responsibility to be revealing symbols of God's love. They claim that God was wrong either in instituting the sacrament of marriage by choosing human love to be the symbol of God's indefectible love or in joining them together in marriage by electing them to be concrete symbols of God's universal and faithful love. Because they failed to develop their initial love and because they no longer desire to be part of the revealing sacramental event that God created with their cooperation in the presence of the Church, they separate themselves from the Church, from the community of believers, and from God.

It is not difficult to see that the sin of divorce may begin long before husband and wife separate from each other. It begins when they start to take each other for granted. They fail to care for each other and let their unconcern grow into dislike and consequently hatred, instead of nurturing creative love, of forgiving by helping the saving love of God to be manifested more and more in their lives.

Since the sin of divorce breaks the sacramental sign, it is preferable to talk about the destructibility of the sacrament, rather than about the dissolubility or indissolubility of marriage. Marriage is simply not dissoluble because divorce is a sacrilegious sin against God and as such, is not under the Church's jurisdictional power in the modern sense of the term. Similarly, neither fornication nor adultery is under this jurisdiction. The Church simply cannot make them permissible under any circumstance. But that does not necessarily mean that they are not under the Church's power of forgiveness.

The distinction between the power of forgiving sins (*in foro interno*) and the power of jurisdiction (*in foro externo*) is not very old. In the early Church there was no separation between reconciliation (forgiveness of sin) and peace with the Church. Only in the twelfth century, we think, the original idea that the forgiveness of sin and peace with the Church, *pax ecclesiae,* are one "gradually disappeared from the consciousness of the Church" (Poschmann, 1964, 159), and some theologians, such as Abelard, rejected the Church's authority to forgive sins in virtue of the keys (Mt 16, 19). According to Abelard, the forgiveness of sins based on personal holiness and the power of the keys was limited to excommunication and to eventual reconciliation with the Church. Abelard and his school could not understand that there is no personal holiness without sacramental grace. It was only with the Second Vatican Council that the interrelationship between sacramental and jurisdictional power took a new turn. Jurisdiction was no longer considered to be exclusively a legislative power but was now considered to be an expression of the Church's conscious presence, as community, in the specific sacramental salvation event. Since Christ had promised to bring salvation within the community of the faithful, the presence of the Church is indispensable for salvation. In this sense it is true that there is no salvation without the Church.

Now, the Church's willingness to be, as community, actively present in the salvation event is expressed by the setting down of certain conditions and circumstances as the *conditio sine qua non* of its presence. The determination of these circumstances is the explicit promise of being there whenever those conditions are realized. Thus, canonical power is only the external expression of the ecclesiological sacramental nature of the Church and of its sacraments. The full separation of jurisdictional power from sacramental power is not correct since it would suppose that the Church could say or do something in one way externally and in another internally.

The unity or even equation of the power of the keys with the power of forgiving sins defended by Augustine (*Sermo,* 392, 3) – and somewhat obscured from the year 800 on by the introduction of private confessions and the gradual disappearance of public penance – might suggest to us once more that the sin of divorce should be considered something which comes under the Church's power of forgiving sins rather than under its jurisdiction only. One should say that divorce is not only illegal. It is a sin against God and against the Church of God, and if there is a causal relationship between the visible Church and the kingdom of God (Poschmann, 1964, 45), peace with the Church means peace with God and vice versa. The question is, therefore, Can the Church give peace to those who have broken and destroyed not only love as human experience (*sacramentum tantum, sacramentum in fieri*) but also love as its progressive sacramental symbol (*sacramentum et res, sacramentum in facto*)?

4.2.2.8 IS THE SIN OF DIVORCE UNFORGIVABLE AND AS SUCH AN EXCEPTION TO MATTHEW 15, 19 AND 18, 18 AND JOHN 20, 22–23?

The Council of Trent declared that through the words "Receive the Holy Spirit. If you forgive the sins of any, they are forgiven; if you retain the sins of any, they are retained" (Jn 20, 22–23), Jesus Christ gave the power of forgiving and retaining sins to his Church (*Canons Concerning the Most Holy Sacrament of Penance,* no. 3; Tanner, 1990, 711–12). Neither the Johannine nor the Matthean text "Whatever you bind on earth shall be bound in heaven, and whatever you loose on earth shall be loosed in heaven" (Mt 16, 19; 18, 18) indicates any limit to this power. Nor was the early Church aware of any sins that would not be included in the words of Jesus. According to Poschmann, in the post-apostolic Church "there is no irrevocable exclusion of sinners" (1964, 24). Mortal sins had to be expiated by appropriate penance, and "it was left to the bishop to determine the form in which the Gospel principles should be carried out, and to hold a just balance between severity in the imposition of penance and the divine readiness to grant forgiveness" (Poschmann, 1964, 45).

To this general practice, Hermas brought some modification by assuming that penance should be given out once only. The reason was that he did not want to give any inducement to commit more sins. Hermas's doctrine of a single penance (*paenitentia unica*) was a novelty formulated on pastoral and psychological grounds. His doctrine was taken up later on as a matter of principle: "what was impossible for psychological reasons has now become so on dogmatic grounds" (Poschmann, 1964, 45). Hermas himself admitted that forgiveness can be extended without restriction to any sin; the only obstacle was lack of sincere repentance (Hermas, *The Ten Similitudes*, 8; Funk, 1901, 573). He listed some sins, for example, deliberate apostasy along with conscious blasphemy of God, which of their nature presupposed a state of mind of direct resistance to God, and so one would be indisposed for penance. The impossibility, therefore, was not on dogmatic grounds but on psychological and moral grounds. In such cases he questioned not the power of forgiving but its usefulness, particularly for the recidivists. By repeatedly sinning, the recidivist made it clear that he or she did not have a sincere spirit of penance, without which forgiveness is useless.

Zeal for perfect holiness, as proposed by the Montanists, more and more favoured the less lenient treatment of the sinner. They did not deny the Church's power of forgiveness; they just did not believe it was practical according to their principle: "The Church can forgive sins, but I will not do so, lest others also commit sin" (Tertullian, *De Puditia*, 21, 7). Tertullian went further and denied to the Church any power in respect to such grave sins as apostasy, murder, and adultery. He was the first to distinguish between forgivable sins, *peccata remissibilia*, and unforgivable sins, *peccata irremissibilia* (ibid., 2, 12–15), a distinction unknown before his time. Tertullian's view was not universally accepted, though to find a sound middle way between excessive rigorism and excessive laxity was never very easy for the Church. The doctrine of single penance facilitated the introduction of the law of the lifelong obligation of penance (Poschmann, 1964, 104).

The result of this penitential discipline was a lifelong postponement until the last days of life as a means of preparing for death. Such an extreme required a new balance (Orsy, 1978, 42–51). The new solution introduced by the Celtic and Anglo-Saxon churches was the praxis of repeated confession to a simple priest with private penance and satisfaction consisting mostly of some short prayers, a form of penance practised even in our days.

From the perspective of the history of the general practice of the sacrament of penance, we can say that there is no theological or historical reason to suggest that there is any sin which lies outside the Church's power of forgiveness. It seems that the sin of divorce is not outside the power given by Christ according to John 20, 22–23 (see also Mt 16, 19). It is not an unforgivable sin. Yet it appears as a sin that the Church, not for dogmatic but for pastoral reasons, refuses to forgive until one of the partners dies. The divorce is "forgivable" only after the death of one spouse, but not as long as both are living. Now we can advance three reasons for a reluctance to forgive the sin of divorce before the death of one of the consorts.

The first is that marriage may be considered to be exclusively a contract not to have sexual intercourse with anyone except with one's consort. Perhaps this is the reason why so many have wanted to see adultery as sufficient cause for divorce. Since adultery breaks the conditions of the matrimonial contract, it obviously terminates it. Such an interpretation is based on Matthew 5, 32, and it finds supporters among the theologians of the Orthodox Church (Meyendorf, 1970), some Reformers, and Modernists (Loisy, 1971, 578–80). J. Moingt tried to defend this view from patristic tradition, but not without critical opposition (1968). The Roman Catholic Church has never favoured this idea. Adultery was certainly always considered a serious sin, though the penance imposed for it considerably decreased with the introduction of private confession and private penance. Basil reports that for the sin of adultery some churches imposed fifteen years of penance, that is, exclusion from the sacraments while leading the life of a penitent. But more lenient penance was imposed on a man abandoned by his wife (*Epistulae* 217, 8–59).The present practice is lenient indeed. One can be absolved from the sin of adultery with a penance of saying, for example, six Our Fathers, Hail Marys, and Glorys to the Father, even if the penitent continues to live with the consort. But if, because of the committed adultery, the innocent consort refuses to live with the guilty one, a lifelong penance of perfect abstinence is imposed on both, and this is not a lenient penance, particularly for the innocent spouse.

According to Roman law, any contract can be dissolved by mutual consent. Thus it follows that the marriage contract could also be dissolved by mutual consent or even by the insistence of only one party if any cause provided in the law prevails. Since divorce was a private matter for adult Roman citizens, in Rome no external party could claim the power of dissolving their marriage. But for the Church it was different. Christ explicitly forbade anyone, either the individual faithful or the community through its official representatives, to exercise the right of divorce because what God has joined together no one may put asunder (see Mt 19, 6). Thus Pius XI was right in reiterating the doctrine of many pontiffs that no human authority can dissolve a consummated marriage of the faithful, because it was God who joined the man and woman in marriage together. The question is, therefore, not that of dissolubility or the indissolubility of marriage but whether the Church can forgive the sin of divorce.

For non-consummated sacramental marriage, the Church progressively defined legal circumstances that could invalidate the marriage as a contract. These were conversion from a non-Christian religion (cf. Gregory III in 1585), solemn religious profession (Alexander III in 1159), marriage contracted with dispensation from the impediment of disparity of cult, and marriage of two non-baptized even without the intention of becoming Christians but with one of them intending to marry a Christian (John XXIII in 1959; Léry, 1960, 266–7).

The command, the prohibition of divorce, is true, but it does not prevent the faithful from sinning by putting asunder what God has joined together in a valid consummated marriage. In such cases, the canonical intervention of the Church cannot be invoked. But do we also have to exclude the sacramental intervention of granting forgiveness for the sin committed? Ambrose clearly expressed the view that the divorce of Christians is not a question of contractual procedure but of real sin, when he said that the divorce of Christians is different from the divorce of non-Christian Romans, for by divorce Christians wreck God's handiwork, *quoddam opus Dei* (*Exposition in Lucam* 8, 2; *PL*, 15, 1765). And with this observation we come to the second reason why we may be reluctant to consider the sin of divorce a forgivable sin before the death of one of the consorts.

The sin of divorce is unforgivable, perhaps, because the first marriage effected something permanent in the married people which neither adultery nor divorce can alter. The Church, by forgiving the sin of divorce, would deny or destroy the work of God, which Augustine called "a permanent reality," *quiddam conjugale*, in marriage (*De nuptiis et concupiscentia* 1, 10; *PL*, 44, 420). For a long time this "permanent conjugal reality" was considered something that even death could not destroy because it would exist forever. This is the theological explanation of why the Oriental Church earlier considered marriage to be something lasting even after death and was reluctant to recognize second, third, or fourth marriages even after the death of the spouse. The repetition of marriage, the symbol of union between Christ and his Church, was prohibited. Both Ambrose (*De viduis*, 11; *PL*, 16, 254–5) and Jerome (*Epistulae* 23, 7; *PL*, 22, 1050) confessed that it was only because of human weakness that second marriages were allowed. One could, however, ask why human weakness would allow a second marriage only after death and not before death? Except for a few churches, a second marriage after death was never considered an unforgivable sin, though some churches for a time imposed a rather heavy penance of several years before a second marriage was contracted (*Gloss on the Gregorian Decretum, Poenitentiale* 1, 14, 2; cf. Haddan, 1869–78, 3, 137).

First, the second marriage and slowly the third and fourth marriages were tolerated after some time, marriages that had previously been labelled adultery (Le Bras, 1927, 2131). In this later time difficulties such as imperfect symbolism or breaking an unrepeatable tie which were created by the second, third, or fourth marriage were no longer considered to be prohibiting.

The contractual interpretation of marriage helped theologians to resolve the difficulties surrounding a second marriage, as well as to allow subsequent marriage after death. Once one of the spouses dies, a subsequent marriage can be valid since, it was said, the dead partner ceased to be subject to the law. The dead person is not a legal person anymore; therefore the marriage contract as contract no longer exists.

But if we consider marriage to be the never-ending love of husband and wife, we may have some difficulty with second and subsequent marriages and better appreciate the theology of the Eastern Church. We may approve more easily what Augustine and Ambrose meant when they talked about *quoddam opus Dei, conjugale quiddam,* permanent conjugal reality – the more so if we believe in the Resurrection and that death cannot destroy or terminate love either as a human experience or as the progressive sacramental symbol of God's love caused and signified by love as a human experience. There is only one thing that can destroy them, and that is sin. Sin, long before death, can destroy not only love as a human experience but also the progressive sacramental love caused and symbolized by the sacramental sign. And if sacramental love is destroyed, there is nothing left which, as a sacrament, could carry on the saving love of God. And if the sacrament has been destroyed forever, there is only forgiveness one can appeal to, if forgiveness can be granted. We therefore arrive at the third reason for a reluctance to grant forgiveness before the death of one of the spouses.

We know from the history of the practice of penance that the only time when the early Church failed to grant forgiveness was when there was a lack of sincere repentance. Now, is it possible to consider divorce a state of direct resistance to God and the divorced faithful as indisposed for penance? Is divorce a sort of deliberate malice, an impenitent state of mind, which would make forgiveness fruitless? We may ask also, if the divorce really is only a lack of internal disposition for penance, how can the death of one partner dispose the other for the reception of forgiveness? According to present practice, after the death of one consort, the other can at once be considered well-disposed to marry again. Therefore we cannot consider divorce in itself an absolutely impenitent state; otherwise, we would assume that internal disposition can simply be supplanted by some external happening without any further request for an internal change of mind.

Clement of Rome knew three kinds of sinful attitude that he thought prohibited the fruitful reception of penance. They were being double-minded, questioning God's power, and not believing that God's punishment will come (Clement, 1953, 48–9). He did not think, however, that the sin of divorce included any of these. The sinfulness of divorce, according to him, is the sin of rivalry, which estranges wives from their husbands and annulls the "oneness of bone of my bone, flesh of my flesh" (ibid., 44–5). Clement recommended repentance even to those whose sins reach from earth to heaven. God can always forgive the sins of those who put their hope in him. It seems that the divorced fall into this category. Their sin reaches from earth to heaven, but they can still put their hope in God. If one does not harden his or her heart but confesses her or his sin, there is no verdict against the individual, according to Clement of Rome, but forgiveness and salvation (ibid., 67).

For Justin, those who enter a second marriage are sinners like those who look on a woman to lust after her (Osborn, 1973, 250). Yet their sin is forgivable since God wishes the repentance of the sinner rather than his or her punishment. Now, if a second marriage is as forgivable a sin as lusting after a woman, then the sin of divorce is not necessarily an impenitent state – the more so since love as a human experience is not entirely within one's power. We are responsible for our love, but we do not love in the same way as we do many other things in life. Love is an interaction with another human being. It is never done alone. It is a kind of reciprocal responsibility of loving someone. It is not a job or work to do or a fast release of pressures. It is the mystery of an individualizing power, "a lasting reality," as Augustine described it, which never lets us continue to be the way we were before. When human love definitively breaks down without hope of revival after many years, people cannot just go back and continue by their own will power to live together. This is more so when the prevailing human society, identifying love with sex, does not support and nurture a love "forever." Perhaps because of the increased number of divorced men and women, we need in our time a solemn feast day celebrating the silent majority of those who experience and witness to the never-ending intentionality of love and to the "infallibility of the fallible human love" (Horvath, 1984, 62–7). Such a celebration would give a most welcome example that human fidelity may triumph even in our time.

But in favour of those who are still alive and whose union has sacrilegiously broken down forever, we should think of the arguments from human weakness and the mercy of God which the early Christian writers used to admit a second marriage after death of one of the consorts. And we could ask again, Why could the divorced faithful after *many years* not be well-disposed and seek mercy like those who have lost their spouses by death?

According to Clement of Alexandria, a second marriage is a falling away from the ideal of Christian perfection, but he praised the Church for not imposing on the widower the burden of a forced celibacy (*Stromata*, 3, 12; PG,

98, 1173). Now, would it not be praiseworthy and merciful also to take away the same burden from those who are really widowed, even though not in a legal sense? Athenagoras knew that man is forbidden both to put his wife away and to marry again. This is a sin against the creation of God since he who "severs himself from his first wife, even if she is dead, is an adulterer in disguise." He resists the hand of God, for in the beginning God created one man and one woman (Athenagoras, 1953, 337). For Cyril of Alexandria, remarriage is a safeguard against fornication (*Catechesis*, 4, 26; PG, 33, 488), but so is it for the divorced as well. Gregory of Nazianzus qualified the first marriage as the Christian rule, the second as indulgence, and the third as transgression (*Orationes*. 37, 8; PG, 36, 292). It took a long time to understand the "right" viewpoint concerning second, third, and later marriages. Innocent III (1208) was the one who made it definitely clear that second and third marriages are not to be condemned (Ep. *Eius exemplo*; DS, no. 794).

The third reason why we may be reluctant to forgive the sin of divorce before the death of one of the spouses may arise from a pastoral and psychological concern. Any permissiveness of this kind could weaken the life of the Church. The Montanist principle can be repeated here: "The Church can forgive sins, but I will not do so, lest others commit sin." There is some truth in this precept, especially when serious penance has disappeared and forgiveness is confused with permissiveness. Once the sense of sin and consequently of penance is not taken seriously, forgiveness becomes equivalent to permissiveness. Since the sin of divorce has such great consequences, it cannot be expiated simply by private confession with a penance of some prayers said for a few minutes. Thus, lack of awareness of the meaning of true penance might delay forgiveness or even lead to the praxis of and, later, the doctrine of the impossibility of forgiveness.

The mystery of forgiveness is the mystery of redemption and has nothing to do with the secular notion of forgiveness. Secular forgiveness simply means remission or cancelling punishment. The biblical notion of forgiveness is different. It excludes neither penance nor punishment (Num 14, 18). The crucifixion and death of Jesus Christ are the revealing signs that God's mercy and remission mean something other than non-punishment. God's forgiveness in the New Testament means a power of enabling someone to sin no more. It is not "I cannot sin" but, rather, "I can not sin." It means that the power of sin over the sinner is broken and the sinner is confident that he or she can follow God's call, since the grace of the Lord is overflowing in him or her. Forgiveness is the experience of the power of being able to follow God's invitation and includes an eagerness to leave the old and sacrifice everything for the new way of existence. It is a real spirit of willingness to take up the cross and do penance, which is the fruit of forgiveness given by God rather than its condition. Without forgiveness there is no penance. A time of forgiveness is also a time of penance.

Unless we understand that forgiveness is not permissiveness, the sin of divorce cannot be considered other than as unforgivable. Therefore, when we talk about forgiving the sin of divorce, we must think of an adequate penance for a really grave sin. On those who denied the faith and separated themselves from the Church, the First Council of Nicaea imposed a penance of many years. During that time they took part with the faithful in the prayers but not in the Eucharistic offering (canon 11; Tanner, 1990, 11). The present praxis of refusal of the Eucharistic communion should be not considered a denial of a right but a penance. Like the "hearers" of the word or the "kneelers" and the "consistents" of the early Church, so the divorced could take part in prayers of the people without receiving the Eucharist until the end of their penance for the sin committed against the indissolubility of the sacrament of marriage. Thus the divorced, helped by the sacramental presence during the mass, could witness to the Church's fidelity to the word of Christ and at the same time proclaim his mercy.

Some lengthy time is needed for the person to heal and for the Church to be sure that sacramental love is really terminated. Because of its innate intentionality, love tries to survive in strange forms, and this makes it difficult to be sure when it is definitively terminated. It is not unusual for one who has left the first marriage after twenty years to realize that she or he has lost his or her best friend, whom he or she loved and misses the most.

If an adequate penance can be established, there is no reason why, after having done all the penance, divorced persons could not be given another chance to gradually build again out of the fragments of their sacramental symbol the definitive symbol of the infallible love of God triumphing over the sinfulness of human beings. It is through the grace of the sacrament of marriage that the temporarily valid word of a man or of a woman may indeed become the definitive and irrevocable word of God (cf. 1 Th 2, 13). The love of a man and a woman will reveal the love of God, which is at work in believers. For ages God has worked patiently, trying again and again to build up the indefectible sign of God's saving love, the Church. With the same patience God builds the sacrament of marriage, which signifies God's Church. God is successful with human beings since God has patience and mercy. God is patient and merciful because he is not permissive. Likewise, unless one becomes aware of the need to take penance more seriously, she or he will not be able to hear God's call for mercy.

In any case, God has time, patience, and the power of forgiveness. It may take some time for many to see definitely that by instituting the sacrament of marriage, God proved God not only a good systematic theologian but also an excellent moral theologian and, above all, a most successful minister of the sacraments. And then one will also see that God is a God of love and mercy and that God's sacraments are the actualization of this love and mercy.

In sum, one can say that marriage as a human reality is a public confession made by a man and a woman expressing freely that they love each other as wife and husband with a never-ending love. If anything contrary is documented later, the present praxis of annulment or divorce is right and desirable. The never-ending intentionality is the indicator that the bride and bridegroom really love each other and that they intend an indissoluble marriage. The indissolubility of marriage is based on the nature of true love.

We have to remember that marriage is not just a contract giving the right to have sexual pleasure with each other. Rather, it is a *credal* faith in a never-ending love for the other. Such a faith and fallible love is reaching out to eternity. It is this reality, expressed in various expressions and rites, that is taken up by Christ as one of his sacraments. It is possible that after years this love has progressively been quenched and has terminated in divorce, a painful, unforgettable experience. Instead of denying years of love, we should take the way of penance and ask for forgiveness in truth and mercy.

4.2.3 The Christian Reality of the Sacrament of Marriage

4.2.3.1 INSTITUTED BY CHRIST

If sacraments are revelations of God and Christ is the full revelation of God, he is the only one entitled to institute a sacrament. In its session 24, on 11 November 1563, the Council of Trent declared that marriage is one of the seven sacraments and was instituted by Christ (*Canons on the Sacrament of Marriage*, no. 1; Tanner, 1990, 754). The proclamation was the outcome of Church's ever-deepening recognition of Christ as its original founder. It was a discovery of the meaning of certain praxis and words in the context of the Church's foundational experience. From the beginning, members of the Christian community were aware that the life Christ gave them was so new that it would take time before they would be able to fully grasp it as a community (Jn 16, 12–13; 14, 26). And this was especially true of marriage. It was old and well-known, yet it was new. Its meaning was connected with the meaning of the new kingdom brought about by Christ. Just as by living with faith, their understanding of the Christ event grew, so also did the meaning of Christ's words concerning marriage in its reference to his kingdom.

According to the evangelists, Jesus referred to himself as a bridegroom (Mk 2, 19–20; Mt 9, 15; Lk 5, 34–35; Jn 3, 29–30). He performed his first miracle at a wedding in Cana (Jn 2, 1–11) and made the wedding feast a symbol of his kingdom (Mt 22, 1–10; 25, 1–13; Rev 19, 7–9; 21, 2.9). It is in light of this connection that he abolished the prevailing custom of divorce, reinforced the original plan of God (Gen 1, 27–29; 2, 24) and deepened its meaning by adding "So they are no longer two but one flesh. What therefore God has joined together, let no human being put asunder." If anyone does, whether man or woman, such a person offends God (Mt 19, 6; Mk 10, 2–12; Lk 16, 16; 1 Cor 7, 10).

Collating the five cases of divorce listed in the gospels, we find three for men and two for women: a man who divorces his wife and takes another wife (Mt 19, 9; Mk 10, 11; Lk 16, 18); a man who divorces his wife and does not marry again, but makes his wife commit adultery (Mt 5, 32; 1 Cor 7, 11); a man who marries a divorced wife (Lk 16, 18; Mt 5, 32); a woman who divorces her husband and marries again (Mk 10, 12; 1 Cor 7, 10–11); and a divorced woman who marries again (Mt 5, 32). Such a detailed specification indicates that marriage was relevant in the life of the foundational Church. The innovation caused uncommon concern for Jesus' followers, as we can sense by the Matthean clause beginning "except" of chapter 19, verse 9.

The exception is known only to Matthew and has a vast bibliography (Horvath, 1970, 400–3). Some have tried to explain the text by analyzing the verb ἀπολύω, to divorce; others have searched for the meaning of the prepositions *μή* and *παρεκτός*, except; and finally, some have clarified the meaning of the noun *πορνεία*. The first group interpreted the verb in the sense of 1 Corinthians 7, 10, meaning not divorce but a simple separation without the possibility of a new marriage. This is the so-called classical solution. Its difficulty is that such a separation was unknown to Jesus' audience. Paul knew about it, but he used the term *χωρισῆναι*, separate, and not ἀπολύω, which means to "send away" (Mt 14, 15; 15, 32.39) or "release," as for a prisoner (Mt 18, 27; 27, 15.17.21).

Another group of authors has studied the meaning of the preposition *παρεκτός* and proposed three different interpretations. The first is the inclusive sense, that is, the case of *πορνεία* is included. Though grammatically possible, such an interpretation is strained. The second bypasses interpretation, that is, Jesus bypasses the question of *πορνεία*, saying nothing for or against the question of *πορνεία*. *Porneia* being a special case requiring its own solution, Jesus preferred to leave it aside. Following this solution, proposed even in the *Jerusalem Bible* (1966, NT, 45–7), in "I am not speaking of fornication," Jesus would admit or defend a current Jewish practice, which he never does elsewhere, and it is hard to understand why he would precisely miss the point of the whole discussion. The third is interpretative interpretation, that is, Jesus would admit the Shammai interpretation as operative for the Jews but would give a new, different legislation for his followers. This interpretation makes less sense in Mathew 5, 32 by denying the difference between "It was said" and "But I say to you" than in Mathew 19, 9. Moreover, the meaning of *πορνεία* is not "fornication." Finally, there was the group that studied the meaning of *πορνεία*. A few interpreted it in the light of *'erwah davar* of Deuteronomy 24, 1, meaning "indecency" more in a physical than in a moral sense. Such an interpretation would again be identical with the Shammai law admitting divorce and thus making Jesus' prohibition meaningless. The more common and more coherent interpretation, which explains why, unlike Mark and Luke, Matthew had to insert his clause, is the one that explains *πορνεία* as *zenut,* illegitimate union, incestuous concubinage, like the one that Herod Antipas had and that John the Baptist gave his life for opposing (Mt 14, 1–12).

Matthew had a special reason for inserting this clause. Without the exceptive clause, Jesus' teaching would appear to reject the Baptist's doctrine that eventually cost him his life. Matthew is especially interested in harmonizing the doctrine of the Baptist with that of Jesus. In Matthew even their inaugural teaching is identical. Unlike Mark and Luke, Matthew says that the Baptist's teaching was like that of Jesus – "the kingdom of heaven is at hand" (3, 2). Following this line of thought, the exceptive Matthean clause makes sense: no divorce except in the case of incestuous concubinage like Herod's, which is no marriage and the wife of which is not really a wife; consequently she had to be divorced. The right reading of Mathew 5, 32 is, therefore, the following: "But I say to you that every one who divorces his wife, except the case of the incestuous concubinage – [like that of Herod with his brother Philip's wife, which is not a marriage and thus he has to divorce her (cf. Mt 14, 4) since that woman is not his wife] – makes her commit adultery; and whoever marries her after she is divorced commits adultery." And the reading of Matthew 19, 9 is: "And I say to you that every one who divorces his wife, except for incestuous concubinage, and marries another commits adultery."

The Matthean clause makes Jesus justify fully the Baptist's teaching and his death with an implied charge of adultery against Philip's wife. Since the story of the Baptist and Herod was not known to the readers of Mark and Luke, the exceptive clause was omitted without causing confusion. Moreover, this meaning of *πορνεία* is supported by Paul's usage of it. In 1 Corinthians 5, 1 he labelled *πορνεία* the sin of a man living with his father's wife. The Assembly in Jerusalem too prohibited this kind of union for Christians (Acts 15, 20.28).

The intrigues prompted by Jesus' teaching concerning the indissolubility of marriage are one more instance illustrating that marriage was for him of special interest and had a plan connected with it. It is not surprising that Paul called it not just a mystery but a great mystery (Eph 5, 32). There are quite a few mysteries that Paul claimed as special revelations made to him. Such is the mystery of Christ the crucified (1 Cor 2, 1–13), the call of the pagans to Christ (Rom 16, 25–26; Col 1, 26–27), the mysteries of the Spirit (1 Cor 13, 2; 14, 22), the mystery of the last day of the Resurrection (1 Cor 15, 51), the work of lawlessness and the lawless one (2 Th 2, 7), the restoration of all things in Christ (Eph 1, 9–10), and finally, the mystery of the relation existing between the union of a man with his wife and the union of Christ with the Church (Eph 5, 32).

The great mystery is a culminating symbol of the relations we find in Pauline theology between shadows and the world to come, the σῶμα, the body of Christ (Col 2, 17; cf. Heb 10, 1), between tent and sanctuary (Heb 9, 8), the bondage by nature to elements and the knowledge of God (Gal 4, 8–9), baptismal ablution and having put on Christ (Gal 3, 27; Rom 6, 1–11) and the Spirit of God (1 Cor 6, 11; Tit 3, 4), and husbands' love for their wives and Christ's love presenting his Church "in splendor, without spot or wrinkle or any such thing, that she might be holy and without blemish" (Eph 5, 25–27).

The first leaders of the Church tried to elucidate the relation between marriage and the Church in the light of their own theology. We read in Ignatius of Antioch's *Letter to Polycarp* (no. 5), written around the year 105, that marriage carries the Church's mark (Funk, 1901, 293). In 203 Tertullian wrote to his wife that marriage is happiness because the Church unites, the Eucharist confirms, the blessing seals, the angels proclaim, and God ratifies marriage and makes it valid (*Ad uxorem,* 2, 6; Tertullian, 1954, 393). Since God united man and woman in marriage, there is grace in both husband and wife, argued Origen in his *Commentary on Matthew* (14, 16; PG, 13: 1230) around 244. It is faith, symbolized by the priestly garment and blessing, which really unites man and his wife, said Ambrose in 385 (*Epistula* 19; PL, 16: 984). By virtue of the priestly blessing, any violation of marriage by the faithful is a sort "sacrilege," replied Pope Siricius in his *Decretal to Bishop Himerius of Tarragona* in 385 (4.5; PL, 13: 1136) in 385. According to Gregory of Nazianzus the hand of the couple in matrimony is joined to the hand of God (*Epistula,* 193; PG, 37: 316–17). Around 400 Maximus of Turin explicitly stated that Christ has instituted the marriage and by his presence at Cana blessed it (*Homilia,* no. 23; PL 57: 274). Jesus went to Cana not just to feast but to sanctify marriage, "which is our birth in body," commented Cyril of Alexandria (*Commentary* on Jn 2, 2; PG, 73, 224) around the year 428.

From these sources it seems clear that for the early theology of marriage, Jesus' presence at the wedding at Cana and his saying that "what God has joined together, let no one put asunder" (Mt 19, 6; Mk 10, 9) were influential and kept it in balance between the contemporary rightist and leftist views concerning marriage. The early Christian writers had to defend the value of marriage, on the one hand, against the rigorists, who preached celibacy for everyone (Encratites) or believed that marriage is from the devil (Gnostics and Priscillianists) or simply prohibited second or third marriages (Montanists, Novatianists), and, on the other, against the extreme liberals proclaiming free love. It is a one-sided reading of the early Christian books to argue that the Church was against the body or sex or that it was too permissive. We should always scrutinize whom or to whom any writing of that age is addressed and see why the author was saying what he or she was saying.

To find a balance was never easy since Christ did not give concrete cases but, rather, principles and directives, the applications of which required reflection and an effort to try out and improve upon some tenets. Faced with new customs and differences, such as, for example, that between Roman law and German practice, scholastic theologians had to discuss what marriage really was. After they worked out a definition of a sacrament, it took time to understand in what sense the new definition could be applied to marriage and to say that marriage is a sacrament in the full sense of the new definition; that is, it is instituted by Christ and confers grace.

In 1139 the Second Lateran Council had to reject the doctrine of all those who condemned legitimate marriage. The council listed the sacrament of marriage after those of the Lord's body, the baptism of children, the priesthood, and other ecclesiastical orders (canon 23; Tanner, 1990, 202). Against the Albigenses and Cathari, who attributed the creation of the material world and marriage to the devil, the Council of Verona (1184) declared the sacrament of marriage to be one of the sacraments of the Church (*DS*, 761).

Some of the early scholastic theologians such as William of Auvergne, Abelard, and Peter Lombard had some difficulty in understanding how marriage could be a sacrament in the full sense. There was, they found, too much passion and wantonness involved, which might be incompatible with grace. Besides concupiscence, canonists suspected simony if the sacrament of marriage would confer grace. Money, in the form of a dowry, is indispensable in marriage, and by marrying, one would buy grace for money.

Progress in solving theological problems was gradual. First, William of Auvergne (1180–1249) admitted marriage as a sacrament not by conferring but by conserving grace. Bonaventure went further and said that marriage confers medicinal grace which, by repressing concupiscence, makes it easier to keep the commandments (*In 4 sent.*, d 26, a 2, q 2). Albert the Great described three probable opinions: the first admits that marriage only signifies but does not confer grace; the second says that it confers grace to avoid sin; and finally, the third says that the sacrament of marriage confers grace for doing good (*In 4 sent.*, d 26, a 14). Thomas Aquinas, in his *Comment on the Sentences* of Peter Lombard, defended the third opinion as probable (*In 4 sent.*, d 2, q 1, a 1, qc 2), but in his *Summa contra gentiles*, he explains it as certain (4, 78; 1934, 543). By considering human beings as belonging to the realm of any living thing as well as to the world of intelligence, he found the synthesis. Conjugal acts can be meritorious (*Summa theol. supplementum,* q 41, a 4), and the sacrament of marriage confers grace and does sanctify. Because of the biological and intellectual unity of a human being, marriage is not just to beget children but to educate and, concretely, for the worship of God (*Summa contra gentiles*, 4, 78).This doctrine was repeated by the Council of Florence. Marriage is one of the seven sacrament of the Church. Its first good is "the procreation and bringing up of children *ad cultum Dei*, for the worship of God" (*Bull of Union with the Armenians*; Tanner, 1990, 550). It contains and bestows grace (Tanner, 541).

Thus theological reflection reached the depth of the great mystery that Paul had seen in marriage: a saving reality of Christ and of the Church. On 11 November 1563 the Council of Trent was able to confess that "marriage in a true and strict sense is one of the seven sacraments of the gospel dispensation, instituted by Christ ... and confer grace" in the Church (*Teaching on the Sacrament of Marriage* and canon 1; Tanner, 1990, 754).

Since it was Christ himself who took the profane reality of marriage and made it a sacrament of his Church, the Church does not have the power to change the human reality of marriage. In its Decree of Tametsi (*Canons on the reform of marriage*; Tanner, 1990, 755–9), being aware that the bride and the bridegroom are the ones who administer the sacrament to each other, the Council of Trent limited the right of the Church to only lay down the conditions under which the bride and bridegroom are able to represent it. Marriage as a sacrament is *ad cultum Dei*, a saving reality worshipping God. *Cultus Dei* means a life worthy of the sons and daughters of God which may determine the size of a Christian family.

Later Leo XIII, Pius XI, and Pius XII and Vatican II more accurately expressed the purpose and end of the human and sacramental reality of marriage by saying that the end of marriage is the *connubium Christi cum ecclesia*, Christ's union with the Church. By virtue of the sacrament of marriage, married Christians not only symbolize but also share "the unity and the fertile love between Christ and the Church (see *Eph* 5, 32)" (*LG*, no. 11; Tanner, 1990, 857–8).

Because of Christian marriage's internal relationship to the basic institution of the Church, the institution of the sacrament of marriage coincides with the institution of the visible Church. The Church as a sacrament was instituted at Calvary when Jesus gave himself up once and for all for the sins of the world and from his open side at once "there came out blood and water," yet on the third day he rose. It was established juridically before the Ascension at the sea of Tiberias and completed on the day of Pentecost. Thus the sacrament of marriage takes its origin from the paschal mystery. It is established as a visible cell of the human and ecclesiastical communities and consummated in the conjugal love of a Christian man and a Christian woman. It is here that the mystical life of the Church penetrates deeply into human relationships. Christ takes the whole of nature, down to the deepest roots, to himself. "Christian matrimony is a mystery that has its foundation in the Incarnation and the

Eucharist and so alone they can fully reveal its rich significance" (Scheeben, 1946, 601–2).

4.2.3.2 THE SACRAMENT OF MARRIAGE

Since there is no sacrament without a cooperative encounter between Christ, the Church, and the faithful, the sacrament of marriage should be described as follows.

The sacrament of marriage is a revealing and saving encounter of God-man, Christ, of the Church, and of the spouses to

1 (*present*)	manifest the virtual signs of the intentionally never-ending mutual love (*symbol*) of a marrying man and woman mutually expressed in words in order
(*symbolized reality and symbol*)	to elevate it to the actual sacramental symbol of the mystical bond of Christ with his Church and to bring about the sanctification of the couple, of the human race, and of the cosmos by
2 (*past*)	commemorating and representing God's love revealed in Christ as unrestricted and total self-giving culminating in his death and resurrection and by
3 (*future*) (*symbolized reality*)	communicating the Triune God's love to the Church and to the world and thus prognosticating the happiness of the eternal kingdom.

4.2.3.3 COMMENT

The presence of all these subjects is required in each sacrament. The actual presence of God is guaranteed by God's infallible word instituting the sacramental symbols. The presence of the Church is indicated by its jurisdictional intervention, and the presence of the minister and of the recipients of the sacrament by their intentions. If one of them is bypassed, the ritual will be null and void.

The intentionally never-ending mutual love of a marrying man and woman, mutually expressed by the words "I take you to be my husband" and "I take you to be my wife," as human reality is the virtual bond that, by virtue of the sacrament, is elevated to be the actual sacramental symbol of the supernatural reality of the mystical bond of Christ with his Church. The natural matrimonial bond existing also in non-Christian marriage by virtue of the sacrament shares the sacramental and mystical reality of the union of Christ with his Church and its indissolubility. This action is not that of the couple any more. It is the action of Jesus Christ, the author of grace, who takes the intentionally never-ending mutual love of the marrying man and woman and elevates it into his own union with the Church and through the Church with the whole human race and the cosmos. It is by the action of Jesus Christ that the sacramental bond is not just a juridical reality any more. It is the reality of the new life brought by Christ, which necessarily brings with it the infusion of grace proper to the sacrament of marriage, modifying accordingly the sanctifying grace, the theological virtues, and the gifts of the Holy Spirit, or will bring them in once the sinful resistance is removed. By the action of Jesus Christ (*ex opere operato Christi*) and of the Church, the sacrament of marriage makes the couple a cell of the Church, which does not only signify but in a true sense continues to "create" the Church and thus becomes an organ for the realization of the Church's ends.

It is because of the permanent sacramental reality that a mortal sin of a marrying person cannot make the sacrament invalid. The effect may be frustrated by the sin, but it will be brought into operation once the sinful resistance removed. Because it is not just the words but the intentionally never-ending love expressed by the words which is the sacramental sign, the marriage itself remains not only signifying but also bringing about grace. Because of its union with the Church's relation to Christ, the sacrament has its permanent reality not as a new sacramental entity, like a new character, but as a qualifying modification of the sacrament of baptism, the prerequisite *conditio sine qua non* of receiving and administering the sacrament of marriage.

The sacrament of marriage, like the other sacraments, takes its sacramental efficiency from the Eucharist commemorating and representing God's love manifested in Christ as an unrestricted and total self-giving that culminated in his death and resurrection. Once the intentionally never-ending love of the marrying man and woman is united by the sacrament with the bond existing between Christ and the Church, it receives the characteristics of Jesus Christ's love. It will be not only indissoluble, never-ending but an indissoluble never-ending, unrestricted, and totally self-giving love that is the self-giving of Jesus Christ, the Son, to his eternal Father. Since God the Father unrestrictedly and totally gave God's life to the Son, the Son becomes no less than God, the second person of the Trinity. Following the Incarnation, his unrestricted self-giving life culminated in accepting death and resurrection. By making marriage a sacrament, he opened a deep level in the nature of love which not only symbolizes but also represents, re-enacting his unrestricted self-giving love, the self of Jesus Christ.

The sacramental reality of this unrestricted and total self-giving love explains why the magisterium of the Church could consistently teach that by virtue of the sacrament, "any conjugal act necessarily remains directed towards the procreation of human life and that any action contrary to this intention is disordered" (Paul VI, 1968, nos 11, 14). Such an argument may sound "romantic," "unrealistic," and "irrelevant" to our human experience, yet it is as real as the God of the loving faith is real and is consistent with the nature of God recognized as love. Since the Church believes in a God of such an unrestricted love, and since the Church is the primary sacrament of Christ, the life of the Church cannot but be Christ's unrestricted self-giving, as expressed in the sacrament of marriage. This is all the more so since unrestricted self-giving is the meaning of the gift of sex.

We have seen that love is the "creative release of new reality affirming the power of the future over the present and past" and that the love of God is the origin of all reality, of creation as well as of redemption. Thus the intentionality of the sacrament is consistent with the intentionality of marriage as a human reality. It is a re-enforcing of the challenge of love. It is a new challenge to remain static within our human existence or to be dynamic, reaching out to a higher level of human existence and love. A structural consideration allows us to distinguish human existence, Christian existence, and God's existence and indicates their symbiotic interaction with ever-increasing challenges. Christian life as a new life brought about by Christ is a life of reason in the present as well as of reason in a future inspired by love. It is seeing the world not just the way it is but the way it should be and will be. The future is a future offered by God to the human race both as a call and as a yardstick for the present, already under the attractive force of the future. It is the vocation and mission of the Church to cooperate with Christ for this future of God, which has already been inaugurated in Christian existence.

Struggle and failure are not necessarily mortal sins. Mortal sin is to deny that God is more than we are and the future is more than the present. It is fashioning God in one's own image and making one's life the standard of Christian existence. In a church based on the sacraments of ordination and baptism, the ordained faithful and the baptized faithful both have their mission. Both have to live up to the challenge of Christian existence. Like any teaching and dialogue, the encyclical *Humanae Vitae* reminds the believer that marriage takes its life and meaning from the Eucharist, the sacrament of unselfishness, and in union with the sacrament of reconciliation, it saves the married from selfishness. Selfishness is a sin because it is an enemy of love. Bishops, priests, and the faithful are asked to be harsh on sin "yet patient and kind with the sinner" (Paul VI, 1968, 501) and to let the "voice and love of the Redeemer" shine through their words and deeds (ibid., 502). The bishops, priests, and faithful all have a mission that is beyond human effort, and all draw their strength from the Eucharist either by taking it or by desiring to take it. It is noteworthy that in the encyclical *Humanae Vitae* one cannot find the words "mortal or grave sins."

The one who says, "God be merciful to me a sinner" may go home justified, rather than the other who exalts oneself (Lk 18, 13–14). Which one is more Christian? Which one is more human? Can both be in one person?

The sacrament of marriage shares the mission of Christ in communicating God's love to the Church and to the world by prognosticating the happiness of the eternal kingdom. Its end is the beatific vision of spending one's life the way God did and does through all eternity.

4.2.4 The Sacrament of Marriage and Sacramental Theology

4.2.4.1 THE SACRAMENT OF MARRIAGE IS A PERSONAL ENCOUNTER WITH CHRIST

The sacrament of marriage is a personal encounter with Christ, who joins the intentionally never-ending love expressed by the words "I take you to be my husband" and "I take you to be my wife" of the bride and bridegroom to the love that he has for the Church, his mystical body, Christ, the head of his Church. He welcomes them and reinforces their entry into the Church, initiated by baptism and strengthened by confirmation. It is the time when God joins the two so that no one should separate them. He brings their intentionally never-ending love to its fulfillment and actualizes the person-creating power of their love to share in the person-creating love of God.

The bride and bridegroom become for each other a unique "somebody," a unique "you," which is the closest "you" to that "you" that God pronounced when God created them and in baptism "named" them by a name to be a person not only of the human race but, as God's beloved son or daughter in God's family, of the Church. Since each personality is created and defined by love, their personalities will now be further differentiated by their mutual love. George, for example, will be the George who is loved by Elizabeth, and God loves George as the one who is loved by Elizabeth. Likewise, Theresa is the one who is loved by Stephen, and God loves Theresa as the one who is loved by Stephen. To express this new identity not only the woman but the man also should have the name of his wife after his name. Through the sacrament of marriage it is Christ who gives them a new identity and a new power to love each other as God loves them and to achieve their new personality. He lets them share the love of God, which brings forth grace, sanctifying them and in them and through them the world. Their love is able to release a new creative reality for the Church and for the world, making the Church and the whole world one great family of love. Thus the sacrament of marriage is a kind of ordination to bring about the family as the cell of the Church, a mini-church, which is the constituent element as well as the aim of the Church.

As in each sacrament, so also in the sacrament of marriage, Christ is the one who is actively present and transforms the visible sign into one of his sacraments. He is the one who baptizes, confirms, consecrates, anoints, and orders to priesthood. So he is the main "celebrant" in the sacrament of marriage also. Though we do not say that Christ gets married each time in each married couple, yet he is present in the sacrament by giving himself entirely to two human beings and through them to the human race. In each sacrament of marriage he gives himself by extending his self-giving in the Eucharist. Through each sacrament, he is living more in this world. He is more with the world and more present in the world. In each sacrament he is the one who loves people more by imparting more grace not only to the ones who have married now but to those who are not Christians but living in marriage or even those who really love each other as wife and husband without being officially recognized as married. It is so since if there is somewhere any good, it cannot be without Christ. He is everywhere wherever some unselfish love is unfolding.

4.2.4.2 THE SACRAMENT OF MARRIAGE IS A UNION WITH CHRIST AND IN HIM WITH BELIEVERS AND THROUGH THEM WITH THE WHOLE WORLD BY VIRTUE OF THE HOLY SPIRIT

All human beings are called to become the new people of God, which, remaining one and unique, is to be spread through the whole world and through every age and gathered into one by the Holy Spirit. It is for this purpose that God sent his Son first and then "the Spirit of his Son, who is Lord and giver of life" (*LG*, no. 13; Tanner, 1990, 859). Thanks to the special gifts distributed by the Holy Spirit (*LG*, no. 12; Tanner, 858), the sacrament of marriage is a sacrament of unity in the Church and in the whole world. As a common human experience, marriage prompts the unity of all married people in the world. It may especially be the sacrament of unity within the Church and within the whole human race wherever there is a husband who loves his wife and a wife who loves her husband. By its sacramentality, marriage becomes a creation-salvation milieu, differentiating as well as allying Christian and non-Christian marriages. To elucidate this concept, we may get help from the theology of non-Christian religions.

Inspired by the Vatican II teaching that non-Christian realities may become vehicles of Christian grace, we can list about thirty models used in the theology of non-Christian religions that explain the relation existing between Christian and non-Christian religions. Of the thirty models (Horvath, 1981, 299–322), let us take the "unconscious" and "conscious" model. According to this model, Christianity can be considered distinct from non-Christianity in the manner in which explicit awareness is distinct from non-explicit awareness of what God is doing in the world. The difference between the awareness and non-awareness of God's salvific milieu in the world is not merely epistemological. One relates to the other as a real, actual, and explicit symbol of salvation to the virtual, potential, and implicit symbols of salvation. Christian and non-Christian may relate to each other just as differentiated human consciousness differs from an undifferentiated human consciousness of salvation. This model suggests that Christ's saving grace is operative in the whole universe through mediation of his primary sacrament, the Church. Evangelization means just a cooperation with grace in the world in order to let it become conscious as fulfillment of the human reality (cf. Acts 17, 23). Evangelization is opening eyes to discover Christ's grace in the world.

Marriage could serve as good example as well as an effective means of the universality of grace. Christian marriage is a sacramental symbol towards which all non-sacramental marriages tend as their full realization. Christian spouses by their sacramental grace enable all non-Christian spouses to give themselves to each other in a unselfish love, and by doing so, they share the creation-salvation milieu of the sacrament of marriage. Thus we can see the sacrament of marriage as the real, actual, and explicit sacrament of the virtual, potential, and implicit symbol of non-Christian, non-sacramental marriages (Horvath, 1970, 392–3). The mission of the Christian marriage is universal. Though not everybody is called to marriage, yet everybody is called to love unselfishly.

4.2.4.3 THE SACRAMENT OF MARRIAGE IS A PARTICIPATION IN CHRIST'S LIFE AND HIS WORK OF SALVATION

"Love one another, even as I have loved you, that you also love one another" (Jn 13, 34) sums up Jesus' life as the infrastructure and mission of Christian marriage. Christ's love prompts the love that husband and wife are able to feel for each other. The love that came as a gift becomes a lifelong task from now on. God creates love and invites them to join God as con-creators in keeping love alive and developing it to its fullness. What God created without them, God will not develop without them. The external attractiveness of a human being may progressively become interior, and the beautiful, lovable, and handsome young girl and boy become beautiful persons, attractive by their increasing goodness. As the years pass, they become more and more one, so that no one and nothing, not even death, can ever really separate one from the other. They grow old together and reach a beauty that is far beyond sexual attractiveness. It is a beauty of gentleness, loveliness, and amiability "by which all human beings may know that the Church is a Church of Christ" (Jn 13, 35). Thus Christian families become the apostles of the Church who "go and make disciples of all nations" (Mt 28, 19). As "a cell" of the Church, they are the most expressive sacramental symbol that represents and accomplishes the Church as the sacrament of God's love.

As we mentioned earlier, love, in answering questions or solving problems, raises new ones. It presents new challenges. And the challenges in marriage are not small. Marriage is one of the most complex realities we know. It is not only a mini-church. It is also a small financial institution, a mini-health centre, an educational academy, a most fundamental social system, a school of psychology, and a site for entertainment. The married woman and man are expected to be not only theologians but also bankers, doctors who bring forth and nurture human life, teachers, sociologists, psychologists, entertainers, and what is more, mother and father, husband and wife. They are expected to be expert in all these areas, yet the most important, the most demanding condition *sine qua non* of a family is to create a love milieu and to maintain it, cultivate it, and increase it day after day in every moment and in every task. To meet such a great challenge of love, to live a life of love and carry out such a task, one has to be a particularly talented, self-assured, and psychologically balanced personality who has more to give than to receive. Yet the challenges that love creates, it can meet and solve. This is the reason that mutual love must be kept, cultivated, and rekindled daily. And love tells us again how this can be done. Each has to live a life for the other and search for the happiness of the other as his or her own happiness. Trust, cooperation, and self-sacrifice are necessary. And this requirement takes us to the next assertion.

4.2.4.4 THE SACRAMENT OF MARRIAGE IS A SACRIFICE RECONCILING THE WORLD WITH GOD

A great human being is one who can love. And the one who can love can sacrifice. We found that the Eucharistic sacrifice was a self-giving. By virtue of the Eucharist, such a self-giving to another human being brings about reconciliation with God and with the world. Because the God-man Christ was so rich and powerful, he could search and work for the salvation of others. So are the ones who administer grace to each other, which is a power of creating others as other. St Paul gave an unequivocal description of the affluence and power of the Christian love that enables a man and a woman to become a "great woman" or a "great man," as any Christian wife and husband have to be. Here is Paul's well-known prescription for human greatness, together with short comments (cf. 1 Cor 13, 4–8):

Love is patient, since it is not afraid of the future;
Love is kind, since it is rich enough to give;
Love is not jealous, since no one else has something that it would not have;

Love is not boastful, since it does not have to cover up by words what it would not have in deed;
Love is not arrogant, since it can respect others for seeing more in them than they themselves do;
Love is not rude, since it is not pushy because it does not have to be the first; it is already;
Love is not self-seeking – it is lacking nothing;
Love is not irritable, since it cannot lose any fight;
Love is not resentful, since it cannot be offended;
Love does not rejoice at wrong, since it cannot benefit from it;
Love rejoices in the right, since it is itself its own justification;
Love bears everything, since it is invulnerable;
Love believes everything, since it knows better and cannot be deceived;
Love hopes all things, since it has the future;
Love endures all things, since it outlives everything;
Love never ends, since it is eternity. (cf. Gregory I, *Moralia in Job,* 10, 7–8; *PL,* 75: 925–6)

Love is like any artistic talent. It is a gift to be cultivated. As any art, love too is a challenge to our inventive mental power called wisdom. It inspires constant discovery of a limitless newness and priceless value of the beloved one. The sacrifice for Jesus, we found, was a love at any price, even at the price of his life, for his Father and the world of his Father. The Eucharist is the sacrament of this love. Being a sacrament, marriage shares in the Eucharistic sacrifice, which tells us that sacrifice is forgiveness and forgiveness is sacrifice. By forgiving each other, husband and wife share in Jesus' work of reconciling the world with God. This is the sacrificial gift of the sacrament of marriage, which is expected to make the never-ending intentionality of love indeed never-ending.

4.2.4.5 THE MINISTERS

The words "I take you to be my husband" and "I take you to be my wife" make it clear that the bridegroom and the bride are the ones who administer to each other the sacrament of marriage. The mutual love by which they love each other is the sacramental sign that is taken up by Christ as a sacrament of his Church and witnessed by a priest or deacon assigned to do so. Therefore we have three "ministers" for confecting a sacrament of marriage: God-man Jesus Christ, the Church, and the marrying couple. The Oriental Church sees the priest as the minister for enhancing the mysterious presence of Christ in the sacrament of marriage.

When Protestant Christians get married, though validly baptized, they are not considered as ministers of the sacrament of marriage, for the simple reason that Protestant traditions do not consider marriage a sacrament. Since they marry in their own denominations, the prevailing intention is that they do not administer a sacrament to each other. Their baptism does not "automatically" make their marriage a sacrament, because the sacramental intention is excluded by the faith of their church. In the same way that one can argue against the validity of the marriage from the denial of the indissolubility of marriage, so one can also argue against validity from the denial of the sacramental intentionality of the marriage. The Church could, therefore, dissolve the marriage of two Protestants the way it could dissolve natural marriages (Léry, 1960). Yet this does not mean that the marriage of the Protestant faithful lacks sacramental grace. They may receive the sacramental grace of marriage through the sacrament of marriage of the Catholic faithful by virtue of the organic unity between the sacraments and their natural symbol, the human mystery of marriage. And those who would believe that their marriage is a sacrament could receive sacramental grace by virtue of their baptism.

4.2.4.6 THE SACRAMENT OF MARRIAGE AND ECUMENISM

By making marriage, as a human experience, one of his sacraments, Jesus Christ brought every marriage into the atmosphere of grace and sanctification. It became a creation-salvation milieu that has sanctifying force. He made it into a universal door for sanctification, a channel of the sacramental grace streaming from the Eucharist and of the sacrament of marriage that remain the attractive force for all the potential marriage sacraments. Virtual marriage can become actual marriage when both bride and bridegroom are baptized and both believe in the sacramentality of marriage. They are the only ones whose love can become the adequate sacramental symbol of the supernatural reality of the mystical bond of Christ with his Church.

Yet all matrimonial bonds existing in non-Christian marriages may and do share the sacramental mystical reality of the union of Christ with his Church and its indissolubility as love everlasting. This universal reality of love, with its intentionality of lasting for ever, may be recognized by believers and non-believers and cherished everywhere in the world. A world council for promoting and cultivating a lasting and ever-deepening respect, love, and peace among husbands and wives in the families of the world would be a most welcome instrument for ecumenism.

4.2.5 *The Sacrament of Marriage and Systematic Theology*

Like the Eucharist, the sacrament of marriage raises issues for any treatise of systematic theology. It gives directions for solving problems and may provide some further understanding of the Christian faith.

4.2.5.1 THE SACRAMENT OF MARRIAGE IS A SYMBOL FOR THE WORLD: A PATTERN OF DIFFERENCE

Marriage is a pattern of difference. There is a man who is not a woman, and there is a woman who is not a man. And the two make up marriage, a fundamental, mysterious reality. God, the one, created human beings; male and female, God created them (Gn 1, 27). The rule for life as well as for knowledge in the created world from that time on is not the solitary "one" but "two"; "one" and the other is the "other one," the "you" and "I." The principle of identity is to be completed by the principle of complementarity, the adjustment of two mutually exclusive approaches, which will serve as a problem-solving paradigm for science and for human realities, for particular and for global problems as well. For example, in describing what electrons are, we sometimes imagine waves, and sometimes we picture particles. But both must be used. And since they are mutually exclusive, one has to adjust the two approaches "in a manner that is not obvious" (Teller, 1969, 78–97).

The simplistic view is to be complemented by "another," by the consideration of "man" and "woman." In any problem-raising and problem-solving in philosophical or theological discourse, marriage as a pattern of difference suggests the need to search for another view and the need to transcend male and female confrontation with the complementary views of the other side by listening objectively to them, *audiatur et altera pars.* There is always another side of the "story." Love demands it.

4.2.5.2 THE SACRAMENT OF MARRIAGE IS A SYMBOL FOR HUMAN EXISTENCE: A CHALLENGE TO COOPERATE WITH THE OTHER AS "OTHER" IN THE COMMUNITY OF THE HUMAN RACE

Marriage is a mini-world of "others." It is a school for living with others and reminds us that we are not alone. They are other people who are not us. They are other people, and in the real life we have to learn to live together with others, to work with others who are really others. Human life is a challenge of being able to live and work together with others whose talents, world views, and moods are different. People have different feelings, yet we are all humans and members of one family, whose birthplace is our planet. Dictatorial, totalitarian systems and idealist, absolutist world views are doomed to failure. They are probably the brainchildren of those who could never learn the lesson the family is expected to teach us.

The sacrament of marriage is a challenge to Christian anthropology to respect cultures, to cultivate individuals, God-created free persons. They are all "others," not "clones" but unique. No one was exactly like any of them before, and there will never will be anyone after. Yet they are able to cooperate with others and create others in one community of others.

4.2.5.3 THE SACRAMENT OF MARRIAGE IS A SYMBOL OF THE CHURCH: SELF-GIVING TO THE COMMUNITY OF THE HUMAN RACE

The Church exists and functions as a people, institution, magisterium, community, service, mystery, and so on. The sacrament of marriage reminds the Church that it is also a family founded and established in love by the loving person of Jesus Christ. Each member is a friend of God, who brought every member, first of all, to love, which is each one's raison d'être. As the married couple have the task of nurturing their love for each other, so the Church too in all its functions, whether teaching, organizing, or in other ways, has the task of promoting a "fervent and ardent love" for God like the one expressed by the *Suscipe* of Ignatius of Loyola (1973, 80) among its members as well as among the nations. There is no member of the human race who does not need forgiveness and has nothing to forgive.

4.2.5.4 THE SACRAMENT OF MARRIAGE IS A SYMBOL FOR CHRISTOLOGY: CHRIST HAS FEELINGS AND A DESIRE TO BE LOVED

The sacrament of marriage is a sacrament of loving and being loved. Christ, the one who created the sacrament, is also loving and wants to be loved. This is the leitmotif of mystical experiences to which the saints of the Church refer and which devotion to the Sacred Heart promotes. It may sound too simple, and to some pitiful, to hear the risen Christ, Lord of the universe, asking for "consolation," for "expiation," or just for the experience of "being loved." Yet if the sacrament of marriage has a mysterious but true reference to the relation Christ has to his Church, the love relation must be two-sided. Unlike the god of classical philosophy, the Christian God has feelings. God is merciful, gracious, slow to anger, abounding in and keeping steadfast love (Ex 34, 6–7) – in a word, lovable. If we love God, it is because God loved us before we read about it in 1 John 4, 10 and reveals this love in a humble request for love. Perhaps on account of the sacramentality of Christian marriage, we can sense that God is not only love but wants to be loved and asks for love. The self-humiliating power of God's love had been manifest in the incarnation, death, and resurrection of Jesus Christ. He is real man and real God, asking for love for God and accepting that on behalf of God. Since he is one with the human race in and through his asking for love, the human race is asking for love. Jesus Christ is a king of the mind and of the will as well as a king of the heart. He is the head of the human race but the head of any family as well as of any reign. It seems consistent that devotion to the Sacred Heart is linked with the celebration of Christ the King and with the consecration of families.

The sacrament of marriage presents a real challenge to Christology. Christ, the real God, the creator of the universe, the saviour of the world, is strong enough to humble himself by asking for human love. Jesus Christ is asking his Church for love because he loves his Church, and the sacrament of marriage is a pledge of that. Marriage and family create a community of mutual love between a woman and a man, and so does redemption. God and the human race are a community of mutual love established by the one who loves and ask for love on behalf of both. It is a human experience that only one who loves dares to ask for love. God's love is searching for the human heart, and the human heart is searching for God's love. Love evokes love. "Love calls forth love" (Teresa of Avila, 1971, 41).

4.2.5.5 THE SACRAMENT OF MARRIAGE IS A SYMBOL OF THE REVELATION OF THE TRIUNE GOD'S UNRESTRICTED SELF-GIVING IN THE FALLIBLE LOVE OF A WOMAN AND OF A MAN CHOSEN BY THE INFALLIBLE WORD OF GOD

God is revealed in each sacrament. In the sacrament of marriage God is revealed in the most fundamental human experience, love. The Trinitarian God's life is the Father's love giving oneself without restriction to the Son and both the Father and the Son to the Holy Spirit. Since the sacrament of marriage is related to Jesus' death and resurrection, marriage is a proper symbol of God's internal life as well as of God's feeling for human beings. It can be an epiphany of God and of God's love for human beings.

The moment of contracting marriage is a revelation that here and now God has chosen this man and this woman, called each by their own names to be from now on the visible symbol of God's love for them as well as for the Church and for the whole human race. The celebration of marriage becomes the "Word of God," announcing that God has joined this woman and this man to become wife and husband. We can say that marriage is the revelation of both God's eternal love and God's choice of one son and one daughter of God to be the visible sign of God's love. The sacrament of marriage is an epiphany of God and a Word of God as well (Horvath, 1970, 97–8).

4.2.5.6 THE SACRAMENT OF MARRIAGE IS A SYMBOL FOR ESCHATOLOGY: MARRIAGE IS KERYGMA THAT LOVE HAS A FUTURE, BUT HATE DOES NOT; THE FUTURE IS STRONGER THAN THE PRESENT OR THE PAST

The Book of Revelation describes the final victory of Christ as a marriage feast (19, 1, 5–9). Some great mystics of the Church, such as St Bernard of

Clairvaux, St Teresa of Avila, and St John of the Cross, have described the highest degree of mystical experience as marriage. God knows and speaks our language and lets it express the *non plus ultra* of God's love for the mystics by words that mean *non plus ultra* in their language. Paul spoke of love surpassing any knowledge and being filled with the fullness of God (Eph 3, 19). Augustine spoke of the supreme knowledge and love of God (*Confessions*, 1993; Gilson, 1960). The language of the mystic Ignatius of Loyola is the mission within and without of the Trinity. Yet what Teresa of Avila and Ignatius of Loyola want to say is the same: love has triumphed. Heaven and earth may pass away (Mk 13, 31; Lk 21, 33), but love will abide (1 Cor 13, 13). In the Resurrection there will be no marriage (Mt 22, 30), but there will be what marriage means: love without end.

The sacrament of marriage's contribution to eschatology is threefold. Firstly, seeing God face to face in heaven (1 Cor 13, 12) is not in a Platonic contemplation of the supreme good but in love. Secondly, eschatology is not a private but a community life of the mystical body of Christ. Thirdly, marriage and virginity and celibacy in their finality are one: the love for Jesus Christ, who is the revelation of the Triune God.

Married people and celibates bonded by evangelical counsels of chastity consecrated to God (Mt 19, 10–12; 1 Cor 7, 32–34) complement each other in the sense of the principle of complementarity, which is an adjustment of two mutually exclusive approaches. Both aim at the same end, the union of Christ with his Church by the symbol of the present age, marriage, or by the image of the eschatological age, celibacy. Yet both draw their force from the Eucharist, together with the sacrament of baptism. Both graces are sacramental. It seems that celibacy does not need a special sacrament because it is the outgrowth of the sacrament of baptism when the baptized are called by their new name (*LG*, no. 44; Tanner, 1990, 85) and by the sacrament of confirmation to a new mission. Being complementary, married people and celibates need each other for the kingdom of God. Neither can remain strong and faithful without the other. They need each other's help, their mutual esteem and admiration, because both are rooted in the same Eucharist. It is understandable that crisis in one brings crisis in the other. The strength of one is the strength of the other.

The "better" of 1 Corinthians 7, 38 and the "happier" of the celibacy (1 Cor 7, 4), cited by the Council of Trent (*Canons on the Sacrament of Marriage*, no. 10; Tanner, 1990, 755), mean the beatitude of the kingdom of Christ (Mt 5, 3–12). Celibacy is not better for everyone but just for those who have been called and to whom grace is given. Otherwise, marriage is the better and happier (1 Cor 7, 36). In the end all will be better and happier in the Resurrection, when sexual life reaches its end.

The sacrament of marriage sets itself in the eternal life of the Church and through the Church in the whole of redemption. For the internal tendency of married love toward eternal life, we find an ingenious presentation by Bernard Lonergan in his article "Finality, Love, Marriage" (1942). He distinguishes three levels: the level of nature, the level of reason, and the level of divine grace. Each level has a horizontal finality through its own actuation. Furthermore, nature and reason have a vertical finality to eternal life in heaven. Thus nature sets its goal in the repetitive emergence and maintenance of life. Reason supervenes to set up its historical, cumulative but not repetitive, spontaneous, ever-varying pursuit of good life. Grace takes over both nature and reason to redirect repetitive, spontaneous, and historical development to the supernatural end of eternal life. Thus sexual potencies through sexual union set their goal in the child, but in a vertical finality the sexual union inserts itself into the actuation of spontaneous potencies in the conservation of life. Yet the actuation of spontaneous faculties prompts friendship between man and woman, which in marriage leads to the education of children. But the friendship between man and woman inserts itself into the increase of personal development through knowledge and values prompting Christian love, which tends to Christian education of the children, which again inserts itself by the increase of the grace of the mystical body, which has its vertical finality in the eternal life of the mystical body, the Church in heaven.

4.2.5.7 THE SACRAMENT OF MARRIAGE IS A SYMBOL FOR PNEUMATOLOGY: SANCTIFICATION OF THE ONE WITH THE "OTHER"AS PERSONS IN A COMMUNITY OF THE OTHERS OF THE HUMAN RACE

The sacrament of marriage as a symbol for pneumatology intensifies the community relevance of all the gifts of the Spirit. The charisma of the one modifies the gifts of the other, and the sanctification of one goes along with the sanctification of the other. Moreover, since the family is inserted into the life of the human race, any charisma is for the community of the human race. Paul recognized this when he warned that "speaking in tongues" should be interpreted and made understandable to others for the benefit of the whole Church, which in his mind served the whole world, and love was the universal aim (1 Cor 14, 1–19).

The Spirit, who is neither the Son nor the Father and much less a woman or man, is the pledge, the authenticity of God as God, a human being as a person, and the Church as a community of persons. Each human being is a member of the body of Christ and the temple of the indwelling Holy Spirit, who besides the Father and the Son, is "another" of the Holy Trinity. The family is a mini-church as well as mini-world, which after Marshall McLuhan's global village should perhaps better be called a global family where each member has equal rights, equal dignity, and concern for others in the one Spirit.

4.2.5.8 THE SACRAMENT OF MARRIAGE IS A SYMBOL FOR MARIOLOGY: MARY AS PRE-EMINENT MODEL FOR BOTH MARITAL AND CELIBATE LOVE

The sacrament of marriage, the sacrament of God's infallible love in a fallible human love, presents Mary's love for God as a pure gift of Christ and reveals any love for God as being so as well. It brings motherhood to Mariology as complementarity to virginity. Mary as mother and virgin is the model of married people and of people bound by the evangelical counsel of chastity. She is not only the patron and supporter of the married and the celibate faithful but the eschatological realization of the intentionally never-ending love, whether marital or celibate. The immediacy of Christ to her made motherhood in this world and virginity in eternal life one. Her future in heaven as virgin already reached her present as mother. This is the logic of the mystery of Mary's love for Jesus Christ. All Christians are called to share the grace Mary has. All have, therefore, to praise and to support both the married in this world and the celibate faithful, expecting the eschatological realization of their intentionally never-ending love for God and every human being. If we, for some insurmountable reason, cannot fulfill what God commands, said Augustine, "let us love him or her who fulfils that and we fulfil that in him or her." So powerful is love (1956, 1811; *PL*, 46, 1627). Married Christians should love and help celibate religious, and religious should love and support married Christians in order to share the fullness of grace of the Eucharistic Christ.

4.3 WHAT IS THE SACRAMENT OF ORDER?

4.3.1 Introduction

Any attempt to answer the question of what the sacrament of order* is has to deal with a great variety of involved questions about the meaning of the terms apostle, apostolic succession, bishop, presbyter, priest, deacon, order, hierarchy, *in persona Christ,* imposition of hands, minister, mission of Christ, redemption, sacrifice, and clergy, all in their historical context. As time has passed, the meaning of these terms has changed. Taken out of their historical contexts, they have been interpreted according to the lexicology of other times. This process has brought about different theological understandings of these terms. Condemnations and schisms followed, and the unity of the Church became a thing of the past. The term *ordo,* when Tertullian introduced it, was not simply an antonym for disorder. During the first centuries, "hierarchy" likewise meant more than ranks subordinated to one another. The words *hiereus* in Greek, *sacerdos* in Latin for Thomas Aquinas, or "priest" in English, each with a definite meaning, were hardly a reminder of the word "apostles." Even today the meaning of the word "priest" is not univocal (Horvath, 1968, 1971a).

What is the priesthood: profession or vocation? Can we define the priesthood by the work a priest is doing? Who is a priest? One who performs sacrificial acts and worship on behalf of a community? A speaker giving sermons? Someone who can say mass? Or a showman performing ceremonial rites? A teacher? The leader of an organization forming a community? The employee of a church rendering services? The executive of church councils and synods? An administrator or manager bringing responses to one's wishes? A minister acting as an attendant? An envoy, legate, emissary, representative, or mediatory agent between humans and God? A revolutionary bringing about radical changes? A transformer turning a community of human beings into a Christian community of love, the law of the cross into the new life of ultimate joy? A prophet helping to promote an understanding of the word of God by translating it into the language of the people? A healing doctor, a medicine man? Someone sharing in Christ's redemptive call entrusted to his apostles? In search for an answer we have to recall history, and in light of the result, we will try to summarize our answer to these questions. We begin with a short general history of the most common notion we use today, the priesthood.

* We consistently use the word "order" in the singular to emphasize the oneness of the sacrament within the threefold participation in it by the bishops, the priests, and the deacons.

4.3.2 The General Notion of the Priesthood

The priesthood was not a Christian invention. Its history goes back to the very beginning of humanity (Sabourin, 1973; Goetz, 1956; Haekel, 1963). In general, the idea of the priesthood is connected with some kind of sacrificial act and liturgical worship. In fact, according to the science of comparative religions, an exact definition of the priesthood includes the acts of sacrifices and worship as its essential elements.

This conventional definition, however, does not include all the aspects of the historical priesthood. For instance, among people of preliterate cultures, there were interpreters of oracles, holy men, and guardians of sanctuaries not necessarily connected with sacrificial rites in addition to the sacrificial and liturgical priesthood. Hinduism is an example. Brahman literature, which covers the period from 1000 to 600 BC, describes the priest as a sacrificer, but the Upanishads (from 600 BC) know only the teacher-priest. Another example could be found in the Greek priesthood, where the priest's duty was mostly liturgical and included the administration of a sanctuary, whereas the *collegium pontificum* of the Romans was primarily a college of theologians. The early priest of the Hebrews was most probably not a sacrificer as we find in the later priestly documents but an interpreter of oracles or a soothsayer who used some means such as an ephod. The Hebrew word *kōhēn* means a soothsayer, whereas *levite* means someone attached to a sanctuary.

The most common notion of the priesthood seems to be, therefore, a person who helps his fellows in their life struggle by ministering special assistance. The priest provides a sort of help "there and then" not available by ordinary skill. Priests were always expected to serve the needs of a group. And as the awareness of human needs developed and changed according to the social and cultural conditions of human civilizations, so did the notion of the priest.

On the first level of human civilization, the stage of gathering food by collecting, hunting, or fishing, the priest was to ensure success in finding food or prey. On the second level of civilization, the agricultural and pastoral one, the role of the priest was to control the wind and the rain, to favourably influence the growth of the crops and the fertility of the cattle, and so forth. On the third level, the city civilization, when people were grouped together to form cities and nations, the role of priests changed again. They were expected to save the city or country from its internal opposition (by sanctioning the social castes) or from its external enemies (by proclaiming the enemies of cities to be the enemies of their gods and labelling conflicts as holy wars). And finally, on the fourth level of civilization, with its intellectual and spiritual values (culture in the strict sense), a priest is asked to help individuals in their spiritual needs of knowing, loving, and feeling, mostly through increasing human potentialities and values.

Yet on all levels the needs are limitless. Groups as well as individuals are never satisfied. They want more and more because the many needs reflect one basic need, the need of the endless, whole reality. The many needs are only manifestations of the greatest need, the need for the entire, infinite, and all-powerful reality, generally called God. This essential need for God has been experienced and expressed in human life in many ways according to the social and cultural development of the human race. As a consequence, the very idea of the priesthood, together with the idea of God, has changed with the consciousness of the needs felt by humans. As people have learned to handle their fields and cattle and to organize and defend their cities, they have made different demands upon their priests. The idea of God changed from God the food provider to God the Shepherd or the King and later to Light, Love, Creator, the founding and attracting Alpha and Omega of the entire human consciousness, and so on. Thus the meaning of the priesthood, as related to the meaning of God, was ever changing too. The changing awareness of human needs brings about a change in the concept of God. This automatically causes a crisis in the priesthood of the time. The existing priesthood becomes meaningless if the concept of God becomes irrelevant in the light of an emerging new idea of the ultimate reality and meaning.

Awareness of human needs and with it the idea of God and the priesthood may be dependent upon one's social and cultural development. And yet time, evolution, historical and economic conditions, and so on only bring out and make manifest one permanent need felt by the human race, the need for the whole, for an ultimate reality transcending time and space. So the universal and timeless duty of the priest seems to be what it has always been and always will be, to help man and woman to encounter God. All other activities are subordinated to the primary priestly activity of bringing humanity and God closer together. If one would like to give to people something less than such an encounter with God, the infinite, that person could be a master but would not necessarily be a priest administering uncommon assistance and helping to transcend human skill. The priest is expected to try something that is beyond human reach. He benefits his fellows by helping them in their greatest need, the need for God, the ultimate; the one to whom one reduces and relates everything and whom one does not relate or reduce to anything else; the one in the light of whom one understands whatever one understands and for whom one would sacrifice everything, but whom one would not lose for anything. In short, the priest is the one who is expected to mediate between God and people.

But is this possible? Can a priest help people in their encounter with God? Is there any reasonable chance of achieving what the priest aspires to? As the human race progresses, does not the idea and the need for God, and with it the notion of priesthood, necessarily become obsolete? Is not the idea of priesthood, the idea of making it possible for humans to encounter God, the end of their intense desire for the endless, for the infinite, the fulfillment of which, however, will never be possible, likewise impossible? Is not the function of the priest thus an illusion and necessarily a failure? For a long time the human mind did not think so. But some two thousand years ago there was a small community that realized that for human beings the priesthood is an inevitable failure and nonsense.

4.3.3 The Radical Originality of the Christian Priesthood

4.3.3.1 CHRIST'S PRIESTHOOD IS THE ONLY EFFECTIVE PRIESTHOOD

The first Christians grasped the radical difference between the Christian and non-Christian ideas of priesthood. The old priesthood tried to bring the faithful to God, but it never truly succeeded because it could never really be in touch with God. Yet they found and believed that there was one who had passed through the heavens, now had his throne in heaven, and was seated at the right hand of God the Father. And he was Jesus, the risen Christ, the Son of God (Heb 4, 14–15). He is God as well as man, and therefore in him God has been made accessible to humans. In him all can encounter God since Jesus is priest on earth and in heaven. Witnessing to the faith of an early Christian community, the Letter to the Hebrews ventured to proclaim that the priesthood of Christ is the only effective priesthood. The priests of old have tried but never succeeded in their intentions. Therefore they never ceased to try again and again (cf. Heb 10, 1–3) to do what Christ did and did once for all (Heb 7, 26. 28). He made a meeting with God forever possible by giving to people what they needed: God in the most perfect way. As the fulfillment of all priesthood, he is the only priest who unites humans to God (Heb 7, 15–25; 9, 24; 10, 11–18). The Levitical priesthood could not cleanse the conscience of the people and so could not enable them to approach God, whereas the priesthood of Christ does cleanse the conscience (Heb 10, 22; 9, 14; 10, 18) and does allow people to approach God (Heb 9, 9–14; 10, 1–22).

4.3.3.2 CHRIST'S PRIESTHOOD IS UNIQUE AND ETERNAL

The priesthood of Christ is not only effective but also unique and eternal. Since the risen Christ "dies now no more" but is living still and will for always and therefore is forever able to unite all men and women with God (Heb 7, 23–25), he needs no successor and he is the one and only priest of the New Testament. That being so, the early Christians, while calling the Jewish priests ἱερεὺς, never addressed their own leaders by that name. Indeed, in the New Testament only Christ (Heb 5, 5–6; 7, 11.15.17.21.26; 8, 1.4; 10, 21) and the baptized Christians are called priests (1 Pet 2, 5.9; Rev 1, 6; 5, 10; 20, 6). The risen Christ being himself the living way by which they can go to the Father (Heb 9, 11) because he has made the encounter with the Father possible, Christians may now draw near to God and enter into the very Holy of Holies, that place where the high priest only was permitted to enter, and that only once a year. Christians now have open to them the way to the Eternal Father. They are thus made priests by Christ (Rev 1, 6; 5, 10), and they do not need a priest, as non-Christians do, in order to meet God. In their encounter with God, then, they can intercede for themselves and for anyone else.

Christians do so, however, with and in Christ, who by his incarnation made God accessible to all and who exercises his priestly mission in Christians as well as in their apostles. Since Christ is the only priest, the ministry of Christians as well as that of the apostles (*LG*, no. 21; Tanner, 1990, 864–5; *PO*, no. 5; Tanner, 1047) is based upon the active priestly presence of the risen Christ. The active priestly presence of the risen Christ in the apostles and their successors was different from that in the Christian faithful. Accordingly, there were two different participations in the unique priesthood of Christ.

4.3.3.3 PARTICIPATION IN THE ONE PRIESTHOOD OF CHRIST

Since there is one and eternal priest, who is alive and exercises his priesthood even today, any priesthood in the New Testament can be only a participation in the one priesthood of Christ. The reason, therefore, for the sacrament of order must be that the one and eternal Priest presented in the New Testament exercises his priesthood in the midst of his priestly people as the head of his mystical priestly body. The distinction between the ministerial and the common priesthood is based upon the distinction between the Head and his mystical body.

4.3.3.4 THE COMMON PRIESTHOOD OF THE FAITHFUL

The Christian faithful are real priests (1 Pet 2, 9) because Christ is present in them as High Priest forming his Church, his mystical body. He perfects them for a work of ministry (Eph 4, 11), supplying to each "joint, fastening and growth" (Eph 4, 15–16). Through Christ they offer spiritual sacrifices acceptable to God (1 Pet 2, 5; Heb 13, 13–16; Rom 12, 1). Christians, as messianic people, are the collaborators of Christ in carrying out his mission. They are expected to be the light of the world and the salt of the earth (Mt 5, 3–16; *LG*, no. 9; Tanner, 1990, 855–6). Yet whatever they do, they do in virtue of the living Christ. All those who believe in him will do the works that he does, still more because he is in heaven at the right hand of the Father (Jn 14, 12). Through their good works and their love, the world will recognize and glorify God (Mt 5, 16) and enter the very presence of the living God.

Thus according to the New Testament, Christians share the effective priesthood of Christ because they can bring men and women to God and help them effectively to meet God. The Second Vatican Council describes in detail how Christians exercise their priesthood (*LG*, nos. 10–12; Tanner, 1990, 856–7). They share in the priestly, prophetic, and royal office of Christ (*AA*, nos. 2–4; Tanner, 1990, 982–5), and as the clergy's fellow workers for the truth (*AA*, no. 6; Tanner, 985–6; cf. 3 Jn 8), they administer to others the grace they have received (*PO*, no. 6; Tanner, 1049), which manifests to all the Saviour's living presence in the world (*GS*, no. 48; Tanner, 1102).

The sacrament of the common priesthood of the faithful is the sacrament of baptism with the sacrament of confirmation. Thus the two sacraments, the sacrament of baptism and the sacrament of order, are the foundations of the structure of the Church, made up of the faithful and of the apostles. The Church is the body of Christ, and Christ is the head of his Church. The sacrament of order is the sacrament of Christ's call inviting every human being to enter into the dialogue of faith with God, and the sacrament of the baptism is the sacrament of faith answering that call, as victorious efficiency of Christ's call through his apostles.

A correlation of the common priesthood of the faithful to the ministerial priesthood of the apostles will provide a further understanding of the priesthood of all Christians.

4.3.3.5 THE MINISTERIAL PRIESTHOOD OF THE APOSTLES AND THEIR SUCCESSORS

Within the body of believers in whom Christ was present as High Priest, there were some called apostles: first of all the Twelve (Mt 10, 2; Mk 6, 30; Lk 6, 13; 9, 1.10; 22, 14), then the primary apostles (2 Cor 11, 5; 12, 11; cf. Gal 1, 17.19), probably those who received their mission immediately from Christ, and finally, the apostles without further precision, seemingly those who were chosen by the primary apostles (Rom 16, 7; 1 Cor 9, 5; 2 Cor 8, 23). It is interesting to note that ἀποστόλος in the New Testament always means a person who is sent and never an object. This is different from its use as adjective in classical Greek (Rengstorf, 1985, 424–54). In the Greek Septuagint the word ἀποστόλος in 1 Kings 14, 6 is a rendering of the Hebrew *šělĩah*, which is the closest term to the "apostle" of the New

Testament. It seems that Greek supplied the term, but the meaning was taken from the Jewish *šělīah*.

According to rabbinical usage, *šělīah* means a representative of a person sending someone on a mission. This meaning of the term gave rise to the proverb in the Talmud, "A man's *šělīah* is, as it were, himself" (*Berakoth* 5, 5; Strack and Billerbeck, 1926, 3, 2). Thus the very notion of *šělīah* lies in a representation of one person by another. In John 13, 20 there is a real identity between Jesus and his apostle. In Hebrews 3, 1 Jesus himself is called "apostle." It means both that he was sent by the Father and that the Father himself speaks and acts in him and through him. According to Mark 9, 41, Matthew 10, 40, and Luke 10, 16, the apostles should be treated like Jesus himself. What is done to them is done to Jesus. The disciples were sent out on a mission to represent Jesus. Their actions proved that they were really representatives, *šělīah*, of Jesus. To be *šělīah* meant more than the simple action of doing a specific work. The man in Mark 9, 38 and Luke 9, 49 casts out demons in the name of Jesus, as did the apostles. However, he was not an apostle because he was not sent by Jesus. Although he did the work of Jesus, he could not do it as *šělīah*, that is, in the person of Jesus.

The apostles were aware that they were *šělīah* of Jesus and that Jesus stood behind their works and words. The miracles performed by them were done by Jesus. And that was the reason why the central point of their preaching was the faith of their hearers in the risen Christ and not their achievement as preachers . Their words were not their words but the words of Jesus Christ (cf. 1 Th 2, 13). They were aware that Jesus was continuing his work in them unto the very end of the world (2 Cor 5, 20).

The idea of *šělīah*-apostle, which marked off the apostles from the other members of the Church, was later expressed by the term *in persona Christ.* The apostles and their successors shared in the priesthood of Christ to such a degree that in them Jesus worked as the head of the Church. Cyprian defined the priest of the New Testament as one who truly acts in place of Christ (*Ep.* 63, 14; PL, 4, 386; Cyprian, 1871, 713), and John Chrysostom said that a priest lends only his tongue to Christ and offers him his hand (*In Joannem homilia,* 86, 4; PG, 59, 473), but the acting priest is Christ. For Ambrose the priest is only a visible image of the Christ who offers the sacrifice (*In Psalmum* 38, 25–6; PL, 14, 1051–2).

The Second Vatican Council used the expression *in persona Christ* as distinctive of the ministerial priesthood. The faithful exercise their priesthood and their mission in the name of the Church (GS, no. 76; Tanner, 1124; SC, no. 85; Tanner, 845) or in the name of the pastor and bishop (AG, no. 16; Tanner, 1026), as distinct from the moment when they act in their own name as citizens (GS, no. 76; Tanner, 1124). Only the bishops and the priests can act in the person of Christ (SC, no. 7, 33; Tanner, 822, 827; LG, no. 10.21.28; Tanner, 857, 865, 872; *PO*, no. 13; Tanner, 1059). For an explanation, the Council of Trent is quoted as saying that "the same Jesus Christ who then offered himself on the cross is now making his offering through the ministry of the priest" (*SC*, no. 7; Tanner, 822). The bishops, by virtue of the sacrament of order, are "vicars or legates of Christ" who have the power of governing, which is the proper, ordinary, immediate power of governing "personally" and not by jurisdiction from the pope (*LG*, no. 27; Tanner, 871). The apostles and their successors were designated by Christ to teach, to sanctify, and to rule in the name "and power" of Christ (*AA*, no. 2, Tanner, 982). The departments of the Roman Curia may operate in the name and with the power of the Roman pontiff (*CD*, no. 9; Tanner, 923), but there is no text that says they act in the person of Roman pontiff. It seems, therefore, that to act in the person of Christ means more than to act in his name. It means what the biblical *šělīah* signified: a real presence of the commissioner, the risen Christ, through his representative. Since Christ is the one who acts in and through the priests, Vatican II consistently called the priesthood of bishops and priests a "ministerial priesthood" in contradistinction to the common priesthood of the faithful (*LG*, no. 10; Tanner, 857). Terminology such as "passive-active" and "personal-sacramental" were carefully ignored by Vatican II. The priesthood of the faithful is equally active and sacramental, and the priesthood of the bishops and of the priests is as passive and personal as the priesthood of the faithful. Through the term "ministerial priesthood," the permanent activity of Christ, the only priest seeking men and women "here and now," at this time and in this place, is indicated. By the reception of order, one becomes a living "minister" of Christ, the Eternal Priest, and so representative of the person of Christ himself, who is carrying out his work of uniting the whole human family (*PO*, no. 12; Tanner, 1057–8) through his ministers (*PO*, no. 14; Tanner, 1060). Only Jesus can carry out what the priest seems to do daily in the Church for the salvation of the human family. Transubstantiation, remission of sin, and justification of any human being by the indwelling Trinity are due solely to the risen Christ, the one and only priest. The ministerial priesthood means, therefore, that the priest is first of all a minister of Christ.

To cast a little more light on the relation of the unique priesthood of Christ to that of the faithful and to that of his ministers, Pius XII, in his encyclical *Mediator Dei*, quoted more than once by the council, said that the priest receives "by virtue of his ordination, through the imposition of hands, the power of being assimilated to the Sovereign Priest in such a way that he represents the person of Our Lord Jesus Christ inasmuch as he is the head of all the members and offers for all of them" (Pius XII, 1947, 538–9) and distinguished in it a descending and ascending movement. In the downward movement Christ places himself as victim upon the altar, and in the upward movement Christ as victim is offered to the Father (ibid., 554–6). In each action, Christ, his minister, and the faithful are actively present, and the mass is an act of Christ and of the Church (*PO*, no. 13; Tanner, 1990, 1059) but each in a different way. In the descending movement the risen Christ as the victim is present on the altar under the species of bread and wine and places himself in the hands of the faithful as an offering to be given to the Father. At this moment Christ is using the ministry of the priest, who is lending his intentions, his tongue, and his hands to Christ, thus representing before the people the person of Jesus Christ, the one and only High Priest. The faithful in this action do not exercise their priesthood except by consenting in the name of the Church, like Mary at the moment of the Incarnation, to the presentation of Christ as victim. In the ascending movement Christ, with the ministers and the faithful, offers himself to the Father. Here the minister and the faithful really offer Christ as the most pleasing offering to the Father. This is the high point of the priesthood of the faithful.

We may say, therefore, that in some sense the "ministerial" priesthood is less than the common, "royal" priesthood of the faithful. The ministers do not act in their own person in the descending movement of Christ and therefore seem "less" priests than when in the ascending movement they act like the faithful in their own person. The distinction that St Thomas Aquinas makes with regard to grace and nature may be enlightening when we apply it to the priesthood of the minister and the priesthood of the faithful (*Summa theol.*, 1–2, q 110, a 2, ad 2 and ad 3). In a sense, the priesthood of the faithful is more a priesthood than the priesthood of the minister. It may be considered nobler in its subsistence since it is more independent in its being. Without losing its participation character, it is the faithful's own priesthood. Therefore it is more a priesthood in itself than the priesthood of the ministers, for the latter belongs, rather, to the personal priesthood of Christ. Therefore the ministerial priesthood is nobler, not as a subsisting priesthood, but as an expression or sign of the "here and now," actively functioning, eternal High Priest, the risen Christ. We can say, therefore, that the participation according to which the faithful and the minister as minister share Christ's priesthood differs not only in degree but in essence (*LG*, no. 10; Tanner, 1990, 857). The priesthood of the faithful lifts up the believing Church as a real priestly community on behalf of Christ, and the priesthood of the minister lifts up the person of Christ as a real priest living and acting now. The mystical body of Christ, by virtue of its head, together with Christ as head of the Church, that is, the whole Christ, fulfills in its own name the priestly function of bringing the human race to God. And yet only by virtue of the sacrament of order, in the degree of the episcopate, the priesthood, or the diaconate, will the faithful be empowered to unite themselves to Christ, so that Christ can be in them to act as head of his Church.

By having said this, we have described the nature of the sacrament of order, not from the point of view of its functions, but from the point of view of the unique eternal priesthood of the risen Christ. The deacon, the priest, and the bishop are, by virtue of the sacrament, empowered to surrender to Christ in such a way that in any of them Christ, the one and only priest, as head of the Church is able to perform his mission. In them and through them the active sacramental and personal presence of the risen Christ as head of his Church is sacramentally realized. The bishop, the priest, and the deacon become successors of the apostles, the *šělīah* of Christ, acting in the person of Christ since in them as in an "instrument," or agent, the risen Christ personally fulfills his mission given to him by the Father.

4.3.3.6 BISHOPS AND PRIESTS

THE FIRST CENTURY

The title *ἐπισκόπος* occurs in the New Testament five times (Acts 20, 28; Phil 1, 1; 1 Tim 3, 2; Tit 1, 7; 1 Pet 2, 25) and is applied mostly to the *πρεσβυτέρους* or "elders" of the Church. This latter term is mentioned nineteen times, mostly after the apostles of second degree in leadership (Acts 11, 30; 14, 23; 15, 2.4.6.22.23; 16, 4; 20, 17; 21, 18; 1 Tim 4, 14; 5, 17.19; Tit 1, 5; Jas 5, 14; 1 Pet 5, 1; 2 Jn 1; 3 Jn 1). The bishops of Acts 20, 28 are the presbyters from Ephesus. In Titus 1, 7 the word "bishop" is the collective name of the presbyters whom Titus had to appoint in every town (Tit 1, 5). The picture of the bishop in 1 Timothy 3, 2 corresponds to the qualifications of the presbyters of Titus 1, 5–9. In Philippians 1, 1, Paul and Timothy salute the deacons immediately after the bishops (refer also to 1 Timothy 3, 2.8). Since we know that all churches had presbyters, the omission of them in the salutation of Paul and Timothy would be inexplicable if the term ἐπίσκοπος did not designate the presbyters at Philippi. Paul and Barnabas appointed presbyters in each church (cf. Acts 14, 23). Presbyters are in Jerusalem (Acts 15, 2.4.6.22.23; 16, 4; 21, 18), Judea (Acts 11, 30), Lystra, Iconium, Antioch, and Ephesus (1 Tim 5, 5.17.19), Crete (1 Tim 1, 5), the dispersion (Jas 5, 14), and Pontus, Galatia, and Cappadocia (1 Pet 1, 1). Moreover, the first church assembly in Jerusalem mentions only the apostles and presbyters. The term "bishop" is not mentioned (cf. Acts 15, 2–35; 16, 4; 21, 18).

It is noteworthy that the twofold enumeration of apostles and presbyters, bishops and deacons, is the usual enumeration of the New Testament. There is no text anywhere in the New Testament that explicitly gives a threefold enumeration of the leaders of the Church. The terms *presbyteros* and *episcopos* are apparently identical also in the Church described by the author of the *Didache* and by Clement of Rome. "Presbyter" is not referred to in the *Didache*. After having dealt with the celebration of the Eucharist, the author exhorts the people to choose bishops and deacons. Since chapter 15 is connected with *οὖν*, therefore, it is clear that the reason for the election of bishops and deacons is to continue the celebration of the Eucharist (*Didache,* 15, 1; Funk, 1901, 32–4). Clement of Rome called the leaders of the Church *προηγουμένους* (Cor 21, 6; Funk, 1901, 128) and named as presbyters (Cor 47, 6; 54, 2; 57, 1; Funk, 1901, 160, 168, 172) as well as bishops (Cor 42, 4; 44, 4; Funk, 1901, 152, 156) those who in the next lines are called again presbyters (Cor 44, 5; Funk, 1901, 156) and who served the community well and might not be removed from the episcopal office (*leiturgia*). The leaders *προηγουμένους* (Cor 1, 3; Funk, 1901, I, 100) are not identical with the old Corinthians.

Thus it seems that the hierarchy of the first century consisted of the apostles and their vicars, the presbyter-bishops and deacons. Although as local hierarchy, the presbyter-bishops had the same powers as the bishops of our day, in the lifetime of the apostles they were not yet successors of the apostles in the full sense but only vicars of the apostles. The apostles, such as Paul, were in constant contact with the churches they founded. This was the case in the Pauline churches. But it was not unknown in a Johannine church (3 Jn 11; Horvath, 1974, 339–40). After the death of the apostles, the presbyter-bishops became the successors of the apostles, and one of them fulfilled the duty of the founding apostle after the model of the Father or Jesus, but not that of the Apostles' College. This structure was attested to by Ignatius of Antioch only in the second century.

THE SECOND CENTURY

In the second century the terms *presbyteros* and *episcopos* are for the most part still synonymous. There is no sign of any limitation on the power of the presbyter. Any superiority of the bishop over the presbyter like that of the following centuries was not known up to this time. The difference was, rather, functional, as the use of the terms *presbyteros* and *episcopos* at that time indicates. The term "presbyter" really signified the status or dignity of the persons. The term *episcopos* indicated the duty of the same persons, who seemingly carried out the official duties in turn. During this time a deacon was the helper of the bishop as well as of the presbyter. The diaconate was the second order in a twofold ministry.

Ignatius of Antioch, in his letters to the different churches, asked from the faithful obedience to bishops, to presbyters, and to deacons (*Tralles,* 2, 1; 3, 1; 7, 2; Funk, 1901, 242, 244, 246; *Smyrna,* 8; Funk, 1901, 282; *Magnesia,* 7; Funk, 1901, 236; *Philadelphia,* 6, 1; Funk, 1901, 270). To the council of the presbyters, he recommended that they should be in harmony with the bishop like strings with a harp (*Ephesus,* 4, 1; Funk, 1901, 216). In fact, the presbyter of Ignatius of Antioch seemed more like a coadjutor bishop of our day rather than a presbyter of today. It should be noted that Ignatius, in order to describe the office of the bishop and of deacon, looks for various models, whereas he has no uncertainty or hesitation with regard to presbyter. At one time he says that a bishop should be modelled on the Father (*Magnesia,* 6, 1; Funk, 1901, 216; *Tralles,* 3, 1; Funk, 1901, 244). At another time he says he should be modelled after Christ (*Tralles,* 2, 1; Funk, 1901, 242). So is the deacon, who having the ministry of Christ (*Magnesia,* 6, 1; Funk, 1901, 234), is the minister of the Church (*Tralles,* 2, 3; Funk, 1901, 244; *Smyrna,* 8; Funk, 1901, 282). The bishop's rule is monarchical. There is no valid celebration of the Eucharist without the bishop or someone else who has the permission of the bishop (*Smyrna,* 8; Funk, 1901, 282). Yet besides the bishop we find the collective name προκαθηένους for the leaders of the church (*Magnesia,* 6, 2–7, 1; Funk, 1901, 232–4). They are the successors of the apostles, modelled on the apostles and mentioned always in connection with the apostles. They are the college or *σύνδεσμον* (*Tralles,* 3, 1; Funk, 1901, 244), the council or *συνέδριον* (*Magnesia,* 6, 1; Funk, 1901, 234), and the faithful must follow them as they would the apostles (*Magnesia,* 6, 1; Funk, 1901, 234).

As in the first, so in the second century the Church is made up of the apostles and the faithful. The apostles are the *šělĩah* of Christ, who will be called priest in the third century. The term may be new, but the content is Christological. The notion of the term "priest" is to be understood in the sense of the *šělĩah*-apostles of the New Testament and not in the sense of the Greek ἱερεὺς, priest. It is not correct, therefore, to think that there was no priesthood in the first century. To avoid an easy misunderstanding of the newness of Christ's priesthood was the reason that early Christian writers avoided applying the Greek word ἱερεὺς, priests, to the leaders of the Church. As it was indicated above, precisely to underline the newness, they formed a new word, "apostle," by changing an adjective to a noun.

The so-called *Second Letter of Clement to the Corinthians* does not mention the bishop or any other leader in the Church except Christ (14, 3; Funk, 1901, 202), Saviour and author of immortality (20, 5; Funk, 1901, 210). In Justin's writings, although the sacrificial character of the Eucharistic meal is clearly described, he names not the bishop or presbyter but the *προεστῶς*, president, who pronounces the words over the water and wine (*Apologies* 1 65, 67; Falls, 1948, 105–6).

Irenaeus, in his book *Against Heresies* (1867), explicitly names the presbyters as successors of the apostles who through their episcopal succession received the sure charisma of truth (4, 26, 5; 1867, 464–5). We may recall here that the Second Vatican Council could rightly apply to the bishops what Irenaeus said about presbyters (*DV*, no. 7; Tanner, 1990, 974). Synonymity of the terms "bishop" and "presbyter" is most evident in the following parallel texts of Irenaeus: "the apostolic tradition is conserved in the Church by the succession of the presbyters" and "the tradition which comes through the succession of the bishops" (Irenaeus, 1867, 260–1). Therefore it seems obvious that for Irenaeus the term *episcopos* still means the office rather than the person who carries out that office. In his letter to Pope Victor on the matter of Easter observance which Eusebius handed down to us, the successors of Peter – Pius, Telesphorus, and Xystus – are called simply presbyters of Rome who presided over the Church (Eusebius, *Church History*, 5, 24; PG, 20, 505).

THE THIRD AND FOLLOWING CENTURIES

From the third century on, we have several documents that mention limitations in the power of the presbyters. The superiority of the bishop becomes more and more explicit. The nature of this superiority has been discussed and argued about from then on until the Second Vatican Council. The presbyters gradually become helpers of the bishops. They can help the bishop not only in his missionary work, as the deacons did, but also in his ministry of celebrating mass and administering sacraments. This new form of diaconate appeared to be more useful than the older form. And as a result, from this time on, the deacons played a less and less important role and the diaconate began to lose its raison d'être and went into decline.

It seems that the leaders of the Church, the presbyters and bishops, were called priests for the first time in the third century (Tertullian, 1954, 7, 2, 1024–5; Dix, 1937, 4–6; Cyprian, 1871, no. 63, 3, 715). As the number of the faithful grew and Christianity gained social status, it was necessary to explain who the Christians were and what their leaders were up to. Being by now conscious that their leaders were unlike the priests of the Roman Empire but in order to let the world know what they were, they found the terms *hiereus* and *sacerdos* more helpful. Yes, they said, their presbyters and bishops were priests and the deacons were their assistants. As the term "priest" gained more acceptance, theological reflection concentrated more on the notion of priesthood, and the doctrine of the sacrament of order became identical with the doctrine of priesthood.

In light of the progressive development of the third century, we can understand that in order to describe the relationship of the leaders of the Church to the faithful, Tertullian introduced the term *ordo,* which had a definite meaning in the social life of that time. It had a collective sense and meant, first of all, the great social high-class orders of Rome, the senators and equestrians. For Tertullian, therefore, *ordo* did not mean the reception of some degree or power but, rather, an admittance into the group or college of the ministers of the Church. Though the idea of order as hierarchical ranks, as we find it in Pseudo-Dionysius influenced by Neoplatonism, was not familiar to Tertullian, he nevertheless admitted a functional superiority of bishops over presbyters. In concluding his treatise on baptism, he says that the bishop has the right to give baptism. So do presbyters and deacons, but always with the bishop's authority. Tertullian did not give the apostolic tradition as his reason. Rather, his reason was the honour of the Church and peace. Otherwise, he said, the episcopal office might become the mother of schism (*De baptismo*, Tertullian, 1954, 17, 1; *CSEL*, 1, 291).

The reason given by Tertullian actually suggests that presbyters also belonged to the episcopal office. In the case of necessity, besides the bishops, presbyters, and deacons, a baptized layman can also baptize, for what is equally received can be equally given. This Tertullian principle will later on in the thirteenth to the fifteenth centuries be called the principle of *adminiculo habiti sacramenti*. In the fifteenth century this principle will be applied to the sacrament of order and allow the ordination of presbyter by presbyter.

Hippolytus of Rome, in his *Apostolic Tradition*, describes separately the ordination of bishop, priest, and deacon. For him the distinction between bishop and presbyter lies in the fact that presbyters cannot ordain (Dix, 1937, 15), unlike bishops, who receive by their ordination the power of being high priest (ibid., 5).

The constitution of the Church in Egypt has no special prayer for the ordination of a presbyter. This lack is also suggested by Hippolytus when he says in chapter 8 that "when a presbyter is ordained, the bishop shall lay his hand upon his head ... and so pray for him according to the aforementioned form which we gave before over the bishop" (Dix, 1937, 13). It looks, therefore, as if presbyters share completely in the priesthood of Christ, and the distinction between bishops and presbyters would be rather disciplinary (Lécuyer, 1953, 41n39).The function reserved to bishops is not permitted to presbyters, but as yet there is no question about the validity of these functions if they are performed without the bishop's permission.

By the fourth century we find more and more documents limiting the functions of the presbyter. The Council of Ancyra (AD 314) states in canon 13, "Neither a chorbishop nor a presbyter of the city, without the permission of the bishop, is allowed to ordain presbyters and deacons in an alien parish" (Mansi, 1889–1927, 2, 518). It seems, therefore, that presbyters could ordain within the limits of their own parish and in another parish with permission of the bishop. Chorbishops, bishops of a country district who already had episcopal ordination (cf. Council of Antioch, canon 10), ordained mostly for the villages and countryside. In canon 13 of the same council we find the same prohibition for the presbyters of a city (ibid., 2, 1311). The expression *neque urbis presbyteris* of that same canon gives the impression that the presbyters of the city were above the chorbishops.

The Council of Neo-Caesarea went further and did not allow a country priest to celebrate in the presence of the bishop or in the presence of the presbyters of the city (canon 13; Mansi, 1889–1927, 2, 541). This ruling suggests that the prohibition did not yet touch the question of validity, for there is no doubt that country priests could celebrate by virtue of their ordination.

Epiphanius, in his *Refutations of All the Heresies* (around 370), states that presbyters and bishops are not equal (75, 4; PG, 42, 508). Arius was wrong, therefore, in saying that presbyters and bishops are equal in order of honour and dignity (ibid., 75.1–3; PG, 42, 504–5). The bishop is father and master by virtue of his ordination, whereas the presbyters with the deacons are the sons who are to administer the business of the church, ἐκκλησιαστικά δύνανται (ibid. 75, 5; PG, 42, 508).

From the fourth century on, the Church was becoming more and more aware of an existing distinction between bishop and priest since some heretics such as Arius denied any actual difference. Jerome did not consider himself heretical when, though recognizing the existing differences, he was certain that these had not existed from the beginning. According to him, they were introduced by the Church to remedy schism and to prevent any individual from rending the Church of Christ by drawing it to himself. Bishops and presbyters were the same in the beginning, but later one presbyter was chosen to preside over the rest (*Epistula*, 146; PL, 22, 1194).

In this Isidore of Seville agrees with Jerome *(De ecclesiasticis officiis,* 2, 7; PL, 83, 787). Amalarius of Metz, about 840, says the same. It is not from the disposition of the Lord but from a custom of the Church that the bishop is over the presbyters and that presbyters are subject to the bishop (*De libris et officiis ecclesiasticis,* 2, 13; PL, 105, 1091). The superiority of the bishop over the presbyter is no longer in question. However, the origin and nature of this superiority is discussed. Later the sacramental character of this superiority will be denied by several scholastic theologians.

From the third century on, as we have seen, the leaders of the Church were called priests, and it was natural that the essence of the apostolic succession was more and more understood in the light of the priesthood. A bishop would be called a priest of the first order, and the presbyter a priest of the second order. When the theology of the sacraments had been elaborated by scholastic theologians, the term "order" became synonymous with the sacrament of priesthood. Hugh of St Victor, Peter Lombard, and St Thomas Aquinas could not see in the episcopate anything more than dignity. "The episcopate is not an order in the sense in which order is a sacrament," says St Thomas Aquinas, "because a bishop is not more a priest than the presbyter" (*Summa theol., suppl.,* q 40, a 5, ad 2). Since the order is related to the sacrament of the Eucharist, in this regard a bishop has no greater power than a priest. The superiority of a bishop is not in relation to the sacrament of the priesthood but, rather, in relation to those sacred actions of the mystical body of Christ that do not belong to the sacrament. Thus it seems that the episcopate has been thrust out of the sacrament of order on the ground of that notion which the first Christians so assiduously refused to apply to their leaders, that is, the priesthood.

With the priesthood related exclusively to the Eucharist, there is another aspect that from the Middle Ages on has caused difficulty concerning the sacramentality of the episcopate. This is ordination of presbyters by presbyters. Hippolytus of Rome and Jerome had admitted that the main difference between presbyter and bishop was that the presbyter could not ordain as did the bishop. But now this power of ordaining did not seem to be so exclusive. Ordinations of priests by other priests took place with the knowledge of popes and were not limited to a certain period.

In the fifth century Cassianus, in his *Collationes* (4, 1; PL, 49, 583–5), stated that Paphnutius, presbyter, ordained his deacon, Daniel, to the priesthood. In the eighth century Willehadus and Liudgerus seem to have ordained presbyters long before their own episcopal consecration (*Monumenta,* 1829, 381–3, 411). In the thirteenth century, in *Glossa Ordinaria in Decretum Gratiani,* we find the principle of *ex delegato Papae et adminiculo habiti sacramenti,* by the delegation of the pope and by the power of the received sacrament, which allowed Popes Boniface IX (*DS*, nos. 1145–6), Martin V (*DS*, no. 1290), and Innocent VIII (*DS*, no. 1435) to delegate ordaining powers to presbyters. According to this principle, each person can confer the sacrament that he has received if the pope gives him delegation. This principle, admitted by many canonists, appeared in the edition of *Gratian's Decrees* published in 1572–85, on the order of Pope Gregory XIII. G. Vasquez mentions that in India some Cistercian and Benedictine abbots could confer all orders except the priesthood in virtue of their papal bulls (Thomas Aquinas, 1929, 6, 243n5).

The question of whether the pope has this kind of power or not has been discussed in the twentieth century as well (Horvath, 1968, 271n81). Those who deny this power generally argue that if a priest could ordain a priest, then there would be no difference between a priest and a bishop, since nothing of the episcopal function could not be fulfilled by a priest. Some theologians, however, said that in spite of the validity of the ordination made by priests, the superiority of the episcopal order is not yet at issue since there is no case of episcopal ordination conferred by a priest. But then others have asked, Is there any need for episcopal ordination if a priest can ordain a priest? Why should the sacramental episcopal ordination be kept if its exclusive function, the ordination of a priest, is not at all exclusive?

The divergence that has existed in the thoughts of theologians and in the Church through the centuries about such a basic institution as the episcopate is surprising. It is no wonder therefore that the Second Vatican Council decided to solve the problem (*LG*, no. 18; Tanner, 1990, 863). The sacramentality of the episcopate was vindicated by the council. Its reality was defined, not exclusively in relation to the priestly function in the

Eucharist, but in relation to the whole mission of Christ. Unlike the priest (*LG*, no. 28; Tanner, 872), the bishop has the fullness of the priesthood (*LG*, no. 41; Tanner, 881), as well as the fullness of the sacrament of order (*LG*, no. 26; Tanner, 870). The bishops are considered successors of the apostles and are entrusted with the whole mission of Christ. In virtue of the sacrament of order, they are incorporated into the episcopal body, preside over the people of God, and take over "the office of the apostles of nourishing the church" (*LG*, no. 20; Tanner, 15–20). The priesthood is, then, one of several missions which Christ received from his Father and which he now exercises through and in his ministers.

Christ, sent by his Father, made the bishops partakers of his consecration and his mission through the apostles and their successors. Thus the ecclesiastical ministry is divinely established, and the bishops, by divine institution, have taken the place of the apostles as shepherds of the Church (*LG*, no. 20; Tanner, 1990, 864; *CD*, no. 20; Tanner, 928). But the question arises as to whether it is by divine institution that this divinely instituted ministry has been handed on to different individuals with varying degrees of participation to be exercised at different levels by bishops, priests, and deacons.

History places many difficulties against an easy yes. The Council of Trent, canon 6, on *The Sacrament of Orders* (Tanner, 1990, 744), states that if anyone says that in the Catholic Church there is not a hierarchy, instituted by divine ordinance and consisting of bishops, priests, and ministers, let him be anathema. The canon deals with order as a sacrament; therefore the difference between priest and bishop is meant sacramentally and not juridically. Now this sacramental hierarchy exists in the Church by divine ordinance.

Several members of that council proposed that instead of *ordinatio divina*, the cannon should refer to *divina institutio*, divine institution, or "by institution of Christ," or at least by "peculiar divine ordinance," since, as they said, everything on earth happens "by divine ordinance." These amendments, however, were not accepted by the majority of the council (*CT*, 1964, 3, 684–91). Divine ordinance does not, in this instance, say anything more than the providence of God. Therefore the divine institution of the hierarchy in its present form of bishops, presbyters, and deacons has not been defined. (The English translation of *divina ordinatio*, by divine appointment, in Tanner, 1990, 744, may be misleading; "appointment" means "institution," rather than divine providence.)

The Second Vatican Council did not intend to decide this question. There is a sentence in the *Dogmatic Constitution on the Church* which seems to indicate that the composers of the constitution may have been inclined to the opinion that the difference between bishop and priest was introduced by the successors of the apostles, rather than by the apostles themselves. In no. 28 (Tanner, 1990, 872) we read the following, "Christ, whom the Father sanctified and sent into the world (see Jn 10, 36), has through his apostles made their successors, the bishops, share in his consecration and mission; and *these legitimately handed on the office of their ministry in varying degrees*" (italics added). The original Latin text reads, "Christus ... apostolos suos, eorum successores ... qui munus ministerii sui, vario gradu, variis subjectis in ecclesia legitieme tradiderunt" (ibid.).

SUMMING UP

Our historical survey suggests that Christ has entrusted his mission to the apostles and made them fully partakers of it. The apostles passed it on to their successors, the bishops, who share Christ's complete mission. Through the sacrament of order instituted by Christ, the risen Christ himself exercises his mission in his minister, the bishop, a successor of the apostles. The bishop, therefore, has not only the fullness of the priesthood but also the fullness of Christ's mission. As successor of the apostles, he receives from the Lord the mission to teach all the nations and to preach the gospel to every creature, which is pre-eminent among his principal duties (*LG*, no. 24; Tanner, 1990, 868). Bishops sanctify the faithful by the sacraments, especially *praesertim*, by offering the Eucharist. They govern the particular churches entrusted to them. They are not vicars of the Roman pontiffs but presidents, *antistites*, of the people they govern. They have the duty also to help the faithful by the example of their manner of life and, as the successors of the apostles, to give their lives for their sheep (cf. 1 Pet 5, 3; *LG*, no. 41, Tanner, 881), a grace not mentioned in connection with priestly ordination.

In view of the growing Church, the sacramental order of the episcopate was divided into varying degrees so that some would possess the episcopal mission in its fullness while others shared in Christ's mission as priests and deacons (*LG*, no. 8; Tanner, 1990, 72). By virtue of the sacrament of the presbyterate, a priest as helper and sharer in the episcopal order shepherds the faithful and makes the bishop, as well as the universal Church, present in the local congregation of the faithful. Thus the presbyter governs and sanctifies under the bishop's authority. This authority of the bishop is not merely juridical since it is based upon sacrament of the order. On the ground of this sacramental sharing of the episcopate, the bishop is father of the priests (*LG*, no. 28; Tanner, 873).

By sharing in the mission of Christ, the presbyter is not only a priest to offer the Eucharistic sacrifice, which is his *praecipium*, chief duty (*PO*, no. 13; Tanner, 1990, 1059). He is also a minister of God's word. He has to preach the divine word to all, which being one of the *paecipua*, principal duties, of the bishop (*LG*, no. 25; Tanner, 869), is also a *primum*, primary duty, of the priest as co-worker with the bishop (*LG*, no. 28, Tanner, 872; *PO*, no. 4, Tanner, 1046). The priest also exercises the function of Christ as shepherd and head, and so he is really and truly a friend and father in Christ to the faithful (*LG*, no. 28; Tanner, 873).

The difference between bishop and presbyter, therefore, is based upon differing participation in the sacrament of order, which in its original form is the order of the apostles. Because of the priest's participation in the same order, he is a minister of the bishop, a concept well-known from the diaconate of the early Church. The form of helping the bishops, however, as we now have in the order of presbyterate, was not known in the first centuries. Under the providence of God, the Church modified it to the way we have it now. The earliest assistants and co-workers of the bishops were known as deacons, and their participation in the apostolic-episcopal order was somewhat different. It is time now to review the history of the first ministers of the bishops, that of the deacons.

4.3.3.7 DEACONS

Vatican II reaffirmed that the diaconate is conferred by sacrament (*LG*, no. 29; Tanner, 1990, 874). From what we have said about the nature of the sacrament of order, it follows that by virtue of sacramental ordination a deacon can act in the person of Christ. The deacon too becomes *šĕlĭah* of Christ since in him as a living instrument the risen Christ, as head of the mystical body, personally fulfills the mission given to him by the Father. This is what the sacramental ordination of a deacon has in common with that of a bishop or a priest. The sacrament of order is one sacrament, and its meaning must be the same for the bishop, for the priest, and for the deacon. Yet at the same time it must have something that is different from the other two. What is it? A deacon cannot say mass, yet he is ordained by the same sacrament of order. What is the diaconate for?

There was a time when the permanent diaconate was not found necessary in the life of the Church. It was just a step towards the priesthood. The Council of Trent ordered the restoration of the permanent diaconate but without success. It was not found to be necessary. The reason why Trent had called for its restoration was not pastoral need but antagonism. The Reformers had denied this order; therefore it had to be reaffirmed. The Second Vatican Council again requested its restoration. Most theologians would agree that the growing shortage of priests is not and cannot be of itself sufficient reason for the restoration and subsistence of a permanent diaconate. It must have a special mission that is an essential part of Christ's mission. What is it? We cannot say, briefly, that it is service, the *diaconia*, in the life of the Church. Why should the deacon be the humble servant par excellence of Christ and not also the priest and the bishop? Do they not share in the ministerial priesthood of Christ? On the ground of their greater share, are not bishops and priests even more than deacons the servants of Christ, the eternal High Priest? If the reason for the disappearance of the permanent diaconate was the creation of a new form of diaconate from the third century on, that is, the presbyterate in its new form, which made the old form of diaconate unnecessary, is the reason of that time forceful in our time as well? Is there now a special need for rediscovering a neglected aspect of the risen Christ's mission to the world? To shed light on these questions, we again turn to the past. The future is always a future of the past. Knowing the past is part of knowing the future.

The historical development of the diaconate in the life of the Church is rather involved. A short and satisfactory account of it in all its different phases is not easy. But we will try to do so and hope that it will be helpful in discovering the role of the permanent diaconate in the life of the Church in the coming age.

THE FIRST CENTURY

The Mystery of Faith The diaconate existed in the very first Christian communities. It is an apostolic institution that we already find in the Pauline communities at Philippi (Phil 1, 1) and Ephesus (1 Tim 3, 8–13) in the fifties and sixties of the first century. According to Paul, deacons must excel in holding the mystery of faith (1 Tim 3, 9). This mystery is one of his central themes. It is that plan of salvation according to which all things in heaven and on earth will be brought together under Christ as head. Christ, ascending to heaven, fulfills all things by reconciling the entire creation with God. Since human beings and their world were alienated from God through sin, the whole creation decayed and disintegrated. But now everything will be brought back to God through Christ and renewed in God (cf. Eph 1, 9–10; 3, 4–9; Col 1, 26–27, etc.). It seems that the deacon may today also have a special role in this mystery of faith in the restoration of the whole cosmos in Christ.

From the time of Irenaeus, tradition interpreted the seven ministers of Acts 6, 1–7 as the first deacons of the Church ordained by the Twelve. However, we should note that these seven are never called deacons in the New Testament. One of them, Philip, preached the good news (Acts 8, 12–13) and proclaimed Christ in Samaria (Acts 8, 5.26–40). The author of the Acts of the Apostles accompanied Paul to Philippi (Acts 20, 6) and visited the elders of Ephesus (Acts 20, 17; 21, 1). Though there were deacons, he does not mention any of them. The seven more probably were the first bishops of the Hellenistic church, which the Twelve visited from time to time to foster their union with Jerusalem (Acts 8, 14–25; Gaechter, 1952).

Service of the Bishop In the time of Paul the diaconate is the second order in a twofold ministry (Phil 1, 1; 1 Tim 3, 8–2; *Didache*, 15, 1; Funk, 1901,

32, 34). The deacons are helpers of the bishops (*Didache,* 15, 1–2; Funk, 32–4). They were elected by the people, as were the bishops. The reason for their election is suggested by the term οὖν, therefore, which connects chapter 15 with the previous one dealing with the celebration of the Eucharist (*Didache,* 15, 1; Funk, 32–4). On the Lord's Day, therefore, the deacons helped in the breaking of bread of the Eucharist.

According to the *Didache,* their ministry was like the ministry of prophets and teachers (15, 2; Funk, 1901, 34), that is, the teaching and the building of the Church. We learn from the letters of Paul that the prophets and the teachers of the New Testament received from the Holy Spirit the special gifts of wisdom (1 Cor 12, 8) and exhortation (1 Cor 12, 10; Acts 11, 27; 15, 21; 21, 9–10). They were the foundation of the Church together with the apostles (Eph 2, 20), and their work was to bring pagans to the obedience of faith (Rom 16, 26). The parallel between deacons and prophets is confirmed by *Constitutiones apostolicae,* a document of the fourth century, where we read that the deacons received the honour due to prophets (2, 3; Funk, 1905, 244).

THE SECOND CENTURY

A Threefold Ministry Ignatius of Antioch is the first to display in his letters a threefold ministry, in which the diaconate is the third order (*Smyrna,* 12, 2; *Philadelphia,* 4; *Magnesia,* 13, 1; Funk, 1901, 266, 286, 240). A deacon represents Christ, he said (*Tralles,* 2, 3; *Magnesia,* 6, 1; *Philadelphia,* 10, 2; Funk, 1901, 244, 243, 272), and is subject to the bishop as well as to the presbyters (*Magnesia,* 2; Funk, 1901, 248). Ignatius of Antioch gave a detailed description of the various functions of a deacon.

Service of the Bishop in Helping the Poor A deacon renders service to the bishop in many ways, such as writing letters and helping in all his duties, even in the word of God. They are also messengers or ambassadors to be sent by one church to another. Ignatius does say not that they are to take care of widows, orphans, and the needy. Yet he reminds them that they are not deacons of food and drink but ministers of the Church of God (*Tralles,* 2, 3; Funk, 1901, 244). If the deacons did take care of the poor and needy during the second century, they did not do so as a service on their own but as helpers of the bishop. To help the poor and to distribute the money collected for widows, orphans, and the needy was at this time first of all the duty of the bishop, as Justin (*Apology,* 1, 67; Falls, 1948, 107) and Hermas (*Similitudes,* 9, 26, 2, 27; Funk, 1901, 622, 624, 620) testify, or of the presbyter, who, according to Polycarp, must not neglect any widow, orphan, or the poor (*Philadelphia,* 6, 1; Funk, 1901, 302). We read in the *Apostolic Tradition* of Hippolytus that it is not the deacon but the bishop who should visit the sick. The task of the deacon is only to report to the bishop concerning those who are sick in the community. For the sick person is much comforted if the high priest rather than the deacon remembers him (Dix, 1937, 37). The care of the poor was special to the bishop also in the fourth century (Council of Neo-Caesarea, canon 14; Mansi, 1889–1927, 2, 548).

THE THIRD CENTURY

Teaching Ministry of the Deacon According to Clement of Alexandria, the office of the deacon is to give spiritual interpretation. He acts and teaches the things of the Lord (*Stromata,* 6, 13; PG, 9, 328).

Sacrament of Baptism In the church of Tertullian, deacons baptized with the power and authority of the bishop (*De baptismo,* 17; 1954b, 291–2).

Sacrament of Reconciliation Cyprian wrote that if a priest was not present, the *lapsi,* the one who had failed to confess being a Christian but had received letters from a martyr, could make a confession, *ἐξομολέγεω,* of his or her sins to a deacon (1871, 1, 524), who was expected to examine the conditions for the individual's readmission to the Church (ibid., 528). And if a priest could not be found and a sinner was dying, the deacon could hear the confession of the dying and lay hands on the dying so that the dying might go to the Lord (ibid., 524). This practice was confirmed by the Council of Elvira in 305, in its canon 32. The reconciliation of the sinner was to be made in the presence of the bishop, but if death was imminent, it might be made in the presence of a priest or by a deacon alone, if the priest so wished (Mansi, 1889–1927, 11).

In the reconciliation of sinners, the deacon acted as the helper of the bishop. Reconciliation was usually a public act in which the deacon and the bishop took part as witnesses (*Apostolic Canon,* Ethiopic version, no. 16). In the case of an emergency, however, the deacon, if delegated by the bishop, could be the sole witness. Moreover, this kind of representation of the Church could be delegated to any Christian, even to a boy (Feltoe, 1918, 42–3). The act of readmitting a person publicly to the Church was not always an exclusive act of the clergy.

THE FOURTH CENTURY

Pastor of Parishes Where there was a shortage of presbyters or bishops, deacons were placed in charge of parishes with the title *plebem regens,* and among other things, they could baptize (Council of Elvira in 305, canon 77; Mansi, 1889–1927, 2, 18). It is probable that some of these deacons illegally began to offer the Eucharist. But before long they were stopped.

Eucharistic Offering The Council of Arles in 314 had to forbid the celebration of the Eucharist by deacons (canon 15; Mansi, 1889–1927, 2,

474). Canon 18 of the First Council of Nicaea even had to forbid the deacon from giving communion to presbyters or to bishops since those "who have no authority to offer" should not give the body of Christ "to those who do offer" (Tanner, 1990, 14–15). During the Eucharist the ordinary office of the deacon was to direct prayers for the Church and the world. If the deacon asked for prayers, everybody really prayed and more efficaciously. The prayers conducted by the deacon were efficacious prayers of the Church (*De prophetiarum obscuritate,* 2, 5; *PG,* 56, 182). At the request of a deacon of Carthage, Augustine wrote his *De cathechisandis rudibus* (*PL,* 40, 509ff.), a manual for deacons doing teaching.

Celibacy From the fourth century on, we have a number of documents from church councils prescribing that deacons must abstain from married life (Council of Elvira, canon 33, Mansi, 1889–1927, 2, 11). According to the *Constitutiones apostolicae,* after ordination the deacons were not permitted to marry (8, 13, 2; Funk, 1905, 514). If at the time of ordination they were not yet married, they had to express their intention of getting married later on before the ordaining bishop. Otherwise they were removed from the ministry if they attempted marriage (*Constitutiones apostolicae,* 6, 17, 1; Funk, 1905, 339–41).

Quarrels between Presbyters and Deacons In the fourth century the distinction of the priests as the new helpers of the bishop in addition to the deacons had become clear. From this time on, in a certain sense the presbyters, removed from the rank of the bishops, took the place of the deacons. It is therefore not surprising that during this century we have several writings that mention quarrels between deacons and presbyters. This was especially so in the Latin church. Thus Jerome, a presbyter himself, in defending the original equality between bishops and presbyters, pointed out the great difference between deacon and presbyter (*Epistulae,* 146; *PL,* 22, 1192–5). The diaconate, he said, had become a great source of revenue and the deacons were better off than the presbyters, who could therefore envy the deacons. According to Ambrosiaster, the deacons pawned off their duties upon the lower orders and tried to raise their own status by assuming the functions of presbyters (*De jactantia romanorum levitarum*; *PL,* 35, 2301–3). Several councils ordered deacons to stay within their own degree (First Council of Nicaea, canon 18; Tanner, 1990, 14–15). Being ministers not only of the bishops but also of the presbyters (Council of Carthage in 398, canon 3; Mansi, 1889–1927, 3, 398), they must remain standing in the presence of the presbyters (Council of Laodicea in 320, canon 20; Mansi, 2, 568).

Perhaps the reason for the ambitious advancement of the deacon is to be found in the instinctive fight for identity in the face of the presbyterate. Deacons had to show their raison d'être to the bishops before the "new deacons." They needed to prove to themselves that they were still important and necessary. Since they were in the bishop's household, this was not too difficult. Being so close to the bishop, they had many means that were completely lacking to the presbyters. As deacons of the bishop, they were able to exercise more power and influence than any country presbyter. As official inspectors, councillors, and messengers of the bishop, they had a knowledge of the affairs of the Church that made them excellent candidates for the episcopate. It was not uncommon that after the death of the bishop, the deacon would succeed him (Lightfoot, 1970, 1040–2), and this appears to have been much more common in the case of the Roman deacons, who, being in the household of the pope, could have had influence not only over the presbyters but over many country bishops as well.

A New Image of the Diaconate The ferment between priest and deacon prompted serious theological reflection on the nature of the diaconate as opposed to the presbyterate. In a spurious Clementine letter of the fourth century (*Ep.* 14; PG, 2, 49) we find the following comparison. If the Church is like a ship, then Christ is the captain; the bishop is the officer in command at the bow, πρωρέυς; the presbyters are the sailors, *ναῦτης;* and the deacons are the overseers of the rowers or boatswains, *τοίχάρχοι.*

When the presbyters took over the internal affairs of the Church, the deacons became like pioneers or frontiersmen, going around looking for those who were not yet members of the Church, and trying to lead them into it (Pseudo-Clement, *Ep.* 12; PG, 2, 47). Their duty was to exhort people to go to church, where the preaching of the priests and of the bishop would cleanse them. Thus the doorkeepers of the physical church building became an office entrusted to the subdeacons, while the deacons became the doorkeepers of the mystical Church, and it was their duty to extend the frontiers of Christ's kingdom. The deacons were now apostles who went after people to bring them to the Church, whereas the bishop with his helpers, the presbyters, nourished, educated, and formed them into Christ. The deacon was the new missionary of the bishop. Unfortunately, this new diaconal activity became neither universal nor permanent in the Church. The developing liturgy and a new monastic spirit became the centre of attention for the diaconate, whose function would soon be restricted to pontifical ceremonies.

THE FIFTH CENTURY

Missionary Mobility of the Deacons The *Codex canonum ecclesiasticorum* says that deacons had to go around exhorting and persuading people to listen to the word of God (no. 64; PL, 56, 736–7). For this ministry the deacon was given the sevenfold grace, *septiformis gratiae robur* (*Liber sacramentorum Ecclesiae Romanae* 28; PL, 55, 115), a term that is still used today in the ordination of deacons.

The pioneer function of the deacon was further developed. The deacon was the first to inspire people to move towards God and to remove hindrances in their way. Next the presbyter, wrote John Climacus, illuminates the mind of the people with the knowledge of God, while the bishop completes this knowledge with the supreme knowledge of the Trinity (*Scala paradisi*, 82; PG, 88, 758). This kind of introductory function of the deacon also is symbolized, according to Dionysius, the Pseudo-Areopagite, in the fact that the deacons lead those to be baptized to their baptism (*Ecclesiastica hierarchia*, 5; PG, 3, 524; Pseudo-Dionysius, 1987, 237–8). Later this introductory role of the deacon will be considered an introduction to the priesthood.

Because of the lack of a clear distinction between early presbyter-deacons and the new forms of deacon-deacons, one can understand the confusion in certain churches about what a deacon can really do. According to the *Heads of Canons* of Abulides or Hippolytus, used by the Ethiopian Christians, the deacon may pronounce the blessing and thanksgiving at the agape if the bishop is not there (canon 35; Abulides of Hippolytus, 1883, 137), but this permission was not found in the *Constitutiones apostolicae* treating the same matter or in the *Canons of the Church of Alexandria* (1883, 140). It seems, therefore, that in the fifth century there were still some churches where deacons in some way or other had the power of the breaking of bread if a priest were not present.

From the fifth century on, the charitable work of the deacons lessened in the Church. The protection and care of the poor, originally part of their office, developed into an institutionalized form directed either by a presbyter or by a layman. Some deacons became merely directors for the goods of the Church (Leo the Great, *Sermones*, 85, 2; PL, 54, 436). However, the majority of deacons dedicated themselves to the liturgy and to singing. The Synod of Rome in 595 reproved deacons who only sang and did not take care of the poor.

THE SIXTH TO FIFTEENTH CENTURIES

Liturgy From this time on it seems that the deacons were more and more confined to the cathedral, and they lived like canons, singing vespers and psalms day and night (Council of Tarragona in 516, canon 7; Mansi, 1889–1927, 8, 542). They were linked more and more with the altar. To prove their importance, they succeeded in making their liturgical function necessary, even indispensable, to the celebration of the mass. A priest by himself could not do what a deacon had to do. For example, a priest could not take the chalice from the altar unless it were given to him by the deacon (*De septem ordinibus Ecclesiae*; PL, 30, 153), and later, in the ninth century, a canon would be introduced according to which a priest could not say mass without a minister (Council of Paris, canon 48; Mansi, 14, 567). The decree of Gregory I laments that deacons in earlier times were ordained for preaching and the giving of alms but now they only sing. In fact, the main condition for being admitted into the order of deacon was to have a good voice, *vox blanda.* A council in Germany around 743 obliged the deacons, like the presbyters, to wear a long clerical vestment (Mansi, 1889–1927, 12, 367), and they were permanently attached to the church assigned to them by the ordaining bishop. Otherwise they would be deprived of their ministry (Council of Worms in 868, canon 19; Mansi 15, 872–3).

From the eleventh century on, the diaconate was only a way to the priesthood. During the Middle Ages the main function of the deacon became to assist the priest, and thus the deacon, once the helper of the bishop, was now the helper of the priest. To understand this change we must remember that at this time the only sacrament of order was that of the priesthood, and the priestly function was focused on the altar in the celebration of the Eucharist and here the deacon served the priest.

THE SIXTEENTH CENTURY: THE COUNCIL OF TRENT

The Council of Trent, dealing with the ministries of the Church on 15 June 1563, summarized a twofold function of the deacon: he receives during the mass the offering from the subdeacon and gives it to the priest, reads the Gospel, and instructs the people concerning the prayers and ceremonies; and he keeps order and is the secretary of the bishop during his sermons. But the deacon himself can also preach, *praedicare,* baptize, and reconcile a public penitent with the Church if a priest is not present. It is the deacon's duty also to help widows, orphans, prisoners, and those in need, either materially or spiritually (*CT*, 9, 601).

We may note here that the word *praedicare* was not used with the words "read, instruct and exhort" of the *Dogmatic Constitution on the Church* of the Second Vatican Council (*LG*, no. 29; Tanner, 1990, 874). It seems that *Lumen Gentium* had a "higher" theology of preaching than the Council of Trent did. Preaching of the gospel was pre-eminent among the principal tasks of bishops (*LG*, no. 24; Tanner, 869). Likewise for the priest, sharing in the mission of Christ preaching was his *primum,* primary duty, as co-worker with the bishop (*LG*, no. 25; Tanner, 872; *PO*, no. 4; Tanner, 1046).

Canon 17 of session 23 recommended to the bishops the restoration of a permanent diaconate. Two reasons were given. The first was the tradition of the Church, attested to in several canons of the early councils. The second was rather polemical. It must be shown to heretics that the functions of this ministry are not superfluous. To hasten the restoration, the same canon forbade diaconal functions to all those who were not yet ordained deacons. The canon concludes: "If it is required for the need and benefit of the Church, bishops are to ordain deacons for the cathedrals and for parishes as well." The support of the deacons must be provided from the revenues of the church (*Decrees on Reform,* canon 17; Tanner, 1990, 750).

But the restoration did not take place. The reason for this failure was the lack of an updated theology of the diaconate and of a felt need for it. Polemical reasons could not overcome the evidence of the past. Unlike pre- and post-Vatican II theology, post-Tridentinian theology showed no interest in the theology of the diaconate. Without such a theology, neither bishop nor candidate for the diaconate could have seen the purpose and the need for this institution of the early church.

THE SEVENTEENTH TO TWENTIETH CENTURIES

The function of the diaconate in the following centuries was laid out and regulated by the *Code of Canon Law* of 1917. Accordingly, a deacon is an "extraordinary" minister of baptism (canon 741), may distribute communion (canon 8452), and may expose the Blessed Sacrament, but he cannot give a blessing with the Sacred Host (canon 1274, 2). He may also preach (canon 1342, 1), but he cannot hold the position of a pastor, which had been permitted to him before the promulgation of the *Canon Law* of 1917.

THE SECOND VATICAN COUNCIL

New interest in the restoration of a permanent diaconate rose during World War II. In German concentration camps many priests and Catholic laymen discussed the difficult situation of the Church and the growing shortage of priests. It seems that married deacons could have done many things of which a celibate clergy was not capable. The efforts of this growing movement in favour of a permanent diaconate culminated in the decision taken by the Second Vatican Council.

Like the Council of Trent, Vatican II recommended the restoration of a permanent diaconate. The reason given was that there are many duties necessary for the life of the Church which can be carried out only with difficulty without the diaconate as a permanent rank of the hierarchy (*LG*, no. 29; Tanner, 1990, 874). These duties, so necessary for the Church, are listed as follows. The deacon has to serve the people of God in the ministry of the liturgy, of the Word, and of charity. In the ministry of the liturgy his duty is to administer baptism solemnly, to be the custodian and dispenser of the Eucharist, to assist at and to bless marriages in the name of the Church, to bring the Viaticum to the dying, to preside at the worship and the prayers of the faithful, to administer sacramentals, and to officiate at funeral and burial services. All of these are to be done to the extent that he has been authorized by competent authority. In the ministry of the Word, the deacon reads sacred Scripture to the faithful, instructs, and exhorts without the specific word *praedicare* being mentioned. Preaching, like the offering of the mass, is done in virtue of the sacrament by bishops and priests. The Second Vatican Council saw a certain parallel between saying the mass *of* Jesus Christ and preaching the word *of* God. The *of* in both cases is not only an objective but also a subjective genitive. The deacon is not a layman anymore. He is also a *šělĩah* of Jesus Christ. Canon 764 of the new *Code of Canon Law* of 1983 recognized that distinction when it stated that "deacons possess the faculty to preach everywhere," and canon 943 names the deacon as the minister not only of the Eucharistic exposition but also of the Eucharistic benediction, which the Council of Trent reserved for the priest.

The duties of charity and administration mentioned in the *Dogmatic Constitution on the Church* are further qualified in the *Decree on the Missionary Activity of the Church* as "social and charitable work" (AG, no. 16; Tanner, 1990, 1026). The reason for the restoration of diaconate given in the *Decree on the Missionary Activity of the Church* differs somewhat from that given by *Lumen Gentium*. It points out that there are men who already carry out the functions of a deacon. It would be helpful to them to be strengthened by the sacramental grace of the diaconate and to be bound more closely to the altar. They would then be enabled to carry out the same ministry more effectively.

Less than three years after the end of Vatican II, Pope Paul VI issued a *Motu Proprio* dealing with the restoration of a permanent diaconate, published on 28 June 1967 (Paul VI, 1967b). He guaranteed that the recommendation of Vatican II would not be mere words, as the recommendation of the Council of Trent was. The *Motu Proprio* indicated explicitly the pastoral care of small Christian communities as the fourth aspect of the diaconal ministry. In the name of the bishop or of the priest, the deacon can preside over small Christian communities. Thus the diaconal ministry became fourfold.

RESTORATION OF A PERMANENT DIACONATE IN CANADA, 1967: AN EXAMPLE

In 1967 the Canadian Episcopal Conference asked the Congregation of the Sacraments for the authorization to restore a permanent diaconate in Canada, listing the following reasons: 61 per cent of Canadians polled on the question expressed their wish to have permanent deacons in their country; a permanent diaconate was expected to provide a more complete sacramental life for the Church in Canada; and there were several pastoral reasons, such as an increasing need of sacramental priestly ministry in the modern society, anonymity in the growing urban parishes, in hospitals, and in educational institutions, the desire to create "relay-communities" (*communities-relais*) between individuals and the huge churches, as a new pastoral service expected to respond to the immediate needs of certain parts of the country, a new rising interest among the faithful in this vocation, and a survey that offered a reasonable guarantee that a permanent diaconate in Canada would be a success and that the bishops could rely on the help of their people and of the existing institutions to initiate and gradually develop this ministry under their pastoral supervision. And the permanent diaconate was indeed a success.

THEOLOGY OF A NEW DIACONATE: AN ANALYSIS

In light of the history of the theology of the diaconate, one could summarize it by saying that deacons are ministers of Christ, vicars of the successors of the apostles (the bishops and the priests), ministers of the Church in the external, horizontal dimension of Christ's calling to build his Church to serve the world (Horvath, 1968). There is enough evidence which suggests that what is peculiar to the deacon as opposed to the priest is a special call that is not explicit in the priesthood yet is included in the mission of the bishop, to whom Christ's whole mission is given. And this is the mission of Christ as Lord of the universe.

According to the Letter to the Hebrews, Jesus is not only the one and only eternal High Priest, the Great Shepherd (Heb 13, 20) and apostle (Heb 3, 1), but also the Lord of the universe (Heb 1, 1–2, 18). He is not only a priest according to the order of Melchizedek who offers sacrifice for sin and propitiates God but also the faithful builder of God's house, as was Moses, who led Israel from Egypt to the Promised Land (Heb 3, 2–4, 13). Not only human beings but the whole of creation is subject to Christ, who will lead all creation into God's rest. After the Resurrection, sitting at the right hand of the Father, he holds the whole universe, leading it into the Sabbath rest of the people of God and freeing it from all kind of labours (Heb 4, 8–10), the result of sin (Gen 3, 16–19). Joshua could not bring the people of God into their final rest in God by the possession of Canaan. Jesus alone, who entered into heaven (Heb 4, 8–10; 10, 12–13), will bring about the day of rest, the final Sabbath for all who do not shrink back (Heb 10, 38–39).

According to Paul, Christ's mission includes the restoration and reconciliation with God of all things either on earth or in heaven that were conquered by the power of sin and death (Col 1, 15–22). The reconciliation with God brought about by Christ affects the whole cosmos, since the sin of Adam had affected the whole cosmos (Gen 3, 14–19; Rom 5, 12–21; 1 Cor 15, 1–28; Col 3, 10; Eph 4, 22–24). The resurrection of Christ is the beginning of the world's resurrection. He conquered the cosmic powers and principalities (Col 2, 15) which ruled and held the old age of death and suffering, and he renews the whole world by a new creation (Rom 4, 17; 8, 18–23.38).

The main idea of the Book of Revelation is no different. Jesus, seated at the right of the Father, will renew all things (Rev 21, 5). Death and Hades will be thrown in the lake of fire, and a new earth and new heaven will be inaugurated where God will dwell with the human race (Rev 20, 13–21; 1, 18; cf. Is 65, 17; 66, 22; etc.).

The synoptic evangelists tell us that Christ restores all things (Mk 9, 12; Mt 17, 11). This is shown by the very signs of his mission. His mighty deeds bring about the complete renewal of the human world (Horvath, 1975a, 249–58). Signs of his kingdom are the blind who receive their sight, the lame who walk, the lepers who are cleansed, the deaf who hear, the dead who are raised up, and the poor who have the word of God preached to them (Mt 11, 4–5).

The Christ of the first Christians, as seen in their writings and art, is the founder of a movement that is not limited to the internal spiritual sphere of individuals. He is the "Pantocrator," the Lord of the world, history, and the cosmos. The works of Jesus are the visible reality of God's new kingdom, which involves a cosmic innovation (Horvath, 1993, 148–53).

The Second Vatican Council was well aware of Christ's "this-worldly" mission. Christ did not want, as we read in the documents, his deeds, which by their very nature are the expressions of charity, to be only good but to be also the signs of his messianic mission (*AA*, no. 8; Tanner, 1990, 987). As a matter of fact, the renovation of the whole universe has been irrevocably decreed and this age already advanced through the mission of the Holy Spirit (*LG*, no. 48; Tanner, 887–8). Christ communicated this mission to the Church, and the Church must be concerned with the whole of people's life, even the earthly part (*GS*, no. 3; Tanner, 1070). It is the task of the Church to labour vigorously so people may be able to build the temporal order. Because Christ's redemptive work involves the renewal of the whole temporal order, it is the mission of the Church not only to bring to people the message and grace of Christ but also to penetrate and to perfect the temporal sphere of the world with the spirit of the gospel (*AA*, no.5; Tanner, 985).

In fulfilling this mission of the Church, the laity evidently have a great part. By their work they have to appropriate the whole universe into a new creation (*AA*, no. 5; Tanner, 1990, 985). In association with Jesus' redemptive work, they have to bring God's creation to perfection (*GS*, no. 67; Tanner, 1116) and the whole material universe to completion in a better way of existence. The laity have to engage in temporal affairs to bring light to them and to order and develop them in Christ's way (*LG*, no. 31; Tanner, 875). Indeed, this duty of sharing in the saving work of the Church is common to every Christian (*LG*, no. 34; Tanner, 877), the religious included (*LG*, no. 44; *GS*, no. 45; Tanner, 885–6, 1099).

But we should not limit Christ's this-worldly mission to the laity and to their secular character. The ministerial, hierarchical priests, who are chosen first of all to give clear witness to the desire for a heavenly home, are not exempt from carrying out Christ's this-worldly mission. The duty that God gave to the shepherds of his people is a true service, called significantly in the sacred literature a *diaconia*, or ministry (Acts 1, 17. 25; 21, 19; Rom 11, 13; 1 Tim 1, 12; *LG*, no. 24; Tanner, 1990, 868). The *diaconia* is the proper mission of the bishop, and the deacon shares it through the imposition of the bishop's hand (*LG*, no. 29; Tanner, 874).

We find that the reason for the sacrament of order is the active sacramental, personal presence of the risen Christ in the midst of his people as head of his mystical body. Now, has not Christ in this sense also to be present in the cosmic restoration of the universe? Has he not to be working for the external material happiness of people not only in the members of his mystical body but also "in person" through the ministerial priesthood? But if the mission of Christ really includes both the spiritual and the material renewal of the human race and his mission in the full sense had been communicated to the apostles and their successors, then this mission should be expressed clearly in the very sacrament of order. If this is so, where could this active presence of Christ at work in the world for the this-worldly happiness of the human race be expressed more adequately than in the sacrament of the diaconate, the sacrament of one of the two helpers of the bishop?

Since the Church must fulfil Christ's mission not only in its laity but also in its ministers, all aspects of Christ's mission, now entrusted to the bishop, must be manifest in the two degrees of helpers of the bishops, that is, in the presbyterate and in the diaconate. In this way, both will be unambiguous signs of Christ's complete mission. In this way the deacon, as sharer of Christ's material this-worldly mission, may have an adequate raison d'être and a special characteristic different from that of the presbyterate. Deacons would thus be the pioneers of the Church, as were the deacons of the fourth century. They were doorkeepers not of the physical church but of the spiritual one, since they could open and extend its frontiers by working the mighty signs of charity of God for others, the external manifestations of the internal renewal brought about by Christ.

The specific characteristic of the diaconate, defined as the active sacramental personal presence of the risen Christ in the world reconciling and renovating us in our material this-worldly dimension, enhances and justifies the traditional fourfold function of the diaconal service. It gives them a theological raison d'être and characteristically diaconal dimension.

In the ministry of the Word the deacon, as pioneer and frontiersman, is sent to preach to those who are not yet active members of the Church and to introduce them into the Church. In the ministry of the liturgy he is to assist the priest, since he does not make the Eucharist present but distributes it among the faithful by translating it into its visible, cosmic dimension. In the ministry of charity he brings about the "here and now" of the eschatological kingdom of God, where history reaches its complete fulfillment and makes the manifestation of the Lord possible. Finally, in the ministry of small Christian communities the deacon, as leader and head, will shepherd the diaconal community to a full ecclesial community, brought to its fullness in the Eucharistic gathering.

The distinction between the spiritual and material dimensions of Christ's mission does not mean a scission in the sacrament of order. The deacon will not be removed from the altar, and the presbyter will not be exempt from his social mission. The poor and lowly are entrusted to the presbyter in a special way (*PO*, no. 6; Tanner, 1990, 1049), and he has an obligation to care for them. But the presbyter will do it always in his own presbyterial dimension, that is, looking primarily and directly at their internal and spiritual renovation. Thus the presbyterial-ministerial vocation will always be different from the diaconal-ministerial vocation. As there are many who are not called to help people properly in their internal innovation (to hear confessions, etc.), so there are many Christians who are not well enough disposed yet to participate properly in the mass. They are like the catechumens of the early times. Many Christians, although baptized, need more introduction and preparation. They can find Christ more easily in acts of charity than in the species of the Eucharist, which is not the beginning but the "culmination of the whole of the Christian community" (CD, no. 30; Tanner, 933).

The presbyters and the deacons are different, not on the grounds that one is called for service and the other is not but on the grounds of the proper dimension of the service to which they are called: one to the presbyterial and the other to the diaconal service. A permanent diaconate does not reduce the number of the priestly vocations. It just provides the possibility of being a minister to those who do not have a priestly vocation.

It is not by chance that it is precisely the Church of today which has become more aware of the this-worldly mission of Christ. Its members are people who are not looking for a "God up there," for a God of otherworldliness, but for a God who is in and of the world. Secularization accentuates the this-worldly dimension of redemption. Now, under the providence of God, the Church more easily recognizes its Christ as servant and healer, the Christ of this world, who at the same time, however, does not cease to be God, the absolutely Other. Since Christ is also an otherworldly God, he can reconcile every man or woman with God, the completely Other, but because he is also the God of this world, he can and will reconcile human beings with the whole cosmos too.

Perhaps this might be the reason why the Church has come to a better understanding of the diaconate's special role today and why it might want to place the diaconal sign before people precisely in our days. Less-institutionalized pioneering diaconal communities inspired by dynamic deacons may become the most efficient forms of evangelization in the twenty-first century.

In sum, we can say that the specific characteristic of the sacrament of the diaconate, as distinct from the presbyterate, is the active sacramental-personal presence of the risen Christ, the eternal High Priest in the world, reconciling and renovating the external, material (horizontal) dimension and the whole visible and cosmic world with God and in God. It differs from the active sacramental-personal presence of the risen Christ, the eternal High Priest in the world, reconciling and renovating the internal, spiritual (vertical) dimension with God and in God, peculiar to the sacrament of the presbyterate. These two aspects are united in the episcopate, to which Christ conferred the completeness of his mission.

4.3.3.8 NON-CHRISTIAN PRIESTHOOD, THE PRIESTHOOD OF CHRIST, THE PRIESTHOOD OF THE FAITHFUL, AND THE PRIESTHOOD OF THE APOSTLES

In terms of the general concept of the priesthood, we may present a greater difference. We see both how much the various forms of the priesthood and order have in common and yet how much they differ from each other. Below we present them in columns, which we hope will illustrate each element. The summary is our understanding of Catholic points of view and calls for other points of views with an ecumenical evaluation of each one's self-understanding and an understanding of the other in order to appreciate the riches of the human race. The community serves individuals, and individuals the community. We want to serve others in order to become more and better than what they are, because that is better for each of us and for the human race.

Non-Christian priesthood	*Priesthood of Christ*	*Priesthood of the faithful*	*Priesthood of the the apostles*
tries to bring people to God by sacrifice	the only one who brings about God's encounter with human beings	brings God to people in virtue of the priesthood of Christ, not in the person of Christ but in his or her own name	Christ, after his resurrection, brings God to people through the ministry of his apostles in person
generic notion of priesthood: for the benefit of people specific notion of priesthood: helping people in their struggle in life by uncommon power, not available here and now			*the bishops* are – ministers of Christ, – successors of the apostles, shepherds, leaders of the Church
strict sense of priesthood: helping people to meet God			*the presbyters* are – ministers of Christ – vicars of the successors of the apostles – helpers of the bishops – ministers of the Church in the internal, vertical dimension of Christ's calling to build his Church in his service to God
			the deacons are – ministers of Christ – vicars of the successors of the apostles

- helpers of the bishops and of the priests
- ministers of the Church in the external, horizontal dimension of Christ's calling to build his Church by serving the world

4.3.4 What the Sacrament of Order Is

Having proposed the specific meaning of the various participations in the one priesthood of Christ, we would now like to present the mystery of the sacrament of order. We will do so in three parts. Firstly, we give a brief summary of the meaning of the key words employed in the history of the theology of the sacrament of order. These are technical words used in any science as an introduction informing the reader about the results of earlier investigations. The aim is not to waste time clarifying a concept already clarified in certain directions and invite further research. Secondly, we present our own description, and thirdly, we comment on it.

4.3.4.1 KEY WORDS FOR THE THEOLOGY OF THE SACRAMENT OF ORDER

The history of the theology of the sacrament of order is a classic example of how misunderstanding of a word that has been taken out of its historical context can bring about an incorrect theological understanding, unnecessary condemnations, schisms, and heresies. We present here some of the key words together with an explanation based on our historical presentation.

An *apostle* means more than a zealous preacher. It is the scriptural evidence that, in addition to the priesthood of the faithful, there was another special participation in the priesthood of Christ. The term *apostolos*, used by New Testament writers not as an adjective but as a noun, unlike in classical Greek (Rengstorf, 1985, 424–5), is one member of the pair "apostle" and "faithful," which are two distinct members of the first Christian communities, marked by two sacraments, baptism and order. It is the *šělĩah* (1 Kgs 14, 6) who is sent and, as such, represents the person who has sent him. It implies a sort of presence of the commissioner in the commissioned that is more than just a legal, juridical commission. It is a real union, a com-union, between the one who sends and the one who is sent. That apostles are *šělĩah* of Jesus means that Jesus stands behind their words and works. We find in the New Testament three kinds of apostles: the Twelve, the superlative apostles (2 Cor 11, 5; 12, 11), and simple apostles (Rom 16, 7; 1 Cor 9, 5; 2 Cor 9, 5; 11, 5–13; 12, 11–12). The Pauline apostles were missionary "episcopal" apostles, whereas the leaders of the Johannine churches were presbyters, local monarchical apostles, except in the Third Letter of John, where an absent presbyter "elder" reaffirms his authority over Diotrephes, the head of Gaius's local community (Horvath, 1974, 339). The term *apostolos* was later rendered by *in persona Christ,* that is, to act in the place of Christ, as distinct from in the name of Christ, *in nomine Christi.*

Apostolic succession means more than a legal and juridical continuity. It means the continuity of Jesus Christ's presence in the successors of the apostles, revealed by God's unbreakable word and symbolized by the imposition of hands, which replaced one's human, God-symbolizing power with Christ's God-symbolizing power (Horvath, 1971a, 49–52). It provides the Church with successors to the apostles, whether they are presbyters, bishops, or deacons. In the lifetime of the apostles, presbyters or bishops were vicars, and after the death of the apostles, they became the *successors of the apostles* in the full sense.

A *bishop,* or *episcopos,* occurs in the New Testament five times and is applied mostly to the *presbyteros* of the Church (Acts 20, 28; Phil 1; 1 Tim 3, 2; Tit 1, 7; 1 Pet 2, 25) in Greek churches, as opposed to presbyters in the Jerusalem church. According to Irenaeus, *episcopos* refers to the office rather than to the person. He was a presbyter in duty.

A *presbyter* is the vicar of an absent founding apostle and later his successor. There is no sign of any limitation in apostolic episcopal power for him until the third century.

Priests, hiereus or *sacerdos,* are called the leaders of the Church from the third century on. By that time their originality had been established, and there was no danger of thinking of them in terms of Jewish or pagan priests. In the period of scholastic theology, the priest became the central concept. The bishop is called a priest of the first order, and the presbyter a priest of the second; episcopal superiority was meant to be juridical, not sacramental. Vatican II established definitively that episcopal consecration is a sacrament. The bishop has the fullness of the priesthood (*LG*, no. 41; Tanner, 1990, 881) and the fullness of the sacrament of order (*LG*, no. 26; Tanner, 870).

The *deacon* is the helper of the bishop-presbyter. It seems that the present presbyterate is a development of the diaconate, rather than a diminution of the episcopate. Both the presbyter and the deacon serve the bishop, one in the vertical and the other in the horizontal dimension of Christ's redemption.

Ordo is a term introduced by Tertullian. It did not mean orderly disposition and regulation, putting in order of various major and minor orders, as Hugh of St Victor, Peter Lombard, and Thomas Aquinas understood the word. In the time of Tertullian it had a definite meaning connected to the social status of the era. Earlier there were the classes of senators and equestrians. Now the leaders of the Church were the third class. The word meant not hierarchy in the sense of Pseudo-Dionysius but an admittance into the group or college of the presbyter-bishops; each is a deacon, a minister of Christ and his people (Mt 20, 25–28).

Hierarchy means more than a gradual order. It means a divine institution, something initiated by God and not by human will. *Institutio divina* differs from *ordinatio divina*, divine ordinance, which is identical with divine providence.

Imposition of hands is more than the handing over of the instruments of the chalice and the paten. The imposition of hands is not *χειροτονία*, stretching out hand, but *ἐπίθεσις*, laying on of hands (1 Tim 4, 14; 1 Tim 5, 22; 2 Tim 1, 6). It may mean curing, blessing, communication of the Spirit, but in the references given, it means a union, a being one with someone whose hands have been imposed.

Clergy, or *κλῆροζ*, does not mean someone who tries to maintain or increase ecclesiastical power within a religious hierarchy. Rather, it means a person called by God (Acts 17, 4) whose lot is God (Is 34, 17; Ex 6, 8; Ps 16, 5; Acts 1, 26).

Pope, pater, or *father*, as a title in a rabbinical and foundational sense, is excluded by Matthew 23, 9. Matthew wanted to make clear that Jesus' teaching and the foundation of his work is not human, but God's teaching and God's foundation. Jesus' followers have one Father as the founder of their community and one Master as their teacher. And this is God, the Father in heaven. Besides Matthew's church, the historical Jesus too may have had a special reason for not wanting his followers to call anyone else father but the one in heaven. For him, God the Father theology was so central that he had to deny that anyone besides him knew "his real Father" (cf. Mt 11, 27; Horvath, 1975a, 182–6; Van Iersel, 1961, 151–7). Thus when the Church introduced the use of the title "father," first for the bishops (cf. the Council of the 318 Fathers at Nicaea in 325) and later for the pope and for the priest, it could not be used except in a typologic sense. The bishop is the type, τύπος, of the father, wrote Ignatius of Antioch (*Tralles*, 3, 1; Funk, 1901, p. 244). That the bishop is modelled on the Father means that he should have the same sentiments, the same love as God, the Father of all, has for God's people. In other words, the bishop has to help and support the faithful as a father does his son and daughter. If there is any model in human experience that fashions priestly life, it is the love a father has for his son or daughter. When this title was extended to the vicar of the bishop, the priest, it meant that he should have the same love for his faithful as God, their only father, has for them. Therefore, when someone calls a priest "father," the priest is reminded of his vocation of working for, supporting, and protecting others lovingly as much as he can and of giving everything, even his own life, if that is required, for another human being.

Sacrifice, in the life of Jesus, is a dedication to God's new way, which replaces the old. It is giving up the human present and past for God's future (Horvath, 1979b, 89).

Redemption is the result of sacrifice for God, reconciling the world to God. It is the whole *mission of Christ*, renewing and perfecting loving relations between God and human beings in the whole world.

The meaning of these key words will, it is hoped, be further clarified by the following description of the sacrament of order.

4.3.4.2 WHAT THE SACRAMENT OF ORDER IS

In answer to our question, What is the sacrament of order? we can say that it is one in which (1) Christ, a bishop as successor of his apostles, and the Church come together (2) to incorporate a faithful person chosen by God into the collegial body of the successors of the apostles by the invocation of the Holy Spirit and the imposition of hands of a bishop, in order (3) to bring about an irrevocable union of the ordinand with Christ and through him with all the human race to perpetuate in the world Christ's permanent calling of people into a dialogue of faith with God by being instrumental of (4) Christ's availability in the Eucharist to grant God's infinite mercy.

4.3.4.3 COMMENT

Christ, a *bishop* as successor of the apostles, and *the whole Church, the foundational one* of "then and there," reaching the place and time of the ordination, come together to

- *incorporate into the collegial body of the successors of Christ's apostles:* a collegial body and state based on the experience and love the first apostles had for Jesus Christ and the mission he entrusted to them as his *šělīah*, that is, persons in whom he made himself available to call his people into a direct dialogue of faith and love;
- *a faithful person chosen by God* through the sacrament of order, the sacrament of calling (cf. vocation, clergy, divinely called), which presupposes a new experience of God's calling distinct from an earlier experience of God in faith, expressed by the sacrament of baptism, the sacrament of faith; the new call is God's new initiative prior to the ordination, the authenticity of which is revealed by the ordination as a true and infallible call of God; the ordination, therefore, as a word of God, is irrevocable; God does not change God's mind about Christ, in whose vocation the sacrament of ordination makes the baptized participate; the inexplicable mystery of the ministerial vocation (why exactly this one and not somebody else) emphasizes again the absolute freedom of God in regard

to the value of the created world; the purpose of this new experience of God is a new sending (*apostolos*) to announce God's calling addressed to mankind;

- *by the invocation of the Holy Spirit and the imposition of hands of a bishop* – the prayer and the imposition of hands are sacramental symbols which signify that by virtue of Christ's Incarnation the Holy Spirit is descending upon the ordinand;
- *in order to bring about an irrevocable union of the ordinand with Christ,* an irrevocable union, understood as the indelible character or mark impressed by the sacrament of order through which the ordinand's God-symbolizing, vestigial, natural power is taken away and replaced by Christ's God-symbolizing power; as a result, the priest will from now on be a priest forever, having something special that people will notice about him; the priest will forever be a question, having something mysterious about him that makes people ask, "What is this?" "Is this possible?" "Is he real, authentic, or a fake?" (so much so that if he ever marries, his wife will forever sense that there is something in him which she never will be able to hold on to completely; these are just a few experiential aspects of the priest's mysterious sharing in Christ of God's symbolizing power);
- *and through him with all the human race*: since Christ cannot be separated from his mystical body, to which though in a different way the whole human race belongs, a priest with Christ will have a special relation to any human being, touching upon his or her greatest need, that is, the person's need of God in its vertical, internal (presbyterial) and/or in its horizontal external, cosmic (diaconal ministry) dimension; the completeness of both is the episcopal ordination (this is the proper meaning of the expression *alter Christus*);
- *to perpetuate in the world Christ's permanent calling of people into a dialogue of faith with God*: the purpose, the end, of the sacrament of order can be expressed as a spatialization and contemporalization of the risen Christ in the different moments of space and time as his tireless calling of people into a dialogue with God here and now; the Word of God, given to humankind in Christ, by the sacrament of ordination resounds forever;
- *by being instrumental of Christ's availability in the Eucharist*: here is the role of priest saying mass; in the mass he will be an instrument (*in persona Christi)* of the Head of the Church, reminding the Church of its being instituted by Christ; this is the meaning of the Church as "hierarchical," that the Church did not make itself and will never will be able to survive on its own; it will constantly depend upon him whose permanent influence is indispensable not only in the past, but in the present and in the future;

- *to grant God's infinite mercy:* here is the role of the priest hearing confessions; he is to proclaim and witness to the faithful and to any sinful person that "God is merciful and loves you"; God in the Eucharist is near to all, forgiving through the sacrament of penance; the priest does this as the minister of Christ and of the Church as well; being a priest, he is to cultivate the sacrament of order as the Church's celebration of its love for Jesus Christ.
- *in saving the world*: Christ remains the actual saviour of each human being; he loves every human being in disaster as well as in good fortune; which is the mystery of love raising questions.

4.3.5 *The Sacrament of Order and Sacramental Theology*

By thinking about our faith, we have rediscovered sacraments as celebrating Christians' love for Jesus Christ and the Eucharist as the model for sacramental theology. Christ's presence in the Eucharist makes the Eucharist the hermeneutic principle to penetrate the mystery of each sacrament and interpret its meaning in the context of the organic unity, the "collegiality," of the sacraments. Not only the sacraments but any apostolic work finds its unity and end in the Eucharist, which is the source, the centre, the eschaton, the culmination of preaching and any Christian activity (*PO*, no. 5; Tanner, 1990, 1047–8). Thus as with the Eucharist, the sacrament of order too is a personal loving encounter with Christ, union with him, and participation in his works and in his reconciling sacrifice.

4.3.5.1 THE SACRAMENT OF ORDER IS A PERSONAL ENCOUNTER WITH CHRIST CALLING

When the Second Vatican Council decided to profess and declare its teaching concerning bishops, it started to do so by commemorating how the Lord Jesus called to himself those whom he wished and appointed them to be with him and share in his power, confirming them on the day of Pentecost, so that the divine mission entrusted to him would continue to the end of the world (*LG*, nos. 19–20; Tanner, 1990, 863–4). These were the apostles, whom at the Last Supper Christ instituted as his successors in his priesthood, offering his body and blood to God the Father with the words "Do this in remembrance of me" (Council of Trent, *Teaching and Canons on the Most Holy Sacrifice of the Mass*, chapter 1; Tanner, 733).

The sacrament of order begins, therefore, with a call. The words *προσκληρόω, κλῆρος* mean being drawn by lot, being called by God (Act 17, 4; 1, 17.26; 1 Pet 5, 3), to be a person whose lot is God (Is 34, 17; Ex 6, 8; Ps 16, 5; Acts 1, 26). And the call, the being called by God, is the beginning of a love affair between God, who calls, and the one who is called, which is expected to last forever.

First, God in Christ begins to call the elected one unassumingly in the midst of the great variety of objects and subjects of one's conscience. Then, mostly gradually but not rarely also abruptly, God becomes the centre of attention and attraction. Sometimes God goes away as it were and comes back again silently, without any considerable noise. When God is gone, God is missed, and the chosen one wonders about the meaning of all this. When God is back and questioned, God answers but not in words or visions. Yet the one who is called gets the message and realizes how much he needs God. The prayer becomes spontaneous. Disquieting yet welcome questions emerge, such as What should I do? Can I be without God? Yes and no. Clarity and doubts alternate. New attractions emerge. Place or event occurs when God touches mind and heart, as a kind of rendezvous, a "come and be with me," special and perhaps remembered for the rest of one's life. After the first, other rendezvous may follow. Joy and sorrow, happiness and sadness, alternate.

The internal call will need external evaluation. Interviews follow, examinations, seminaries, studies, discernment, admissions to the ordinations, and finally the day of ordination. The divine and infallible word arrives: "Yes, I called you." "I have chosen you since the beginning of the world," and "I will be with you now." "You may leave me, but I never leave you, because I keep my words, and you will be my priest for ever." "Anyway I love you, because I cannot hate ..."; "and you have to proclaim my love and mercy to generations to come" (Ps 71, 18). "Wherever you will be, I will be and call you again and again, because you became my everlasting call to the human race for a dialogue of love which I initiated when I died on the cross out of my love for you and for any human being."

And whether the young priest, the young *cleric,* the one who had been called, verbalizes all this or not, he will realize that his life is no longer just his. He belongs to someone and many someones. His life becomes from that time on more "happenings" than "planning." His destiny is associated with the destiny of the Other. A kind of love is poured over him from all directions immediately, or sometimes after a period of transitory wondering and confusion – unless he deceived the Church and without love for Christ, stretched out his hand for the free gift of God, and then doubts, pain, and guilt emerge – a celibate priestly life begins its journey towards the life of eternal love.

The time of the first "honeymoon," when the newly ordained enjoys the power and the success of priestly activities, may last for many years. Attention, admiration, and the love of the people of God will surround the young priest. And the years will fly by. Twenty, twenty-five, years will have passed by since the day of ordination, and the time for assessment of the forgone life has arrived. It is a time when celibate priestly life and married life alike become a monotony of the déjà vu. "Is that all I could get?" "What was that all about?" "What is the result?" Married people can look at their children, the family they founded. But the priest? The quick "thank you, father" has passed, and only God knows those invisible good deeds. "They were all for Jesus Christ, but how about me?" one asks. "I should have a life for myself as well." "What happened to the first call?" It seems that people and God have abandoned the priest at the same time. Life is empty and cold. The aging body needs help and warmth. It is again a time for choice.

First, a cold coexistence. "I do what I have to do for you, but you have to understand I have to do what I have to do for my life, for myself." Next, "I can live without you," says the *Mittagsdämon.* And one day I wake up and I feel so different. Faith is so far away, almost or really gone. A new call is there, and a choice is made. Married people get divorced, and celibate priests get married.

Or husbands and wives rediscover that the best friend, the reliable one, is the one with whom they have spent the greater part of their lives. It was the time that made them what they are and will be during what is left of their lives. And the celibate priest rediscovers that the one who has called him and with whom he has lived for a long time, Jesus Christ, is still his best friend. He meets Christ again with the words "Into your hands I commit my life again as I did before. Stay with me. The day is now far spent and it will be evening very soon"(Lk 23, 46; 24, 29).

This is the time when people such John of the Cross, Teresa of Avila, Henry Suso, and Ignatius of Loyola became saints and great mystics. Christ never abandons his people, much less his priests. His love is everlasting. The old lover calls and calls again. The greatest lover knocks at the door. And both the mystic and the renegade priest feel the same and may reply to the humiliating love of their Lord, "I despise myself and repent in dust and ashes" (Jb 42, 6). And there will be great joy in heaven, for a priest who was lost and is found (Lk 15, 32). Or ...?

4.3.5.2 THE SACRAMENT OF ORDER IS A UNION WITH CHRIST AND IN HIM WITH BELIEVERS AND THROUGH THEM WITH THE WHOLE WORLD: THE MEANING OF THE IMPOSITION OF HANDS

Since apostolic times, the mission Christ entrusted to his apostles has been transferred to their successors by the symbol of the imposition of hands. By the imposition of Paul's hands (2 Tim 1, 6), together with those of the council of elders (1 Tim 4, 14), Timothy was designated to be Paul's successor. The Greek word is used not *χειροτονία*, stretching out one's hand for voting, but *ἐπίθεσις τῶν χειρῶν*, laying on of hands. The special grace conferred by it to Timothy was the task of leading the Christian community, the ministry of the Word, bearing testimony for Jesus, and the care for personal sanctification. Timothy was expected to elect qualified bishops (1 Tim 3, 1–7) and deacons (1 Tim 3, 8–13) yet without laying his hands hastily upon anyone (1 Tim 5, 22). He led the community in their supplications, prayers, intercessions, and thanksgiving for all human beings (1 Tim 2, 1–15).

From the beginning, even in the time of scholastic theology and the Council of Florence, the union with the risen Christ as the substance of the sacrament of order has been signified by the imposition of hands. Yet the same union with the risen Christ was expressed by the Council of Florence in the handing over of the chalice with wine and the paten with bread (matter) and the words "Receive the power of offering sacrifice in the Church for the living and dead" (form) as the essence of the sacrament valid for the time being (Council of Florence, *Bull of Union with the Armenians*; Tanner, 1990, 549). It is known that Thomas Aquinas and the scholastic theologians all affirmed that the imposition of hands was also essential to the administration of the sacrament. It signified the "effect" of the sacrament, that is, the grace that made the consecration of the body and blood of Christ possible (*In Sent.* 4, dist. 24, q 2, a 3; *Summa theol*, 3, q 84, a 4). Such a specification of the sacramental symbol by new terms to correct contemporary misunderstanding was within the timely service of the Church (cf. Pius XII, 1948).

The meaning of the imposition of hands is manifold, but its basic meaning is a union, " being one with" or "being in one." It is a kind of inseparability between the one who imposes his hands and the one upon whom the hands have been imposed. In the case of ordination, it is a sort of identification with him, a union of love with Christ, a special being of the risen Jesus Christ with his minister through his apostles and their successors. Thus the imposition of hands by a bishop is the authentication of the call of Christ, sending his minister to his faithful and through them to every human being in the present and in the future. It is the sending to all nations (Mt 28, 19) and to all creation (Mk 16, 15).

Even though one minister may be directly sent to a particular group or nation, his mission has to be always open to the whole world. Each one who is called and ordained shares in the universal mission work of Christ. It is on the basis of Christ's mission to the whole world with no limit that any Christian church, be it Roman Catholic or Orthodox, Anglican or Protestant, Reformed or Evangelical, has an internal grace within which it is moved towards an ecumenical union and unity.

4.3.5.3 THE SACRAMENT OF ORDER IS A PARTICIPATION IN CHRIST'S LIFE AND HIS WORK OF SALVATION THROUGH THE INDELIBLE CHARACTER IMPRINTED BY THE HOLY SPIRIT FOR THE "MULTI-SPATIALIZATION" AND "CONTEMPORALIZATION" OF CHRIST'S MISSION

According to the *Decree on the Ministry and Life of the Priests* (PO, no. 2; Tanner, 1990, 1044), priests are sealed with a special mark or character imprinted by the Holy Spirit and thus are configured or patterned to Christ the priest, so that they may be able to act in the person of Christ, the head of the mystical body of Christ. It was Augustine who first used the word *character,* distinctive mark, to express the mystery of the sacrament of order. He interpreted the χάρισμα of 2 Timothy 1, 6, given to Timothy by the imposition of hands, as a gift distinct from grace; therefore, unlike the Donatists, he thought that a renegade priest in sin could also validly consecrate and perform priestly functions. After ordination, the ordained, therefore, is believed to have something that cannot be lost by mortal sin. It may be called a spiritual indelible mark, so that one who was once a priest can never become a layman again (Council of Trent, *Canons on the Sacrament of Order,* no. 4; Tanner, 744). The Donatist deviation was instrumental for the Church in reflecting on the mystery of the sacrament of order.

If it is not just the sacramental grace, we can ask, what is then the indelible character, the seal imprinted by the Holy Spirit, the configuration to Christ, a "being patterned" to the priesthood of Christ? What happens to the priest in ordination that he, even in mortal sin, is able to share in Christ's life and in his work of salvation? This is one more mystery of the sacrament of order. Being imprinted by the Holy Spirit, the indelible mark should be understood as a sharing in the mystery of the Incarnation, the mystery of consecration, and the mystery of sanctification. Since it is so, we may use the same problem-solving paradigm we found in each one of the three mysteries. We already mentioned earlier that to join two or three into one as intimately as possible without sacrificing the reality of either one, theology used a special removal and replacement thought model (Horvath, 1971).

For example, to explain our faith in the one God and three divine persons we remove three individual essences that should be proper to each real divine person and replace them by one divine essence functioning as the one essence of the Father, the Son, and the Holy Spirit. Similarly, in the mystery of the Incarnation we remove the reality of the "person" that should have pertained to the human nature of Christ and replace it by the reality of the second divine person. Such a removal and replacement ensures the union between the divine and the human in Christ without change and confusion, without division and separation (Council of Chalcedon, *Definition of the Faith;* Tanner, 1990, 86). The reasoning over transubstantiation is similar. The substance of bread and wine is removed and the function of the substance of the risen body of Christ takes over as their replacement. And once more we have a union of the divine and the human. Finally, in the mystery of sanctification, following the scholastic explanation, the human nature, considered not as a principle of human existence but as *species impressa,* that is, as the direct principle of the act of believing and loving God in Jesus Christ, is replaced by the divine nature, which in a quasi-formal way makes possible that one believes and loves God in Jesus Christ the way God does (Rahner, 1969, 153; Flick, 1962, 482–94; Scheeben, 1946, 613–65).

The union of Christ with his priest is evidently unique, and it cannot be reduced to any other known form of union. It is manifestly different from the union of the Three Persons with each other in the consubstantial unity of the Trinitarian life. It differs also from the union of the two natures in the hypostatic union in Christ. And it differs as well from the union that exists between the body of Christ and the Eucharistic species. Finally, it differs from the union of Christ with the justified faithful, since in the case of the priest, the union in question is compatible with the existence of mortal sin. It is clear that one cannot think that the priest's individual nature or his personality, or his substance, or his nature as direct principle for the acts of knowing and loving, can be removed and replaced in the sacrament of order. In effect, a theologian can think of only one element to which the process of removal and replacement seems applicable. And this is *the human natural power to symbolize God as existing*, which will be replaced by *Christ's God-symbolizing power as calling every human being into the dialogue of faith.*

Each human person has been created by God in God's image (Gen 1, 26), and so each human being points beyond him or herself. His or her own existence is a certain *trans-appearance* of God. Each one is a sign, a symbol of God. Now, in virtue of ordination, the natural God-symbolizing power is taken away and replaced by Christ's God-symbolizing power. God's image of human nature is transformed by the sacramental grace into a new image of Christ's God symbol, Christ's sign-event. The priest's being takes on a new, extraordinary power of being able to point beyond its ordinary, denotative and expressive power to Christ's God.

The presence of Christ is already a reality in the baptized. This presence is modified in ordination so that the individual becomes a powerful symbol-event, challenging others and inviting them towards God. Because of the new symbolizing power, Jesus Christ, the God-man, shines through, and God's voice sounds in human existence in a new way, inviting other human beings into a dialogue of faith. The being of the priest becomes a new revelatory configuration of signs, raising questions about the incarnate God and by the same token manifesting the challenging power of God to human beings. There are, of course, some functions that of themselves are eminently symbolic of Christ's initiative and of the Church's dependence upon Christ; the celebration of the mass and the absolving from sin are the most expressive and, as such, evidently priestly functions. Nevertheless, the priest's symbolizing activity cannot be reduced to and identified only with such functions.

If the natural God-symbolizing power can be called a God-shadowing power, Christ's own God-symbolizing power should be called a "God-presenting" power and his God-remembering God's real presence. Consequently, the union of God with the priest is of such a nature that once the priest has accepted God's invitation to be the symbol of his calling initiative, the priest will be forever predestined to represent, to re-enact, Christ's challenging initiative. Thus no matter what the circumstances, even in a state of sin, the priest is actuating his new God-symbolizing power and testifying to Christ's active calling by raising questions and problems. Therefore the priest's function is not primarily to perform special actions but to reveal and symbolize to the world the nature of the Church and to make Christ's calling to dialogue resound with every human being. In this way the priest, as Christ's minister, participates in his life and his work of salvation by "multi-locating" his presence and "contemporalizing" his mission.

Just as the Church could not exist without the baptized, so it also cannot exist without ordained ministers. If one would take the position that, for the sake of argument, the Church could exist without the actual celebration of the mass, one should say that the Church could not exist without ordained ministers. This is the Eucharistic Christ's dependence on the baptized and ordained faithful. Again, even if we wish to suppose that the Church were able to admit that a baptized faithful person without ordination could celebrate the Eucharist *per modum actus,* by this action the layman would not any more become a priest than the proxy would contract marriage by pronouncing the words that form the symbols of the sacrament of marriage on behalf of the contracting party. The priest has, indeed, a special role for the Church in the revelation of God, and the Church will never remain without priests.

To answer the question as to why someone would become a priest, we can say that no one becomes a priest because he wants to do something. One becomes a priest because he has been called by God to symbolize Christ's sacramental presence in the world in calling every human being into the dialogue of faith. One can refuse and not follow this calling; but once he has accepted it and has been ordained, there is no way he can separate himself from the mission of Christ, which is his priestly mission. In positive terms, Christ's destiny is the priest's "destiny" of constantly calling every human being into the dialogue of faith (Horvath, 1971a, 47–52).

4.3.5.4 THE SACRAMENT OF ORDER IS A SACRIFICE RECONCILING THE WORLD WITH GOD BY ANNOUNCING THE TIRELESS CALL OF THE MERCIFUL GOD

By offering his body for others and pouring out his blood for the forgiveness of sins, Jesus through his life and death was "a true and proper sacrifice." And since he is the same one who offers himself as victim on the cross and the one in the mass made present by the ministry of his priest (*Teaching and Canons on the Most Holy Sacrifice of the Mass*, canon 2; Tanner, 1990, 733), it is obvious that the priesthood of the New Testament is a sacrificial priesthood. The priest is a minister of Christ, who broke down and breaks down the dividing wall of sin between God and human beings and between one human being and another.

The above argument presupposes a notion of time open to eternity. The crucified and risen Christ, sitting at the right hand of the Father, who is eternity, is able to be present "here and now" where the priest is offering mass. Eternity enters "here" time. And the same Jesus Christ, the perfect sacrifice once for all, accepts the characteristics of time without ceasing to be the risen one. This mystery is the basis for different understandings, Catholic and Protestant, of the meaning of the notion of the apostles and their successors, the priesthood, Christ's sacrifice, and the mass. We may agree that eternity is not endless time and time is not simply the present instance of eternity. Time is not eternity and eternity is not time, and faith in a God who became man has to respect the validity of such an argument. Thus the Incarnation remains a permanent challenge to the human mind.

In the history of Christian thinking we find four instances that transcend an obvious incompatibility of time and eternity: the early Christians' faith in the resurrection of Christ; the book of Bible we have at hand today, mostly in translations, and its relation to the word of God; the Eucharistic presence; and the theology of Jesus Christ as eschatological unity of time and eternity. A short presentation of each should suffice here.

4.3.5.4.1 Early Christians' Faith in the Resurrection

For the early Christians, the experience of Jesus' resurrection was more than just the experience of apparitions. It was also a recognition of Jesus' beatifying presence in the kerygma, in his deeds, and in his *šĕlĭah*-apostolic Church. The presence was a new one. It was a new closeness of the Jesus of Nazareth whom they had met before and who now was working in them and through them. They were aware that the same Jesus who had commissioned them before his death now, after his death, stood behind their works and words. This is the reason that they began to preach, not about the kingdom of God in general terms, but about a faith in the risen Jesus Christ which became the central point of their message. Paul's theology expressed this faith clearly. For him, it was obvious that by his death and resurrection, Jesus Christ conquered space and time. He had ascended into heaven, yet in the breaking of bread and in each of his apostles Christ continued to build his Church among Jews and gentiles until the consummation of the world.

4.3.5.4.2 The Bible and the Word of God

The resurrection experience of the early apostles is attested in 1 Thessalonians 2, 13, where we read that the words the Thessalonians heard from Paul had been accepted, "not as the word of a human being, but as what it really is, the word of God, which is at work in the believers." The early faithful were aware that the Lord, who now was in heaven, had spoken through his apostles, and the words of the Bible were not limited to the manuscripts of Paul's letters. It was extended somehow to the copies made and later to the translations when they were read by the believers. It was the same Lord Jesus, the risen one, who is freed from the fetters of space and time and transcends the "now" and the limits of time of the "after now." The word of Christ, the word of the apostles as the word of God, the bread as the body of Christ, is the same one mystery of the Resurrection. The early Christians did not present any explanation. They simply witnessed to their faith. It was the scholastic theology that tried to present some explanation for the Eucharistic presence.

4.3.5.4.3 The Eucharistic Presence

We have seen how Thomas Aquinas, by using the concept of substance and quantitative dimensions presented an explanation of how one and the same Jesus Christ can be in heaven with the Father and present with us on earth. Jesus Christ is the same one who is in preaching as many times as the word of God proclaimed and who is offering himself wherever the Eucharist is celebrated. On the basis of Einsteinian insight, a further approach can be made in support of the first Christians' experience of the risen Christ following the first day of resurrection (Horvath, 1993).

4.3.5.4.4 Jesus Christ, the Conqueror of Time and Eternity, Is the Eschatological Union of Time and Eternity

The Newtonian absolute, substantial notion of time is like a limitless great receptacle containing the concrete, measured times, one after the other. It reduces time to space as to its ultimate. Measured times may be linear, one after the other, so that the past is past and can never return, or circular so that whatever has been will be again. Such a concept raises a few problems for faith. Since only God is eternal and everlasting and there is no God besides him, the prophets proclaimed and the Church believes, that there will be an eschatological end of time. In the Newtonian concept of time, it was a problem to explain the unique position that Jesus Christ has in the history of the world. But inspired by further research on the notion of time, a new notion may be proposed which is coherent with both the Einsteinian insight and the Christian faith in Jesus Christ as the conqueror of time and eternity (Horvath, 1993, 60–4).

We can see that the purpose of the kerygma of the early Church was to transcend the time between the "past" when Jesus preached and the "now" when the proclaimed word was announced by bringing both into the future, which was not the future of men and women but the future of God, a future made by God. And this was possible because in the kerygma God's eternity appeared as power related to Jesus' presence. Thus the kerygma was not only a preaching about Jesus but the realization of the presence of God in the world of the community of Jesus Christ. The eternal God was associated with the time of Jesus, and the time of Jesus Christ became the "eternity" of the presence of God

The possibility of the kerygma as the presence of the past historical Jesus, together with the presence of God's future, suggested that through the kerygma of Jesus Christ, everyone's time could be related to eternity. The discovery of this possibility opened the door for the evangelization of the gentiles with no exception whatsoever. Through Jesus' time, God's time, that is, God's eternity, became available to every time. The universal dimension of the kerygma was a necessary outgrowth of experiencing Jesus, the proclaimer, in the proclaimed word anywhere and at any time. Jesus was not only a fact of the past but a word event now, and the two could be identified. Now, the identification of Christ as word event (the proclaimed Christ) with Jesus as past event (proclaiming the eschaton of God) meant that Jesus' time had conquered the past and the present. In contrast to profane history where the past is sublated by the remembering present, the present historical now is reached and vanquished by the time of Jesus, which as God's time, became the redeeming standard for the present as well as for the future.

By his death and resurrection, the first Christians recognized the identity of the historical Jesus with the transhistorical Christ and consequently as the one who conquered time and eternity. Thus Jesus, being the eschatological union of time and eternity, is able to be present as gift and sacrifice for sin (Heb 5, 1) and to bring about forgiveness of sin without any limit through the ministry of the priests (Jn 20, 22–24). Yet the sacrificial priesthood of the ordained priests does not mean that they have to crucify Christ or any substitute again. Rather, it simply announces the efficiency of the forgiveness of sins related to the Eucharistic Jesus. Both the Eucharist and the forgiveness of sins become realities by the power of the Holy Spirit, indicating that both are God's doing and therefore true and real.

The sacrament of order as sacrifice is more than saying mass and hearing confessions. It is sharing in the life and work of Christ. It is a life for the benefit of one's fellow human beings by breaking down the dividing wall between God and humans. The life of a priest is a sacrifice for peace and forgiveness. He is to be a friend of all, bringing peace to every one. It is remarkable that Vatican II asked the bishop that, by virtue of the fullness of his priesthood, he should not be afraid to offer the greatest sacrifice, giving his life for his people (*LG*, no. 41; Tanner, 1990, 881), a request not made in the following paragraph describing the priest's call for holiness. Yet bishops, priests, and deacons, by virtue of the ordination, should all announce and witness to the call of the tirelessly merciful God, who gave God's Son as a sin offering. And this sin offering transcended and transcends the time of the past. Forgiveness is, even now, God's doing and therefore real.

4.3.5.5 THE SACRAMENT OF ORDER AND ECUMENISM

Ecumenism is first of all a cooperation in action. And the minister of Christ should cooperate with Christian and non-Christian ministers, so far as they are all for the benefit of all their fellow human beings. They may do so since Vatican II acknowledged that the spirit of Christ has not refrained from using other communities and churches as a means of salvation whose efficacy comes from that fullness of grace and truth that has been entrusted to the catholic Church (*UR*, no. 3; Tanner, 1990, 910). An interreligious prayer may be a response to the invitation of the Holy Spirit embedded in the invitation of the leader of another religious community. "An interreligious prayer is intended," we read in the concluding statements of Bangalore 1996 and Bose 1971, "to foster human unity, its practice also makes even more urgent the search for Christian unity, prayer, and Eucharistic fellowship. Disunity in the Church hinders the Church's work for the unity of all people" (*Bulletin*, 1998, 235).

Although the Roman Catholic Church believes that, because the sacrament of order is lacking, there are ecclesial communities that have not retained the authentic and full reality of the Eucharistic mystery, yet "when they commemorate [Jesus'] death and resurrection in the Lord's supper," they profess that "it signifies life in communion with Christ and look forward to his coming in glory" (*UR*, no. 22; Tanner, 1990, 919–20). The celebration of the Lord's Supper is, therefore, more than just a prayer. It is a real "symbol" that may be understood as an authentic Eucharistic sacramental reality if we are to be able to appreciate Christ's manifold presence in our world and the meaning of the *šĕlīah* of Christ.

But as we noted, the difference between symbol and sacrament is considerable. Those who believe that the Eucharist is a sacrament can understand those who see it as only a symbol; therefore their participation in a non-Catholic Eucharistic celebration may be authentic but virtually incomplete, whereas those who do not believe in the real presence, with its sacrificial implication, would find themselves out of place in a Catholic

Eucharistic celebration. Their participation cannot be authentic and is, therefore, not commendable. Those who cannot believe in the real presence are to be respected, and in their turn they should respect those who do believe in the real presence. Without sharing the faith of a community, one cannot be a real participant in that community's confessional celebration but only a spectator. But the Eucharistic celebration is not a show. It is not just a friendly gathering either. It is the celebration of unity of faith of the community, and as such, it should be respected as a true identity implying an authentic and full unity.

There are so many celebrations that can express our unity with other human beings, believers and non-believers, Christians, Jews, and Muslims, and so on – the more so since we are all in a sense Christian, Jew, Muslim, Hindu, Protestant, and Catholic. We have so much in common (Horvath, 1975a, 274–5). The persecution of one religion is, therefore, the persecution of all religions and all human beings.

Ecumenism should be neither a covert proselytism nor the foundation of a new religion with new worshipping. Rather, we all should respect each other the way we are and help each other to be authentically what we are. Unity is not our doing but God's. It is a reconciliation, and God is the first and principal author of it. We must receive the gift of unity and consent to it in faith (2 Cor 5, 20). Is this a good ecumenism? Is not a cooperation in action for the benefit of the human race the most successful ecumenism?

4.3.5.5.1 The Anglican Order

The Anglican mass is different, even though Anglican ordination is a complex issue. In the history of the theology of Anglican ordination, there are nine periods of special importance to be distinguished: pre-Reformation England, the New Ordinal of 1550, the Edwardian Ordinal of 1552–1662, the altered form of 1662, the Oxford Movement, the bulla *Apostolicae Curae*, Anglican ministers ordained by Orthodox bishops, the recognition of the validity of South Indian orders in 1955, and post-Vatican II Anglican-Catholic dialogue.

Pre-Reformation England used the Sarum Ordinal of the Salisbury Pontifical, which is substantially identical with the Pontifical of the Western Catholic Church. The New Ordinal of 1550, decreed by the Act of Parliament on 31 January 1550, was modelled on the Sarum. The Edwardian Ordinal of 1552 was a revised version of the New Ordinal under the influence of reformers such as Thomas Cranmer, William Tyndale, and John Hooper, and the implied sacramental theology is disputed. Article XXV, for example, states, "There are two Sacraments ordained of Christ our Lord in the Gospel, that is to say Baptism and the Supper of the Lord," yet the other, one of them being order, we read in a transposed clause of 1563, are "sure witnesses and effectual signs of grace" (Hardwick, 1881, 323–4). And when we come to communion, we find that the body of Christ is given and taken and eaten only in a heavenly and spiritual manner (ibid., 331), which can be interpreted in a Catholic sense as well. The article that sounds most unambiguously reformist is XXXI, which says, "The offering of Christ once made ... Wherefore the sacrifices of Masses, in the which it was commonly said that the priest did offer Christ for the quick and the dead ... were blasphemous fables, and dangerous deceits" (ibid., 1881, 333).

If the presence of Christ is not recognized in the mass and the mass seems to gain a value independent of Christ, the reformed position is logical. The sacrificial value of the mass is from Jesus Christ present in the mass and not from the rite of the mass as such. Thus neither the form of the order nor the intention of the revisers was unambiguous. It was for this reason that one hundred years later the Edwardian Ordinal was altered. The altered form of 1662 added to the episcopal consecration, after having changed "Take the Holy Ghost" to "Receive the Holy Ghost," the words "for the office and work of a Bishop in the Church of God" and to the priesthood, "for the office and work of priest in the Church of God" (Raynal, 1871, 101–2) Leo XIII, in his encyclical *Apostolicae Curae*, acknowledged the validity of the corrected form but denied the validity of the 1552 ordinal.

Those who argue in favour of the validity of Anglican ordination would like to stress apostolic succession, which the Church of England wanted to keep (Hughes, 1968). Those who argue against it point to the defect in sacramental form and sacramental intention (Clark, 1962) and question the apostolic succession. But perhaps the question Günther Gassman (1964) asked is the fundamental one: Is Anglicanism in its real origin a Protestant or a Catholic movement? And if the majority of Anglicans would agree that Anglicanism is a Protestant movement, the question of the defects in the consecration forms and the intentionality of apostolic succession may become secondary.

What is particularly attractive in Anglicanism is that it has kept the question of the validity of the Anglican priesthood alive, perhaps indicating that even though Anglicanism was originally a Protestant movement, by its Catholic interest in the validity of the sacrament of order, it has managed to keep both the Catholic and the Protestant traditions in complementary tension. That this was the case became particularly evident when a great number of Anglican clergymen asked Orthodox bishops to ordain them. With a valid form, validly ordained Anglican bishops could validly ordain priests. And now it is not certain for a Catholic which Anglican priests have a valid ordination.

The interest of the Anglican clergy and the Anglican faithful is a grace of the Holy Spirit. Since in sacramental theology, probabilism cannot be a problem-solving principle, a conditional ordination of any Anglican priest who joins the Catholic Church is a consistent way of proceeding. In the case of a great number of Anglican priests who wish to join the Roman Catholic Church, a common concelebrated renewal and/or conditional ordination of bishops or priests would be most expressive. A collegiality of Catholic bishops would welcome the collegiality of the Anglican bishops or priests. It would not be a reordination but, rather, a thanksgiving for a earlier consecration or celebration of first ordinations. For the Church, such a celebration would be God's revelation of who is a priest or a bishop forever.

But such a celebration presupposes a communion in doctrine between the Catholic and Anglican churches. There are some favourable signs that the two churches are coming closer to each other day by day, and one day they may have a Joint Declaration similar to the one between the Lutheran and Roman Catholic churches on the Doctrine of Justification jointly signed on 31 October 1999. In the preamble it shrewdly stated that the condemnations put forward both in the Lutheran Confessions and by the Roman Catholic Church's Council of Trent are still valid today but that the two churches "have come to new insights." (nos 1, 7) The churches do not take these condemnations lightly, and they do not disavow "their own past and that those condemnations do not apply the common teaching present in the declaration" (no. 10). Such a remark should be an example for future cooperation. Yet the example of the Council of Florence should make us cautious. Consensus among theologians is not enough for a union. It has to include consensus among the faithful of the churches involved.

4.3.5.6 THE SACRAMENT OF ORDER AND WOMEN

We have noted that the vitality and eagerness of Anglican church leaders and their faithful for a valid reception of the sacrament of order is a call of the Holy Spirit. Is the movement urging the ordination of women to the priesthood similar? Since the beginning, women were never absent from the life and work of Jesus and of his first apostles. No one can claim that they hated or despised women. They were celibates, yet they loved women. Paul called Persis the "beloved one." Jesus loved Martha and Mary, each in her own way. He liked to talk to woman (Jn 4, 3–27). He saved the woman caught in adultery from being stoned. He felt compassion for the poor widow (Lk 21, 1–4) and did not mind that a woman poured ointment on him (Mt 26, 6–13; Lk 7, 36–50; Jn 12, 1–8). He liked women and women liked him (Lk 11, 27). We may consider this in a certain sense a novelty in that age. Jesus' message was not directed only to men. Any women who listened and accepted his word were for Jesus like his sister and his mother

(Mt 12, 50; Lk 8, 21). Paul was not different. He talked to women (Acts 16, 13), who found him likeable (Acts 16, 15c).

The Acts of the Apostles speaks of women as leaders of house churches, which were significant for the extension of the early Church (1 Cor 16, 19; Rom 16, 5; Col 4, 15; Phlm 2; Acts 16, 14–15. 40; MacDonald, 1996, 30–1). Margaret Y. MacDonald skilfully demonstrates in her book *Early Christian Women and Pagan Opinion* (1996) how the early Christian women were seen by the pagan Greco-Roman world and how "public reaction to early Christian women may have influenced their lives" (30–2; 164–5; 170–5).

Celsius, a philosopher of the Greco-Roman world, referred to Christianity as a belief created by a hysterical woman identified as Mary Magdalene. He was not the only Greco-Roman who found that Christian women initiated a household-based female movement which became a menace to the well-established Roman society. The Romans considered religion public and a male affair. But the second-century critics of Christianity recognized that the early church rendered a domestic issue public and "attacked Christianity for blurring the conventional distinction between public male space and private female space" (MacDonald, 1996, 31).

4.3.5.6.1 Non-institutional Ministries of Women

In the first centuries women had non-institutional and institutional ministries in the Church.

MANY WOMEN

Among the non-institutionalized ministries, we find "many women" who simply followed Jesus when he went around through villages and cities proclaiming the good news (Lk 8, 1–3). Out of their means, τὰ ὑπάρχοντα, they ministered, διακονέω, and provided for Jesus and for his followers. They witnessed his death (Mt 27, 55; Mt 15, 4) and his resurrection (Mt 28, 1–10; Mk 16, 1.6.9; Lk 24, 10; Jn 20, 1.11ff.). They were with the apostles expecting the coming of the Holy Spirit (Acts 1, 14). Following Jesus' example, Peter, Barnabas, and Paul too were accompanied by "sister (believer)–women" (ἀδελφὴ γυναικός) who helped them "to refrain from working for a living" (1 Cor 9, 64) and also in the work of spreading the gospel. Paul mentions several women who worked with him. One of them was Phoebe, whom Paul calls "our sister." He does not call her a deaconess but a helper of the church at Cechreae. She needed help (παραστῆτε) at Cechreae but in turn she helped many before (προστάτις ἐγενήθη), including Paul (Rom 16, 1–3). The expression οὖσαν διάκονον is a special grammatical construction. The "one being" is feminine, yet the service, διάκονον, is masculine (Rom 16, 1). It is noteworthy that the term "deaconess" was not used before the third century. Paul names a woman, Mary, who worked hard among the Romans (Rom 16, 6). Tryphaena, Tryphosa, and Persis worked also "hard in the Lord" (Rom 16, 12). Work in the Lord and work in the gospel, like that of Euodia and Syntyche (Phil 4, 2–3), means apostolic work. Clement of Alexandria informs us that women such as Euodia and Syntyche ministered to the women living in a special women's department separated from men (*Stromata*, 3, 6; PG 8, 115). Their relation to individual apostles was personal rather than institutional, unlike that of the widows (1 Tim 5, 9–16).

PROPHETESSES

We have noticed already that, together with the eleven in the upper room, there were women also waiting for the Holy Spirit. After the descent of the Holy Spirit, Peter recalled that in the messianic age sons and daughters would prophesy (Acts 2, 17). In the early church, indeed, there were women who prophesied. Philip the Evangelist, one of the seven of Acts 6, 5, had four unmarried daughters who prophesied (Acts 20, 9). Not for teaching (1 Cor 14, 34–36) but for prophesying did Paul give instruction to women (1 Cor 11, 5). His response was simple: follow the prevailing customs (1 Cor 11, 16) and keep the veil on.

Both teaching and prophesying were special gifts of the Holy Spirit. The purpose of teaching was to present the Christ event as acceptable by faith and make it intelligible as truth acceptable to the human mind, whereas prophecy was to help the community in making decisions for the present and the future in a search to know the will of God. So Agabus the prophet indicated what the will of God was for Paul in Jerusalem (Acts 21, 10.14). The prophets of the church at Antioch learned from the Holy Spirit that Paul and Barnabas should be sent to the mission among the gentiles (Acts 13, 1–3). The prophets Judas and Silas exhorted and strengthened the church of Antioch with many words (Acts 15, 32). So did the prophetesses in their communities, helping them to discern the will of God in their daily agenda. Like the prophets, they were not constituted by election and ordination but were called directly by the Holy Spirit (1 Cor 14, 29–33). In Pauline literature the prophets are mentioned after the apostles but before the doctors (1 Cor 12, 28; Eph 2, 20; 4, 11; Rom 12, 6; Acts 13, 1).

From the second and third century on, the ministry of the prophets faded away when the Montanists and Gnostics appealed to the inspiration of the Spirit and called themselves prophets or prophetesses. Their spirit was no longer the spirit of Jesus Christ because the Christ event, they said, had been replaced by the Spirit event. The role of the apostles and doctors was taken up by the prophets and prophetesses. Before long the Montanists and Gnostics were considered heretics, and we do not hear much of the prophets and prophetesses any more in the early Church. But we learn more about widows, virgins, and deaconesses.

4.3.5.6.2 Institutional Female Ministries in the Church

WIDOWS, VIRGINS, AND DEACONESSES

From the earliest times we find in the local communities widows who were supported by the Church (Acts 6, 2; 9, 38; 1 Tim 5, 16c). It was one of the charitable services of the new church. There were also widows who were supported by their own families (1 Tim 5, 16a–b). Furthermore, there were young widows who were encouraged to get married again (1 Tim 5, 11–15). And finally, there were widows, members with a special status, a kind of "order" mentioned mostly after the apostles and deacons. The members of the widowhood were elected (καταλέγω) following the criteria laid down by Paul (1 Tim 5, 9–10). Their vocation was similar to the "many women" of the gospels – work of charity and hospitality for itinerant apostles and the Christian faithful (cf. Rom 1, 7; 16, 2). They provided the place and occasion for celebrating the breaking of the bread and perhaps kept the Eucharist for the sick. Polycarp encouraged them to consider themselves "the altars of God" (θυσιαστήριον θεοῦ) and reminded them to be prudent about the faith of the Lord (Polycarp, *Phil.* 4, 2.3; Funk, 1901, 301). The *Disdascalia apostolorum*, an early church order of the first part of the third century, exhorts the widows that being the "altar of God," they should not walk around visiting one house after the other to chat, but stay at home like an *altar of God* or an *altar of Christ* to pray to God (3, 6; Funk, 1901, 190). "Faith of Christ," "altar of Christ," "pray," and "special services for women" are the distinctive notes we find in early literature dealing with the widows. All of this suggests the special closeness to Christ characteristic of the later deaconesses and nuns, the outgrowth of the first institutionalized ministry of women.

Clement of Alexandria named the widows among the "elected persons" (*Paedagogus*, 3, 12. 97; PG 8, 676)) of the Church following the presbyters, the bishops, and the deacons. Tertullian applied his word "ordo" to the widowhood, recognizing it as a special social group or status (*Ad uxorem* 1, 7; PL 1, 1286). It was a *secta*, a way of life, a separate group distinct from the bishops, presbyters and deacons, yet belonged to the clergy (*Monogamia*, 12; PL, 1, 947–8), who had ecclesial but not priestly dignity (Origen, *Homilia in Lucam*, 17; PG, 13, 1846–7).

From the second century on, young girls, "virgins," began to join the group of widows. Ignatius of Antioch, in his letters to the church of *Smyrna* (12, 1; Funk, 1901, 287), greets the virgins as so-called widows (*παρθένους τὰς λεγομένας χήρας*) . Tertullian also knew a virgin less than twenty years old who had joined the widows (*De virginibus velandis*, 9; Tertullian, 1954, 2, 1219). *Didascalia apostolorum*, of the early third century in Syria, is the work that for the first time mentions deaconesses. We find the new Greek word and learn that a virgin should be a deaconess. Only if there is no suitable virgin might a widow of good reputation take her place (6, 17; Funk, 1913, 341).

It seems that at this time a deaconess became the head of the college of widows. As time passed and more and more virgins joined the order of widows, it progressively became the order of deaconesses. John of Chrysostom confirms this change when he says that there was now the chorus of virgins as there was formerly the chorus of widows (*Homilia 3 in illud widua eligatur*; PG, 51, 323). It seems that Chrysostom was one of the last still writing about widows. As celibacy prevailed more and more among the clergy, deaconesses were elected from the virgins and became leaders. Their function was similar to that of the widows. It consisted mostly in assisting women in baptism and in their needs. When the deaconesses tried to act like the deacons and assisted around the altar, the prohibitions did not fail to follow. Gelasius Papa energetically denied this right to them in 494 (PL, 59, 55ff.).

When the institution of deaconesses was to replace the institution of widows, it borrowed the name of the deacons and with it the ceremony of the deacons. The First Council of Nicaea in 325 made it clear that deaconesses ought not receive the imposition of hands; so they were in all respects to be numbered among the laity (canon 19; Tanner, 1990, 15). Nonetheless, there were some ancient and medieval Oriental and Roman Ordinals in which the rite of installing a deaconess was almost identical with that of the ordination of a deacon: imposition of hands, invocation of the Holy Spirit, imposition of a stole, and receiving communion from the bishop (Mayer, 1938, 56–63). The Carthusian nuns' reception of the stole at the time of their profession is a survival of the "ordination" of the early deaconesses.

The order of deaconesses lasted in the Western church until the twelfth century and in the Oriental Church somewhat longer. It was revived in an updated form at Kaiserswerth in 1836 for the Lutheran Church, followed by the Methodists, the Church of Scotland, and the Church of England. The formation and the training of Protestant deaconesses is to help them in taking care of the sick and the poor, teaching, and helping out in parish work.

RELIGIOUS ORDERS OF WOMEN

With the foundation of the Benedictine Monastic Order, women found a new organized way of participating in the life and work of Jesus Christ. The consecration of abbesses began to replace the ordination of deaconesses. The various forms of the religious orders and congregations helped woman to serve the Church in evangelizing, ministering to the needy and the sick, and educating children. Schools and hospitals became the memorials of the Catholic nuns' skills. Their achievements, for which they may never receive well-deserved recognition from their Church, the state, and their beneficiaries, made the world in which we live more human.

The theology of the work of nuns enhances the strength and meaning of the special closeness of God, witnessed already by their early ancestor, the institutionalized service of widows of the apostolic age. They had also been called the "altars of Christ," symbolizing stability based on the nearness of Christ. To the Church since then women and their service have meant stability and the nearness of Christ. Their royal priesthood has witnessed Christ's tireless call for mercy through the ages.

The Church feels that the beauty of a woman is always more than the beauty of an attractive young girl. With age, it becomes deeper and transforms all her being. So too the wisdom of a woman is more than the knowledge of a successful businesswoman. It is more sophisticated and more universal. Finally, the strength of a woman is more powerful than the muscles of a she-woman. It is more mysterious. Perhaps this is why preliterate men wanted to gather in "men-only" assemblies. To fulfill the mission received from Christ, the Church needs women more than ever before.

"ELECTED" CATHOLIC WOMEN FOR THE THIRD MILLENNIUM

Catholic women and religious sisters have to rethink and find their place in the Church of the third millennium. Some will be always elected, like the first widows, to help the Church more directly than housewives and mothers are able to do. Yet they will be not to supplement but to complement what the world can achieve in science, business, politics, social life, spirituality, parishes, schools, and hospitals and to add to all that a special dimension of what the closeness of God means. They may not be called widows, virgins, deaconesses, or sisters, but perhaps just the Lord's "elect," the name of the first institutionalized helpers of the apostolic church (cf. also ἐκλεκτῇ κυρίᾳ, "elect lady," in 2 Jn 1). As they were then, so they will be elected by God to be members of a society of complementarity, the specifically female role in the world.

Elected women are elected to complement the Church as any woman as a woman is called to complement man in the world. Complement means something different from, something more than, what is complemented. Complementarity is the adjustment of two mutually exclusive approaches (Teller, 1969, 78–97). Man is not woman and woman is not man, yet the "adjustment" of the two is the key to success, peace, and happiness in the world. A woman may not replace a priest, but she is to complement the service the priest is to make to the Church. And this is what the modern Catholic woman, the modern Catholic religious sisterhood, has to discover. It should be a new association or society of complementarity, a new cooperation with science, business, and politics, with the marginal people of the society, with the spiritual life of a parish, and so on. There are to be discovered new methods and principles of developing science, social and ecological environment, theology of God and the world, and so on through the collegiality of the *electas*, which God has yet to reveal to us in the third millennium, the millennium of the women.

Life and history have a way of providing for all people a "golden age" to make a considerable contribution to the common good of humanity and to reveal the mystery of God and God's creation. Not one of them has the final say yet each past has a future since history is resurrection and resurrection is history.

In order "to let the heritage of the Bible be opened more widely" (*SC*, no. 51; Tanner, 1990, 831), the document *Pontifical Biblical Commission*'s *Interpretation of the Bible in the Church*, published on 14 May 1993, presented various methods of interpreting the biblical texts positively yet marking each one's limitations. Like biblical studies, women's studies display a great variety of interpretation according to the different methods. Each method has a perspective that helps one to know and appreciate human existence more. Reading Margaret Y. MacDonald's *Early Christian Women and Pagan Opinion* (1996), one may ask, Will Christian women present a menace to well-established modern society as the first Christian women did? There is much more involved here than saying a mass in a church. How will the public reaction to Christian women in Africa, Asia, America, and Europe influence their lives? It will probably be seen in the time to come. But that the early Church owed a great deal to women is well documented in the Pauline writings. Christianity presented a great chance to the women of that time; so will it also do for the women of the future.

4.3.5.6.3 Women Priests?

The question of women priests in the Church is not new. It goes back to the second part of the second century, to the beginning of Montanism, an apocalyptic movement of prophets and prophetesses around the year 172. Also called Pepuzians, they had male and female priests. Epiphanius learned that Christ had appeared to a woman from Pepuza as a woman and had given her a special wisdom. Some of them had a special devotion to Eve, the first woman, and some worshipped Mary, the mother of Jesus, as a goddess and offered sacrifices to her. Epiphanius attributed such a faith to the devil (*Adversus haereses*, 2, 1; *PG*, 41, 879–82). The Montanists were condemned by several Asian synods and also by Pope Zephyrinus. Irenaeus listed among the heretics the Marcionites, who allowed women to concelebrate the Eucharist, which sometimes ended up, according to Irenaeus, in carnal union between the priest and priestess (*Adversus haereses*, 1, 13; *PG*, 7, 579–86). The Marcionite Christology was Docetist and, like the Gnostics, denied the real value of the Eucharist as well as priestly ordination. Women who dared to teach and baptize into this new religion Tertullian called heretics and their ordination reckless and empty (*De prescrip-*

tione haereticorum, 32; PL, 2, 56). So did Augustine, not because they were women, but because they taught some doctrine contrary to Christ's teaching (*De haeresibus*, 1, 26–31; PL, 42, 30).

One can say, therefore, that in the early Church the ordination of women was a praxis of heretics and the Church could not agree with it. Such condemnation, however, was general. Practitioners were called heretics on doctrinal grounds. From the condemnation of the Montanists, Marcionists, and Pepuzians as heretics, some authors have argued that the concept "only man can be validly ordained" is a doctrine *de fide definita*, a revealed truth (Sola, 1962, 674). But one can say that they were condemned as heretics not for ordaining women but for teaching heretical doctrines about the Eucharist and ordination. Yet we have to note that some early theologians already argued against the ordination of women by Jesus Christ, who did not ordain even his mother to the priesthood. We notice that when Epiphanius, Irenaeus, Tertullian, and Augustine argued against the ordination of women, they did not argue for the theological notes. There was no theological consensus and no council took the issue up for discussion.

Constitutiones apostolorum around 400 argued against the ordination of women from 2 Corinthians 14, 34–40 with 1 Timothy 2, 12–14 and 1 Corinthians 11, 6. Man is the head of woman, and woman is the body of man. The ordination of women would make the body the principle of the head This would be against the order of creation. It is all the more objectionable since in Christianity there are no goddesses to whom pagan women in general sacrifice (3, 9; Funk, 1913, 201). *Constitutiones Apostolorum* suggested that both the natural law and the divine law prohibit the priestly ordination of a woman. We should note here, though, that the same *Constitutiones* prohibited a woman from baptizing, which had been allowed them from the earliest times. The argument of the symbolism of man as head of the women was repeated by Patristic writers and Scholastic theologians, who tried to find new arguments against women priests.

Bonaventure seems to have been the first who argued from the identity of gender. Christ was male; therefore the priest who presents him must be of the same gender (*In 4 Sent.*, d 25, a 2, q 1). Thomas Aquinas repeated the old argument that woman is inferior to man and cannot represent the excellence of the head of the Church, Christ the Lord (*Summa theol. suppl.*, q 39, a 1). Latin canon law simply states that a woman is not a valid recipient of ordination (canon 1024).

One should note that once the sacrificial relevance for a religion disappears and the teaching role is emphasized, women join religious leaders. In the Brahman literature, for example, which covers the time from 1000 to 600 BC, the priest is a sacrificial priest. In the Upanishads after 600 BC the priest is a teacher-priest, and women take part in free discussion. It seems that sacrificial ritual knows of no women priests, whereas religions based mostly on knowing welcome women priests. Thus it is understandable that the Reformers permitted women to preach the word of God as pastors of congregations.

The theologians' arguments about why women cannot be ordained are only secondary. The real issue is that there is in the Church a negative tradition lasting over two thousand years. The decisive question is whether such a prohibition is of divine or human origin. In other words, is the prohibition from God such that the Church can never change it, or is it only a human law that the Church has the right to change it whenever it seems useful?

Thomas admitted that there were certain theologians who claimed that woman could validly though illicitly be ordained. Yet he thought otherwise (*Summa theol. suppl.*, q 39, a 1). Bonaventure said that it is more probable that a woman cannot be ordained validly. The prohibition is by divine law (*In 4 Sent.*, dit. 25, a 2, q l). Francisco de Vitoria held that it was of divine law, but to say the contrary he did not find absurd (Dix, 1937, 20–1). For William A. Van Roo the male subject belonged to the substance of the sacrament. The Church therefore cannot change it (Van Roo, 1957, 125). Ludwig Lercher proposed as theologically certain that women cannot be ordained to the priesthood (1950, 2. 315). Yet it was not clear what syllogism led him to conclude his proposition from a revealed truth by means of a natural truth. Other believed that it was a common and certain thesis among the theologians (cf. Doronzo, 1962, 394–6).

In his apostolic letter *Ordinatio Sacerdotalis,* published on 13 May 1994, John-Paul II said that he had no authority to change the church's two-thousand-year-old tradition about ordaining only men to the priesthood. He made it clear that he believed it was by divine law that the Church cannot validly ordain women to the priesthood. John Paul II reiterated what he had already said in his *Exhortation on the Laity, Christi fideles Laici,* on 30 December 1988, that a woman cannot receive the sacrament of order is the practice that the Church has always found "in the expressed will of Christ, totally free and sovereign, who called only men to be his apostles." At that time John Paul II cited Paul VI's speech to the Committee for International Women's Year, saying that the pope cannot change what Christ did, yet he wanted to promote the role of women in missionary evangelization in the life of the Christian community (*Origins,* vol 18, no 35, 188). According to a response from the Congregation for the Doctrine of Faith to his *Ordinatio Sacerdotalis,* John Paul II made it clear that he believed that this doctrine belongs to the Deposit of Faith. It has been set forth infallibly by the ordinary and universal magisterium and is therefore to be held always, everywhere, and by all as belonging to the deposit of faith.

Hermann Joseph Pottmeyer, a member of the International Theological Commission, said in a short essay published in the *Tablet* (2 November 1996, 1435–6) that the presumption is justified that it was only at the request of Cardinal Ratzinger that Pope John Paul II did not make an *ex cathedra* statement about the impossibility of ordaining woman in the Roman Catholic Church. The pope himself was sure that this was a doctrine that could be defined *ex cathedra.* Pottmeyer in the same article suggested that a universal council should be called to solve the problem once for all providing a sign of the will of God in this matter. But, one can ask, after more than one papal statement on the ordination of women, could an Ecumenical Council decide otherwise? Could another pope in his conscience approve the decision of a Council allowing the ordination of women to the priesthood in the Roman Catholic Church, notwithstanding previous papal statements?

So long as there is no *ex cathedra* papal statement, the answer is not difficult. A new insight is needed which may justify the validity of an old insight. Progress, however, is not expected in presenting more arguments pro and con but in a mutual ability to share one's own conscience with others and let one see what the other sees and vice versa. To put it another way, are there really two kinds of love for Jesus Christ involved? And if yes, can the love for Jesus Christ become a problem-solving or a question-raising paradigm or both? It is at this point when one's thinking about faith calls for a loving prayer.

A practical case may be insightful. Suppose that there is a faithful Catholic woman who comes to a priest or to a bishop and says that she has a vocation to the priesthood in the Roman Catholic Church. What can the priest or the bishop say? One should ask, where may such a desire come from? From the devil? From her natural ambition? Or from God? May such a desire or vocation come from God? Thinking of Thérèse of Lisieux, could a priest or bishop say to the woman, "Just pray, foment, and cultivate your vocation for the priesthood in the Roman Catholic Church quietly, privately, even though you can be sure that you never become a priest?" Yes. He can and should say that. A grace, even if it is never activated, is never in vain. As the scholastic axiom is true when it says *nulla potentia frustra,* no ability or talent is in vain, so a theologian can say *nulla gratia frustra,* there is no grace that is in vain. No grace is without purpose. In the present writer's view, a Catholic woman's desire to become a priest may still come from God and God may grant the wish the way God granted the wish of Thérèse of Lisieux, who became a missionary without leaving her convent. We never entirely know the ways of God, who certainly loves women as Jesus did. And God's ways are not our ways. Thank God for that.

4.3.6 The Sacrament of Order and Systematic Theology

4.3.6.1 THE SACRAMENT OF ORDER IS A SYMBOL FOR THE WORLD: CALL

The sacrament of order is not a symbol for the world as "order" opposed to chaos. It is not even a symbol just for religion and the Church. It is a symbol for the world as a call. A call is a transcendental notion of being. The Father calls the Son, the Son calls the Father, both call the Holy Spirit, and the Holy Spirit, together with the Father and the Son, calls the world. The creation of the world is a call. Instead of an *exitus* and *reditus*, instead of an emanation like that in late Platonism or in modern process philosophy, the creation is a call to God out of nothing. It gives priority to the final cause over the efficient cause. The being is not a mechanical process following the law of pushing, commands, and orders but an existence of freedom, attraction, and invitation. It is an invitation from someone to someone to be rather than not to be. Wanting a child is a call of someone into existence which precedes the action of bringing it about.

The call is not just a call to be. It is an invitation to cooperate, to work together with the creator to make the world better, to make it more what it was created for. In classic Catholic philosophy, being is one, true and good. But it may remain an abstract concept unless it turns into a dynamic action to become one, true and good, in the way for which it was created to be one, true and good.

On the surface level, this is the fundamental law of the "capital" or the investment: a call to invest more money or labour. At a deeper level, life in general is a call to be healthy, educated, successful and so on. Friendship is a call to move from loneliness, from depression, from inability to wholeness, fullness, perfection. A call is the way of existence: to be always more than one was and is now. A call moves the cosmos and the biosphere. It is inserted in the world of animals and cosmic worlds moving them out of the past and present into the unknown future and always following each one's call.

At the basic fundamental level, a call is inserted by God in the heart of every creature and in every human being. It is experienced as a restless yearning, as a universal law of gravity, a sense of being away from where one is to where one would like to be. It is a desire for the indefinite, the unlimited, the infinite, God. It is restlessness, as Augustine expressed it, for every human being until he or she can rest in God (Augustine, 1993, 3). Since that call is universal, the love of God is the very essence of human life. And the priest is called to call that love of God out of each human life.

4.3.6.2 THE SACRAMENT OF ORDER IS A SYMBOL OF HUMAN EXISTENCE: A CHALLENGE TO INITIATIVE

When we read that male and female were created in God's own image (Gen 1, 27), we may interpret the words to mean calling our future into being. God created us to love our future and take the initiative in the world, in our society, and in our life. It is Christian hope that lets us dare to take the initiative for that future. It is a hope that is not just an expectation but a trust that God's help will never fail to assist in human daring. It may not turn out the way one calculated, yet there is no doubt that the postponement of the promised help means new help surpassing expectations.

The sacrament of ordination may sound like sending. Yet really it is a call to go and work with Christ, whose call is an encouragement: "do not be afraid, be bold, I promise, I will be with you always to close of the age" (Mt 28, 20).

4.3.6.3 THE SACRAMENT OF ORDER IS A SYMBOL FOR THE CHURCH: CONSTANT DEPENDENCE ON THE HISTORICAL JESUS AS ITS CREATOR

The sacrament of order is a reminding symbol for the Church that it is not self-made; it was made by Christ. Whereas the sacrament of baptism together with the sacrament of confirmation brings about the charismatic, moving the Church forward into the future under the guidance of the Holy Spirit; it is the sacrament of order that makes the priest and through him the Church in a sense "conservative," looking to Christ, who came to be for every human being an everlasting standard of the future. It makes the Church "Christocentric," Christed, a Church made by Christ. Whether the Church is a people, an institution, a community, a service, a mission, a sacrament, or a falling in love with God, the priest makes any of these models Christed, reminding all that without Christ they can do nothing (Jn 15, 5). This is the meaning of apostolic succession, and this was the meaning of the expression about the priest as "alter-Christus," that is, making Christ present and presenting Christological meaning for everything.

4.3.6.4. THE SACRAMENT OF ORDER IS A SYMBOL FOR CHRISTOLOGY: CHRIST'S CALL IS ONCE FOR ALL

To say yes today and no tomorrow is human. It is a sort of privilege of living in time. Christ lived in time and made his time the expression of eternity. His eternity entered into time and his time into eternity. So too his call to the priesthood enters time. It has the characteristic of yes and no because Christ enters into a dialogue with a human being in time. Yet once both the called and the caller have said yes together and the yes is the yes of Jesus Christ, the call enters eternity and becomes a call once for all.

Here we sense again the mystery of the presence of the sacrifice at Calvary in the mass. The sacrifice of Christ at Calvary entered eternity, but the Church's response is both in time and in eternity as well. Similarly, Christ takes up the yes of the ordinand, pronounced in time, and joins it to his priestly yes, pronounced at the cross to his Father. And so the yes of a human being in other times becomes a yes once for all with the call made once for all.

4.3.6.5 THE SACRAMENT OF ORDER IS A SYMBOL FOR THE REVELATION OF THE TRIUNE GOD: WHEREVER THIS PERSON IS, THERE CHRIST WILL BE AS SAVIOUR

The sacrament of order reveals God as the one who cares and directs God's own people, which after Christ is the entire human race. As God called Adam, Abraham, Moses, and his prophets and sent Jesus Christ with the Holy Spirit, so is God personally calling and sending every priest of Jesus Christ. In the sacrament of order there are two kinds of revelation taking place. The first is that wherever this man is, God is available as Saviour. And the second is that the God who is made available is the God of Jesus Christ, a God who loves human beings. He forgives and offers eternal life by sharing life with more and more people and brings unity in the pluralism of the world by the Spirit of Jesus Christ.

Yet not only the priest but every human is a priest. For being called by God to God and only for God, each human being is a revelation of God as being created by God for God. To create someone for less than God would be against the holiness of God as love. The uniqueness of each human being is revelation of God as unique and as love. Love personalizes and makes one sacred and free – in a certain sense, absolute. The freedom of each human being comes from being created by God free, unique, and the slave of no one. If one serves, he or she does so freely by love, creating someone or something divine. And the priest of Jesus Christ calls this uniqueness out of each human being to become the son or daughter of God and lord by sharing the lordship of Jesus Christ.

4.3.6.6 THE SACRAMENT OF ORDER IS A SYMBOL FOR ESCHATOLOGY: ACTIONS IN THE PRESENT CAN HAVE A DECISIVE IMPACT ON THE FUTURE

Because Jesus Christ conquered time and death and made the end present to any instance of time, priestly ordination is an action done not only in the present but in the future as well. It is not the bishop but Christ who is the one who ordains a priest forever. The possibility of an ordination *ad tempus*, for a given time, supposes eternity as endless time and eschatology as an event of time, bringing about no difference between our present life and the life to come. Consequently, our actions in time would make no difference for the future. They would not deserve even in the state of sanctifying grace, either eternal happiness or eternal punishment. Christ's merit would similarly not be infinite or eternal by itself but merely by external decree of God the Father. But this is not the way it is.

Human life does makes a difference in the future. A past is never just a past. It is the parent of the future. Human beings do not live in vain. The way they live does make an impact on the future. This is so on account of the mystical body of Christ, which receives life from Jesus Christ who is God, who was and will be so forever (Rev 1, 8) and shares his eternal life with people (Jn 14, 3) freely according to their works (Rom 2, 6). Sins forgiven on earth are forgiven in heaven. Yes to the love for God lets the Triune God make a home within the universe (Jn 14, 23). The words "This is my body" and "This is my blood" let them become true through the words of Christ. Christ made and makes human life a worthwhile drama with the possibility of triumph or tragedy.

4.3.6.7 THE SACRAMENT OF ORDER IS A SYMBOL FOR PNEUMATOLOGY: CHRISTOLOGICAL PNEUMATOLOGY, THE REVELATION OF SIN

The sacrament of order is a symbol for pneumatology in liberating the future from its past. The future depends on the past yet never becomes its slave. The Spirit is always new. The sacrament of order exhibits pneumatology both as the forgiveness of sins and as the revelation of sin, which only Christ can forgive. The Spirit is to convince the world concerning the sin of ignoring the call, concerning righteousness that the call is a call of Jesus from his Father, and concerning the judgment that the call is once for all (Jn 16, 7–11). Jesus's call is a call in the Spirit. The Spirit is not to force. It means freedom and anticipation of the future as living in joy, peace, and love. Christ has conquered the world (Jn 16, 33) and let created beings triumph over the evil of natural disasters, human cruelty, stupidity, and hatred.

4.3.6.8 THE SACRAMENT OF ORDER IS A SYMBOL FOR MARIOLOGY: MARY AS "CO-REDEMPTRIX"

The sacrament of order is a symbol for Mary's being called by God's special love for her. God called her. She accepted the call and took the initiative to cooperate with Christ in his redemptive work precisely as a woman in her complementary role to the work of Christ. She became God's co-worker, co-redemptrix with Christ. She is this not as an equal but as complement in the sense of complementarity as the adjustment of two mutually exclusive approaches: her God became her Son, yet her Son was still her God. Such is the mystery of redemption. In Mary one can see what Christ can do in and with a human being. She is a revelation of Christ in the Christian anthropology of the new life in Christ. Since it was a special, free love of God for Mary that made God call Mary and since Mary replied to this special love by her special love for God, the sacrament of order is a symbol for Mary and Mary is a symbol for the "apostles" of Christ.

4.4 WHAT IS THE SACRAMENT OF FORGIVENESS?

4.4.1 *Introduction*

The sacrament known as the sacrament of penance or the sacrament of reconciliation or simply confession may be called the sacrament of forgiveness (Orsy, 1978, 17). The terms "confession," "penance," and "reconciliation," in their contemporary use, have a connotation that fails to convey the real event taking place in this sacrament, the realization of perfect love for God. Penance is just part of the sacrament, which more often takes place after sins are forgiven. Confession of sins to "another human being" is much less than what God is doing in this sacrament. It may, indeed, be difficult to understand that God can be angry and would need to be reconciled. Rather, people are angry with their neighbours, and the reconciliation should take place not in the church but in their homes (Mt 5, 24).

Forgiving is a biblical term used by Christ who, came to call not the righteous but sinners (Mt 9, 13; Mk 2, 17; Lk 5, 32) by proclaiming it (Mt 18, 12–14; Lk 7, 47; Jn 3, 17; 12, 47), granting it (Mt 9, 2–6; Mk 2, 5–11; Lk 5, 35–39; 7, 47–50), and delegating it to his apostles (Jn 20, 22–23; Mt 22, 16.19; 18, 18) to preach it in his name to all nations (Lk 24, 47; cf. Acts 2, 38; 5, 31; 10, 43; 13, 38–39; Eph 4, 32; Col 3, 13; 1 Jn 2, 12).

Forgiving is a human reality. Christians are asked to forgive each other (Mt 6, 12–15; Lk 11, 4) because otherwise God will not forgive their trespasses (Mt 6, 15; cf. Mt 18, 21–22.35; Mk 11, 25–26; Lk 6, 37; 11, 4; 17, 3–4; Col 3, 13). Forgiving may have many forms and expressions, and Christ did not determine the way Christians have to express their forgiveness. It was left to them to follow the custom of the people they belonged to and lived with. Now, this common human reality of forgiving was taken up by Christ and made a symbol for one of his sacraments when he breathed on his disciples and said to them, "Receive the Holy Spirit. If you forgive the sins of any, they are forgiven; if you retain the sins of any they will be retained" (Jn 20, 22–23). As at the time of the Incarnation (Lk 1, 35), so here also the name of the Holy Spirit reminds us that the human reality of forgiving has a deeper reality and meaning. It transcends the purely human dimension. The forgiving will be not just the forgiving of a Christian or of any human being but the forgiving of Christ in heaven, as he made clear by his words (Mt 16, 19; 18, 18). It will be a forgiving by God lifting up the imperfect love of the repenting sinner into a perfect love for God. The mystery of the fourth sacrament of Christ is the mystery of God's merciful love for sinners revealed in the Eucharistic words of God's Son dying for the forgiveness of sins (Mt 26, 28).

4.4.2 Ways of Forgiving

4.4.2.1 THE PRELITERATE AGE: PROPITIATION OF THE ANGER OF THE ANCESTORS

Since the beginning, people have experienced success and failure, good and evil in their life. Not the good but the evil was mysterious and needed explanation. They searched for and came up with their "bad deeds" as the reason for their bad luck. The Lugbara, of the Sudanic Linguistic Family, came to believe, for example, that *ezaten,* sin, is contracted by "bad deeds" which "rejected true agnatic kinship values" (Middleton, 1960, . 19). Sin was an offence not against the supreme God but against the ancestors. It weakened the harmony and unity of the community. Sacrifice, in general a sharing of food with the ancestors, was a form of cementing the group's solidarity (ibid., 68). To expiate the anger of the ancestors, the Herero priest took a mouthful of blessed water and spurted it over the transgressor who confessed his sins against the tribal laws (Veder, 1966). The Yakö Bantoid of Southern Nigeria gave some bronze manillas, or pottery flasks, or a reproduction of the head of the petitioner, made of clay, to *ase,* calm, a benevolent spirit, who in turn, reconciled people angry with each other "by cooling their hearts" and thus changing the destructive egoistic passion into a benevolent heart (Forde, 1964, 265). Not forgiveness but propitiation was the purpose of the Thonga offering as well (Junod, 1962, 39).

What words and actions did for people in preliterate culture, writings did for people in the literate age. The purpose of all three was to create harmony and unity among the conflicting forces and tendencies people experienced in their daily life. Releasing feelings and creating harmony among conflicting forces and emotions prompted language, crying out for help in the form of petition and prayer (Berggren, 1975, 107–8; 206–8). Prayers, confessions, and psychotherapy are all visible symbols and expressions of reaching out to others for help and peace. Each provides an elaborate form of avoiding conflicting forces, restoring and conserving good relations with the world in which people live. In the preliterate stage this referred mostly to relations with the ancestors. But for Israel it referred to God, the real "ancestor," who had called Israel into existence, and good relations with Yahweh were life or death for them (Dt 30, 15–20).

4.4.2.2 THE PRE-PROPHETIC TIMES OF THE OLD TESTAMENT: OBEDIENCE TO THE LAW

THE DECALOGUE

One of the earliest codes of prohibitions, prescriptions, rewards, and punishments is the Decalogue of the Ten Commandments (Ex 20, 1–17; cf. Dt

5, 1–21). In it we can list eight prohibitions (no other God, no idols, no taking God's name in vain, no killing, no adultery, no stealing, no false testimony, no coveting) and two prescriptions (keeping the Sabbath, honouring one's parents). There is one reward offered: long life for honouring one's parents. The punishment of a jealous God visited the iniquity of those who hated God on the community up to the third and the fourth generations. For stealing committed by Achan at a battle, the community was punished by a defeat at Ai, and the criminal was stoned to death (Jos 7, 1–26). The reward for those who loved God and kept the commandments was that the same God showed steadfast love to thousands (Ex 20, 5b–6). No forgiveness is mentioned in this context.

THE YAHWIST CODE OF THE LATE PRE-MONARCHIC PERIOD

The Yahwist Code (Ex 34, 17–26) lists three prohibitions (no molten god, no blood offering with leaven, no Passover leftover) and four pre-prescriptions (keep the unleavened bread feast, make the first fruit offering, keep the Sabbath, and appear before the Lord three times a year, not empty-handed). The reward would be that God would cast out nations before Israel and enlarge its borders.

As an introduction to the Yahwist Code in the book of Exodus, we find an early structure of forgiveness recalling times when Israel broke the covenant (Ex 34, 6–9). The first moment was the recognition of God as merciful, gracious, slow to anger, and abounding in steadfast love for thousands, forgiving iniquity, transgressions, and sins. This recognition of God is a kind of credal formula, often repeated in the Bible (cf. Num 14, 19; Neh 9, 17.31; Ps 85, 15; 103, 8; Jon 4, 2). Yet the merciful God was able to punish the iniquity of the fathers upon their children to the third and the fourth generations, but by confessing sinfulness and asking for forgiveness the way Moses did, God forgave (Ex 34, 8–9). On account of Moses' prayer, the broken covenant was renewed. Sanctions or punishments are not mentioned this time. For the petition of a righteous member of the community, the sins of the community might be forgiven (cf. also Gen 18, 32).

This episode is a kind of symbol of God's forgiveness in Christ. Christ, the new Moses, reveals in his life and death God as graciousness yet as the one who "by no means clears the guilty" (Ex 34, 7), goes into the midst of his people, identifies himself with them, pardons their iniquity and sins, and takes them for his inheritance. He made a new covenant, and it was for his righteousness that the sins of the world are forgiven. Before all people he did "marvels such as have not been wrought in all the earth or in any nation" (cf. Ex 34, 10) in the "mighty deed" of his resurrection. Sanctions and punishments are not mentioned in this context, suggesting that satisfactions are not punishments but, rather, identification with Christ, who took the sin of the world on himself.

OTHER CODES OF THE OLD TESTAMENT

The Code of the Covenant or Elohist Code (Ex 20, 22–23, 33) follows the Decalogue except for its announcing the death penalty for killing, striking one's own father, cursing one's father or mother, and kidnapping a person. Anyone afflicting a widow or orphan risks God's wrath burning and killing him or her. If any other harm is done to someone, the *lex talionis* applies: life for life, eye for eye, tooth for tooth, hand for hand, foot for foot, burn for burn, wound for wound, and stripe for stripe (Ex 21, 22–25), as the judges determine. The reward for keeping the law is that God will come to God's people, will bless them and set their borders from the Red Sea to the Sea of the Philistines and from the wilderness to the Euphrates, and will deliver the inhabitants into their hands. Serving other gods makes them sin against God, which will be a snare for them (Ex 23, 33). Zimri, the son of Saul, was killed for having brought a Midianite woman into his family (Num 25, 1–17). But when Moses married a Midianite woman and his sister Miriam rebelled against him, for punishment she was only expelled outside the camp for seven days (Num 12, 1–16), because Moses cried out to the Lord for her (Num 12, 13). But again, when Korah rebelled against Moses, he and his followers were punished by death (Num 16, 1–50).

The Holiness Code (Lev 17–26) ordered that anyone who sacrificed any of his children to Molech, an Ammonite deity, be stoned (19, 21; 20, 1–4), and if anyone ignored the ordinance, he and his family should be cut off from among his people (20, 4–5). The Deuteronomy Code (Dt 12–26) in general had an exhortatory tone except when it dealt with those who wanted to serve other gods. In such a case there was no forgiveness. Relatives should be the first to put the guilty one to death (13, 9), because forgiveness had its limits.

Does forgiveness have its limits in the New Testament too? one may ask. After having received the power of forgiving sins from the risen Lord, were the apostles absolutely free to forgive any sin? What did Jesus mean when he said that the sin against the Holy Spirit cannot be forgiven (Lk 12, 10; Mk 3, 28; Mt 12, 31)? Is it not the kind of sin but only the penitent's own unrepentant will that makes forgiveness impossible? It has to be so. Otherwise the forgiveness given to the apostles would be a magic power working against the human will as well. But this cannot be, because God the redeemer respects the human freedom that God the creator gave to human beings.

SACRIFICES: RITES OF PURIFICATION

Forgiveness presupposes a certain notion of sin, and sin implies an idea of God. Sacrifice seems to be a universal means for forgiveness. It is propitiation, obedience, but more than those two. It is a recognition of the other as other. It is the first step in unselfishness and respect for the other. And we touch here upon the common element of the notion of sacrifice in its secular and religious sense. I can make a sacrifice to my friend, to my country, and to my enemy as well as to my God. In each case I place something or someone else before me.

In the Bible, while there is no one common notion for the different kinds of sacrifices as we have in Latin and in English, still the idea of "preference" given to the other can be discovered in the meaning of all the close to three hundred references R.J. Thomson could find in the Bible outside the Levitical Law (1963). We mention here just the burnt offering (Lev 1, 3–17), the atonement that "puts a cover over one's sin" (Ex 29, 35–37) with the sin offering (Lev 4, 1–5, 13; Jg 20, 26) and guilt offering (Lev 5, 1–6, 7). The two goats to be offered symbolically bear the sins of the people. The one is offered to God as a sin offering and the other, with the sin of the people placed on it, is to be driven into the wilderness, the home of the demon Azazel (Lev 16, 1–34). The sin offering is made for purification from various forms of uncleanness – childbirth, leprosy, contact with death, and so on (cf. Num 15, 22–31) – which meant separateness from the community and were committed unwittingly (Lev 5, 1–6), yet purification is indispensable because of the holiness of God present among God's people. No forgiveness but purification is required, which meant expiation, abolishment of debt, and reunification with the community (Paschen, 1970, 195). The guilt offering is for an offence against God and/or the community that requires retribution, such as the golden tumours and golden mice offered by the Philistines for having captured the ark (1 Sam 5, 1–6, 21).

4.4.2.3 THE TIMES OF THE PROPHETS: PRAYERS FOR FORGIVENESS OF SINS AND CONVERSION TO GOD

With the prophets, the age of conversion and forgiveness was inaugurated. For deliberately committed sin, the prophets announced forgiveness to those who recognized their sins and, as penitents, asked God for forgiveness. The prophets were the ones who talked constantly about the forgiveness of sins. They announced that God would forgive the sins of those who returned from their evil ways to God. Forgiveness was more than non-punishment. It was an action of God, who can create a new spirit and a new heart (Ezek 11, 19) and can wash the sinner so that the sinner "shall be whiter than snow" (Ps 51, 7).

Hosea asked Israel to return to the Lord and pray by saying to God, "Take away all iniquity; accept that which is good and we will render the fruit of our lips" (Hos 14, 1–2). Psalm 32 is a confession of sins as well as a thanksgiving for forgiveness and for healing, a proof of forgiveness given (vv. 1–5). And then the psalmist exhorts the congregation to follow his example of praying for forgiveness (vv. 6–11). Psalm 51 has a similar structure: appeal to God's mercy (vv. 1–2); recognition of sin (vv. 3–5); asking for forgiveness by washing the sinner whiter than snow, creating a clean heart, and placing a new and right spirit within him (vv. 7–10); putting the psalmist in the presence of God (v. 11); giving him back the spirit with joy of salvation (vv. 9–12); and praising God (vv. 14b–15) and teaching others to do the same, that is, confessing and asking for God's forgiveness (vv. 13, 16–17). It is a remarkably exact presentation of the process and result of the sacramental forgiveness granted by Christ.

In his hymn of triumph celebrating Israel's restoration, Isaiah called for repentance and return to the Lord that God might have mercy and forgive sins generously (Is 55,7). He used the word *šalah,* of which God is always the subject. It means that God remits castigation, punishment (Ezek 18, 30), and lets the sinner return into service and communion with God (cf. Jer 29, 12–14; 36, 3). Yet God's forgiveness does not exclude divine judgment (see Num 14.18).

The other word for remission is *naśa,* bearing the sin. The sin is not forgiven (cf. Ezek 10, 17; Lev 5, 1), but it is taken away from the sinner, like a scapegoat sent to perish in the wilderness, the world of demons (Lev 16, 22). The servant of Yahweh in Isaiah is doing both; he bears the sin of many and carries it away as well (Is 53, 10–12). He carries the sorrows, is smitten by God and wounded for our transgressions, is cut off from the land of the living, makes himself an offering for sin (Is 53, 10). Unlike Jeremiah (cf. his laments in 11, 18–19; 15, 10–21; 17, 14–18; 18, 18–23; 20, 7–13; 20, 14–18) or Job, the Servant of Isaiah suffers silently like a lamb, the image of suffering without resistance. By itself it does not mean a sacrificial animal, as it does in exilic texts. The term used in Isaiah 53, 7 is *śeh lattebah,* a lamb for slaughter, but it does not necessarily suggest Passover. A third word for the remission of sin in the Old Testament is *kipper.* Literally, it means to cover, to wipe away. If God is its subject, it may mean that God deletes, deterges sin (Ps 65, 3;78, 38; Ezek 17, 63; Ps 79, 3; Jer 18, 23).

The remission of sin in the Old Testament may, but not necessarily, mean no punishment, the lifting of the sin without internal renewal, or ignoring it on the merit of a righteous member of the community. It may also mean internal renewal, new spirit, and new life. In any case we can see, that forgiveness was and is a central issue for the secular and religious world. It was this human call that Christ replied to by his gift of forgiving and taking away the sin of the world.

4.4.3 The Sacramental Reality of Forgiveness

On 25 November 1551, during its fourteenth session in the first chapter, the Council of Trent declared the faith of the Catholic Church by saying that "the Lord instituted the sacrament of penance at that particular moment when, after his resurrection from the dead, he breathed on his disciples, saying: 'Receive the holy Spirit; if you forgive the sins of any, they are forgiven; if you retain the sins of any, they are retained' (Jn 20, 22–23)" (Tanner, 1990, 703, 711).

The meaning of the scriptural text of John 20, 22–23 is defined in canon no. 3 directly by referring to the forgiving and retaining sins and negatively by excluding the meaning of simple "preaching the gospel" (Tanner, 1990, 711–12). The meaning of the Greek verb ἀφίημί is to "let go, remit, forgive" and of κρατέω, to "retain, not changing situation." The full meaning emerges from its scriptural context.

Forgiveness is a human reality, and as such, it is the symbol of sacramental forgiveness. The sacramental meaning of forgiveness therefore has to include the meaning of the visible symbol of forgiveness. Forgiveness must be a forgiveness. The Lord's Prayer confirms this. If we do not forgive them their trespasses, neither will God forgive us our trespasses (Mt 6, 12–15; 18, 35; Mk 11, 25–26; Lk 11, 4; 17, 3–4; Eph 4, 42; Col 3, 13; cf. Mt 5, 23–24). It is not without reason that Christians are asked to forgive one another and anyone; otherwise God will not forgive their trespasses.

Yet sacramental forgiveness is more than human forgiveness. It transforms it, elevates it and gives it a new reality. It brings about the presence of God. God is the one who forgives since there is no sin that is not a sin against God. Thus forgiveness becomes a "sacrament," a mystery of forgiveness as well as the mystery of sin. The theology of forgiveness is complementary to the theology of sin, just as the theology of the Eucharist is complementary to the theology of the sacrament of forgiveness. We may detect this by further analyzing the meaning of John 20, 22–23.

4.4.3.1 "FORGIVE" AND "RETAIN"

"Forgiving" and "retaining"of verses 23a and 23b are conjoined not by καί or ἤ, and/or, but by ἄν with the aorist subjunctive, which means "haply," "in case that," you remit, "in case that" you retain. The two are therefore supplementary explanations. When the Church forgives sin, it retains it by making forgiveness dependent on the penitent's disposition. And when the Church retains forgiveness, it does so with the intention of forgiving. Each of the two has the intentionality of the other. The sacrament of forgiveness is not magic, because it is a sacrament of God's love, and love appeals to love, as recounted in Psalm 51.

Verse 23 is connected with the saying that the mission Jesus has received from the Father he gives now to his disciples (Jn 20, 21), which by "when he said this" (v. 22) is joined again to his breathing the Holy Spirit. There cannot be, therefore, two forgivenesses, one in heaven and one on earth. Forgiveness on earth is identical with forgiveness in heaven because both are given to the apostles by the same Holy Spirit. In other words, there is no forgiving by God that is not a forgiving by the Church. And vice versa, there is no forgiving by the Church that is not a forgiving by God. Moreover, all forgiving on earth is forgiving by the Church because no forgiving on the earth is possible without the virtue of the Eucharist (cf. Jn 15, 5). And consequently, all forgiving shares in the sacramental grace of the sacrament of forgiveness.

Christ gave his mission to those disciples (Jn 20, 21) to whom he promised to give it in his farewell speech before his death (Jn 17, 18) and whom he sent to reap what he had laboured for (4, 8) and who were to be received as him who sent them and the one who sent Jesus himself (13, 20). They were *šēlĩah* apostles who followed Jesus in his lifetime on earth and of whom one was John, the "disciple whom Jesus loved" (Jn 21, 20), and those with Peter, to whom the power of binding and losing was promised earlier. Note that the favourite term in John's gospel is not the word "apostle" (13, 16) but μᾶθητής, disciples.

4.4.3.2 "BINDING" AND "LOOSING"

What was promised to Peter – "I will give you the keys of the kingdom of heaven, and whatever you bind on earth shall be bound in heaven, and whatever you loose on earth shall be loosed in heaven" (Mt 16, 19) – was promised to the disciples (Mt 18, 18), whose instruction became Jesus' main concern after Peter's confession. The second promise was followed by instruction about forgiveness (Mt 18, 19–35). The two sayings may suggest that they are two executive elements of the one mission of Christ: Peter and the community of the apostles.

"Binding" does not mean refusing forgiveness but laying down the conditions without which sins cannot be forgiven. And "loosing" means readmitting a person into the community by forgiving sins. It means leading the sinner back to the community of the sons and daughters of God. The text reflects penitential praxis familiar from the Old Testament with its three instances: excommunication, separation from the community (cf. 2 Th 3, 14 a–b; 1 Cor 5, 1–13); repentance with examination and determination of penance (cf. 2 Th 3, 14c.15; 2 Cor 2, 5–6; 2 Cor 13, 10); and readmission to the community, reconciliation, forgiveness, (2 Cor 2, 7–11), later by imposition of hands. The novelty was that the Christians knew that the sins were also forgiven in heaven, and the forgiveness for them meant a new life in Christ, a sharing in God's life. In other words, the mystery of the forgiveness of sins revealed both the mystery of sin and the mystery of God.

4.4.3.3 TAKING AWAY THE SIN OF THE WORLD

Christ as the lamb of God came into the world to take away the sin of the world (Jn 1, 29). He is the pre-existing (Jn 1, 30), eternal Son of the Father, who sent him to take away the sin of the world (Jn 3, 16). The verb αἴρω means to take away, to remove, like a scapegoat (Lev 16, 22), which bore the sin of many and carried it away (Is 53, 2–12).

To take away the sin of the world was Jesus' life program. "He began to preach, saying, 'Repent, for the kingdom of heaven is at hand'" (Mt 4, 17; Mk 1, 14), "the acceptable year of the Lord," when all debts are wiped out (Lk 4, 19.21). The formula ἀφίημι τὰς ἁμαρτίας, forgive sins, has returned since that time in Jesus' life and death, in the work of the apostles, and in the liturgical prayers and chants of the Church. The sin is revealed and recognized as universal. If some say that they have no sin, they deceive themselves and make Jesus Christ into a liar (1 Jn 1, 8–10).

4.4.3.4 FORGIVENESS AS HEALING AND SHARING IN THE NEW LIFE OF CHRIST

The forgiveness of sins was not forgetting or ignoring sins as if nothing had happened. Rather it was justification, reconciliation, redemption from a miserable way of existing of the *past,* leading to a new life, sanctification in the *present,* and salvation-resurrection-glorification in the *future.* It was a holistic healing as Jesus led one from his or her illness to a whole life symbolized by restored health, the sign of sins forgiven (Mt 9, 1–8; Mk 2, 1–12; Lk 5, 17–26; Jn 5, 14).

Forgiving sins is one with Jesus' mission. According to the Synoptics and Pauline and Johannine sources, Jesus' work and all that he offered to his followers can be summarized as the action of moving peoples from sin (Mk 1, 15; Lk 1, 77; Mk 2, 1–22; Mt 9, 1–8; Lk 5, 17–26; 7, 47–50; 24, 47; Mt 16, 19; 18, 18; cf. Mk 14, 22–25; Mt 26, 26–28; Rom 1, 24–32; 5,14; 7, 1–8.39; Gal 5, 17–21; 1 Cor 5, 5–13; 2 Cor 5, 19; Tit 2, 12; Jn 1, 29; 21, 15–17; 1 Jn 1, 9–10; 2, 12; 3, 5; 4, 10; etc.) to the presence of God, to peace, charity, chastity, happiness, and joy, a new relationship to other human beings as well as to the whole cosmos by the action of justification, new creation, regeneration, liberation, sanctification, reconciliation, purification, expiation, resurrection to eternal life, the cancelling of sin in cooperation with God (Horvath, 1979b, 90–3). He really came to call sinners (Mk 2, 17).

The author of the Letter of Barnabas described Jesus as a leader leading his people out of the old world into a "new promised land of milk and honey" (Funk, 1901, 54, 56). Thus Jesus could easily be understood as the Way (Jn 14, 6), and his new foundation, the Church, likewise as the Way

(Acts 9, 2). The Council of Trent, in session 6, described well the justification of a sinner as "a transition from that state in which is born as a child of the first Adam to the state of grace and of adoption as children of God" (Tanner, 1990, 672). Any sin is a termination or challenge to justification, and so any confession is a reinstallation or strengthening of the justification received by baptism. Sacramental forgiving includes the notions of justification, sanctification, redemption, and salvation – in a word, the new life in Christ. And the new life in Christ cannot be understood without the theology of sin and the sacrament of forgiveness.

In the context of Jesus' mission, sin is revealed as being more than just disobedience to a law or a great injustice and violence committed against a human being and the world created by God. Sin is the rejection of a better future of integrity, generosity, and authenticity offered by God in Jesus Christ in favour of a present world affected by the sins of selfishness, inauthenticity, and incontinence under the ruler of this world (Jn 16, 11; 12, 31;14, 31). Sin is against faith, charity, and hope. It is unbelief that God loves and cares about me. It is greediness, craving for what belongs to others. It is despair and fear of tomorrow.

Forgiveness of sins means that I can believe again that God loves and cares for me and so does God's world. Forgiveness of sin means that I can love again and discover that I have so much to give and that it is much better to give than to receive. And finally, forgiveness of sins means that I can hope again and be free from fear. I can trust in God, others, and myself by opening a happy future as a home for me and others. In brief, forgiveness means that my faith can conquer unbelief; my love can conquer hatred, and my hope can conquer despair and hopelessness.

4.4.4 The Sacrament of Forgiveness in the History of the Church

4.4.4.1 PUBLIC PENANCE

Christ's actions and sayings made it clear to the Church that it had the mission of forgiving sin yet without determining how to do it (Orsy, 1978). The gravity and responsibility of carrying the mission was much heavier than simply letting the Church say indiscriminately to anyone, "Your sins are forgiven" (Rahner, 1975). This was particularly true in a time when persecutions became frequent and violent and the number of the apostates grew with the number of the martyrs and penitents.

Because of the early Church's Jewish heritage, the most obvious first step was to follow the traditional rabbinical penitential system. A Syrian bishop, probably formally a physician, provided a compendium of the first stage of early penitential discipline in his *Didascalia* (Funk, 1905). A person who committed a serious sin was excommunicated and separated from the community of the Church. Examination followed. Canonical penance was determined and the community began to pray for the publicly reprimanded repentant. At the end of repentance (*Didascalia*, 2, 15.16.20.24), reconciliation was made by the bishop by the imposition of hands, as in baptism (*Didascalia*, 2, 41). The *Didascalia* lists seven sins that required public penance: bad treatment of slaves and the poor, producing idolatrous objects, sexual sins, calumny, misuse of office, and fraud.

Tertullian and Cyprian somewhat earlier reported a similar discipline, but they were less lenient than the author of *Didascalia*. This practice was called public penance. It did not mean public confession of sins, because the sins were public. Rather, it had to do with the special pastoral and liturgical disciplinary status of the penitent. Being aware of its Jewish origin, the Church followed the rabbinical penitential rite. Yet being aware also of being the mystical body of Christ, it considered reconciliation with the community and forgiveness of sins to be identical with sharing the new life in Christ. The only obstacle was the lack of authentic repentance.

Because of Montanist and Novatian rigorism, on the one hand, and the moral laxness of a growing number of Christians, on the other, the praxis of "one penance" (*paenitentia unica*) prevailed in some churches. Tertullian alone distinguished between forgivable sins (*peccata remissibilia*) and unforgivable sins (*peccata irremissibilia*), such as apostasy, murder, and adultery (Tertullian, *On Modesty*, 2, 12–15; *PL*, 2, 983–5), a distinction that never became the doctrine of the Church, though finding the middle way between excessive rigorism and excessive laxity was never easy in the history of the Church.

Since the sacrament of baptism was known also as the sacrament of forgiveness of sins leading into the new life of Christ, the sacrament of forgiveness was called another sacrament of baptism, a laborious kind, a second plank after shipwreck for those who had fallen after baptism (see Council of Trent, *Sacrament of Penance*, chapter 2 and canon 2; Tanner, 1990, 704, 711). It is understandible that some early Christians found it difficult to understand that one who entered into the new life of Christ could fall again and have an open door for a second time. This kind of thinking is remarkable. It is reveals the mystery of forgiveness of sins as an authentic being reborn, a real entering into the everlasting life of Christ. The mystery of forgiveness of sin is indeed a mystery of heaven. But it is easier to grasp the difference between the two sacraments of forgiveness if one sees both as rooted in the Eucharistic Christ, who has been given to take away sins of any kind and more than once as long as we are in time.

4.4.4.2 PRIVATE PENANCE

Since rigorism did not prevent laxity, the public penance was gradually shortened and left for Lent. From 800 on, a new form of penitential discipline was introduced. It was the first step in moving from penance to confession. The change was prompted by the social changes following the collapse of the Roman Empire. The number of the faithful grew, and Christians dispersed over a vast territory. No priest could visit, much less a bishop, more than once a year or over many years. When finally a priest came, he could not do more than give some exhortations, and since he did not know the people, they themselves had to confess their sins. If the priest did not know when would he be able to come again, he had to give absolution and ask the penitents to do their penance whenever they were able to. So the faithful received absolution before the penance was completed. The importance of penance decreased and that of confession increased. The praxis was initiated by the Irish priests. At first it was censured, but later it was universally accepted (Orsy, 1978, 35–51; Poschmann, 1964, 124–38).

4.4.4.3 SCHOLASTIC SYNTHESIS

During the first millennium, readmission to the Church was understood as identical with the forgiveness of sins. As the Scholastic theology of the sacraments was developing, the general notion of the sacrament raised a few questions about the sacrament of the forgiveness of sins. The first question was about the sacramental symbols; the second had to do with what the sacramental symbols would bring about. Since only God can forgive sin, Abelard could not understand that the current or any ecclesial authority could forgive sins. He, and with him Scholastic theology, began to separate the power of the keys from the absolution of sins. "Binding" and "loosing" were reinterpreted so that binding meant excommunication and loosing, liberation from the excommunication of the Church.

The early biblical understanding of binding and loosing had been reinterpreted. Peter Lombard understood the power of the keys of binding as imposing a penance. Since only God can forgive sin, absolution could be only declarative. Martin Luther supported this interpretation. To bring the two forums, external peace with the Church and internal forgiveness of sin, closer and to give some efficiency to the absolution, Hugh of St Victor introduced a distinction between *culpa*, guilt, and *paena*, punishment. Guilt is interior, impiety or unrepentance, which absolution cannot forgive. What absolution can absolve from is the punishment, the liability to future damnation.

Thomas Aquinas proposed a synthesis by determining the matter and form of the sacrament of forgiveness. The personal acts of the penitent, such as sorrowful confession and satisfaction, are the matter, and the power of the keys, the absolution, is the form. Both are the instrumental cause of grace and of the movement of the free will, changing attrition to contrition. The free movement of the will, the *paenitentia interior*, symbolized by the external actions, further symbolizes (*res et sacrament*) the act, bringing about grace and with it forgiveness of sin. A schematic presentation would be as follows:

sacramentum tantum the visible symbol	acts of the penitent: sorrow, confession, exterior penance (matter), and the act of absolution (form)
res et sacramentum symbolized and symbolizing	movement of free will (*paenitentia interior*) – attrition
res tantum symbolized reality	infusion of grace, perfect love of God, remission of sin

(Thomas Aquinas, *Summa theol.*, 1, 2, q 113, a 8; cf. 4 *Sent.*, d. 17, q 1, a 4, sol 1 and sol 2; Poschmann, 1964, 169–74)

The justification of the sinner or the forgiveness of sin, Thomas Aquinas said, is God's greatest work (*Summa theol.*, 2, q 113, a 9). The sacrament of the forgiveness of sins is instrumental in applying Christ's merit to the penitent. It changes the faithful from having attrition to becoming contrite by transforming the selfish love into an unselfish love of God by allowing the confessing faithful to participate in Christ's true love for God, manifested in his death and resurrection (Horvath, 1988, 497).

4.4.4.4 THE COUNCIL OF TRENT

The scholastic research and disputes were instrumental in formulating the doctrine of the Council of Trent on the sacrament of penance during session 14, on 25 November 1551. After having explained its need, the institution, and the difference between the sacraments of penance and of baptism (chapter 1 and 2), the council described contrition μετάνοια, conversion, confession, absolution, and satisfaction as the different parts of the sacrament required for the integrity of the sacrament and forgiveness of sins (Tanner, 1990, 704–9). We present each in its extended version (Alszeghy, 1983).

4.4.4.4.1 Μετάνοια, Conversion

The original meaning of μετάνοια is conversion, often translated as repentance (Mt 3, 2), which, in distinction from attrition, was also called contrition by the Council of Trent (Tanner, 1990, 705). Conversion in general means a change in a way of thinking, one's value system (Wanamaker, 1999, 23–31). We disapprove of what we have approved of so far and now appreciate above all that which we did not appreciate until now.

Jesus' Sermon on the Mount gives a detailed explanation of conversion and presents the Christian life as a constant conversion (Mk 1, 15; Mt 4, 17; Lk 13, 4). Paul reminds us that conversion is not a reward but God's gift of gracious invitation to return to him with a free reply (1 Cor 4, 7; 15, 10; 2 Cor 3, 16; 5, 18; Rom 6, 23; cf. Jn 15, 3; cf. Council of Trent, *Decree on Justification*, chapters 4–5; Tanner, 672).

According to Ezekiel, conversion is turning away from transgressions committed against God to receive a new heart and a new spirit (Ezek 18, 31). The patristic tradition explained conversion by the lost son's return to the father's house (Lk 15, 11–32). It can be motived by need and fear or by love. The first was motivated by selfish and the second by unselfish love. Conversion begins when the lost son leaves the "far country" to return to his father. When he returns exclusively to get food for his empty stomach, he is like the one who goes to church to avoid eternal fire. God is just a means for one's personal advantage. This is attrition. It is not perfect yet not sinful. It is even a gift of God, but by itself it is not enough for justification and for the forgiveness of sins. But when the lost son returns to his father because he realizes that he has sinned against his father and made him lose his son, whom he loved, he does not think any longer of his father's gift. He just wants to meet his father, who, he now realizes more than ever before, loves him so much. When this unselfish motivation becomes predominant, his attrition becomes contrition, perfect love that wipes out sins.

Such a transformation is prompted by the sacrament of penance, which induces the grace inviting the penitent to conversion (Council of Trent, session 14, *Sacrament of Penance*, chapter 4, *On Contrition*). The council admitted that it sometimes happens that this contrition is made perfect by love, and a person is reconciled with God before this sacrament is actually received; nevertheless, the reconciliation is not to be attributed to the contrition "without a desire for the sacrament being included in it" (Tanner, 1990, 705).

Attrition, according to the council, is imperfect contrition. It is attrition since it is not explicitly out of love for God. It originates from a consideration of the ugliness of sin or a fear of hell and punishment. Being a hope for pardon, it is a gift of God and an impulse of the Holy Spirit, not yet actually dwelling in the penitent but moving and helping him or her on the path toward justice, and with the sacrament of penance it is raised to a justification, which is a perfect love of God (Tanner, 1990, 705).

The sacrament of forgiveness renews the value system accepted by the sacrament of baptism. Both move one from temporal values to love of God and other human beings. One can experience a progressive evolution from personal needs to the self-discovery of personal riches for being able to love unselfishly the way God does. In Augustine's words, it is a progressive discovery that " we are restless till we rest in God" (1993, 3). It is for this reason that forgiveness had a pre-eminence in the teaching and life of Jesus Christ and also in speculative sacramental theology.

The love *for* God that wipes out sin by virtue of the sacrament of forgiveness is a gift *of* the love God has for the penitent and each human being. It is a constant call of God, progressively moving the human heart to return to God freely. The Council of Trent, in its decree on *Justification*, lists some of God's loving calls leading one towards the sacrament of forgiveness. The first is an initial faith, believing that God is willing to forgive, revealed in and through the redemption of Jesus Christ (Rom 3, 24). The next is recognizing one's own sinfulness and need for love and slowly turning away from sins to love God, be with God and follow God's will (Tanner, 1990, 672–3).

These actions and impulses of the Holy Spirit moving towards love and justice are already the sacramental graces of the sacrament of forgiveness to be received later. It seems that here is an effect anterior to its cause. Indeed, the notion of "before" and "after" in sacramental theology had been relativized (Horvath, 1993, 72). We can explain this process by the presence of the Eucharistic Christ, who is active before and after any sacrament and transforms the visible symbol into a sacrament. God's love is anterior to any human love. An attrition made perfect by love reconciles the sinner with God before the sacrament, yet not without the sacrament of forgiveness of sins. A real love for God above everything which wipes out sins is a real detestation and sorrow for the sins committed and a loving determination to do whatever is recognized as God's will (Jn 14, 21). And such a determination is already present by virtue of the sacrament to be received. This is possible because of the presence of the Eucharistic Christ, the foundation of the unity and transcendental universality of the sacraments. The presence of the Eucharistic Christ makes possible that the Church can always believe that if one repents because of his or her love for God, he or she will be saved, even though in the given circumstances, confession is not possible. So, for example, anyone who died during the preparation for baptism or during penitential excommunication would enter heaven.

This is something that Baius did not believe, and his assumption could not be accepted by Pius V in 1567 (*DS*, nos. 1031–3). It is therefore true that contrition is always connected with the remission of sins, and the sins of the catechumen can be forgiven even before reception of the sacrament of baptism. Thus reception of the sacrament of forgiveness is not always required for the remission of sins. This even more so because even the sacrament of forgiveness brings about the forgiveness of sins by raising one's imperfect love to the perfect love the Church has for God. And this love of the Church is the gift of the Eucharistic Christ to his Church. The sacrament of forgiveness does not forgive sins without the presence of the Eucharistic Christ and his perfect love for the Father and the human race. So both statements are true. There is no forgiveness of sin without the perfect love of God. and there is no perfect love of God without the sacrament of forgiveness. And there is no forgiveness without the sacrament of forgiveness.

It may be noted here that Felix M. Cappello, SJ, renowned former professor of canon law at Gregorian Pontifical University in Rome and a confessor much in demand at the Church of San Ignacio in Rome, in a lecture given to the priests of Rome in preparation for the Roman Synod in 1963, strongly emphasized that perfect contrition, a sorrow for sins for the sake of love for God, "is not difficult, it is easy."

4.4.4.4.2 Confession

By stating that the sacramental confession of sins is of divine right (chapter 5, session 14, *Sacrament of Penance* with canons 6–8; Tanner, 1990, 705–6, 712), the Council of Trent affirmed that the confession of sin is part of the sacrament of penance and it is not just a certain ritual of penitential practice. A decision about forgiveness or retention of sins (Mt 16, 19 and 18, 19) can be made only if the faithful had declared his or her sin not just in general but specifically and in detail. This has been the conviction and the practice of the universal Church since the beginning, as we read in the counciliar documents (Tanner, 705–6).

The confession of sins is the faithful's opening to grace, to the presence of Christ. The naming of each and every sin is an ongoing opening up of oneself more extensively and more deeply to the grace of the forgiveness of sins and to the Holy Spirit, moving penitents to love God with all their heart, with all their soul, and with all their mind and strength (Mt 22, 37–39; Mk 12, 30–32). Thus the power of the love of God transcends the words of the priest, yet the priest's words remain instrumental in bringing the presence of Christ to the deepest dimension of faithful's being in a most intimate way and freely. In reply to the confession, the words addressed by the priest to the faithful are encouraging words, echoing again the words uttered earlier over the head of the baptized – "this is my beloved son, daughter, with whom I am well pleased" (Mt 3, 17) – and reminding of God embracing the lost daughter or son in love (cf. Lk 15, 20).

The repentant confession of sins is a sort of reply to the profession of faith pronounced at baptism and now repeated in the introduction to the *New Rite of Penance* (1973). Both the profession of faith and the confession of sins are confessions of love. Love reveals holiness and it confesses sins. By the profession of faith, God is introduced as the loving creator and merciful redeemer, and by the confession of sin, a daughter or son of God presents herself or himself as a repentant sinner marked by sins that she or he admits as exclusively her or his own. This is the initial love that the Council of Trent referred to as the impulse of the Holy Spirit modified by and modifying the sacrament of the merciful love of God. As love reveals sin, so confession makes life conscious by achieving a self-knowledge through sins "before the divine mercy for all to be pardoned" (*On Confession*; Tanner, 1990, 706).

4.4.4.4.3 Absolution

The Council of Trent defined the act of absolution as "like a judicial one in which a verdict is pronounced by the minister as if a judge" (chapter 6, *On the Minister of the Sacrament and on Absolution*; Tanner, 1990, 707). Absolution is not a judicial act in a univocal sense. It is only *ad instar actus iudicialis,* like a judicial act, pronounced by the priest *velut a iudice,* as if he were a judge, that is, in an analogical sense only. That the absolution is like a judicial act and the priest pronounces a verdict as if he were a judge means, according to the Council of Trent, the following.

First, it does not mean a judicial act in a political sense, being distinct from the legislative and administrative power as if the priest were a judge in a disputed matter. Rather, it means that the priests "discharge as ministers of Christ the function of forgiving sins by the power of the holy Spirit" and not by their own power (Tanner, 1990, 707). The power is the power of the only judge, the Eucharistic Jesus Christ, and the priest is just his *šělĩah*-apostle, who does it in the name of the Father and of the Son and of the Holy Spirit. It is therefore incorrect to interpret the "I" of the verb "absolve you" as referring in an absolute sense to the "I" of the priest, as if Jesus Christ were absolving in one confessional and his priest in another, and the two were equal and independent of each other, absolving subjects in hearing confessions.

Since the sacrament of forgiveness brings about love for God, the words of absolution said in the singular "I" must refer to the person of God, as they do at the moment of consecration. It is only Christ, the God-man, who can accomplish what happens in the confession. The words are the words of a priest, but the priest cannot and should not "play God." Precisely the judicial character of the absolution means that the priest forgives sins in the person of Christ. Therefore the one who "binds" and "looses" is Jesus Christ, the one who is present in the Eucharist He is the one who has the power to lay down the condition of participating in his Church's love of God, the only sacramental sign of being admitted into the internal life of God now, in time, and ever after, in the beatific vision. Consequently, Catholics also confess only to God and not to another human being, because no human being can forgive sins. They confess to Jesus Christ, the incarnated real God and man, present in the Eucharist and through the Eucharist in each of his sacraments (Horvath, 1988, 496).

That the power is that of Jesus Christ explains why did Jesus gave the

Holy Spirit on the occasion of giving the power of forgiving sins and sent his apostles the way he was sent by the Father (Jn 20, 21–22). This is why Paul judged "in the name of Christ " (1 Cor 5, 4), "in the presence of Christ" (2 Cor 2, 10). He used the authority that the Lord had given to him (2 Cor 13, 10), and Christ was speaking in him to the sinner (2 Cor 13, 3). Therefore it is Christ who binds and looses. The actions of the priest and the penitents are just the visible sacramental symbol, the visible gesture of Christ's saving activity.

Secondly, the absolution is a like a judicial act because it does not declare or exhort that sins are forgiven. It brings about the forgiveness of sins and creates a new situation where not sinning is possible. It is a reconciliation. Καταλλάσσω (2 Cor 5, 18) as a transitive verb means changes outside the agent. We cannot reconcile ourselves with God. Only God can reconcile one to God. It is up to the penitent to accept God's initiative of taking him or her back into a loving relation to God and into a unselfish sacrificial service to the world. In virtue of this change, the sinner becomes a non-sinner, "unjust becomes just, from being an enemy becomes a friend (*Decree on Justification,* chapter 7; Tanner, 1990, 673). We cannot simply change another and, if someone has something against us, reconcile the other to us, restore friendship and peace (Mt 5, 23–26). God has to offer friendship to each one and reconcile each, and God makes us able to forgive each other. The priest is instrumental in reconciliation, which is a change and a renovation.

Thirdly, the idea that absolution is like a judicial act means that the priest has to take his actions seriously and not "in jest." He has to judge whether the penitent is a serious penitent. He may assume this by the mere fact that the penitent has come to confess his or her sins and not the sins of others. Yet he should help the penitent to be sorry and ask seriously for the mercy of God. Whereas the judge in the secular sense analyzes external acts and circumstances and declares the defendant guilty or not guilty, the priest has to sense what is going on in the heart of the penitent and whether the impulse of the Holy Spirit is detectable.

Fourthly, that absolution is like a judicial act means furthermore that the priest does not have to scrutinize the penitent about the sins the penitent did not accuse him or herself of. He is not a inquisitor or prosecutor who has to prove that the defendant has committed one or more sins the priest can think of or suspect. So the priest does not have to investigate the marital life of the penitent in the confessional (Chapelle, 1996). If the priest is asked anything, he should reply simply and briefly. But his task is to place the penitent before the merciful God and let him or her experience the power of the grace of the sacrament. The availability or non-availability of a confessor may be not only physical but moral as well. In such a case, as in that of contrition, confessing the sin not confessed this time but at the earliest convenience is justifiable and recommended.

Finally, that the absolution is like a judicial act means that binding and loosing do not directly mean the power of absolving or of refusing absolution. The two go together. The priest binds by loosing and looses by binding. Binding means that the priest, also representing the Church, determines the condition of loosing and undoing the injustice done to the community by the commission of sin. Each sin is not only a sin against God but also against the Christian community and the human race. Accordingly, the priest gives "penance" or satisfaction, which the penitent has to make to undo injustice done to this world and to share in Christ's saving activity in the present world (Horvath, 1988, 497–9)

4.4.4.4.4 Satisfaction

As on the confession, so too on satisfaction, the Council of Trent's teaching is presented within the context of its interpretation of the Reformers' doctrine. They knew well that only God can forgive sin and any instrumental cooperation with God would be a temptation for the Church to "play God." Following the Abelardian trend of thought, one might not understand how any ecclesial authority could forgive sins. Though initially both Luther and Melanchthon valued the penitential practice of private confessions (cf. *The Confession of Augsburg*, 1530) but because they had not accepted ordained ministry, the Reformers denied the sacramental penance administered by ordained ministers. Instead they believed that any of Christian faithful could strengthen each other in faith and that God would forgive their sins (cf. *Canons Concerning the Most Holy Sacrament of Penance*, no. 7; Tanner, 1990, 712).

In reply, the council said that precisely the great abundance of divine generosity made the faithful able to make satisfaction through Jesus Christ before the Father (*On the Works of Satisfaction,* chapter 9; Tanner, 1990, 709), and the penance imposed in satisfaction is not a purely human tradition. By making satisfaction, the faithful follow Jesus' example, so that by suffering with him, they may be glorified with him (Rom 8, 17). The works of satisfaction, the council continued, are also *ad praeteritorum peccatorum vindictam et castigationem,* for atonement and punishments of past sins. Penance was obviously not unknown in the history of the early Church. Tertullian, Cyprian, and Anselm found important reparative punishment for past sins. They argued that sin deprives God of his right to be honoured and justice demands that this right of God be restored. The Eastern Church never followed this kind of argument. And indeed, the reparative function of satisfaction as far as God's honour was concerned was not proposed as an infallible dogma by Trent.

The Council of Trent wanted to honour this tradition without teaching that God is revengeful. Rather, it was a recognition of the present world order, where it is expected that injustice will be punished and undone. For this reason, the council made a clear distinction between forgiveness of sin and temporal punishment and the eternal punishment remitted with the remission of sin and guilt by the sacrament of penance (*Decree on Justification,* chapter 17; Tanner, 1990, 677; canon 30; Tanner, 681). Whereas the sacrament of baptism remits with the forgiveness of sins both the eternal and the temporal punishment, the sacrament of penance remits only the eternal, not the temporal, punishment in order to let us be more industrious and appreciative of the gift received (*Teaching Concerning the Most Holy Sacrament of Penance,* chapter 2; Tanner, 704; chapter 8; Tanner, 708; canons 12, 15; Tanner, 713). The temporal punishment was interpreted as a certain reparation of damage and injustice done to this world as well to God, and both were deserving of at least some symbolic recompense. This is all more true since the sinners should rightly judge and condemn the evil done and so identify themselves with the crucified Christ. In such a context even a small penance may not seem meaningless or ridiculous. It is a token and a modest, loving sharing in Jesus' uniquely meritorious life, suffering, and death.

4.4.4.5 VARIOUS WAYS THAT LOVE FORGIVES SINS IN THE LIFE OF THE CHURCH

Beside the sacrament of penance, the Council of Trent explicitly recognized three other sacraments as forgiving sins: baptism (*Teaching Concerning the Most Holy Sacrament of Penance,* chapter 2; Tanner, 1990, 704), the anointing of the sick (*Teaching on the Sacrament of Last Anointing,* chapter 2; Tanner, 710; canon 2; Tanner, 713), and the Eucharist (*Teaching and Canons on the Most Holy Sacrifice of the Mass,* chapter 2; Tanner, 733; canon 3; Tanner, 735). Though they do this, they do not do it independent of the sacrament of forgiveness. As a result of the organic unity existing among the sacraments and of his Eucharistic presence, Christ transforms each sacrament into a sacrament of love that wipes out sins. Yet the sacrament of forgiveness will remain the one in which the forgiving power of any of the sacraments finds its sacramental realization.

The same is the case for many other forms of love, called charities; all tend intentionally to the forgiveness of sins. These include also the countless liturgical prayers of the Church for forgiveness of sins and a great variety of penitential rite celebrations, the acts of forgiving other human beings (Mt 5, 23–24; 6, 12–15; Mk 11, 25–26; Lk 11, 4; Mt 18, 21–22.35; Mk 11, 25–26; Lk 6, 37;17, 3–4), loving other human beings, including one's enemies, unselfishly helping them (Mt 5, 44–48; Lk 6, 27–36), even giving one's life for them (Jn 15, 13), listening to and proclaiming the word of God (cf. "May the words of the gospel wipe out our sins," the priest's concluding prayer after having read the gospel), suffering and dying with and for Jesus (cf. the first martyrs of the Church redeeming the penance of fallen Christians), giving alms and donations or taking active part in church activities and enterprise (cf. crusaders and iIndulgences), or just praying for the sinners and/or for the dead. Each and all these are rooted in and prompted by the Church, the people of God, as the primary sacrament and instrument of forgiveness.

4.4.4.6 THE SECOND VATICAN COUNCIL

As an introduction to Vatican II and an appreciation of both the Council of Trent and Vatican II, we find instructive and inspiring what the Lutheran historian Jaroslav Pelikan wrote before Vatican II in his book *The Riddle of Roman Catholicism* (1959) about the sacrament of penance.

> Through the administration of these three steps – contrition, confession, and satisfaction – the church has a splendid opportunity to apply the healing power of the gospel to the concrete needs of the penitent. In the hands of a conscientious pastor, the sacrament of penance makes divine grace meaningful without minimizing the individual's responsibility for his sin. It is, at its best, a truly evangelical means for "the cure of souls," one whose benefits Protestantism has discarded too easily, and one for which a friendly chat with the minister is not satisfactory substitute. Psychologically, too, private confession is sound, enabling a person to "come clean" about his guilty feelings and to know that he has forgiveness from God in spite of anything he may have done. The therapeutic value of this is difficult to overestimate. Members of the church will testify how useful they found this, and former members will admit how much they miss it. Here, as nowhere else in the entire Roman Catholic system, the delicate balance between God's gifts and God's demand can be maintained and individualized ... Like the other sacraments, penance accentuates the riddle of Roman Catholicism by bringing out the best and the worst in the church: the best, which is its concern for imparting the grace of God and its understanding of human frailty; and the worst, which is its tendency to "play God" and to tyrannize its members with the law. (Pelikan, 1959, 120–1)

Replying to this riddle was a task that Vatican II undertook when it ordered the rites and formulas of the sacrament of penance to be revised so that "they express more clearly what the sacrament is and what it brings about" (SC, no. 72; Tanner, 1990, 834). The council tried to evaluate the faith of the contemporary church. Christian life challenged theology to ask questions about the real effect of the sacrament, whether the present praxis was in direct line with the faith of the apostolic church, what one should do to allow the conversion, the reality of the sacrament, to be more experiential, relevant, and meaningful.

The council had seen the Church in a new light. The Church as the people of God is "in Christ" as a "sacrament or instrumental sign of intimate union with God and of the unity of all humanity" (*LG*, no. 1; Tanner, 1990, 849). It is a primary sacrament and instrument to reveal and bring about universal forgiveness between God and humanity, and within humanity. It is the Church's vocation to bring peace in the world by mutual forgiveness. In the light of John 8, 7 and 1 John 1, 8, mutual apologies are needed instead of mutual accusations.

For the revised penitential rite, Vatican II asked that it express more fully both sin as an offence against God and its consequences in society. Penance should be not only inward and individual but public and collective in penitential services (*SC*, no. 109; Tanner, 1990, 839). The social dimension of any good and bad deed should be recognized. The Church and the world are wounded by sin. Reconciliation should be a reconciliation with the Church and the world (*LG*, no. 11, Tanner, 857; *PO*, no. 5, Tanner, 1047). The social and universal dimension of the various forms of charities forgiving sins, particularly the sacramentals and indulgences, are to be emphasized. The Church has set up sacramentals, the council insists, which in special circumstances, at the discretion of the bishop, can be administered by suitably qualified lay people (*SC*, nos 60, 79; Tanner, 832, 835). Sacramentals are "sacred signs through which, rather like with the sacraments, effects brought about primarily on the spiritual level are symbolised, and obtained through the prayer of the church. Through them ... various features of life are sanctified" (*SC*, no. 60; Tanner, 832). They are to intensify and deepen the effect of the sacraments. In chapter 3 of *Sacrosanctum Consilium*, sacraments and sacramentals are presented side by side to mark the relationship between them, between the accidental rites and the substance of the sacraments (cf. *SC*, nos 60–82). The prayer for the sinner is a petition returning again and again. Renewal of vows, baptismal and funeral rites, the rite celebrating marriage, and so on, are symbolic expressions of love and mutual reconciliation with the Church and world. They are concern for others, and so are indulgences.

The purpose of temporal punishment, which was to be discharged in this world or in purgatory (Council of Trent, *Canons Concerning Justification*, no. 30; Tanner, 1990, 681), is a certain reparation of the damage and injustice done by the sin to this world. The sins are forgiven by God, but "the created world demands justice, since in virtue of the Incarnation what is done to the world has been done to Jesus Christ. The so-called expiatory acts and deeds are gestures of the Church showing that the Church takes seriously the judgment of the world as well as the judgment of God. The Christian community can do this and even has to do it, because being a union of saints and sinners it is in time and eternity as well" (Horvath, 1993, 139). On the basis of the principle of solidarity, Vatican II emphasized the social aspect of sin and wanted to make everyone aware that all human beings are one in the Church; the individual and the community together have to repair damage done to the world and make it ready to enter into eternity (ibid., 140–53).

Indulgences may have served selfish purposes and became scandalous to many. Yet they were inspired by a faith in "the community of saints and sinners" in which one faithful person can benefit from the penance or satisfaction of another. Beside mortification, bodily lacerations, and prayers, an obvious penance may be the financial loss of one turned into gain of another. The martyrs gave their lives for others. The rest may give money to redeem or uplift others.

To promote contributions to enterprises such as the construction of buildings, such as hospitals or churches, or the defence of territories by crusades (Horvath, 1994, 40–1), the Church offered indulgences. It was an exchange of sacrifice and gifts within an interplay of generosity and greediness (Poschmann, 1948). Yet voices were raised against aberrations and abuses. Lateran IV, Trent, and Vatican II all insisted on reform. Paul VI (1967a) introduced the reform and recognized indulgences as further conversions and ways to forgiveness. Plenary indulgences are rare because of a lack of adequate dispositions on the part of the faithful, he said. Partial indulgences are no longer measured by the time spent in purgatory or the time spent doing penance, as was the case in the early church. Rather, the penitent's own good deed performed during that time will be doubled by the Church as Christ's sacrament and instrument for the forgiveness of sin.

4.4.4.7 THE NEW RITE OF PENANCE, 1973

The New Rite of Penance was promulgated by the Sacred Congregation for Divine Worship in 1973. It has three parts: an introduction placing the penitent in the presence of God, of the Church, and of the world by recalling the mercy God has shown in Christ to the world and to the penitent; a description of the three rites: individual penitent, a community rite of several penitents with individual confession and absolution, and a community rite with general confessions and absolution; and appendices (Orsy, 1978, 131–60).

The new rite is a welcome integration of the various penitential praxises we find in the history of the Church. It encourages the faithful to become aware that they are members of a community and are all sinners and responsible for the sins of the others, and that with their confession they carry before God their sins, which share in the sins of the world, and ask God to forgive them in the name of Jesus Christ.

4.4.4.8 THE MYSTERY OF CONFESSION: AN ANALYSIS

A study of confession suggests the following:

1 We should remember that when we go to confess our sins, we announce and proclaim that God is merciful and that God's kindness has no limit. Confession is a grace of God. God asks us to confess our sins. We go to confess our sin because God has invited us by the grace of the confession we are going to make.

2 The sacrament of forgiveness of sins is an efficient way to transform our selfish love of God and of the world into an unselfish love for God to love God and other human beings with all our mind, heart, affection, and strength.

3 Confession is a sharing in the love the Church has had for God since the time of Jesus Christ.

4 Since only God forgives sins, we do not confess sins to human beings but to God, who is actively present there to listen and to say a few words just to us. This is the reason for confessional secrecy, so that the priest does not have to know who has confessed sins to him. Dark, anonymous confessionals are expected to symbolize that we do not confess to a man. As Jaroslav Pelikan remarked, a chat with the priest will never be a satisfactory substitute for the sacrament of forgiveness of sins (Pelikan, 1959, 120).

5 My confession has a community dimension. The Church and Christ are actively present in my confession. In me the Church is confessing its sin, since I am a member of the Church. The Church needs my confessions in order to make Christ's forgiving grace present in the world. In my sins I take the sin of the world to Christ. As I am a member of the human race, in me and through me the world and the Church are confessing their sins. I am responsible for both the Church and the world.

6 I am doing this because Christ takes upon himself my sins and the sins of the world. By taking them away, he leads me to the Father.

7 The meaning of frequent confessions is based on a right understanding of the historicalness of human existence. Conversion is not instantaneous but a process of developing in time. A real conversion needs time. One has to understand that one's life so far has not been perfect and can be improved. The life that was destructive should be made constructive. And this is the time for it because God made this time for it (2 Cor 6, 2).

8 Frequent confession is not useless. It is possible that we do not see its result because of our shortcomings as a result of our psychological heritage and circumstances and our being in the world. But precisely this is my challenge to "to save the world which is mine." Such is the meaning of the confession of venial sins.

9 Because of the organic unity of the Church and of the world and the uniqueness of Christ, there is an organic unity among all my confessions. Each confession is the actualization of all my past confessions and the anticipation of my future confessions.

10 Furthermore, my confession and the forgiveness of my sins are an anticipation and realization of my last confession of both my particular judgment at the moment of my death and my universal judgment at the end of the world. They are a prognostic sign of the end of the world for me.
11 My confession thus is a commemorative event of the past, a demonstrative sign of the present, and a prognostic sign of the final day, my entry into heaven, into the presence of God.
12 The sacrament of forgiveness of sins is God's gift for the third millennium, as it was before and will be thereafter.

4.4.5 *What the Sacrament of Forgiveness Is*

At the *surface level,* Christ, the Church, as community, represented by a priest or a bishop, and a faithful believer come together; at a *deep level,* by allowing the confessing faithful (confession) to participate (absolution) in the Church's true love for God and of every human being (ecclesiological dimension), the sacrament of forgiveness is a further actualization of the sacrament of baptism) in that through the power of the Holy Spirit, they transform the selfish love of a faithful person into an unselfish love for God (*ex attrito fit contritus,* anthropological dimension), stirred up at the *basic level* by experiencing God's gratuitous love (theological dimension), revealed in Jesus Christ (Christological dimension), which forgives sins.

4.4.5.1 COMMENT

The celebration of a sacrament is always a community event. Christ (*ex opere operato*), the Church (jurisdiction), the minister, and the faithful (intention) celebrate together and bring about the sacrament. The absolving priest, as a *šēlīah*-apostle representing Christ, and the Church together with the confessing faithful are the visible symbols that represent and bring about the movement of the free will, called *paenitentia interna,* or attrition, which being already an impulse of the Holy Spirit moving the penitent to a sorrowful love for God.

This initial love for God is joined by absolution to the love which the Church has as a gift that Jesus gave his Church through baptism. The sacrament of forgiveness, therefore, forgives sins by bringing about love for God in the penitent. It brings about conversion, which gradually modifies the faithful's value system and influences concrete decisions that move the penitent more and more from the temporal good to a search for God in everything.

Psychology tells us that the motives of our actions and decisions are not always fully conscious, and that we are more conscious of willing than of why we will. The sacramental words of the penitent and of the priest may work on a psychological level, even after confession and absolution, and let one enter and participate in the Church's loving God. And this makes both private and general confessions and absolutions desirable.

Since the individual and personal exercise of freedom is indispensable, individual confessions are necessary. But so also is the Church's witness to its perfect love for God before the whole world. Community confession and absolution makes explicit the idea that the private confessions and absolution are participation in the Church's love. Like any sacrament, the sacrament of forgiveness has a community aspect as well as an individual, personal aspect.

Sacramental confession is not limited to the minutes spent in the confessional. It begins with an Advent-like preparation and ends in an Easter and Pentecost-like joyful admiration of the miraculous event of the sacrament penetrating the whole being of the penitent during thanksgiving. As a result of such a process, the connection between the love of God and the sacrament of forgiveness becomes habitual and rooted more and more in the paschal mystery and the event of Pentecost. Being anchored in the Easter and Pentecost events, the sacrament of forgiveness becomes an ever-growing conscious participation in the Church's true love for the forgiving God and for every human being. It becomes obvious that there is no perfect love for God and human beings which is not ecclesial and sacramental.

In reverse, from this premise it follows that the Church needs my confession. In my confession and through my confession, the Church again experiences God's gratuitous love, which the same Church is to make available to all those, Christians and non-Christians, who without confession might receive the grace of perfect love (contrition). Since the sacraments are the actualization of the Church's life, by confessing my sins, I enter into the whole Church's experience of God's forgiving love. As a result, each confession of mine will be in a real sense the actualization of all the confessions of others as well as of all my previous confessions and the anticipation of my *last* confession at the moment of my death (particular judgment) and at the end of the world, when my confession forms part of all confessions of humankind (universal judgment). As the particular judgment can be considered one's last private confession, so the universal judgment is the Church's last and final confessional experience of God's unearned, forgiving love, which since Christ's resurrection is already ongoing. *The last judgment began with the crucifixion of Christ.*

Our salvation, our entry into heaven, is our final confession. Thus each celebration of the sacrament of forgiveness is a realization of both the final judgment and our entry into heaven, into the presence of God. In a word, each confession is the beginning of the beatific vision. Yet the sacrament of forgiveness is more than one's salvation. By confessing, the faithful identify themselves with all those who are in and outside the Church and wish to join and enter it more intensively. Reception of the sacrament of forgiveness of sins is somewhat similar to what the Church as a community does on Ash Wednesday and on the first day of Advent (Jungmann, 1932). It leaves the Church, as it were, in order to enter it once more and stir up the experience of its first love in order to become once again conscious of God's forgiving love in Jesus Christ, as a gratuitous and forgiving love, independent of the worthiness of the sinner and the Church's ability to return it on its own merit. Thus the sacrament of forgiveness is the realization and proclamation of the *Soli Deo gloria* by a Church completely in love with God and wishing without any pretension that glory stay with God alone, *ut stet gloria soli Deo* (Luther, 1883–1928, 5, 532; Horvath, 1988, 499)

4.4.6 The Sacrament of Forgiveness and Sacramental Theology

4.4.6.1 THE SACRAMENT OF FORGIVENESS IS A PERSONAL ENCOUNTER WITH CHRIST

Each sacrament is a personal encounter with Christ, but each has its own special features. The sacrament of forgiveness is obviously an encounter with the sin-forgiving Christ. In it Christ is confronted with sin or, more concretely, with the sinner. It is a unique encounter with Christ, the judge of the living and dead, who revealed the mystery of sin in his crucifixion and death.

Purifying, washing away, redemption, justification, sanctification, and salvation are all actions of Christ and let us sense the mystery of sin and forgiveness. Both sin and forgiveness are mysteries, but forgiveness is a greater mystery than the mystery of sin. Sin determines our whole being and so, but much more, does forgiveness. The mystery of meeting the forgiving Christ in the sacrament of forgiveness shares the mystery of meeting the Eucharistic Christ. Yet it is not a transubstantiation. Rather, it is a transformation of the mystery of selfish love into the mystery of the loving God and every human being in the world God created. It is a way of loving God and people the way Christ loves them with his unselfish redeeming love. Our being determined by the selfish love of sin will take on the characteristics of Christ's love.

It is such an encounter that Ignatius of Loyola presents in his colloquy at the end of his first meditation on sin of the first week of his *Spiritual Exercises.* The exerciser, aware of being a sinner, looks at the crucified Christ and in a burning love for Christ asks, "What have I done for Christ? What am I doing for Christ? What must I do for Christ?" (Ignatius of Loyola, 1973, 32). The forgiving Christ acknowledges and reveals the destructive power of sin and the human dream in it. He liberates the selfish love and raise it to a constructive, creative love, a love he has. He lets goodness triumph over evil once more. This is a feeling of power and joy that the penitent feels after confession, an awareness that God has forgiven. We may elucidate this concept even more. Christ did not ignore sin. He did not destroy it. He faced it by forgiving it. One can ask what he really does by forgiving. The Greek words for forgiveness, the noun αφεις and the verb ἀφίημι, lexicographically do not carry this positive meaning. The verb means to "leave it the way it is" (Mt 5, 24; 8, 22; 18, 1 2; Mk 1, 18.20; Jn 14, 18, etc), "let one do something" (Lk 6, 42), "abandon" (Rev 2, 4), "tolerate" (Rev 2, 2), or "give up" (Rom 1, 27). Yet even Rudolf Bultmann, in his article for the *Theological Dictionary of the New Testament*, rightly gave a positive meaning to αφειςς and ἀφίημι by saying that "forgiveness as an eschatological event renews the whole man in whom sin was not just something isolated and occasional but the power which determined his whole being" (1970, 512). So is justification. The righteousness of God, as a real gift, becomes the righteousness of the penitent. In the expression "the righteousness of God," the "of God" is an objective genitive. It is, therefore, not a pre-Christian justification but a new, Pauline creation (Bultmann, 1964, 12–16).

The eschatological age began with the paschal event of Christ and is not to be waited for at the end of the world. The forgiving Christ is the one who justified in the past, is sanctifying now in the present, and will save in the future (Horvath, 1977, 295–6), all at once, since he is the eschatological unity of time and eternity and "the sacraments are the eschatological realizations of his redemption." Christ has redeemed time by making it the expression of eternity and eternity the meaning of time (Horvath, 1993, 63, 72). This is why we can say that in each confession, in each sacramental forgiveness, I meet Christ, the only judge, opening eternity for everyone. In the presence of Christ I enter the threshold of time and eternity and reach the end of my time and the gate of heaven (ibid., 117–24).

The next three fundamental axioms of sacramental theology applied to the sacramental forgiveness are explicit formulations of the personal encounter with the forgiving Christ.

4.4.6.2 THE SACRAMENT OF FORGIVENESS IS A UNION WITH CHRIST AND IN HIM WITH BELIEVERS AND THROUGH THEM WITH THE WHOLE WORLD BY VIRTUE OF THE HOLY SPIRIT

The presence of the forgiving Christ is a union with the forgiving Christ. His presence is not like the presence of an object in our consciousness. As the creator and divine forgiver, he cannot be newly present to us without being newly united with us in our being. This does not only mean that our being and life have an internal tendency or impulse to be "merciful, gracious, slow to anger, and abounding in steadfast love and faithfulness forgiving transgression and sin." It also means that we feel solidarity with the community of sinners and the world affected by the power of sin. As sin unites the world in hostility, so forgiveness unites it in affection and cooperative satisfaction. When someone who was one of the sinners receives sacramental absolution by virtue of the sacrament of forgiveness, he or she becomes united with the forgiver in discovering sin, in facilitating its confession, and eager to repair the damage done in the world. The co-sinner is changed into co-redeemer and co-satisfactory by prayers and by deeds in carrying the cross of reparation, which was and still is Christ's life and work of salvation.

4.4.6.3 THE SACRAMENT OF FORGIVENESS IS PARTICIPATION IN CHRIST'S LIFE AND HIS WORK OF SALVATION

The sacrament of forgiveness as participation in Christ's life and his work of salvation gives concrete meaning and program to the Pauline "it is no longer I who live, but Christ who lives in me" (Gal 2, 20). After the sacrament of forgiveness, not human forgiveness but God's forgiveness is the model for forgiving those who trespass against each other. One has to forgive those who trespass against him or her seventy times seven (cf. Mt 18, 22). With God's forgiveness, the time has come to go into the world and participate in Christ's life and his work of salvation by forgiving (Mt 5, 9).

Each sacrament is not only a sanctification but also a mission. So the sacrament of forgiveness is a mission to forgive. As a peacemaker, the faithful person is to bring about peace. After he or she has received the sacrament of forgiveness, forgiveness is a Christian duty. Its omission is a Christian scandal (Mt 18, 21–35).

Peace and forgiveness are correlative terms. Among human beings affected by original and personal sins, there is hardly any peace without forgiveness. Even those who love each other as times passes get bored with each other, irritated by each other. But people who receive the sacrament of forgiveness have a special mission and impulse to become instruments of peace and forgiveness. The world is full of wars, oppressions, depression, injustice, murders, exterminations of peoples. It seems that sin dominates the world. Yet the faithful are invited to face sin the way Christ faced it: not by ignoring it, not by denying or underestimating it, but by forgiving it and cooperating in its satisfaction. Forgiving is not easy. It is not always in our power, much less in the power of the one who is to forgive. Both to forgive and to be forgiven require sacrifice.

4.4.6.4 THE SACRAMENT OF FORGIVENESS IS A SACRIFICE RECONCILING THE WORLD WITH GOD

Like peace and sacrifice, so sacrifice and forgiveness are also related terms. The Council of Trent argued that mass is sacrifice because there is forgiveness of sin. And there is a theological reason for that. Sin absolutizes the relative and forgiveness relativizes the non-absolute. Such a non-absolute is one's "ego," and forgiveness is the recognition that one's ego is, indeed, not absolute. The confession that we all are sinners has to be two-sided. "You and me," "me and you," we have both sinned. On behalf of the Roman Catholic Church, John Paul II dared to make such a confession during Lent of 2003. As long as the human race does not reach such an universal recognition of everyone's sinfulness, there will be no peace in the world and no peace in our souls.

We argued earlier (4.1.3.5) that sacrifice is a human reality and means that all the sacrifices endured and offered by human beings during the history of the human race appropriated in their intersubjective and revelational dimension all sacrifices as personal and universal. On the revelational dimension, we found sacrifice to be an epiphany when God and human beings disclose themselves to the other in virtue of their common and mutual self-communication through Jesus Christ. In that moment all sacrifices share in Jesus' work, reconciling the world with God and the world with itself. This is the universal , propitiatory at-one-ment in forgiving (2 Cor 5, 18–20)

4.4.6.5 THE SACRAMENT OF FORGIVENESS AND ECUMENISM

Denominations, sects, and schismatic and heretical churches stem from values rightly or presumably missed by a parent church. These differences bring forth on both sides encroachment and one-sided, exaggerated accusations. But the time of mutual accusations should be followed by times of mutual self-accusation and mutual self-confession. The parable of the lost son is the biblical lesson for the sacrament of forgiveness (Lk 15, 11–32). With a little modification, we may present it as a biblical lesson for ecumenism. For the sacrament of the forgiveness, the father of the two sons is the image of God. For ecumenism, we may consider the two sons and their attitudes the image of the various groups and it does not really matter which one side takes up one brother or the other (1 Jn 1, 8). The real lesson is that both have to follow their Father in his joy at their homecoming. And each will bring to the Father's house all that each has, good and bad. The real point is that they are all at home, their good is made a common good, and their sins are the object of common confessions. Such a homecoming of the Jews, the Moslems, and the Christians is expected by God, the Father of all three, each bringing home the money they received with interest in order to make it their common good (Mt 25, 27).

We can say this because we find that there is an organic unity between each singular use of the sacrament of forgiveness and all administrations of the same sacrament of forgiveness whenever and wherever they occur. We find that there is also a sacramental organic unity between one forgiving and another being forgiven (Mt 6, 12) and all forgiveness and being forgiven of the human race. There is unity in all the sacraments of forgiveness, and all forgiveness ever given or to be given in the world comes from the one Eucharistic risen Christ present in the Church (Mt 28, 20), without whom there is no sacrament. One cannot be without the other, because the Eucharistic Jesus Christ is the one who confects any sacrament through the ministerial cooperation of his *šĕlĭah*-apostle, the priest or bishop, and the faithful, who with the Church share Jesus Christ's great love for the Father expressed in his death and resurrection. He is the one who is able to wipe away all sins. He is the one who alone in his death and resurrection achieved the perfect love of God and made it available to any human being. Thus Jesus' death and resurrection were and remain for ever a great benefit for the world, and so is the sacrament of forgiveness of sins.

4.4.7 *The Sacrament of Forgiveness and Systematic Theology*

4.4.7.1 THE SACRAMENT OF FORGIVENESS IS A SYMBOL FOR THE WORLD

That forgiveness is a symbol for the world means that our world cannot exist without mercy and forgiveness. No philosophical or scientific system can be considered realistic unless there is room in it for forgiveness. Our world is a coherent whole with a unique coordination and cooperation of opposing and contrary forces. And the human world is part of the cosmic world and cannot ignore the laws of the universe. The most violent and cruel regimes sooner or later have to learn that forgiveness and mercy are stronger and longer lasting than blood and death, and have to reform themselves accordingly. It may seem that the most powerful and efficient means to conquer evil is evil. Yet in historical perspective one can agree that forgiveness is more powerful in overcoming evil than vengeance. The history of Christianity should support such a view.

We can say that mercy and forgiveness are more fundamental to being and human existence than power. In a limited form we find them wherever there is life. They may take the form of a selfish destructive power, but really they are nothing else than a limitless and endless mercy or forgiveness to oneself. A dictator is one who forgives everything to himself or herself. And when he or she makes an exception for someone else, he or she ceases to be a dictator, and the exception is the beginning of the end of the merciless dictator. Dictators know this. But whatever they choose, they cannot last. The choice the dictator has is really just how far she or he can afford to extend mercy and forgiveness. The more one is rooted in the fullness of universal being, the more one feels like being more merciful.

It may be a long step forward in culture and in wealth before we can abolish the death penalty and war and replace both with forgiveness. To feed murderers may be very expensive, yet it is more humane since it lets mercy and forgiveness triumph. So it is with abortions. The merciless killing of innocent human embryos pleases no one. But "merciful forgiveness" cannot always transcend one's "ego self-defence mechanism." And so it is with any lack of forgiveness. Not everyone can afford limitless forgiveness. Only God's forgiveness is limitless. Yet even God willingly paid a heavy price by offering God's own Son for the forgiveness of the sin of the world. Thus it became clear that the aim of forgiving sins is always love: to love and to be loved. And this love was expected to be heightened by Jesus Christ dying on the cross for the forgiveness of sins.

The same end is served by "penance," which really is satisfaction. Satisfaction does not have to be terrifying. Fundamentally, it is the expression of a grateful love that wants to do something good. That the human penitential system and the sacrament of penance seem to approach each other may be a sign that forgiveness is a universal human reality and a paradigm for solving problems. It was made so by the Christ event. Evil and merciful forgiveness are not limited to the sacrament of forgiveness. They are a human reality. It is the mission of the sacrament of the forgiveness to insert the grace of divine forgiveness into human history by undoing the damage done and to transform penance into "satisfaction of love."

A convicted murderer given a lifelong prison sentence who confesses his sins may receive for penance saying six Our Fathers and Hail Marys with Glory to the Father. Yet penances given in the confessional are more than saying prayers. First of all, they are expressions of being really sorry for the committed sin and of detesting one's crime before Christ and asking for forgiveness. The prayers are, therefore, an act of faith, participating in the cross of Jesus Christ. They are tokens of the gifts and pledges of a new life of reparation transcending the nature of the damage done. They all issue from the gratitude of a love and mercy as real as Christ's death for our sins.

Sacramental forgiveness is not leniency or underestimation of the seriousness of sin. Its intention is to stir up gratitude and love expressed in action and deeds. Even penitential prayers should not be said as a painful monotonous recital but as a loving commemoration of the Church and other human beings, sinners or friends, living or dead, whom we have offended and we ask forgiveness for. He who is forgiven little loves little, and we may expect that he or she of whom much is forgiven will love much (see Lk 7, 47) and the satisfaction will be accordingly. But this is not always so. Some are ashamed and do not want to remember their sins. They want to forget. Such an attitude is understandable before other human beings but not before God. There is a time to forgive and a time to be forgiven and do the work of love. And unfortunately, there is a time to lose the last chance, but there is also a time to pray not to lose it.

4.4.7.2 THE SACRAMENT OF FORGIVENESS IS A SYMBOL FOR THE HUMAN EXISTENCE: THE CHALLENGE TO HAVE STRENGTH AND COURAGE

Forgiveness is not always easy, especially if damage has been done to us. We read or hear in the news that people have been murdered. We do not think that we have to forgive any of the murderers we read about. But the relatives of the victims are interested, first, to know who did it and to bring the sinner to justice. In such a case, forgiveness is not expected. Yet forgiveness has to begin sometime. Jesus Christ had the strength and courage to call someone to be "his friend" who would betray him and lead him into his death. This does not mean that we have to take a murderer in our own house. The sinner has to learn in his or her own home that there are people who have the courage to say, "Peace be with you," and to think that it is not impossible that one day she or he may become "a good" responsible human being. That there are people who believe that it is not an impossible dream that not only in a musical play but in real life too Aldonza may become Dulcinea (Wasserman, 1966, 81). We may know people who do not kill each other physically but cannot stand each other mentally. They differ so much that one is the negation of the other. They are the "merciless intellectual murderers." Their relations are always strained. Whenever they meet in a room, the room is at once full of tension. It would be best for them, one would say, if they were far away from each other. Yet their mutual forgiveness and cooperation could be a great benefit for many others. The Church needs them especially because they are as different as Peter and Paul. Precisely because they are different, they may reflect the mystery of the Church. Two mutually exclusive approaches of two talented persons could make great services for themselves if they were able to forgive each other. Forgiveness means nobility, self-transcendence. Only strong and courageous individuals are able to forgive.

Forgiveness is a moving force for progress, for a new beginning. And the sacrament of forgiveness is God's guarantee that there is no sin which may close once for all any possibility, any new chance. Forgiveness is very divine and very human. The first opens the possibility of eternal life and the second welcomes it.

4.4.7.3 THE SACRAMENT OF FORGIVENESS IS A SYMBOL FOR THE CHURCH: FORGIVENESS IS A MISSION

The Church is both holy and sinful; therefore it has to carry out the mission of forgiving sins. It does so first in its members and then through its members in the world. The Church has to be a forgiving Church because by its forgiving God forgives sins and does not do so without the

Church of God's own Christ. The sacrament of forgiveness of sins is an essential mission of the Church.

Thus the Church needs the confessions of its members because in a person's confession the Church faces the mystery of sin and the mystery of the world without Christ. Through each confession the Church is once more in the presence of Christ and asks for his forgiveness. By doing so, it again stirs up its love for Christ, who died on the Cross and rose for each and all the sins of the world.

The forgiveness granted by God through the Church prompts one to be an instrument of forgiveness. It lets the faithful become conscious of the impact that sins have made on them, on the Church, and on the world. It makes one understand the teaching of St Paul that the faithful's personal morality and sins are not measured only by the morality of the world. Being united with the Church and with Christ, one offends and hurts not just the common justice by which he or she is obliged to the world but also the holiness of Christ and the new world that faith has made real with its new demands and blessings. And this new reality is the reality of the mystical body of Christ. All Christians are members of Christ, the temples of the Holy Spirit, because the Spirit is within them (1 Cor 7, 15.19) and this is real for the believer.

Sins and forgiveness are a cosmic reality. The sacrament of forgiveness opens up oneself and lets grace enter where weakness abides. It brings about renewed faith that a life without weakness and sin is once more possible. It bring about new hope, new trust, new love for a future stronger than the past. Faith with love and hope is able to disarm nature's forces (Gen 1, 8; Rev 21, 1).

4.4.7.4 THE SACRAMENT OF FORGIVENESS IS A SYMBOL FOR CHRISTOLOGY: CHRIST'S PREROGATIVE OF LOVE AND JUSTICE

Forgiveness of sin reveals a new feature of Christology. How and why did Christ dare to say that he can forgive sin and announce that "your sins are forgiven"? Why and how could he love sinners? He loved sinners, one can suggest, because they revealed his uncommon love for the Father and his perfect dedication to justice as his indisputable privilege. He joined once and for all his forgiving love with his great and unique "penance" made for his followers as well as for his enemies by his death on the cross and resurrection. Instead of condemning them in dying, he excused them for their ignorance (Lk 23, 34). In his anger he could and did curse them (Mt 11, 21; 21, 19; 23, 13–36; Mk 11, 14; Lk 6, 24–26; 11, 42–47), yet he learned not only obedience (Heb 5, 8) but forgiveness also. He joined love and justice and made forgiveness one of his sacraments and thus forgiveness became characteristic of his "Way." The mystery of the Incarnation, hypostatic union, revelation, redemption, sanctification, salvation, and glorification – each and all of these find their significance for human beings in forgiveness, the distinctive pledge of the love God has for the human race.

He proclaimed that love from the very beginning of his life (Acts 2, 38; 5, 31; 10, 43; 13, 38; Mt 16, 19; 18, 15–18; 28, 18–20). It was an innovation that could be hardly introduced by his community, which built up ecclesiology on its Christology. If there was anyone who could persuade the Church that it had such a power, it had to be the one who was convinced that love is stronger than hatred and that love with "logos," is the epistemology of that new ontology. The Johannine gospel suggests that when Jesus said that nobody has ever seen God except the Son, who is "in the bosom" of the Father and made that known, so the Word logically had to be "full of grace and truth" (Jn 1, 18, 14). It was the Word's exclusive special right, privilege, and power that others had to believe in and experience his justice. One can understand that forgiveness makes evident that ecclesiology is Christology and Christology is the revelation of the Holy Trinity.

4.4.7.5 THE SACRAMENT OF FORGIVENESS IS A SYMBOL FOR THE REVELATION OF THE TRIUNE GOD: FORGIVING LOVE IS FREE AND INDEPENDENT OF THE WORTHINESS OF THE SINNER

A forgiving love that is free and independent of the worthiness of the sinner reveals unambiguously the absolute transcendence and independence of God from the created world. God does not need anything. When God forgives, it is done graciously and freely. It reveals God as absolutely perfect, rich, and invulnerable. No one can use God's free forgiveness against God. Any misuse may hurt only the one who misused it but never the God who has forgiven. From this it follows that only God can truly forgive. And this free God's love, which the world cannot give, is actualized in the sacrament of forgiveness.

Forgiving that is free and independent of the worthiness of the one to be pardoned is the only real forgiveness. Forgiveness is really forgiveness if it is not a business, not a *do ut des*. To be able to imitate God's forgiveness and mercy (Lk 6, 36), one has to share the generosity of God and God's fullness to forgive freely without waiting for anything in return. This implies a sharing in the nature of God (2 Pet 1, 4), enabling one human being to forgive injustice unselfishly. Human forgiveness may create vassals. God's free forgiveness makes the sinner free.

4.4.7.6 THE SACRAMENT OF FORGIVENESS IS A SYMBOL FOR ESCHATOLOGY: THE MERCIFUL SHALL OBTAIN MERCY

If there is final forgiveness, the end of the world cannot be doom and gloom. Even though sin exists and its power is real, Eschatology will be the fulfillment of Etiology. The final goodness will be the fulfillment of the original goodness of the Creator. The final fight will be won not by force but by forgiveness. The *ur*-being of existence and its law was and remains forever forgiving love. The end of human history, as well as that of the cosmic world, will be the revelation that each of us was ever loved by God in the Church of Christ like no one ever was before or ever will be after (Horvath, 1993, 150–3). The Eucharistic love will find its final realization and expression in the universal judgment of the world when mercy shall prevail (Mt 5, 7). Yet there will be no final restoration, *apocatastasis*, since forgiveness is free. It is given only to those who want to be forgiven. And there is sin that cannot be forgiven because there can be people who do not want to be forgiven. Forgiveness implies sins committed, and there can be people who would never admit that they are sinners and need mercy.

4.4.7.7 THE SACRAMENT OF FORGIVENESS IS A SYMBOL FOR PNEUMATOLOGY: THERE IS NO FORGIVENESS WITHOUT THE HOLY SPIRIT

The sacrament of forgiveness is a symbol for pneumatology, meaning that pneumatology is Christology and Christology is pneumatology. Christ's forgiveness cannot be without the Holy Spirit, and there cannot be forgiveness by the Holy Spirit without Christ. The first would raise questions about the universal and infinite dimension of Christ's divine redemption, and the second about the historical foundation and validity of sin and its forgiveness.

The fact that there is no forgiveness of sin without the Holy Spirit reveals the transcendental, supernatural nature of sin. Sin is not just a transgression of a command. It is the denial of love as the foundation of being and redemption by confessing hatred as foundation of being. This is the mystery of the irreversible damnation of the Satan with whom Jesus denied any relation. The theology of the unforgivable sin against the Holy Spirit (Mt 12, 32; Mk 3, 29–30; Lk 12, 10) is the negative expression of the positive affirmation that sins can be forgiven only by the Holy Spirit.

Spirits without a body, such as Satan, and spirits with a body, such as human beings, can have actions that transcend time and have an impact on eternity. Forgiveness cannot be imposed on anybody. There is a time when forgiveness is desired, and there is time when forgiveness is not desired. Doing good or evil forms one's identity or personality. It is possible that sin is identified with one's personality so much that one cannot give up sin without ceasing to be what he or she has become. "I just cannot deny what I am," "I cannot put all my life in parenthesis," "I am my sin and my sin is me," and "I just cannot believe that there is or can be forgiveness or any need of it" are statements a human being can make. Forgiveness may seem too easy, on one hand, and on the other, it may threaten "the achievement" of a lifetime.

We noted earlier that the action of the Holy Spirit is required for the mystery of the Incarnation, for the inspiration of the Scripture, and for carrying out Jesus' saving work. It is necessary for faith to recognize that Jesus and not "me" is Christ. Each human being has the power of making a god out of her or himself. What this involves is the belief that it is not God but I myself who am the fullness of being. Bultmann described the grace of revelation as the recognition that God is God and I am just a creature (1960, 85–6). Human existence is a dramatically and dangerously great chance for adventure because human beings may win or fail. Forgiveness may not be easy. One must first forgive the other and then forgive oneself and then receive the forgiveness of God. It is expressed in the words "I am glad, my God, that *you* are God, and I am your creature who needs your forgiveness."

4.4.7.8 THE SACRAMENT OF FORGIVENESS IS A SYMBOL FOR MARIOLOGY: MARY IS THE REFUGIUM PECCATORUM, OR REFUGE OF SINNERS

The sacrament of forgiveness glorifies God's love as free and independent of the worthiness of any human being (Lk 1, 46–55). So does God's love for Mary. And such is the love that Mary has for any human being whom her Son has redeemed. Refuge means someone to whom one can have recourse in difficulty. Does the refuge of sinners mean, therefore, that Mary is the one to whom bank robbers, murderers, defrauders, money launderers, criminals, prostitutes, abortionists, adulterers, fornicators, liars, and people who never go to church can take recourse?

There is more than one reason why is Mary the refuge for sinners. The first is that being the mother of the Saviour of the world, in a spiritual yet real sense Mary can be considered the mother of every human being, and a mother is the best advocate because she finds difficult to believe that her son or daughter is a criminal. Another reason is that a mother can always hope, particularly for her children. And this is true of Mary, who is praised in the Scripture for her faith: "blessed is she who believed that the promise made to her by the Lord will be fulfilled" (Lk 1, 45). Such a faith or trust is the first step toward conversion of any sinner. It is a trust that one can do better in spite of countless relapses, that one is better than what he or she thinks of him or herself. It is a kind of daring vision that the future of his or her "I" is not necessarily her or his present ego, that a rotten life does not make it impossible to reach or return to a powerful, youthful, innocent optimism, free of anxiety and fear. And here is the third reason that justifies the fact that Mary can rightly be honored as a refuge for the sinner.

Mary is an immaculate virgin and thus an example, model, and sure sign of hope and *solatium*, optimism (*LG*, no. 68; Tanner, 1990, 898), for all sinners. And so she is "the beginning of the Church," which is to be also in heaven in the communion of the saints. With Mary all the members of God's holy people united by the Eucharistic presence may intercede for one another and hope for the return of an "innocent youth." Mary is, therefore, the sure sign that the whole Church intercedes for sinners. Like the martyrs of the early church, she prays together with the whole Church (Acts 1, 14) for the power and grace of the sacrament of forgiveness in the Holy Spirit.

But what is the theological value of such a discourse? The Second Vatican Council noted that the "Church constantly holds its course towards the fullness of God's truth" and that "under the assistance of the holy Spirit" there is "growth in understanding of ... both the words and the realities they signify" (*DV*, no. 8; Tanner, 974). Obviously, such a reality is Mary, the mother of Jesus Christ. The noted progress comes about "through contemplation and study by believers, 'who ponder these things in their hearts' (see Lk 2, 9 and 51)," "through the intimate understanding of spiritual things which they experience," and through the preaching of those "who, on succeeding to the office of bishop, receive the sure charism of truth" (ibid.).

All these three ways of progress in understanding faith are obvious in understanding the mystery of Mary, the mother of Jesus Christ, who as a woman, mother, and female human being, has a special prerogative, privilege, and power of attraction. She is the one in whom justice and love embrace each other, and the eternal human love of a woman who cannot believe that the sins of her beloved sons and daughters are unforgivable remains an indispensable symbol for the revelation of God's love for human beings.

John Paul II expressed this concept convincingly in his *Encyclical on Faith and Reason,* when for the understanding of faith he joined Mary with the role of philosophy and called both to "offer [their] rational and critical resources that the understanding of faith, may be fruitful and creative." "For between the vocation of the blessed Virgin and the vocation of true philosophy there is a deep harmony. Just as the Virgin was called to offer herself entirely as human being and as woman that God's word might take flesh and come among us, so too philosophy" is called to offer its rational and critical resources, "its autonomy in no way impaired" (John Paul II, 1998, no. 108, 40).

4.5 WHAT IS THE SACRAMENT OF THE ANOINTING OF THE SICK?

4.5.1 Sickness and Health

Sickness, bodily and spiritual, has from the beginning been considered a threat, and the human mind has tried to reason about it (Bowker, 1970). For African traditional religions, sickness is a punishment by the offended ancestors and spirits. One has to learn how to expiate them, but one has to know also that there are some means, some medicines, to cure the ailment. Nature, the universe, is fundamentally good and supportive to human beings. It was made so by a gracious God, and if humans respect nature, they will find plants, spirits, and all kind of beings that help people to restore their health.

For Hinduism, the cause of suffering is much deeper. Suffering is an ontological reality. It is the essence of the universe. Conflict is inherent in existence and life is a chain of killing and being killed. There is an universal disorder, and sacrifice serves as a means to restore order at least temporarily until the final rest and peace is reached through several incarnations. Buddhism discovered and taught how to break the unbreakable chain of suffering and that one can reach happiness not with God's help but by well-thought-out methods and faithful discipleship. For Sufi Islam, suffering and self-mortification are welcome because they make us aware of God, whereas for Shiite Muslims, suffering, especially martyrdom, is a sure way to eternal happiness in heaven.

The books of the Old Testament show a great variety of ideas about suffering. The Book of Proverbs summarizes the old tradition that suffering is a punishment for sin: "The fear of the Lord prolongs life, but the years of the wicked will be short" (10, 27). This is the philosophy of Job's friends, with which the author of that book does not agree. Neither did Jeremiah. He had seen that the "wicked prosper and the treacherous thrive" (12, 1). Ecclesiastes could not understand why it is that one fate comes to all and is the same for the good and for the sinner (Ec 9, 2–3). Second Isaiah proclaimed the redemptive value of the just one's suffering. The Lord revealed that the "suffering servant" will bear the sins of many, make intercession for the transgressors (Is 53, 12), and lead his people back to God (Is 53, 1–13). After the destruction of Jerusalem, the apocalyptic literature promised reward for suffering in the next life (Enoch 102, 6–11; 4 Ezr 4, 26–27).

In Orthodox rabbinical literature, suffering is a punishment for the sins of Israel (Schweid, 1991, 186–7). Yet it is more than that according to the new theology of the Holocaust. It is the problem of why "God is hiding His Countenance in the face of radical evil" (ibid., 202). It implies a "claim of eternal presence beyond history," "the enigma of faith, and beyond it the enigma of the Jewish believer's loneliness before a hiding God" (ibid., 203–8). This sounds like a remarkably close parallel to the loneliness that Jesus Christ suffered in his life and agony, to his "daring new conceptualization of the divine presence," which he proclaimed to the world, as well as his "eternal presence beyond history." One can find a parallel symbolism between the Christian theology of the uniqueness of Jesus Christ's suffering and the Jewish theology of the uniqueness of the Jewish people's holocaust. Is Jesus Christ the fulfillment of the true Israelite destiny, or are the Jewish people the fulfillment of the true Jesus Christ's destiny?

According to the gospel narratives, Jesus had a special care for the sick and gave a great deal of attention to them. He tried to alleviate their suffering. Even though he did not deny some relation between original sin and sickness, he did not consider sickness just a punishment for one's sins (Jn 9, 3). For him, God was not absent in sickness and sickness could be a means of grace. And what is more, he identified himself with the sick (Mt 25, 39.43), and so union with the sick became a union with Christ (Mt 25, 36–45; 2 Cor 1, 3–7). Thus God did not abandon the sick, and sickness was a milieu of salvation and not of damnation.

The apostles were sent to anoint the sick with oil and heal them, as we read in the gospels (Mk 6, 13; cf. Lk 10, 34). Their mission of announcing the good news included healing and taking care of the sick (Mk 16, 15–18). And the Church continued to do the same. In the letter of James we find the description of how the early Church took care of the sick. If there was a sick person in the house, some invited a presbyter of the Church, who prayed and anointed the sick one with oil in the name of the Lord, who was expected to raise him or her up. If the sick committed sin, the same Lord would forgive them (Jas 5, 14–15).

Anointing in the name of the Lord meant that it was the Lord's doing and that the prayer of faith and the prayer of the Church would save, (σώσει) the sick, restore the sick physically and spiritually. The Lord will raise (ἐγείρω) the sick the way he did the epileptic who was like a corpse (Mk 9, 26–27) and Peter's mother-in-law, who lay ill with fever (Mt 5, 14–15). The verb ἐγείρω means physical cure and resurrection as well. Finally, sins will be forgiven (ἀφίημί). The Council of Trent referred to this text as the scriptural reference for Jesus Christ's institution of the anointing of the sick as one of his sacraments (*Teaching on the Sacrament of Last Anointing*, session 14, chapter 1; Tanner, 1990, 710; Vorgrimler, 1967, 1978). Faithful to the mission of Christ since the beginning, the early councils ordered bishops to build hospitals. At that time hospitals, as well as sickness, were considered a preparation for death and not a place of healing. Thus the anointing of the sick, together with the Eucharist, was also a kind of viaticum for the dying.

It was only in the twentieth century that the notion of sickness and health changed considerably. Progressively, sickness was not any longer a door to death but a challenge to recover health. Likewise, health was more than the absence of sickness. It became a duty to perform. Hospitals were no longer called shelters for the sick but health centres. Conveniently, the name of the sacrament of the last anointing has been changed to simply the anointing of the sick with the renewed hope of getting one's health back spiritually and physically. As the notion of sickness has changed, so has the faithful's understanding of the sacrament of the sick

4.5.2 *The Sick and the Sacrament of the Sick in the History of the Church*

Since the time of Jesus, the sick have reminded the Church of Christ and have remained the special care of the Church (Babos, 1983a). For a long time the Church was the only community or institution that consistently tried to take care of the sick and the elderly.

James 5, 13–15 provides evidence that already in the first century the Church took care of the sick. A silver tablet with seventeen lines of Aramaic text from the first century contains a prayer for cure and forgiveness that is similar to James 5, 15 ('Découverte,' 1963, 73, 490). From that time the care of the sick included the use of a certain oil blessed for the sick. A Coptic version of the *Didache* thanks God for oil given by his son, Jesus. The *Apostolic Tradition* of Hippolytus, from the year 215, knew about oil for the sick (Dix, 1937). But it was only in the time of Constantine that the Church was able to build *nosocomia*, places for the sick, and *gerocomia*, homes for the aged. Canon no. 75 of the pseudo-apostolic Arabic Nicene canons declared that each city should build facilities for the sick and the poor. We know that St Basil erected *Basiliad* in Caesarea, Cappadocia, in 370, and in Rome Fabiola Pannachius opened a hospital near the Tiber river (Nasalli-Rocca, 1966, 159–60).

The Sacramentary of Serapion, bishop of Thmuis, had a prayer for the blessing of the oil. In 416 Pope Innocent I made a reference to the anointing of the sick done by a presbyter with oil blessed by a bishop. Caesarius of Arles, in his Sermon no. 261, followed James 5, 14–15, and instead of the forgiveness of sins, he gave priority to restoring health. The rite prior to the Gregorian reform with an invocation of the Holy Spirit upon the oil is described in *Decretum Gelasianum* of the early sixth century. Eligius (590–660; *PL*, 93, 69) and Bede (673–735; *PL*, 93, 69) both spoke out against the superstitious use of the anointing of the sick. The Hôtel-Dieu hospital in Paris was founded at this time.

The Gregorian Sacramentary of the ninth century listed the anointing of the sick closely after the sacrament of penance. It recommended that if the sick person did not get better, the anointing should be repeated up to seven times. Nevertheless, from this time on the main effect of the anointing of the sick was expected to be help for the sick in facing death, and the anointing of the sick became a last anointing of the dying.

In the Profession of Faith prescribed for the Waldenses by Innocent III in 1208, the anointing of the sick is listed with that name as one of the sacraments. Innocent IV, in one of his letters of 1254, already named it *unctio extrema* (DS, 833), last anointing, a name kept until Vatican II. From the time of Innocent IV the sacrament has consistently been listed as one of the seven sacraments (cf. Council of Florence, 1439, *Bull of Union with the Armenians*; Tanner, 1990, 548–9). The Council of Florence just handed over to the Armenians a text taken from Thomas Aquinas (see especially *Summa contra gentiles*, 4, chapter 73; 1934, 537–8).

In light of the definition that for the Scholastic theologians, such as Hugh of St Victor, Peter Lombard, and Bonaventure, sacraments are signs bringing about grace, the effect of the last anointing had to be grace for the salvation of the soul and not for the healing of the body. To bring into harmony the tradition of the early church and the new understanding of this sacrament with the biblical understanding of sickness as a consequence of sin, Aquinas felt it necessary to say that this sacrament is set against bodily infirmity so far as this follows from sin and hinders spiritual healing. Since the Church did not anoint any one condemned to death in good health, Aquinas concluded that the sacrament called last anointing had to be ordained *ad sanandum,* to bodily healing. Precisely because it is ordained to healing, it can be repeated more than once and is applied to the different parts of the body. For the same reason it is administered only to the sick *sub specie corporalis medicinae,* under the form of medicine for the body. And as in each sacrament, so in this sacrament too the signification of the sacrament must be observed. Just as the action of washing is symbolic in baptism, so is bodily healing in this sacrament. Furthermore, the matter used in this sacrament is oil, which has a well-known healing power for the body by soothing pains.

Since the effect of the sacraments is a perfect cure and the abundant grace of perfect healing, continued Thomas Aquinas, it is fitting that many priests be present and say the prayers together in order to procure the whole effect of the sacrament. If only one priest is present, he should be there on behalf of the whole Church and administer the sacrament in the power of the entire Church, whose minister he is. This sacrament completes the healing inaugurated by the sacrament of penance and delivers from the guilt of temporal punishment as well as from sins one does not remember and from the daily sins without which we cannot live in the present life. Therefore it is properly called the last sacrament, concluded Aquinas. It consummates the healing in both soul and body in the same way that we participate in God's life in heaven (*Summa contra gentiles, 4*, chapter 73; 1934, 537–8).

Thomas's success in harmonizing new insights with old traditions may explain why during the Council of Trent the word *dumtaxat*, only, was changed to *praesertim*, especially, for not unduly delaying the anointing. Thus this sacrament is "to be used for the sick, especially for those who are so dangerously ill that they seem to be about to depart from life; and consequently it is also called the sacrament of the departing" (chapter 3; Tanner, 1990, 711). It is "the final complement" of penance and of the whole Christian life (*Teaching on the Sacrament of Last Anointing*; Tanner, 710). In canon 2 the sacrament is called, as in the early tradition, the anointing of the sick which alleviates the *sick* instead of the "dying," and it is a grace not only of healing of "a past age" but of the present time as well (Tanner, 713).

At the same time the council retained the name the "last anointing," and in canon 1 it affirmed that it is "truly and properly a sacrament instituted by Christ" as suggested by Mark (6, 13) and commended and announced by James (5, 14–15). The grace effected by the Holy Spirit takes away sins as well as the remains of sins. It comforts and strengthens the soul of the sick person by arousing in him or her great trust in the divine mercy. Because of this support, the sick person bears the inconveniences and trials of the illness more lightly, resists more easily the temptation of the devil, and sometimes regains bodily health "when it is expedient for the salvation of the soul" (Tanner, 1990, 710). Finally, the presbyter of James 5, 14 is not to be understood as an elder or some leader of the community who would not be a bishop or a priest (ibid., 711).

Following the early tradition of the Church, Vatican II called this sacrament again the sacrament of the sick and placed it in a Christological and ecclesiological context by exhorting the sick to associate themselves "to the suffering and glorified Lord and to make a contribution to the good of the people of God" (LG, no. 11; Tanner, 1990, 857).

4.5.3 *The Sacramental Reality of the Sacrament of the Anointing of the Sick*

4.5.3.1 THE PRE-EMINENCE

As we said earlier, each sacrament has a pre-eminence. The pre-eminence that the sacrament of the anointing of the sick has over the other sacraments is its symbolizing of God's mystery, which Vatican I called God's incomprehensibility *(Dogmatic Constitution on the Catholic Faith,* chapter 1; Tanner, 1990, 805). A sort of trans-symbolization of the sick person is taking place. This will be discussed shortly (Knauber, 1975; Horvath, 1989).

4.5.3.2 THE FOUR AIMS AND THE FOUR ACTIVE PERSONS PARTICIPATING

Like any other sacrament, the sacrament of the anointing of the sick can be described anthropologically, ecclesiologically, Christologically, and theologically. Anthropologically, it is for human beings. It comforts and strengthens the sick person by arousing in him or her "great trust in the divine mercy to bear more lightly the miseries and pains of illness, strengthening in temptation, forgiving sins, if there be any still to be expiated, removing the remains of sins and restoring health when it is expedient for the salvation of the sick person " (Council of Trent, *Teaching on the Sacrament of Last Anointing,* chapter 2; Tanner, 1990, 710).

The ecclesiological description presents the sacraments as life functions of the Church in which the Church's life is actualized and expressed. It is in this sense that Vatican II says that through the sacred anointing of the sick and the prayers of the priests, "the whole Church commends the sick to the suffering and glorified Lord that he might relieve them and restore them to health (see Jas 5, 14–16), and it exhorts them freely to associate themselves with the passion and death of Christ (see Rom 8, 17; Col 1, 24; 2 Tim 2, 11–12; 1 Pet 4, 13), and so to contribute to the good of the people of God" (*LG,* no. 11; Tanner, 1990, 857).

The Christological consideration of the sacraments turns our attention to the fact that each sacrament is a kind of earthly extension of the risen body of Christ, a sort of gesture of Jesus, who becomes sacramentally yet visibly present to us in the sacrament of the anointing of the sick person, who is joined to the suffering and glorification of Jesus Christ. And since Jesus Christ is the revelation of the Triune God, the sacrament of the anointing of the sick is the revelation of the inner life of God and shows us the incomprehensibility of the God of Jesus Christ. A sick person is a symbol of eternity who is God.

In presenting our summary reply to the question of what the sacrament of the anointing of the sick is, together with a commentary on it, we would like to recall once more that the validity of any sacrament, and thus that of the sacrament of the anointing of the sick, requires the active presence of Christ, the God-man, the Church as the hierarchical community of the faithful, the sick, and the minister performing the sacramental event. The absence of any of the four would invalidate the sacrament.

4.5.4 *What the Sacrament of the Anointing of the Sick Is*

The description we present again follows a pattern of three levels, known in structuralist consideration as surface level (structuralized non-structuralizing), deep level (structuralized and structuralizing), and basic level (structuralizing non-structuralized) (Horvath, 1977, 284–5; Lane, 1970, 15). The first is the visible rite of actions and words, the second is the new life of faith, charity, and hope (and sometimes the sacramental character), and the third is the uncreated grace, that is, Jesus Christ in Trinity. The three levels are one. Distinction is prompted by the way our reason operates: divides and unites.

surface level (*sacramentum tantum*) symbolizing not-symbolized	Christ, the Church as people of God, the minister, and the sick faithful, through the symbol of the anointing with the blessed oil and of the accompanying prayer of the priest, come together in order to
deep level (*res et sacramentum*)	– redeem our selfish ego defence mechanism put into operation by apprehension of the image of death emerging in the
symbolized and symbolizing	– experienced sickness through the release of the power of the resurrection of Jesus Christ, who
basic level (*res tantum*) symbolized not-symbolizing	– spent a great deal of his ministry going around curing the sick in order to reveal the transcendent incomprehensibility of his heavenly Father and his eternal home.

4.5.4.1 COMMENT

In the sacramental action of the anointing of the sick, there are three symbols involved: oil, the sick, and the prayer. The first and the third are easy to understand (Horvath, 1989). The oil implies a threefold symbolism. First, it is a symbol of healing, of life, gladness, and joy. Being blessed by the bishop (or a priest acting as his representative), it suggests that the anointing will be the action of the whole Church. Secondly, oil symbolizes the gift of God and his blessing, which means that God is "eulogizing us with a certain warmth of heart." In other words, God is giving us God's friendship, which is life, joy, and therefore forgiveness of sins. Thirdly, oil is a symbol of the Holy Spirit bringing about the eschatological age, the nearness of God to us. The prayers that are the form of the sacraments verbalize the symbolism of the oil: "Through this holy anointing may the Lord in his love and mercy help you with the grace of the Holy Spirit. Amen."

The first and third symbolisms are logically coherent, but the second, the symbolism of the sick, is somewhat unusual. In the sacrament of the anointing of the sick, something takes place that is unique and cannot be found in the other sacraments. We would like to call this original event the trans-symbolization of the human meaning of the visible symbol. In the other sacraments the visible symbols retain their natural meaning. Water means cleansing to all of us, washing and refreshment of life. The oil in confirmation is for strengthening. The bread and wine are nourishing. Absolution or reconciliation is the forgiveness of sins. The imposition of hands in ordination is union with Christ. But in the sacrament of the anointing of the sick a human person who is not well enters into a revelatory constellation in which God reveals what human beings (anthropological), what the Church (ecclesiological), what Christ (Christological), and what God (theological) are in the revelation of Jesus Christ. In the other sacraments the visible condition of the recipient does not enter as visible symbol in the sacramental event. Being non-Christian for baptism, or being sinful for penance, etc., is not visible as being sick in the case of the sacrament of anointing of the sick is, where the sickness must be perceptible.

All sacraments are sacraments of the death and resurrection of Jesus Christ, and each has a pre-eminence (Thomas Aquinas, *Summa. theol.*, 3, q 65, a 1 and 3; 1948, 402–7). The sacrament of the anointing of the sick has a special pre-eminence in symbolizing here and now, in our time and space, the death of Jesus Christ precisely as the symbol of resurrection. Here the symbol of the end of life becomes the symbol of the beginning of eternal life. One could find some motive here of why Jesus showed so much love and care for the sick. His role as redeemer and saviour through his death and resurrection found in the sick its most powerful expression.

By instituting the sacrament of anointing the sick, Christ took the symbol of the present world, a symbol of weakness, and transformed it into a new symbol of the world to come. The natural symbol is reinterpreted and the non-symbol becomes a symbol. In this sense the sacrament of the anointing of the sick is the "end" of the sacramental symbolism, and it becomes the "last" sacrament, since the symbolism as we know it comes to an end with it. It is the negation of the logic of symbolism.

There is a new sense in it, which only faith can grasp. It seems that Christ wanted to tell us that God's symbolism transcends our imagination and our understanding of the depth meaning of symbolism. God penetrates the depth of the visible reality, where our senses cannot follow God. Only faith can do so by sharing God's intelligence and symbolizing power to unearth the meaning of the risen life. Thus by virtue of faith the believer can see the sick person, the non-symbol of life, as a symbol of life. This is what the grace effects in the sacrament of the anointing. We can understand this better if we consider the transformation taking place in the sick as a result of the sacramental grace.

The nature of the sickness may be different, yet each sickness carries in itself the image of death which threatens our existence. As a result, our body, or rather, our whole self puts its ego defence mechanism into operation. Through the biological mechanism, the psychological and spiritual self-defence mechanism is activated as well. On each level, death is sensed as the final annihilation of this ego defence mechanism, its final defeat, and the struggle for survival is intensified. Thus we can say that any sickness we experience is a sort of apprehension of the image of death in various degrees of intensity. In order to see how the grace of the sacrament of anointing is operating and how it is challenging death as the final annihilation of this ego defence mechanism, let us first examine the various functions of the natural self-defence mechanism as they are known in psychology (Holmes, 1984, 347–50; Toman, 1979, 252):

1 denial of reality: one refuses to admit the truth (I am really not sick; I will not die);
2 daydreaming: one escapes into a satisfying world of fantasy, instead of facing reality as it is (I watch television day and night; I read science fiction or crime stories);
3 rationalization: one gives false but socially approved reasons to justify questionable behaviour (I would not be sick if ... I can explain it from my background);
4 projection: one blames others for personal shortcomings and attributes to others one's unacceptable impulses (the nurses drive me nuts);
5 repression: one excludes painful or dangerous thoughts from one's awareness (I do not think about it);
6 regression: one tries to gain sympathy or avoid problems by retreating to infantile behaviour (I need you, you are like a mother to me);
7 reaction formation: one denies faulty impulses by going to the opposite extreme (I do not eat too much; I am very organized; I am not afraid);
8 emotional isolation: one avoids hurt through apathy or detachment (I could not care less; I do not give a d—);
9 identification: one increases feelings of worth by identifying oneself with important people or institutions (I got a letter from the president; I die for my country; I am a saint).

Now, the grace of the sacraments operates on the various forms of self-defence mechanisms and transforms them so that the denial of reality will give progressively more room to *recognition of reality*, daydreaming to *facing reality*, rationalization to *contextualization*, projection to *responsibility*, repression to *active cooperation in improving the given situation*, regression to *growth*, reaction formation to *incorporation and sublimation of impulses*, emotional isolation to *altruism*, and identification to *personal identity discovery*.

The process of this transformation, put into action through the grace of the sacrament, follows the pattern neither of magic nor of drugs used in medication. A more suitable image would be that of the health resort with its salutary ecological milieu in which the cure is provided by the healing atmosphere of the region. By establishing or reliving in a more experiential way the saving relation brought by the Christ event with the surrounding world, the anointed person leaves, as it were, the hospital, "the dwelling place of the sick," and goes "home" to the Church, the community of the sons and daughters of the Resurrection (cf. Lk 20, 36), and shares their life of faith. It is true that there is nothing particular in this, since prayers, sacraments, and charities in general all serve the same purpose. But in the case of the sick, it all becomes more existential, more experiential.

All this is the work of faith of the Church, God's gift. The self-deceptive and reality-distorting ways of coping with the problems of life are replaced with the courage to face directly the difficulties of life and to deal with them realistically by establishing unselfish relations with others, characteristics of the risen life promised to us by Christ. The grace given in the sacrament of the anointing of the sick is not just any kind of grace but specially the grace of the resurrection of Jesus Christ. Consequently, this sacrament more powerfully reveals in its symbolism the reality of the death and resurrection of Jesus Christ than the other sacraments do. It is a sharing in the resurrection. It is an entry into it. The sacrament of the anointing of the sick is a further symbol of baptism by its transcendental significance.

4.5.5 The Sacrament of the Anointing of the Sick and Sacramental Theology

4.5.5.1 THE SACRAMENT OF THE ANOINTING OF THE SICK IS A PERSONAL ENCOUNTER WITH CHRIST

The sacrament of the anointing of the sick, like any sacrament, is a personal encounter with Christ. And this truth should be recalled on any occasion when this sacrament is administered. It is Christ who brings about the sacrament of the anointing of the sick. The presence of Christ is more than just simple healing. It is the presence of the one who loves the sick, those who are alone, who suffer and are not well. He liked and he likes to be with them. His presence means that God is present in sickness, in death, in the grave, and in heaven. One should therefore not be afraid. If God is with us, who is against us (Rom 8, 31)? Where God is, there is life. Having God is having life. When we are sick, we like to hold the hand of someone who loves us, because somehow we feel that with the loved one we are safe. We like to hang onto someone, because we feel that if we hold onto someone, we belong to those who are alive. We are in the atmosphere of life, we touch life; therefore we cannot die.

Christ's presence is more than charismatic healing. It is not just healing of the body by the spirit of God (cf. 1 Cor 12, 7–11). Rather, it is an invitation to work together with him for eternal salvation. There is a close relationship between charismatic healing and sacramental healing. Because Christ is one, charismatic healing is not independent of sacramental healing. Both are through the Eucharistic Christ, who still has compassion for those who are suffering and who goes around healing every disease and infirmity (cf. Mt 9, 35) by communicating his Spirit of life. Christ's presence in the sacrament of the anointing of the sick is a call to live and to work with him in suffering for the salvation of the world.

4.5.5.2 THE SACRAMENT OF THE ANOINTING OF THE SICK IS A UNION WITH CHRIST AND IN HIM WITH BELIEVERS AND THROUGH THEM WITH THE WHOLE WORLD

By getting sick, one becomes a member of the "community," the "collegiality" of the sick. Though the sick person may have the impression that he or she is isolated, yet he or she has entered into a new union, the union of full-time sick people. It is a solidarity that transcends the family and one's professional and national borders. This new bond is strengthened by the sacrament of the anointing of the sick. The encounter with Christ is the beginning of a new union with him, who had chosen suffering to save the world. This purpose may bring about a much closer union. It is a vocation, a new job, a new apostolate, a new apostleship of prayers and offering.

But it is also a vocation to fight and defeat sickness and regain health. It is salvation in the full sense: saving the world from sin by sacrifice but also saving the world from death and infirmity. The organic unity of each bestowal of the sacrament of the anointing of the sick comes from the presence of the same Christ and the common task of extending the grace of the Holy Spirit to any healing in the world. Because sickness and, concretely, the sick person are sacramental symbols, like the human reality of marriage, so the human reality of sickness and of the sick person too is a salvation milieu that Christ has provided as a further new contact with the profane world in order to insert his paschal mystery into it.

4.5.5.3 THE SACRAMENT OF THE ANOINTING OF THE SICK IS A PARTICIPATION IN CHRIST'S LIFE AND HIS WORK OF SALVATION

Vatican II commends the sick to associate themselves with the passion and death of Christ and cites Romans 8, 17; Colossians 1, 24; 2 Timothy 2, 11–12; and 1 Peter 4, 13. By so doing, they become fellow workers with Christ, moving the whole creation to redemption (Rom 8, 18–23) to complete what is lacking in Christ's suffering for the sake of the mystical body and to enjoy eternity as fellow heirs with him and to rejoice and be glad when his glory is revealed.

Such a theological argument and reasoning becomes more personal, meaningful, and attractive if the sick person begins to give thanks for suffering as for a great gift. With the light of the Holy Spirit the sick may discover that the suffering in his or her life was and is indeed a special time of grace. Salvation means the nearness of God, and suffering may be a special instance of sensing God's presence, his kindness, and God's special love for someone. Experiencing God's goodness and kindness may be really humiliating, since we may find ourselves utterly unworthy of such a privileged love. And so, as the council exhorts us, we will contribute to the good of the people of God (*LG*, no. 11; Tanner, 1990, 857).

4.5.5.4 THE SACRAMENT OF THE ANOINTING OF THE SICK IS A SACRIFICE RECONCILING THE WORLD WITH GOD

Out of his great love for the Father, Jesus accepted the chalice and drank it. This was his sacrifice which brought about love and forgiveness for the sins of the world. Sickness, suffering, and death may prompt envy, despair, and hatred for the healthy, for the living, for the world. The experience of being loved by God should make the sick person generous to the world. He or she may want to share all that he or she has with others, with the world. Such a sick person becomes forgiving, forgiving the sins of others, and so makes a contribution to forgiveness in the world. And this forgiveness is the reward for one's sacrifice prompted by the person's love. By offering and joining his or her cross to that of Jesus Christ, the sick person becomes a sacrifice, reconciling God with the world and the world with God.

4.5.5.5 THE MINISTER

The mystery of the sacrament of the anointing of the sick is a great mystery. It completes healing in both soul and body and brings the kingdom of Christ and world reality to a close unity. It completes the forgiveness inaugurated by the sacrament of forgiveness and the Eucharistic presence of Christ, who went about curing sickness and disease. It delivers from sins, from guilt of temporal punishment, and carries forward the sacrament of baptism as an entrance into the suffering Church by opening the door to the mystery of resurrection. In such a context one can appreciate and discover the significance of canon 5, concerning the sacrament of the anointing of the sick, of the Council of Trent, which says that only a priest ordained by a bishop can be the proper minister of this sacrament (Tanner, 1990, 713). The intention of the canon was to exclude any interpretation that explained the "presbyters" of James 5, 14–15 in a lexical sense – that is, the elders in any community – and not in its scriptural sense as *šĕlĩah*-apostle (ibid.). The exclusive sense obviously does not mean that a bishop should not be brought in to anoint a sick person.

The theological reasoning behind the canon is that the sacrament of the anointing of the sick forgives sin, and forgiving sins is proper to the priestly and episcopal dimension of the sacrament of order. Most authors agree that the Council of Trent did not definitively exclude the possibility that a deacon too could be the minister (Ziegenaus, 1975, 362–3; Vorgrimler, 1978, 219). Yet it seems that such a change would require the creation of a new diaconate by the Church similar to the creation of the presbyterial diaconate in the third century. Whether such a change would serve a pastoral need is not without doubt. The sacraments are for people but not in an exclusive sense. They are for the Church, for Christ, and for God, as we have argued before. The anointing of the sick should not be placed at the same level as medication or drugs that biologically cure diseases. Its healing does not work like a pill. Rather, it creates a healing atmosphere that heals and cures. And this is the community of the Church with the priest as its representative, using oil to signify the mystical body of Christ. The sacrament of anointing the sick is a solemn occasion of celebrating the sick person as the symbol of the suffering Church. And so that the sick person may deserve a visit from the priest, who is able to hear his or her confession and presents the vertical dimension of salvation in a time when God's transcendence and mystery is sacramentally summoned up. Visiting the sick may be more a priestly responsibility than part of the diaconal administrative business of the parish.

4.5.5.6 THE SACRAMENT OF THE ANOINTING OF THE SICK AND ECUMENISM

Suffering and death make us one. We are inclined to think that we are the only one who suffers and the only one who dies. Indeed, we suffer and die alone, because nobody can suffer and die for us. The way we suffer and the way we die constitute our personal achievement and our dignity. Yet if we open our eyes and our heart, we recognize that there is no one and never was and never will be anyone without suffering and death. It is our common origin, common way, and common destiny. We are one in suffering and dying. We all are full of fear and anxiety, and we all are needy, poor, and marginal in more than in one sense. We are all mortals, all dying since the moment we were born. Each suffering we endure deprives us of what we thought makes our existence sure and lasting and brings us closer to every other suffering human being.

Here lies the most realistic foundation for ecumenism. If we all suffer, in spite of any other appearance, and if we all have to die, let us help each other to live and to die in this world with dignity, honestly as brothers and sisters in life and in death. And the sacrament of anointing the sick, be it in new or in old ritual, makes a great contribution, so that even if we did not live for others, we may die for each other (Horvath, 1993, 102–4).

4.5.6 *The Sacrament of the Anointing of the Sick and Systematic Theology*

4.5.6.1 THE SACRAMENT OF THE ANOINTING OF THE SICK IS A SYMBOL FOR THE WORLD: THE WORLD IS MORE THAN WE KNOW ABOUT IT

The sick person as a symbol of eternal life may be a surprising sign to us. Yet our world is full of surprises. Even the surprises that matter may yet deliver, said Edward Teller, are close to infinite (Teller, Teller, and Talley, 1991, 220). And much more life and many more people may yet deliver surprises. The longer we live and learn and meet more people, the more we have, if we are honest with ourselves, to enlarge, to modify, or even completely to rework the horizon that we have been working out of since the beginning of our conscious life.

And this is much, much more the case with revelation and faith. The inhominization of the Incarnation (Horvath, 1976, 448–9) as revelation is "an experience of the expected-unexpected. It is expected on account of the word of God and unexpected on account of the general course of life. This being so, the symbiosis of the unexpected and expected is characteristic of the biblical experience and consequently the permanent element of our Christian life. Christian life may be described as the continuous experience of the unexpectedness of God's expected promise" (ibid., 1976, 446).

Since the innermost reality of any being that makes being exist is love, as we stated at the beginning of our analysis (see 1.3 above), each being has its fundamental mystery in God. And if the knowledge of God's mystery prevents God from being bored during all eternity, and if even we are going to do "what God was always doing" (Horvath, 1993, 153), it will do so with us as well. God's mystery with God's world will be much more than what we know now. It is too wonderful to understand and to justify the way it is (Job 42, 2–6).

4.5.6.2 THE SACRAMENT OF THE ANOINTING OF THE SICK IS A SYMBOL FOR HUMAN EXISTENCE: A CHALLENGE TO NEVER GIVE UP

If by using the triad of faith, charity, and hope, human existence could be characterized as an existence of hope (the young planning for the future), love (the adult in the present), and faith (the old living in the past), Christian existence should be rather described as an existence of faith in Christ (of history), of charity (love of the Father who gave and gives us God's own son), and of hope (the Holy Spirit's pledge for the future; see Eph 4, 4–6). Hope, which is not expectation but trust that God will never abandon me and which gives me the strength to overcome any obstacle and suffering or even death, will keep my faith and charity alive through the challenging times. The earth may go around the sun and the sun around the centre of its galaxy, yet one's life is going straight ahead. The future is always more than the past. Suffering may be a relapse, yet one's personality moves ahead. It is "I" who through death and the grave move ahead to eternity.

The old person may look back to the past, but the young one is still hoping. Life is ahead of him or her and not behind. So it is for any Christian. For a Christian, life is always ahead. The Christian is never old. The Christian is always young, someone who is still able to dream impossible dreams. The Christian will never give up. His or her trust will overcome the world passing by. Seeing someone who is sick and dying is a real challenge to hope for more than one's life could offer so far.

4.5.6.3 THE SACRAMENT OF THE ANOINTING OF THE SICK IS A SYMBOL FOR THE CHURCH'S LOVING THE SICK, THE POOR, AND THE MARGINALIZED

Sick, poor, and marginalized are reversible terms. The sick person is poor and the poor person is sick. The marginalized person is sick and poor. All three terms mean someone who is not in charge of his or life, one who cannot support him or herself and needs help. The Church is expected to support the poor, the sick, and the marginalized because it was sent for that purpose. It was founded to serve the needy. The Church is expected to give and not to receive. Above all, it is expected to give what no one else has and only the Church has, trust and hope. Before God, every human being is poor, marginal, and a sinner who needs forgiveness, someone who needs help to get up and walk. It was not silver or gold but to "walk in the name of Jesus Christ of Nazareth" that Peter gave the man lame from birth (Acts 3, 6). Saying to the world again and again, "Get up and walk in trust" keeps the Church relevant and alive.

4.5.6.4 THE SACRAMENT OF THE ANOINTING OF THE SICK IS A SYMBOL FOR CHRISTOLOGY: CHRIST AS SAVIOUR CARES FOR THE SICK PERSON

Salvation means health and resurrection, "getting up" for eternal life. All humans are mortal. Immortality is not a natural condition of human beings. It is a gift from Christ (Horvath, 1993, 39–41). The sacrament of the anointing of the sick is a reminder that Christ's salvation means the whole human person in body and spirit. So the resurrection will be not just an immortality of the soul but the entry of a human person with body and soul into the eternity of God. The curing of diseases was always connected with faith and forgiveness of sins. So the opposite is also true. Forgiveness of sins brings about the curing of the body in the sense that the sinner, freed from the burden of sin, trustfully begins to take care of him or herself and of others.

The Christ one meets in this sacrament is the Christ who loved and still loves the sick and therefore did and still does spend a great deal of his ministry going around to cure the sick in order to reveal the transcendence of his heavenly Father and his eternal home. The sacrament of the anointing of the sick is the realization of this Jesus' love towards the sick, whom he especially loved. And the reason behind this special love is that like his crucifixion and his death; so the sick, the real poor, reveal his love for the Father. The sick person, as the real poor, loses the character-forming determinations he or she acquired long ago and the attachments linking him or her to certain circumstances. Once freed from these circumstances, she or he is able to accept and return the unrestricted love of Christ to the Father without any reservation (Lk 23, 46). Thus the sacrament of the anointing of the sick is the memorial and revelation of the gracious love that Christ, the "absolute" poor on the cross (Mt 27, 35), offered to his Father. It is this love of the poor Christ on the cross for God that made Christ lovable and loved by all God-loving human beings, who always wanted in love to return to God God's greatest gift, the love for God.

4.5.6.5 THE SACRAMENT OF THE ANOINTING OF THE SICK IS A SYMBOL OF THE REVELATION OF THE TRIUNE GOD AS INCOMPREHENSIBLE

The sacrament of the anointing of the sick is the negation of the logic of symbolism. A non-symbol is transformed into a symbol. The symbol of despair becomes a symbol of life. It seems a kind of taking back of all that sacramental theology, as revelation of God, tried to establish. We said above that marriage is revelation of the Triune God as God's unrestricted self-giving. Priesthood is the symbol of God's tireless calling of human beings into a dialogue with God. Forgiveness tells us that God's love is gratuitous, free and independent of the worthiness of the sinner and his or her ability to return it. Now, the sacrament of the anointing of the sick presents God's incomprehensibility, which cannot be grasped except in faith because it transcends the way we know our world (cf. Luther, 1883–1928, 7, 519). It sounds like a negative theology saying that we know more about what God is not than what he really is.

We have to admit that our minds like surprises. We expect that God has secrets, endless secrets; otherwise we might be not interested in God. Edward Teller once said that the attribute of God he felt most strongly about was God's knowing all secrets. About an everlasting God, the most appealing aspect is, he continued, that there will be always more secrets to be discovered through never-ending surprises (Teller, Teller, and Talley, 1991, 220). Perhaps this is not only possibly but necessarily so. Otherwise we might think of a God who is just a boring self and will us bore as well. From the beginning, Christians believed that God is incomprehensible, yet they hoped to see God face to face in the beatific vision. To explain that the two are not mutually exclusive, we can make a distinction between the way as human creatures we see God face to face and the way God sees God "face to face." Our sharing in God's nature is not and never will be identical with God's existence. So God is and remains always incomprehensible to us. But is God incomprehensible to God? If God's logos is less than God, the answer is yes. If God's Logos is consubstantial with God, the answer is no.

But we can have another way of approaching God's incomprehensibility. God's knowledge is a personal knowledge, and personal knowledge always involves trust. The person is always *ineffabilis*, ineffable, unutterable. A person never can be resolved to a formula of words. No matter how much a scientist can know about me, and it does not matter how many millions of people know me, the way I know myself is always my own knowledge, which remains always mine. I can let people share with me, but I can never really give myself away fully. I am a human person, and as a person, I share the incomprehensibility of God. Likewise and even more our sharing in God's incomprehensibility remains forever an incomprehensibility. But incomprehensibility is in a sense a precondition of love. Love creates ineffability. Love invents incomprehensibility. Love is the foundation and the fruit of God's incomprehensibility. Incomprehensibility is eternity, and love is the threshold of time and eternity.

4.5.6.6 THE SACRAMENT OF THE ANOINTING OF THE SICK IS A SYMBOL FOR ESCHATOLOGY: TIME IS THE REVELATION OF ETERNITY

Sickness, the image of mortality and death, could become the symbol of salvation and of eternal life because by Christ's Incarnation, time became the revelation of eternity. As the divinity of Christ became the meaning of his humanity, so eternity became the meaning of time. And as the humanity of Christ became the expression of his divinity, so time could become the expression of eternity (Horvath, 1993, 62–4). Because of the analogy of being, two contradictory beings, such as God and a human being (God is God and not a human being and a human being is a human being and not God), may convene in being, and at the same they may differ in the same (cf. Lateran IV, chapter 2, *On the Error of Abbot Joachim*; Tanner, 1990, 232). In virtue of the Incarnation, God became man and a man could be called God; thus by the same Incarnation, eternity and time were joined in eschatological union who is Jesus Christ. In him time became the expression of eternity and eternity, is the meaning of time. Mortality in time became immortality in eternity, and a sick person a symbol of eternity.

4.5.6.7 THE SACRAMENT OF THE ANOINTING OF THE SICK IS A SYMBOL FOR PNEUMATOLOGY: THE SICK, THE POOR, AND THE MARGINAL AS A TEST CASE FOR THE AUTHENTICITY OF A THEOLOGY OF THE HOLY SPIRIT

The contribution that the sacrament of the anointing of the sick has for the theology of the Holy Spirit is that all gifts of the Spirit have to have an incarnational, bodily dimension. Instead of taking this world to the next, the Spirit brings the other world into the present one. It was the Spirit who made the Incarnation of Christ real, and it was the same Spirit who called the mystical body of Christ into existence. It is coherent and consistent with this that the Spirit is the one by whose power the presence of Christ is ascertained, witnessed, and brought about in the sacraments and the invisible is made visible to be a revelation of the invisible.

Therefore it is consistent, too, that the "charismatic" church remains the church of the poor, the sick, and the marginalized people of this world. Love likes to be poor. It likes to give by emptying oneself to be poor, a servant, without considering doing that to be unjust, ἁρπαγμός, to oneself (Phil 2, 6). It is called the poverty of spirit of those who are poor in spirit, οἱ πτωχοὶ τῷ πνεύματι (Mt 5, 3). It is consistent also that there cannot be an essential difference between sacramental grace and charismatic grace and, for the same reason, between so-called mystical and non-mystical grace, except for the degree of humility in receiving it. All are the graces of the Eucharistic Christ by the Holy Spirit.

4.5.6.8 THE SACRAMENT OF THE ANOINTING OF THE SICK IS A SYMBOL FOR MARIOLOGY, CALLING TO MIND MARY'S BODILY ASSUMPTION INTO HEAVEN

The sacrament of the anointing of the sick means salvation for mind and body. Its aim is the restoration of health in soul, mind, and body by creating a milieu of sanctification and love. A sick person needs help. The more serious the sickness is, the more help the sick person will need. Sick people are all exposed to the graciousness of others. This exposure to the graciousness of others is the symbol of our being at the mercy of God for God's grace.

Mary delivered herself to the mercy of God (Lk 1, 38) and made herself the recipient of God's favours. The more she received, the more she relied on God. Her acceptance of becoming the mother of Jesus Christ made her more the "handmaid" of the Lord, more "powerless" in front of her God. The more humble she became, the more gifts she received and so excelled in grace and humility. God exalted her "as one of low degree" and filled her with good things (Lk 1, 52–53). God let Mary be a co-worker in redemption during her life on earth and even after that when she appeared to a poor little girl as the one who loves the sick, the poor, and marginalized "sinners." Thus Vatican II could recognize her as being one "enriched by this supreme office and dignity of being mother of God the Son," and as also the one who is "outstanding among the humble and the poor of the Lord" (*LG*, nos 53, 55; Tanner, 1990, 892–3). Mary's assumption in body and soul into heavenly glory was the necessary condition of being the universal mediatrix of all graces, including the grace of our bodily resurrection. Bodily resurrection is the only way to be present to the world always and everywhere in body and soul, but particularly at the hour of death (Horvath, 1993, 123–4).

The truth that the greater one is, the humbler he or she will be became a leading motive for Christianity and for any theological treatise. Christ himself gave an example at the Last Supper when he washed the feet of his disciples and said, "You call me Teacher and Lord; and you are right, for so I am. If I then, your Lord and Teacher, have washed your feet, you also ought to wash one another's feet" (Jn 13, 13; Lk 22, 26; Mt 23, 11–12). It is in this sense true that Christology is Mariology and Mariology is Christology (Horvath, 1972, 295–9), and Christology is Christian Anthropology. It seems that only great women and great men can be really humble and able to receive the gift of eternal life, the resurrection of the soul and body. The sacrament of the anointing of the sick is a sacrament of love, the threshold of time and eternity. It is the sacrament of the those who can say, "God, into your hand I commit my spirit" (Lk 23, 46).

4.6 WHAT IS THE SACRAMENT OF BAPTISM?

4.6.1 *Introduction*

From the sacraments we have scrutinized so far, we know that the Father, the Son, and the Holy Spirit are a God who is pleased to be with the human race (Eucharist), a God of unrestrictedly self-giving (marriage) who tirelessly calls human beings into a dialogue (order), forgives gratuitously and independently of the worthiness of the sinner (forgiveness), and is incomprehensible by transcending the way we know our world (anointing of the sick). Now from the sacrament of baptism we learn that God is a person in the Father's generosity, a person in the Son's integrity, and a person in the Holy Spirit's authenticity. The sacrament of baptism is the reply of *faith* to God's efficient *call* for dialogue. It is one of the two sacraments constituting the Church as a people in dialogue with God. The sacrament of order is the sacrament of God's call, and the sacrament of baptism is the sacrament of answering God's call.

4.6.2 *Baptismal Symbolism*

4.6.2.1 JESUS' BAPTISM

Baptism as a rite of initiation was not a Jewish practice. New Testament writers considered circumcision (Gen 17, 9–14) to be a counterpart to Christian baptism as an outward sign of belonging to the Jewish people (Rom 2, 25–29; 4, 11; Col 4, 11; Phil 3, 3). The Essenes, known from the Qumran scrolls, practised baptism of ablution as a sign of cleansing and purification. Their book, the Manual of Discipline, makes it clear, however, that ablution was not enough without internal obedience to God's commandments. The baptism of John the Baptist was similar, but there is no evidence that he was a member of the Jewish sect.

Jesus accepted John's baptism as an indication of a sort of affinity with one of the existent Jewish spiritual movements. It was a rejection of any discipleship or belonging to the leading groups of Pharisees, Sadducees, and scribes. He went to John the Baptist to show his belonging to his contemporary world and at the same to liberate himself from it. John the Baptist was the only man of his time whom Jesus praised, yet he did not fail to make clear that the least of his followers is "greater than he" (Mt 11, 11).

Jesus' baptism was a theophany and a Christophany at the same time. After John the Baptist's witness (Mt 13, 14), God and the Spirit of God, descending and alighting on him, now witnessed to Jesus. The four gospel traditions found it important to report the event (Mk 1, 10–11; Lk 3, 21–22; Jn 1, 32–34). It reminds us of the opening theophany of the creation, when before the creation God's spirit moved over the waters. The gospel narratives too announce the beginning of the creation of a new world. The Spirit emphasizes that the new creation was for the world initiated by Jesus, who is the Son of God, and everybody is expected to listen to him. The time of the theophanies of the old is over and they give place to Christophanies. The Nativity was the first Christophany witnessed by simple people, the shepherds, implying that Jesus is for everyone and his kingdom has no class distinction. The second Christophany, the Epiphany, suggested that Jesus and his kingdom belong to the world of the sciences as well. The baptism was the third Christophany, revealing that Christ's home is heaven since he belongs to God the Father and to the Spirit of God. This Christophany is strengthened by the Christophany of the Transfiguration, ensuring that Jesus is the meaning of the old theophanies. The final act of the new creation, the foundation of his Church, the new people of God, is the Christophany of Jesus' death and resurrection. It is not surprising, therefore, that the same Spirit who was at the beginning of the creation and at the introduction of Jesus Christ into this world is present at the establishment of God's Church on the day of Pentecost.

The Christophany given to Paul on his way to Damascus with the words "Saul, Saul, why do you persecute me?" (Acts 9, 4) made him understand that the Christophanies from that time on would be followed by "anthropophanies," the revelation of Christ's union with every human being (cf. Mt 25, 40.45). So the theophanies of the old led through the Christophanies of the New Testament to the anthropophanies of the personal encounter with Jesus Christ and his Church in the sacraments. The sacraments join the faithful with Jesus Christ in sharing his life, his work of creation, redemption, and sanctification. The newness of this life is not just a simple extension of the old affected by failures and sins. It is a complete break with the old, and this complete break is signified by the sacrament of baptism as baptism into Jesus' death.

4.6.2.2 BAPTIZED INTO JESUS' DEATH AND BURIED WITH HIM

Those who were baptized into Jesus Christ, we read in Paul's letters, were baptized into his death and buried with him. To be united with him in a resurrection like his, the baptized have to be united with him in his death and burial (Rom 6, 1–11; Col 2, 11). Through him, *διὰ*, in him, *ἐν*, towards him, *εἰς*, and with him, *σὺν*, are the expressions Paul used to describe the close unity between Christ and the baptized, who from now on suffer with (Rom 6, 6), die, and are buried with him (Rom 6, 4), are raised with him (Col 3, 1), rule (1 Cor 6, 3) with him, and share in his glory (Rom 8, 17).

Christ's life is communicated in baptism, and the Christian is sharing Christ's origin, his destiny, and his journey towards it. The "anthropophany" becomes again a Christophany.

Paul was very much aware that his encounter with Christ changed his life for ever. It was a grace that transformed his sinful hatred into a graceful love and freed him from the power of human addiction to drunkenness, quarrelling, jealousy, lust, and murder and gave him peace, kindness, patience, gentleness, and self-control, which he recognized as the fruit of Jesus' Spirit (Gal 5, 16–26; Rom 13, 12–14; Col 1, 13). Baptism is indeed a baptism in the Spirit of Christ, the fruits of which will last during the entire life of the baptized, dormant or active, growing or weakened. As the first sacramental encounter with Christ, it leaves its "scars" on the soul for ever. Paul rightly compared it to circumcision (Col 3, 11). The transformation, as radical as death and resurrection (Col 2, 12–15), is marked by a name given in baptism. The baptismal name is, however, just a symbol of that name which God gives to each human being by calling him or her into life. The baptized is not only a child of God but a unique, individual person. This name is now a secret. It will be revealed in its entirety at the moment of death by the entering into eternity.

4.6.2.3 THE NAME

When we were born, we were born into the society of human beings that determined our being as a human being. Our father and our mother called us into life and into a family. Their names determined our name as a member of a human family. We are a human person who has a father and a mother. From that time on, our personal identification carried the names of our parents. To make us a distinguishable member of their family, our parents give us a personal name. So we have our full name.

We were not born with our name. The name was given to us without our involvement. It was arbitrary. But as we grow, we become more and more identified with our name. We become our name and our name becomes us. Our name is now our presence. Through our name we are present to anyone who utters or remembers our name. There will be times and places when our presence will be just our name. So long as our name is remembered, we live there at least in memory. According to African traditional religions, this is the lifetime of the ancestors. When no one remembers an ancestor anymore, the ancestor will be lost in the world of the nameless spirits.

We live in our name. When we hear our name, we reply or hide. Once we die, we will hear our name once more, and we will reply and eternity begins. Knowing our name means having a certain power over us. This power may be a power of love that lets us live, grow, and flourish or a power of envy and hatred that intends to subjugate, belittle, destroy, and kill. We are our name. We should, therefore, love our name as well as the names of all those people we love. Their names mean their presence to us. There will be times when they can be present to us only in their names. We may whisper their names in love. But we may curse their names in fury as well. We may write down their names in loving remembrance or scribble them in order to cross them out. Names are always more than just words. They are symbols, sacred or cursed. They signify people whom, without exception, Christians have to love, because God loves all of them. It is because God loved them that God called them into life. God never hates what God created. Otherwise they would never have been created. God may correct them, warn them that they may be freed from their wickedness and put their trust in the Lord (Wis 11, 24–12, 2). Whatever they reply, God will never hate them because God cannot hate anybody.

A name is a powerful presence. It is a sort of sacrament, and we should pronounce it with respect and love for that person whom we name. And so was the name of Jesus for the first Christians. It meant his presence among them (Acts 2, 28; Horvath, 1975a, 199–203). It was a sort of sacrament of the risen Christ. They loved that name and they rejoiced when they "were counted worthy to suffer dishonor for the name" (Acts 5, 41). They had no doubt that the one who had that name was alive and worked with them, for them. He worked miracles with them (Acts 3, 6–8). By his name sins were forgiven and the gifts of the Holy Sprit imparted (Acts 2, 38; 4, 30–31). He made them different from any other group. They were Χριστιανός, Christians (11, 26), who called his name (Acts 9, 21); they loved him and followed him.

Since that name was almost everything for them, in distinction to the followers of John the Baptist, they baptized in the name of Jesus Christ (Acts 2, 38; 8, 16; 10, 38; 19, 5; 22, 16). With the name of Jesus, they belonged to the family of Jesus. Because for them he was the Son of God (cf. Acts 9, 20; Jn 1, 34), they understood that they share in the sonship of Jesus, and thus they were the sons and daughters of God (Gal 4, 5–7), partakers of the divine nature (2 Pet 1, 4).

It seems that baptism in the name of Jesus Christ alone is a Pauline formula, whereas baptism in the name of the Father and of the Son and of the Holy Spirit is a synoptic one. The synoptic Trinitarian baptismal formula of Matthew 28, 19 should be interpreted in the light of Jesus' baptism together with his transfiguration. The context of both is Judaic. God and God's Spirit support Jesus' claim of being the Son of God who is to be listened to. The synoptic setting for the baptism of Jesus is solemn and impressive. God the Father (Mt 3, 17; Mk 1, 9; Lk 3, 22) and the Spirit of God (Mt 3, 16; Mk 1, 10; Lk 3, 22; Jn 1, 34) reveal Jesus' sonship. John the Baptist attests to the same (Jn 1, 34). In the transfiguration in the presence of Moses and Elijah, the same words of the Father are repeated and the disciples are ordered to listen not to Moses or Elijah but to Jesus, the real Son of God (Mt 17, 5; Mk 9, 7; Lk 9, 35). Thus it is understandable that the members of the community of Matthew's gospel were baptized in the name of the Father, the Son, and the Holy Spirit (Mt 28, 19). Jesus, as the Son of the Father, was presented with his Father and with the Holy Spirit, who brought about his incarnation and led him throughout his life as a witness for the believers (1 Cor 12, 3). The Matthean Trinitarian baptismal formula is more explicit and is supported by the baptism of Jesus. It is the one that has prevailed and is used even today in most Christian churches. It is a more expressive symbol of both the great love the early Christians had for Jesus and the mystery of the new "synagogue," the new *ecclesia,* carrying the name of Jesus, the Son of the Father, pledged by the Pentecostal Spirit. [5]

Baptism in the name of Jesus supposes a deeper Christology. It reflects the Pauline "in him the whole fulness of deity dwells bodily" (Col 2, 9) and the Johannine "he who has seen me has seen the Father" (Jn 14, 9; cf. Moltmann, 1974). Here Jesus does not need any authority to support him. It is more the meaningful in the Pauline Christology of being baptized in the baptism of Jesus. Being baptized in the baptism of Jesus means, firstly, having died with him on the cross (2 Cor 5, 14; Col 3, 12) and being buried with Christ (Rom 6, 3–4) and, secondly, being all baptized by one Spirit into one body, whereby all, Jews and Greeks, slaves and free, are one. Here is the foundation of the Pauline doctrine of the baptism as entering into the Church, the mystical body of Christ (1 Cor 12, 12–13).

Baptism in the name of Jesus and in the name of the Trinity are both baptizing in the name of God, which means that the baptized belong to God and God belongs to the baptized. As a result, God will be named by God's people and God's people by the name of God. God is called the God of Abraham, Isaac, and Jacob (Ex 3, 6), and the people, according to Jeremiah, are called by God's name (Jer 14, 9). Those baptized in the name of Jesus, whether in his name alone or in his name within the Trinity, are all his people, carrying his name. Baptism is therefore both personal and communitarian. What circumcision was for the people of the Old Testament (Gen 17, 9–14), baptism is for the people of the New Testament (Rom 12, 5–9; 4,11; Phil 3, 3). It is a mark that is not visible yet is real of someone who has been baptized and belongs to Jesus Christ and to his people for ever.

4.6.2.4 BORN OF WATER AND THE SPIRIT

Baptism literally means dipped, immersed in the water that symbolizes purification (Ezek 36, 24–28; Ps 51, 9; Dt 23, 10ff.). Water may kill and means death (Ps 29, 10; Mk 4, 37; 2 Pet 2, 5), yet it means also life, resurrection, and new life. So being born anew of water and of the Spirit can mean to be the sons and daughters of God (Jn 3, 3–6) and to move out of being in time into being in eternity as the sons and daughter of resurrection (Lk 20, 36). It is indeed a new creation (2 Cor 5, 17).

By being born of water and the Spirit, one becomes a member of Christ (1 Cor 6, 15; 12, 17), and as a result, the baptized becomes *lordly*, having Christian behaviour (Rom 6, 1–11). The characteristics of a lord are dignity and generosity, boldness and assurance, felt only by one who is of the "highest birth and rank" (Augustine, *Letters* 98, 5). It is the Christian *noblesse oblige.*

Further, by being baptized the baptized becomes a member of the Church and joins through a sacramental bond all members of the Church (1 Cor 6, 15; 12, 17) who have lived and are living in time and space (Augustine, *In Ps.* 30, 3; 61, 4; 85, 5). Each human being who ever lived, now lives, and will live will become his or her brother or sister, sharing each one's joys and sufferings, merits and shortcomings. They are all one in their way home.

Finally, the baptized become the temple of the Holy Spirit, sharing God's eternal life (1 Cor 6, 19). They are justified and redeemed by Christ of all their sins, original and personal. Through the presence of the Holy Trinity, baptism is the first sacrament for the forgiveness of sins.

4.6.3 The Sacrament of Baptism in the History of the Church

Because of its prefiguration in circumcision and its symbolism of dying with Christ on the cross (Rom 6, 3–4) and being buried, baptism was to be received just once. It was not repeatable. Because it represented an incorporation into a new family, the people of Jesus Christ, during the first centuries baptism frequently was a household event (Acts 16, 34; cf. 9, 35) and included children and infants as well. This was all the more so since Jesus loved children (Mt 19, 13–15; Mk 1, 13–16; Lk 18, 15–17), whom he considered a sort of symbol of his kingdom (Mt 11, 25; Mk 10, 14; Mt 18, 2–3; 1 Cor 14, 20) and welcomed as members of his new "church." It seems that shortly after Jesus' resurrection, without any special rite, infants and the children were baptized together with their parents. Only since the fourth and fifth centuries has the Church prepared a special rite for the baptism of the children as a logical development of the theological dispute about original sin in the time of Augustine.

With the Donatist controversy, the question came up as to whether or not baptism conferred by heretics and schismatics was valid. The Donatists were originally Numidian bishops, named after one of their members, who believed that the Church is only the Church of the "holy" and so sacraments conferred by sinful ministers cannot be valid. Against them, Augustine rightly argued that since Christ is the true minister of the sacraments and particularly of baptism, the validity of baptism is not affected by the faith and worthiness of the minister. Likewise in his dispute with Pelagianism about St Paul's doctrine on original sin (Rom 5, 6–21), Augustine could demonstrate the need for the baptism of infants. Since any newborn contracts original sin, which can be remitted by the grace of Jesus Christ given in baptism, infant baptism was theologically justified. Thus it followed also that baptism is necessary for eternal salvation. This necessity was specially argued from John 3, 5, which says that "unless one is born of water and the Spirit, one cannot enter the kingdom of God."

For the salvation of infants who died without being baptized and for that of the many non-Christians who died without even having heard of Jesus Christ, the baptism of desire was an answer. As the martyrs who died before they were baptized could be saved by a sacrament to be conferred in the future, so the people of the world, one could argue, will be saved by Christ's sacrament of baptism operating in the Church. This is all the more so since Christ manifests himself, said Augustine, through the people of the whole world not in great glory but in great trials and sufferings (*Ostendit se esse per omnes gentes toto orbe terrarum non in magna gloria, sed in magna tentatione; Enarrationes in Psalmos,* 60, nos 2–3; CCSL, 39, 766), since more people can share in the latter than in the former.

Augustinian theology could not take a new turn until, under the influence of Arabic thinkers, the Aristotelian scientific world view challenged the Church. The physical world claimed the status of reality above or at least besides that of the soul. The *res,* the thing, was identical with reality, and grace, in order to be real, had to become *res,* a great scandal for Augustinian Lutheran theology as well as for post-scholastic Catholic theology. Once again the updating of one epoch became "out of touch" in the light of the next "new" scientific concept of reality. And the Church had also to take this one into consideration.

Christ entered into the world to save it by his presence instead of leaving it with his selected ones for heaven. Accordingly, Scholastic theology in its time had to work out an "objective" theology by carefully trying to save the Patristic tradition. It gave to the material world a more positive role in the redemptive work of Christ by virtue of the sacraments, and thus it became the forerunner of the *Gaudium et Spes* of Vatican II (Tanner, 1990, 1069–135).

Thomas Aquinas's treatise on Baptism (*Summa theol.*, 3, q 66–71), with its fifty questions, remained the guideline for theological treatises for many centuries to come. The effect of baptism, said Thomas, is that Christ illuminates the baptized, who participates in the generosity (*fecunditas*) and grace of the Church (3, q 69, a 5). The sacraments are presented in the Third Part of the Summa as the continuation of the presentation of Christ, in the light of whom Thomas reinterpreted Patristic and Philosophical traditions. Yet Christ is present not only at the end but also from the first page of his *Summa theologiae* according to the Thomistic principle that "what is first according to intention will be last in execution" (*Quaestiones quodlibetales*, 8, 1.2. ad 1). Thomas's *Summa* is, therefore, a Christological theology in its entirety (Horvath, 1966, 7–8n24; see also 279–83).

Because Christ is the one who baptizes, even a non-baptized human being can baptize. We read in the *Summa* (3, q 67, a 5) that Christ may use the cooperation of any human being, a great principle for ecumenism. Christ, his grace, and Christian values extend beyond the ritual boundaries of the sacraments yet are never independent of the presence of the Eucharistic Christ. Thomas's presentation of baptism is quite complete. Baptism remits both original and personal sins but not the consequences of original sin – ignorance, concupiscence, suffering, and death. It confers habitual grace, theological and infused virtues, together with the gifts of the Holy Spirit. It is the baptismal character that forms the baptized in the image of Christ and makes him or her share Christ's priesthood.

Reform theology of baptism varies somewhat. The Augsburg Confession states that baptism is necessary for salvation. The Book of Common Prayer follows Catholic teaching on baptism. Because of his fundamental principle that faith alone justifies, Luther could not see that baptism was necessary. Ulrich Zwingli held that baptism was only a sign of admitting one into the Church community. According to John Calvin, baptism gives assurance for the elect that they participate in the gifts of Christ. During the nineteenth and early twentieth centuries some Protestant pastors became liberal in applying various baptismal formulas. In Germany after the collapse of the Third Reich, Protestants who wanted to join the Roman Catholic Church were asked to agree to be conditionally baptized in the Catholic Church.

The Council of Trent, in its *Decree on Baptism*, limited itself only to defend some Catholic practices challenged by the Reformers. In the canon 2 the meaning of the water mentioned in John 3, 5 was positively defined as not a metaphor but "true and natural water" (Tanner, 1990, 685). In the *Decree on Justification* we read that "Jesus Christ merited justification for us by his most holy passion on the wood of the cross, and made satisfaction to God the Father on our behalf," and that the sacrament of baptism, the "sacrament of faith," is an instrumental cause without which "justification comes to no one." Justification is not only the justice of God by which God is just but a justice "by which has God made us just," so that the faithful are truly just and "each one receiving individually his/her own justice according to the measures which the holy Spirit appoints to each one as he wills" (chapter 7, Tanner, 673). It is therefore an internal justification that really wipes out sins and brings about a renewal of one's inward being.

The preparation for baptism is already, we read, "roused and helped by the divine grace" of justification. Luther's "fiducial faith" may have prompted the description given by the council in chapter 6 on the *Manner of Preparation for Justification,* which clarifies the nature of subsequent baptismal justification. Accordingly, the nature of the grace of this preparation proleptically anticipates the nature of the grace of baptism. The initial grace, which invites, moves one freely to believe that he or she is a sinner yet can be justified by God's grace and mercy for Christ's sake, whom she or he begins to love as the fount of all justice. So the sinners begin to hate and detest their sins and are ready to be moved to begin a new life and keep God's commandments (Tanner, 1990, 672–3).

The doctrine of Trent on baptism would not be complete without considering its doctrine on original sin, given during session 5 on 17 June 1546. In light of Romans 5, 12, canon 4 defended the doctrine that everyone is baptized not just for the forgiveness of sins but for the forgiveness of original sin particularly, which is concupiscence, a tendency to sin. It is not a "sin in the sense of being truly and properly as such but in the sense of being a result of sin and inclines to sin" (canon 5; Tanner, 1990, 666–7). For Trent as well as for Augustine, the source for the doctrine on original sin was Paul's teaching that all things, τὰ πάντα (neuter), which may refer to people and all creation, are consigned to sin (Rom 5, 6–21; 3, 9–10; Gal 3, 22), which, as we have already remarked, was a way for Paul to let Christ be loved by everyone one as a loving saviour.

The Second Vatican Council's *Dogmatic Constitution on the Church* recalls the ecclesial dimension of baptism. Through baptism, the faithful are incorporated into the Church and are, by the baptismal character, given a place in the worship of the Christian religion. "Reborn as children of God, they have an obligation to profess publicly the faith they have received from God through the Church" (*LG*, no. 11; Tanner, 1990, 857). And here as its source the council refers to Thomas Aquinas's *Summa theol.* 3, q 63, a 2.

The New Order for Baptism (1969, 1972) presents baptism as a dialogue of the people of God with God in the Proclamation of the Word as the call and in the Profession of Faith as the reply of the Church to the call of God (to be discussed in volume 2 of our *Thinking about Faith*).

4.6.4 What The Sacrament of Baptism Is

Summing up, we are able to propose our answer to the question of what the sacrament of baptism is. The description is followed by a short comment.

surface level *sacramentum tantum* symbolizing non-symbolized	Christ, the Church, represented by the minister and the faithful,the godparents with the candidate's parents and friends, and the candidate come together so that, in the symbol of baptizing (immersing) and naming the Triune God,
deep level *res et sacramentum* symbolized and symbolizing	they bring about the candidate's being buried in Christ's death to the world, as a world of the original sin of greediness, pride, and incontinence, and joining Christ in the new life of resurrection, a world of the community of faith, charity, and hope, (*LG*, no. 8) of integrity, generosity, and authenticity (Rom 6, 3–14) and made one
basic level *res tantum* symbolized not symbolizing	with the unity of the Son, the Father and the Holy Spirit (*LG*, no.4).

Baptism is always an event for the Church. Given its importance, solemnity is always recommended. The Church as a whole accepts and makes one more human being a full member of the Church. It is the celebration of one more transition from the state of original sin we all are born into to the "state of grace and of the adoption as children of God" (Rom 8, 23) through Jesus Christ (Council of Trent, chapter 4; Tanner, 1990, 672).

The state of original sin we describe as the lack of the generosity of charity, of the integrity of faith, and of the authenticity of hope. The first is greediness, the second is pride, and the third is incontinence. Greediness is avarice, an excessive acquisitiveness, a mark of internal spiritual poverty. Pride is an excessive appreciation of one's own worth, which is the sign of a deep, internal inferiority complex. And incontinence is a lack of self-restraint in food or sexual appetite, a symptom of disharmony in conflicting tendencies. Such is the state of original sin, still experiential in the world until the end of time.

The new life of resurrection in Christ is faith with integrity, a state of being complete, love with generosity, of cheerfulness in giving, and hope with authenticity, of being exactly what we are expected to be. All three are based on the deep level of God's life merited by Christ and to be shared by all who are called to justification, first by the baptism and later by the sacrament of forgiveness (Horvath, 1977, 284–99). By baptism, an adult or infant is placed in the milieu of the forces of grace triumphing over greediness, pride, and incontinence. All who were formally consigned to the sins of greediness, pride, and incontinence now are consigned by baptism to the generosity of love, to the integrity of faith, and to the authenticity of hope. And thus all have a personal relation to God the Father in charity, to Jesus Christ in faith, and to the Holy Spirit in hope (Eph 4, 4–6).

4.6.5 The Sacrament of Baptism and Sacramental Theology

4.6.5.1 THE SACRAMENT OF BAPTISM IS A PERSONAL ENCOUNTER WITH CHRIST

By the sacrament of baptism, one becomes Christian, a member of the mystical body of Christ, moved from a purely human existence to a Christian existence with all one's sins forgiven. Christian existence is not just a purely ontological reality but also a new awareness that brings about a new value system with a specific epistemological, Christed world view. This change is called "baptismal character," which lets the baptized share in the priesthood of Christ with an ability to express faith and sanctify the world by his or her pastoral care for others.

No human being would be able to do any of these things without Christ's active presence. The sacrament of baptism is a special personal encounter with Christ, who in person opens the doors of his Church to the baptized and with the doors to the Church the doors of heaven as the new home for the baptized. From that moment on, the baptized belongs to the family of God, and as a member of this household, he or she receives a share of Christ's work in saving the world. There is now a "new" Christian, a "young Christian" with "new" plans for the Church, and in it for the world and for the baptized. In the baptized, Christ begins his life on earth, as it were, from a new Bethlehem and Nazareth to go around the world doing good and entering death and resurrection in order to complete his work on earth (Babos, 1983b).

The name of Jesus Christ in the Trinitarian unity from now on is not just the name of someone gone long ago but of someone who is with the baptized. The baptized becomes Jesus' name. As the God of ancient times was the God of Abraham, now Jesus' name will be the Jesus of Peter Smith, or the Jesus of Mary Lynch, and so on, which means Jesus, the Savior of Peter Smith or Jesus, the Saviour of Mary Lynch, and so on. The name of the Saviour of the one " here and now" is a real name, because the new name does what it says. Thus the name of Jesus becomes the name of the baptized. The newly baptized gets a new "family" name. He or she will be called Peter or Mary of Jesus as the most noble origin and family name that a Christian can have. The baptized family extends into time and space as far as any Christian lives now and has ever lived before and ever will in the future. And what is more, it extends up to God, who will never leave the baptized. Baptism gives to the baptized a closeness to God. It gives, as it were, the grace of having at any time a direct line to God and having the right to call the God of the universe "My God, my Lord, my Saviour." This closeness is given also to the baptized infant, who too can with those little lips call on God as "our Father" and may walk in the presence of God with a "natural" familiarity with God. It is for this reason that the sacrament of baptism is the sacrament of faith as well as the sacrament of prayer, an interaction of faith and love. Faith ascertains the presence of God, and love provides joy.

And here one may sense the great gift of baptism. As someone who is baptized, she or he can take for granted that there is a God, the ultimate reality and meaning of the world, and can say, "God cares about me, God loves me. God listens to me, never interrupts me, yet answers my prayers. This is not always done in the way I want, but I can see later that it was better for me. My trust is never disappointed. God is so 'human,' and speaks my language. God's presence is always assuring, pleasant, and joyful. When a cross is laid upon my shoulders, it turns out to be one more way to increase our mutual love and to serve the benefit of other people. Faith is to have a friend. It is to have a God who is faithful and never gives up loving me. God is with me in life and will be in my grave and in life ever after."

The author of the hymn *Jesu, Dulcis Memoria* in the late twelfth century observed that only one who has experienced it will understand what it means to love God. And any baptized person can experience that. A short but assiduous prayer does so: "My Lord, give me the grace that I may love you and let my reward be that I love you more."

Faith is not a "natural" thing. Rather, it is one of the great wonders in the world. How is it possible to pray to and love a God one has never seen? Faith is "the victory that overcomes the world" (1 Jn 5, 4), and the one who believes in Christ is the one "who will do the works" that Christ does, and "greater works than these will he do" (Jn 14, 12).

4.6.5.2 THE SACRAMENT OF BAPTISM IS A UNION WITH CHRIST AND IN HIM WITH BELIEVERS AND THROUGH THEM WITH THE WHOLE WORLD BY VIRTUE OF THE HOLY SPIRIT

The newly baptized joins Jesus Christ and with him the human race more closely. By entering the Church, the newly baptized also enters the world more closely. Baptism is a new birth both for heaven and at the same time for the family of the human race, for "all the nations of the earth" (*LG* no.

13; Tanner, 1990, 859). She or he becomes a member of the people of God, which include the world (*LG*, nos. 13–16: Tanner, 859–61), sinners not being excluded, since Jesus came to search out and save them (Mk 2, 17; Mt 18, 14; Lk 15, 7). There is no human being without some belief. The baptized can include all these in a universal "we" by saying, "God, we believe, but help our unbelief." She or he will be able to be one of them whenever this person says something positive and does good for others.

4.6.5.3 THE SACRAMENT OF BAPTISM IS A PARTICIPATION IN CHRIST'S LIFE AND HIS WORK OF SALVATION

"The Church into which people enter through baptism" was "founded by God through Jesus Christ as a necessity for salvation" (*LG*, no. 14; Tanner, 1990, 860). It was and still is the mission of Christ that "the entire human race may form one people of God, come together as the one body of Christ, and be built into one temple of the holy Spirit" (*AG*, no. 7; Tanner, 1017). The baptized person is called to participate in the same work of helping the entire human race to form one people of God, one body of Christ. Each baptized is doing so by sharing the baptismal grace with others, baptized and non-baptized. Any faith in human goodness is an implicit faith in the humanity of Christ and thus it is an initial baptismal grace.

The baptized shares Christ's life and work of salvation, firstly, by constant prayers for the baptized and for the non-baptized that they all may become more authentically that which they are and make their values a common good to others yet without infringing on their rights. Secondly, they do the same by offering mass and joining with Christ to help the needy, whether baptized or not, in the way, for example, Mother Theresa did. Thirdly, they begin to take "pastoral care" of all people, both Catholic and non-Catholic, by considering the other not as someone to receive from but as someone to give to and to be helped on the way to Christian fulfillment, all the while loving people not just in the way they are but also in the way they are expected to be in God's providential plan.

4.6.5.4 THE SACRAMENT OF BAPTISM IS A SACRIFICE RECONCILING THE WORLD WITH GOD

The baptized are called to be actively present at Christ's offering in the mass. This is the reason that from the beginning Christ's followers could not be satisfied with small sanctuaries where the ministers, following the example of the pagan Roman priests, alone performed rituals on behalf of their people. No, they needed a basilica, a palace of public assembly, where the whole community could come together with the bishops, priests, and deacons to offer Christ as the greatest sacrifice of their love to God the Father. They offered Christ as a sacrifice of praise and thanks for themselves and for the world. They offered Christ as a propitiatory sacrifice for their sins and for the sins of the world, promoting reconciliation and peace in their lives, in their workplace, in their country, and in the world. They offered Christ as the sacrifice of a peace offering (Lev 3, 1), the peace for all, by making all one race in the world (Eph 2, 14).

The baptized should never feel strangers and sojourners in a church but all fellow citizens with the saints and members of the one household of God (Eph 2, 14–22). They are invited to break down with Christ the dividing walls of hostility, to create in themselves a new human being reconciled to God in one body by Christ's cross, and to bring the hostility to an end. Hatred, lack of charity for others, is not a Christian way of existence. Being the sons and daughters of God by the special grace of baptism, Christians are to be peace-makers (Mt 5, 9). They are not just peaceable but εἰρηνοποιοί, peace-makers, those who work to make peace.

Creating peace is a special art. It includes the legal talent of giving justice to each and being an advocate for everyone. It supposes a special problem-solving insight with a vision of future possibilities. It is a charismatic gift of the Holy Spirit, the Advocate, who lives in each baptized person (Eph 2, 22) and distributes God's charisma to each according to her or his vocation. Thus Sunday mass for the baptized is not a show. Rather, it is a strategy meeting of peace-making. It is where we reflect on the past and plan for the future, always gaining strength from the sacrifice of Christ, our peace offering.

4.6.5.5 THE MINISTER

Since for the candidate baptism opens the door of the Church, it seemed logical that the bishop or at least the priest should be the ordinary minister of baptism. In earlier times some, such as Tertullian, thought that even a deacon should not baptize. Yet because of the great need for baptism for salvation, a view gradually prevailed that anyone, including a non-believer, can baptize if he or she in baptizing has the right intention of doing what the Church is doing in baptizing. It was argued that since Christ is the one who baptizes, there is no need for a holy bishop or for any bishop, not even for a Christian, to accept one into the Church by the sacrament of baptism.

Such a concept may be an eye-opening one for ecumenism, and it supports the effort to extend the boundaries of sacramental grace beyond the visible Church. It assumes that Christ will cooperate with non-Christians by bringing about one of his sacraments as a means of salvation. The only condition is that they will share the intention of the Church without believing in the Church and what it teaches. For validity, it is required only that there is an urgent necessity, such as that the candidate is dying and no priest is available, and that the candidate is baptized in the name of Christ within the Trinity. This conviction assumes also that Christ will cooperate with non-Christians by bringing about the salvation of the world.

4.6.5.6 THE SACRAMENT OF BAPTISM AND ECUMENISM

The task of peace-making with God and with the every human being is a common good. For that purpose any baptized person is called to cooperate with every human being according to the best talent each has. Each receives a special gift enabling him or her to use his or her analytical objectivity, the inventive rationality of Christian prudence, and the circumspect love of Christian wisdom to cooperate with others in order to transform natural greediness, pride, and incontinence into human generosity, integrity, and authenticity. These are values that each human being independent of race, philosophy, and religion is striving for. At the same time these are the specific experiential human values of the transcendental Christian faith, charity, and hope. It is a universal common task to remedy human spiritual poverty, an internal inferiority complex, and the symptoms of disharmony of conflicting egoistic tendencies for self-affirmation.

4.6.6 The Sacrament of Baptism and Systematic Theology

4.6.6.1 THE SACRAMENT OF BAPTISM IS A SYMBOL FOR THE WORLD: THE NAME IS REAL

Names are not just words. They mean a human individual, who might be close to us yet as a human person is ineffable, mysterious, incapable of being expressed in words. Each human being is an "another world." He or she is always much more than that we know and can grasp. This is a mystery to him or to her. A human person is more mysterious than infinite time and space. By giving a name to someone, we only distinguish one individual from the other but never express him or her. Each person transcends us. We think superficially when we assume that by a few labels we can correctly categorize human beings and so have nothing more to learn about an individual we have met.

The name is a name of a person. If a person is reduced to his or her name, she or he means no more than just a number among the countless human beings. What the name really signifies is a mystery, a wonder, a miracle, a hidden treasure, a mighty, powerful, marvellous, startling, prodigious, terrifying yet at the same time uplifting being whom only God could create. A human person is, indeed, a revelation of the holy and mighty living God. It is this last reality that baptism lays bare inasmuch as it affirms the value of a human being as transcending any other value of the world. The person remains an ultimate that cannot be reduced to numbers, to chemical and physical entities, or to a cosmic event. By saying that a person is ultimate, we have said everything we can, yet we feel that we have said nothing. We know so little. What is a human person? An image of God? More: he or she is a beloved son or daughter of God sharing God's mystery as a member of the human race. Since each human being is a person, Christian society is democratic, yet no one can be defeated just by a number. The dignity of the human person is the foundation and the end of Christian philosophy. And so is it for Christian epistemology. As an example of Christ, a Christian is never a slave but a free "co-creator" of the society of the family of God.

The name is sacred because we were called into existence by God with a name of "the beloved son or daughter of God." We will be more and more impregnated by that name until our baptism reaches its consummation in our death. When we die and are buried with Christ, the Christophany of our baptism will be revealed fully and clearly as being "face to the face" (cf. 1 Cor 13, 12), and I will understand myself as God understood me (1 Cor 13, 12) in God's likeness (2 Cor 3, 18; 1 Jn 3, 2).

What we have just said about names and persons is true in an analogous sense about mathematical or scientific symbols or religious icons of the world. Symbols are all words, titles, and names of the world that we use to initiate a meaningful conversation with the same world. Any being existing in the world is a question that scientists try to "baptize" with names in order to enter into a mutual communication with the world and get closer to its deeper, mysterious reality. By doing so, scientists and linguists try to domesticate the world by changing it into a home for human beings. It is a way to let the world to speak a human language. They humanize the world and at the same time materialize, secularize human life and human beings in the original meaning of the word *saeculum.*

The Bible already suggests this when we read that God made each human being in God's image and asked Adam to subdue and dominion the world (Gen, 1, 26–28) by giving names to the various creatures (Gen 1, 26–28; 2, 20). Naming a being is a placing of it in the wholeness of world. It is a welcome greeting of one being by differentiating it from others and at the same time placing it in the totality of universe marking its limitation. Naming is a way of saying, "You are this and nothing else." Once you want be something else, you will die (Gen 2, 17). God has no name because by creating, God gave names to anyone else who is not God. Even Jesus Christ was named by God, who called him in his baptism " the son of God" (Mk 1, 11). God as being means that being belongs to God. Being is the name of being related to God. Thus God is known as the one who baptized the world by naming beings as necessarily related to God and, as such, sharing the being of the world. Being baptized in water relates a human being to his or her earthly origin, water, which is life and death. Being baptized in the name of God is relating someone to God and life for ever.

When a human being names the world, he or she does so as an image of God and thus relates the world to God. By naming the world, human beings sanctify the world. By giving the world the name of being, the being belonging to God the origin of being, which means that the world is the world of God. So baptism is a symbol of the world, and each baptism is the echo of the creation of the world.

4.6.6.2 THE SACRAMENT OF BAPTISM IS A SYMBOL FOR HUMAN EXISTENCE: A CHALLENGE TO TRANSCENDENCE

The sacrament of baptism is not only a revelation of what we are in the sight of God but a task to become what we shall be. It is a symbol of human existence, which is never a static position in the present but a restless passing from the here and now to an approaching, yet unknown tomorrow. Cultures of all ages knew something called by the general term "spirit." This was what God breathed into human beings (Gen 2, 5) and what seems to always move creation and people ahead. It is the never-ending human curiosity, a never being already there.

John the Baptist baptized with water, but the baptism of Jesus was with the Holy Spirit. It means that the Spirit of baptism is to move humans from a purely human existence to a Christian existence, which is more than human mind and heart may desire. It is to reach out to the infinite since it can be satisfied with no less than God. It is the spirit of discovery, the fearlessness of the beyond, the unknown. It is a boldness in search of adventure since the baptized person knows that no matter how far he or she may go, he or she will never leave the house of God because in the present and in the future there is always a direct line to God. Human transcendence is his or her being rooted in the creation of the world as symbolized by baptism.

4.6.6.3 THE SACRAMENT OF BAPTISM IS A SYMBOL FOR THE CHURCH: GROWTH

The message of the sacrament of baptism for Ecclesiology has to do with ever growing and moving ahead, an ever reaching out to God. This is not just a missionary activity but a progression in faith, charity, and hope, integrity, generosity, and authenticity, on the way to Christian perfection. Ecclesiology is to be ascetical, mystical, and moral as well. The baptismal grace as grace is of the same kind. The grace given to a baptized person is a mystical grace, a grace of prayer and fidelity to the Church as sacrament. It is a grace for calling that, in spite of all past failures, pride, quarrels, immorality, ever-returning sin (Horvath, 1994, 51), there is always time to begin to regain baptismal innocence and to live for others. One's real happiness is working for the happiness of others.

Such a call is the universal call to holiness in the Church (*LG*, chapter 5; Tanner, 1990, 880–4). All the faithful are invited and bound to strive towards holiness and the perfection of their particular state of life. All have to control their emotions, holding back from the pursuit of perfect charity, being attached too much to riches in a way that is against the spirit of being poor in spirit (*LG*, no 43; Tanner, 884).

4.6.6.4 THE SACRAMENT OF BAPTISM IS A SYMBOL FOR CHRISTOLOGY: THE MEANING OF THE FILIATION WITHIN THE TRINITY; THE THEOLOGY OF THE SON

In the revelation of his baptism and transfiguration, Jesus' filiation was revealed and confirmed. He is the beloved Son of God the Father. "My son" is a name, and as a name, it is identical with Jesus Christ. He called himself simply "Son." Only the Church, referring to him, had to say the "Son of God" to avoid any misunderstanding that Jesus is "the son of the Church" (Horvath, 1975a, 172–86). "Son" is Jesus's name, his personality in the presence of God the Father. The sacrament of baptism summons us to a more penetrating theology of the Son, of the filiation.

What does it mean that one divine person's name is Son? Filiation implies paternity. Yet there is no femininity. It is not a family. And this may be considered not a culturally conditioned terminology without any significance of a transcendental nature. The second divine person in the Trinity, we read in Romans 8, 29, is the first-born Son. For the Church this meant a natural communication of the essence, a generation, of one substance with the Father, distinct yet one with the Father as the Father's own. Filiation is a process of determination about what it means to have such a relationship within one God. "Son" and "begetting" are biblical terms and cannot be replaced by other terms without losing revelational information. Patristic and Scholastic theology raised the question and explained generation by "uttering" as an act of intellect, an act of reaching out to someone (Horvath, 1966, 80–3).

Filiation and paternity are obvious expressions of love relations. They mean that there is a love relation between two persons. Further, they are expressions that God is love and in God there cannot be anything else but love. Father and Son are the personifications of God's nature as unrestricted self-giving to the other. Love is not just an addition to God's existence; it is the essence of God's being. Thus love is the origin of God's being, and of any being. It is the absolute condition of existence. No being is conceivable without love. Love, which is the origin of being, is a love that transcends sexual love on the creaturely level. Love between man and woman, between father and mother, or between father and son or daughter is a temporal and spatial expression in time to be sublated in eternity. It seems that this is the meaning of Luke 20, 35–36; Mark 12, 25; and Matthew 22, 30.

The feature of the Christology requested by the sacrament of baptism is Jesus Christ, who loves God the Father with all his heart, with all his soul, and with all his strength and mind and who loves us as he loves his Father (Mt 22, 37–39; Mk 12, 30–31; Lk 10, 27). His death was his testimony to that love (Mt 27, 46 with Lk 23, 46). Probably this is one of the main reasons that the early Christians loved him so much and their love laid down the foundation of Christianity. The meaning of filiation is a love of self-giving, a "going out" as expressed in John 19,17: "and he went out, bearing his own cross." There is a person who merits love and compassion for having a unique power of burning one's heart (Lk 24, 32), raising love for himself.

4.6.6.5 THE SACRAMENT OF BAPTISM IS A SYMBOL FOR THE REVELATION OF THE TRIUNE GOD: THE FATHER AS GENEROSITY, THE SON AS INTEGRITY, AND THE SPIRIT AS AUTHENTICITY

Baptism in the name of the Father and of the Son and of the Holy Spirit reveals to us the kind of God we believe in. By analyzing the relevant scripture references, we find that the Father means generosity, the Son integrity, and the Holy Spirit authenticity (Horvath, 1977, 290–4). The Father is the one who gives (generosity) completely (the integrity of the Son) God (the authenticity of the Holy Spirit).

The characteristic of the Son is that he is a perfect image of the Father. It is the integrity of the Son that the Son is God in the same sense as the Father is God by sharing one and the same essence. Seeing the Son is seeing the Father (Jn 14, 8). The Son is unlike a creature. Nothing in him fails to be God as the Father is God (Horvath, 1993, 79–80). And the characteristic of the Holy Spirit is authenticity. The Spirit witnesses that Jesus is the Lord, is ἀρραβὼν, a pledge of ἀρραβῶνα *τοῦ πνεύματος*, and a guarantee (Eph 1, 14; 2 Cor 1, 22; 5, 5) that the Father and the Son are exactly what their names claim, a real God of generosity, integrity, and authenticity.

The three are the reaffirmations of what kind of love is God, and they are expected to be the hallmark of Christians baptized in the name of the Triune God. They are "a people made one by the unity of the Father and the Son and the holy Spirit" (*LG*, no. 4; Tanner, 1990, 851). God's love is generous, perfect (integrity), and authentic, reflected in the Church as a community of faith (Christ), love (Father), and hope (the Holy Spirit) (*LG*, no. 8; Tanner, 854).

4.6.6.6 THE SACRAMENT OF BAPTISM IS A SYMBOL FOR ESCHATOLOGY: THE TRINITARIAN LIFE IS ETERNITY

When the celebrant asks the candidate for the reason why he or she has come to be baptized, the candidate's reply is "eternal life." "Eternal life is," says the celebrant, "to know the true life and the one he sent, Jesus Christ. God raised him from the dead to be the Lord of life and of all things, seen and unseen. In asking for baptism today you ask for this life." There may be many reasons why people are attracted to Christianity and ask for baptism, but the most specific gift that Christ offered to his followers was eternal life. Now eternal life is to know Jesus Christ, we read in the liturgy of baptism. But knowing him is not just scientific knowledge. Knowing a person is having faith in that person. And having faith in a person is loving that person and being able to live with him or her forever. Being able to be with Jesus Christ forever is eternal life. Being baptized in the name of Jesus Christ means in a full sense being baptized in the name of the Father, whom Jesus loves, and in the name of the Holy Spirit, who is the love of the Father and of the Son.

Baptism is sharing not only the faith the Church has but also the love the Church has for Jesus Christ. And baptism opens the door for a never-ending eternal love for Jesus Christ, the origin and the end of all beings, seen and unseen. This love is what the Trinitarian God is and what the Trinitarian God is doing for all eternity. God's love is inexhaustible, incapable of being worn out. So is God.

4.6.6.7 THE SACRAMENT OF BAPTISM IS A SYMBOL FOR PNEUMATOLOGY: THE SPIRIT IS A PERSON WITH A REAL NAME

The contribution the sacrament of baptism is expected to make to the theology of the Holy Spirit is that the Spirit is a person, yet never alone. Though always with the Father and the Son, yet the Spirit has his own distinct divine name. Having a divine name, the Spirit is worshipped and glorified with the Son and the Father. The name "Spirit" is a real, personal name. It means advocate, giver of life, experience, liveliness, and transcendence. The Spirit makes the new life in Christ experienced now, in the present tense. This experience is the fruition of the baptismal grace called the fruits of the Spirit. They are love, joy, peace, patience, kindness, goodness, faithfulness, gentleness, and self-control (Gal 5, 22–23). Wisdom, science, faith, healing, miracles, prophecy, discretion of the spirit, tongues, and interpretation are "all inspired by one and the same Spirit who apportions to each one individually as he wills" (1 Cor 12,7–11). By one Spirit the faithful are all baptized into one body and "made *to drink* of one Spirit" (1 Cor 12, 13), bold, optimist (cf. Acts 2, 13) people of the future (Barth, 1969, 27–40). Yet these are not new graces. Rather, they are the intensification of the grace given by the sacrament of baptism and of the Eucharist. The "drinking of one Spirit" of 1 Corinthians 12, 13 was probably inspired by the "eating this bread and drinking the cup" of 1 Corinthians 11, 26.

We may summarily say that the work of the Holy Spirit is that the faithful experience their love for God as well as, or much more than, any human love they have experienced. It is a burning love of which St Augustine, St Theresa of Avila, St Ignatius of Loyola, and many other mystics have talked. It is an optimism with love for others and a deep feeling of unworthiness. Whereas Christ's work is for the present, the work of the Spirit is, rather, facing the future. It is the Spirit who lets Christians love human beings not for the way they are now but for the way they may be in the future in their final actualization.

4.6.6.8 THE SACRAMENT OF BAPTISM IS A SYMBOL FOR MARIOLOGY: THE IMMACULATE CONCEPTION

The sacrament of baptism brightens the relations between the mystery of Mary and the mystery of the Church. Mary, with a burning love for God and for others and with her deep feeling of unworthiness, is the image and the fulfiment of baptismal grace of the Church, which she received before she was born. Mariology is not only Christology but Pneumatology as well. Redemption in the past and salvation in the future are present in Mary's time. She is already what the Church hoped for. What has been given to her already will be given to others. The reality of her future is the true sign of a sure hope (*LG*, no. 68; Tanner, 1990, 898).

Mary's immaculate conception reveals the mystery of our baptism. Through Mary, the sacrament of baptism illustrates not only its own universal necessity but also its trans-temporal and trans-spatial dimension. By saying this, we do not want to say that Mary's immaculate conception was the result of an anticipated baptism, as if the sacrament were a reality existing independent of the Church of Jesus Christ somewhere in a Platonic world. Rather, the incarnated Eucharistic Christ, the one who actively wipes out original and personal sins in each baptized person, was the one who "wiped" out even the realization of original sin in Mary in the Church which Christ initiated in that instance. In Mary's immaculate conception the salvation history of expectation has been changed into the fulfilled salvation history. The woman promised in Genesis, 3 15 has appeared. Thus Mary could become full of grace yet not independent of the Church of

Christ and his sacraments. She was never outside the Church and its graces. Rather, she is the first and "con-constitutive" member of the Church, which is divine and human, sacramental and spiritual. It in this sense can we say that Mary is the mother for Christ's sacramental Church. Again, she is the sure hope that there can be salvation for every human being of goodwill through Christ's sacramental Church. By baptism, which wipes out every sin, original and personal, the baptized participate in Christ's sinlessness, shared by Mary eminently in her immaculate conception. Thus Mary is once more the prototype of the redeemed faithful.

4.7 WHAT IS THE SACRAMENT OF CONFIRMATION?

4.7.1 *The Sacrament of the Fullness of Grace*

The feast day of the sacrament of confirmation is Pentecost, the last day of the paschal celebrations. The paschal season begins with the Eucharist and ends with confirmation by the Holy Spirit, the authentication of the fullness of the Church's sacramental life. It is the time when the Church begins to live in communication with others (Thomas Aquinas, *Summa theol.*, 3, q 72, a 2). For this reason the sacrament of confirmation bestows the fullness of the Holy Spirit and could not be given before the resurrection and ascension (ibid., ad 1; Thomas, 1948, 464). It is the sacrament of the fullness of grace (ibid., ad 2), perfecting salvation (ibid., ad 3) by implanting a Christian individual into the community of the Church not just for personal sanctification but for a spiritual sharing with the whole world.

The Second Vatican Council expressed the same faith by saying that "the faithful are bound more completely to the Church; they are enriched by a special strength of the holy Spirit, and in this way are under a more pressing obligation to spread the faith by word and deed as true witnesses of Christ" (*LG*, no. 11; Tanner, 1990, 857). It is through the sacrament of confirmation that the apostolic vocation of the faithful is expressed without any difference of sex, race, or culture. It is for this reason that the sacrament of confirmation is the "last sacrament," the fulfillment of all the sacraments for speculative theology. It is the revelation of God as the one communicating God's Trinitarian life in the Church as the community of faith, charity, and hope.

4.7.2 *The Sacrament of Confirmation in the History of the Church*

The classic scriptural reference for confirmation is Acts 8, 14–17, where we read that when the apostles heard that Samaritans believed and had been baptized yet "the Holy Spirit had not yet fallen on any of them," Peter and John were sent to lay their hands on them to let them receive the Holy Spirit. The reception of the Holy Spirit was so experiential and tangible that one Samaritan, called Simon, wanted to pay for the power he saw that Peter and John had. We find another case of the bestowal of the Holy Spirit separate from baptism in Acts 19, 1–7. Some disciples in Ephesus were baptized in the name of the Lord Jesus, and after that Paul laid his hands upon them, the Holy Spirit came on them "and they spoke with tongues and prophesied" (19, 6). These bestowals of the Spirit were after Pentecost.

The reception of the Holy Spirit in various occasions, such as missionary work (Acts 8, 29.38; 13, 2), healing (Acts 4, 8–12), conversions (Acts 9,

17), making decisions (Acts 11, 12; 15, 28), appointing bishops to care for the churches (Acts 20, 28), praying to God as Father (Rom 8, 15–16; Gal 4, 6), and building up the Church (1 Cor 14, 12), was a messianic gift promised by Christ (cf. Jn 14, 26–16; 13–15; Acts 2, 17). In John's gospel the Holy Spirit is called Advocate or Counsellor, in Greek with a masculine ὁ, he, and named ἄλλον παράκλητον, another counsellor (Jn 14, 18, 26) who had been poured out on the day of Pentecost in the most visible and experiential way (Acts 2, 1–47).

Pentecost, fifty days after Passover, was the feast of harvesting (Lev 23, 22), of ingathering at the year's end (Ex 34, 22), the anniversary of the giving of the law, and the completion of the paschal mystery. It was on this day that, according to the Acts of the Apostles, the Holy Spirit was given to the Church in fulfillment of Christ's promise that on the last day God would pour out God's Spirit upon everyone. There were a few tangible signs of that. Firstly, there was a sound from heaven. God's presence in the Bible is made clear by hearing rather than by seeing (Gen 3, 9–10; Ex 3, 4; 1 Kgs 19, 12). It sounded like, secondly, the rush of a mighty wind (Num 11, 3; Jn 3, 7–8; Mk 4, 41; Mt 8, 27; Lk 8, 25; Horvath, 1975a, 170) and filled all the houses. Further, there appeared to them tongues as of fire, which were distributed and rested on each one. Fire is a sign of God's presence and so appeared in the burning bush to Moses (Gen 3, 2–5) and later on Mount Sinai (Ex 19, 18). (4) Fourthly, all present were filled with the Holy Spirit and began to speak in "other tongues." Each of the listeners heard them in his or her own language. The apostles were speaking in their own language, ἡμέτεραις γλώσσαις, yet different people could hear their own language (Acts 2, 8.11). It was a miracle of hearing and not of speaking. The λαλεῖν ἑτεραις γλώσσαις, speaking in other tongues, the gift of Pentecost (Acts 2, 4) was different from the gift of λαλέω γλώσσαις speaking in tongues (Acts 10, 46; 11, 15; 19, 6).

The gift of tongues is not the Pentecostal gift given only on the day of Pentecost. It is the gift of which Paul spoke (1 Cor 12, 10; 1 Cor 14, 5–19.22; Mk 16, 17) and said that it needed interpretation. It is an uttering of words that do not mean anything in any language. They are uttered under an overpowering religious emotion of thanks and praise, prompted by an intensification of the baptismal grace, which permeates the whole being of the speaker. It is the first instance of prophecy that needs to be interpreted through the gift of interpretation. Paul gave his views on it when he said, "I thank God that I speak in tongues more than you all; nevertheless in the church I would rather speak five words with my mind, in order to instruct others, than ten thousand words in a tongue" (1 Cor 14, 19).

The miracle of Pentecost was the inauguration of turning the babel confusion of languages of all the earth (Gen 11, 9) into the one language of Christ. Peter on that day boldly gave his witness to Jesus Christ as the Messiah, whom "God made both Lord and Christ." There were Parthians and Medes and Elamites, residents of Mesopotamia, Judea, and Cappadocia, and of Pontus and Asia, Phrygia and Pamphylia, Egypt, Libya, and Rome, Cretans and Arabians, both Jews and proselytes. People were "cut to the heart" (Acts 2, 37) and they were baptized. An international church was founded and its previous number went up that day from one hundred and twenty (Acts 2, 15) to three thousand (Acts 2, 41).

Ephesians 1, 14 and 2 Corinthians 1, 22 and 5, 5 name the spirit's function as ἀρραβὼν, ἀρραβῶνα τοῦ *πνεύματος* a pledge, guarantee of the spirit. It is the authenticity of oneself based on reflections, penetrations of one's heart (1 Cor 2, 10–11; Prov. 20, 27). In other words, it is an imprint, a seal of the Holy Spirit, marking Christians as Christians (Gal 5, 16–25; 6, 8; Rom 8, 1–17; cf. Gen 38, 18), or a signet (Gen 41, 42), like that authenticating a judicial document (1 Kgs 21, 8). Thus the bestowal of the Holy Spirit as confirmation of the baptismal sharing in the life of the Church was part of the initiation into the new life, celebrated with the imposition of hands (cf. Acts 19, 6) and with anointing as σφράγις, sealing signet, and guarantee of the spirit.

Hippolytus of Rome in the third century describes the imposition of hands as an important part of the liturgy of confirmation. The anointing got more importance first in the East and later in the Western church as well. The church in Europe progressively found the anointing more meaningful as the symbol of the sacrament of confirmation (Fransen, 1975).

According to the Bible, anointing with oil was a sign of the consecration of prophets, kings, and priests and it fits very well with the effect of confirmation, making the faithful serving the Church like a soldier defending the Church and extending its borders. The anointing with the oil of chrism, olive oil mixed with balsam, signified the gifts of the Holy Spirit and the ownership of Jesus (see Dt 32, 34) once for all. This was the foundation of the doctrine of the indelible mark conferred by the sacraments of confirmation and baptism.

The Council of Elvira, now Granada, in Spain around the years 300–6, ordered that if a deacon baptized someone, the baptism should be completed by the imposition of hands by a bishop. Even at that time the rite of the present sacrament was considered to be the fullness of baptism. Yet it is only from the eleventh century on that the sacrament of confirmation has had its own liturgy separate from baptism. The anointing on the forehead, sign of a fearless and proud confessor of the faith with the sign of the cross, was first combined with the imposition of hands. Later the imposition of hands was replaced by anointing. Anointing became the proper sacramental sign of confirmation until 1752, when Benedict XIV reintroduced the imposition of hands.

The specific effects of confirmation, borrowed from Thomas Aquinas, are described by the Council of Florence in 1439 by the *Bull of Union with the Armenians.* The chrism, made from oil and balsam blessed by a bishop and considered the matter of the sacrament, was a symbol of the gleaming brightness of the Christian countenance of lordship and joy and explained in the words "I sign you with a sign of the cross and I confirm you with the chrism of salvation in the name of the Father and of the Son and of the Holy Spirit." The ordinary minister is the bishop, and the effect is to strengthen confession of the name of Christ, as the apostles did on the day of Pentecost, and glorify in the sign of Jesus's cross, made on the forehead of the confirmed (Council of Florence, session 8; *Bull of Union with the Armenians*; Tanner, 1990, 544–5).

Since the Reformers could not recognize the sacrament of confirmation, testified by the New Testament, as one of Christ's institution, the Council of Trent found it necessary to declare that the sacrament of confirmation is not an empty ceremony or a form of religious instruction but a true and proper sacrament. It affirmed also that the bishop is the ordinary minister of confirmation, yet it did not deny the Eastern rite giving the right to assign the priest as the ordinary minister of confirmation (Tanner, 1990, 686).

In its document on the Church, the Second Vatican Council disclosed the ecclesial dimension of all the sacraments and so also of the sacrament of confirmation. "With the sacrament of confirmation, we can read, they (the faithful) are bound more completely to the Church; they are enriched by a special strength of the holy Spirit, and in this way are under more pressing obligation to spread the faith by word and deed as true witnesses of Christ" (*LG*, no. 11; Tanner, 1990, 857). According to the new rite promulgated in 1971, there is a prayer for the coming of the Holy Spirit, which is followed by the imposition of hands. The anointing is done on the forehead with chrism and the words "Be sealed with the gift of God, the Holy Spirit."

4. 7. 3 What the Sacrament of Confirmation Is

Summing up the sacrament of the fullness of grace in the history of the Church, we are able to propose an answer to the question of what the sacrament of confirmation is.

surface level *sacramentum tantum* symbolizing non-symbolized	Christ and the Church, represented by the minister and the baptized faithful, through the symbol of sealing with chrism, come together to bring about
deep level *res et sacramentum* symbolized and symbolizing	a baptized faithful person's incorporation in the Church's language event, constituted by the manifold expressions of the Church's faith in the languages of the world, to move the Church boldly to its self-realization as a community of faith, charity, and hope (LG, no. 8) in unity with
basic level *res tantum* symbolized not symbolizing	the person of the Holy Spirit witnessing Christ, the Son of the Father, as the language of the languages.

4.7.3.1 COMMENT

There is an anointing in the sacrament of order, in the sacrament of the sick, and in the sacrament of baptism. And so there is one in the sacrament of confirmation, which completes all three, each one in its own way. The chrism blessed by the bishop joins the baptized more fully to the universal Church. The olive oil mixed with balsam symbolizes cleansing and healing in the anointing of the sick and strength and consecration in the order. The sacramental symbolism of the anointing and sealing of confirmation means strength, confidence, and courage in working for the unity of the human race (*LG*, no. 1; Tanner, 1990, 849). Being sealed symbolizes a more complete belonging to Christ by sharing in his mission and the Church's work for unity. The imposition of hands and the sign of the cross signify "the promise of divine protection in the trial" (*Catechism of the Catholic Church*, 1994, 242). This is the level of the sacramental visible sign of the confirmation.

In the light of Pentecost, the universal Church can be seen as a language event made up of the many languages of the world expressing the reality of the Eucharistic Christ. Thus by the sacrament of confirmation the baptized is more fully incorporated in the Church as the language event of the various languages of the world in order to cooperate boldly in moving the Church to its self-realization as a community of unity in faith, charity, and hope in words and deeds by furthering generosity, integrity, and authenticity as the human dimension of charity, faith, and hope. This does not mean only the various languages spoken in the world but also the languages of the changing cultures, subcultures, different social classes, age groups, mentalities, and world views.

Finally, the deep level of the sacramental reality of confirmation symbolizes the basic level, where the Holy Spirit is acting to reveal Jesus Christ as the language of languages and making the world one in believing in Christ. The sacrament of confirmation makes the baptized Christian a special instrument of the Holy Spirit for the Pentecostal unity of languages. It is by the grace of the Holy Spirit that the baptized faithful become witnesses to Christ by being attractive leaders of the world in both solving problems and opening new chances and possibilities for the world in Christ. Perhaps this is what Paul meant when he talked about Christians as εὐωδία, ὀσμή, the fragrance and aroma of Christ (2 Cor 2, 14–17).

4.7.4 The Sacrament of Confirmation and Sacramental Theology

4.7.4.1 THE SACRAMENT OF CONFIRMATION IS A PERSONAL ENCOUNTER WITH CHRIST

The sacrament of confirmation, like the other sacraments, is a personal encounter with Christ but with a special feature. In his or her confirmation the baptized faithful encounters Christ by his sending the Holy Spirit. As Christ works until the end of the world, so he sends the Holy Spirit. And he does not send the Holy Spirit only at the moment of reception of the sacrament of confirmation but at any time after that when the grace of the sacrament of confirmation operates in the baptized for the unity of the world and the Church. It is an encounter with Christ within the life of the Holy Trinity as the Son receives the Father's self-communication in expressing the Son as the Son of the Father, and from their mutual, loving "spiritedness" proceeds the Holy Spirit, authenticating the inalienability of both through the Spirit's own inalienability as well as contemporizing, making present, the revelation of Jesus Christ in faith. Thus the Holy Spirit dwells in the believer together with the Father and the Son (Jn 15, 23).

The Holy Spirit makes present the revelation of Christ in faith by transforming the "there" and "then" of the historical Jesus into a saving "here" and "now" of any time and any place. Jesus' human history, when every "now" becomes past, has inaugurated the eschatological age when the human past, present, and future are reached and vanquished by the event of his life The sacrament of confirmation is an encounter with the risen Christ present in faith by virtue of the Holy Spirit (cf. 1 Cor 12, 3).

4.7.4.2 THE SACRAMENT OF CONFIRMATION IS A UNION WITH CHRIST AND IN HIM WITH BELIEVERS AND THROUGH THEM WITH THE WHOLE WORLD

"And there appeared to them tongues as of fire, distributed and resting on each one of them. And they were all filled with the holy Spirit" (Acts 2, 3–4). The tongues rested on each one of the about one hundred and twenty members of the first Church, whom the risen Jesus Christ had asked to stay in Jerusalem until they would be be "baptized with the holy Spirit" (Acts 1, 4–5). They were all baptized with the Holy Spirit in the same way without any discrimination. And likewise, without any difference or discrimination, the various linguistic groups heard them speaking in their own native languages. The manifestation of the Holy Spirit on the feast day of Pentecost became the revelation of the union of all believers in the Eucharistic Christ and through him with the whole world. It was not a speaking in tongues but a miracle of hearing of the Pentecost when each was speaking his or her own language yet all heard their own language. And this unique event of hearing became the foundation of the sacramental church for every time and for every space.

The sacrament of confirmation has its pre-eminence in this union of the Christian faithful with the whole world. The democratic equality within a most personal individualism of the baptized is the grace of baptism. Yet its fullness is expressed by the sacrament of confirmation. The equality with a unique personality living in the community of Christ, signalled by the indelible character of baptism, is now perfected by the indelible character of confirmation not by multiplying but by modifying the character imprinted by baptism. The Holy Spirit is revealed by the sacrament of confirmation as the spirit of the contemporalization and universalization of the Church for every time and space.

4.7.4.3 THE SACRAMENT OF CONFIRMATION IS A PARTICIPATION IN CHRIST'S LIFE AND HIS WORK OF SALVATION

The Holy Spirit, most personal and individualistic in distributing gifts, at the same time has the most altruistic personality. Wherever the Holy Spirit is mentioned in the New Testament, the task is just to promote the cause of Jesus Christ. As the Advocate, the Spirit will not teach anything new but will let all that Jesus had said and deeded to his Church (Jn 14, 26) be remembered. The Spirit takes what is Jesus' own and declares it to us (Jn 16, 8–15). Thus the sacrament of confirmation will be just a fuller participation in Christ's life and his work of salvation.

The miracle of Pentecost is a prognostic sign of what the Church is expected to bring about instrumentally. The work will not create one human language that all nations of the earth will understand and take for their own language. Jesus Christ is confined and not confined to one language (Horvath, 1994, 42). He is not even a dictionary that lists all the words spoken by the human race. Rather, he is a person, and as a person, he is the language of all languages, having the ability to prompt love in any language.

In 1312 the Council of Vienne rightly prescribed that an abundant number of Catholics be well versed in many languages to be able to present the faith adequately to every nation (Tanner, 1990, 379). But the miracle of Pentecost does not only imply an obligation to learn and speak the language of another nation. It means much more that each nation, each linguistic group, by its own hearing of Christ's message, will develop its implicit Christology operating in its world view and its own concepts of ultimate reality and meaning into an explicit Christology of Christ as its Saviour. By these Christologies all nations are expected to make a contribution to the Christology of the Church, expressing Jesus Christ as the real Saviour of all the nations of the world. Christ is to become the Messiah not for one but for every nation living on this globe. He is expected to be the realization of all their aspirations and dreams. Yet all these aspirations and dreams are not the cancellations of another's aspirations and dreams. Rather, they are the manifestation and actualization of the great varieties and potentialities of the human race, including the experience of double love the early Christians had, a love for Christ and a love Christ had for them and for the whole world. Christ has love not just for one person but also for a nation, and one can believe that no one ever loved his or her nation more than Christ did and does. This is the corollary that Jesus is the Saviour of the world.

4.7.4.4 THE SACRAMENT OF CONFIRMATION IS A SACRIFICE RECONCILING THE WORLD WITH GOD

Both the sacrament of baptism and the sacrament of confirmation share in the Eucharistic sacrifice, reconciling the world with God. To humans seeking God by reaching out to heaven (Gen 11, 4; Horvath, 1975a, 86–7) the sacrament of confirmation replies by presenting a God who seeks peoples and reaches out to all the nations by the descent of the Holy Spirit. The descent of the Holy Spirit reinforces the Incarnation. The reconciliation effected by the second divine person is revealed and extended by making the whole world the "elected chosen ones." It is a further sign of how much God loves the world of human beings. After the second person, the third person was sent into the world. As a result, the whole world became a home for God where God can dwell. God's chosen people are universalized, and from now on everybody is a chosen one, a beloved one of God.

The sacrament of confirmation confirms that Jesus' redemption, justification, and salvation are not limited to a few chosen ones. God is not for those who can reach out to heaven. God is open to the whole world. God is for everyone, made accessible to every nation, to each individual here on earth. Everybody is a neighbour to everybody else, and to do any good to another is a good done to God. The whole world becomes God's household.

For the first Jewish Christians this was not easy to understand and accept without great concern. The dispute between Peter and Paul lets us sense the great sacrifice it meant for faithful Jews. It looked like a great threat of losing their own faith and with it their own identity. Peter needed a vision to defend his leadership (Acts 11, 1–18; Gal 2, 11) and another experience of a descent of the Holy Spirit on the gentiles (Acts 11, 44–48). The controversy over the admission of gentiles continued until the apostles and the elders gathered in Jerusalem and settled the question. Membership in Judaism was not identical with membership in the new "Way."

The sacrament of confirmation requires a similar sacrifice from all the baptized. A confirmed Christian, while still remaining faithful to his or her family, country, and culture, has to love with ordered love the people of other families, countries, and cultures. After Pentecost the chosen people are not only our friends, our own country, our language group, but beyond that, every human being, Catholic or non-Catholic, Christian or non-Christian. The confirmed Christian has to offer the sacrifice of love and help people to overcome racism, hatred, and discrimination.

For this reason the renewal of baptismal promises during the celebration of the sacrament of confirmation has a further emphasis. It implies the rejection of any hatred, the hatred of any human being, with a positive reaffirmation of loving any human being, good or bad, friend or enemy (Mt 5, 44; Lk 6, 27.35–36). Such a rejection and profession should be part of any religion, any ideology or human system. Hatred of any human being should be crossed out of any creed or holy scripture, if we believe that God cannot hate because hatred is the denial of God's being. Perhaps in the celebration of confirmation there should be a direct question addressed to the candidate: Do you promise that you will love any human being and reject the hatred of any human being?

Yet the sacrifice of the sacrament of confirmation is not different from the Eucharistic sacrifice. After Pentecost the sacrament of confirmation is a universalization of the sacrifice of the Eucharist as a sacrifice of thanksgiving, praise, and propitiation for the sins of Catholics and non-Catholics, Christians and non-Christians. The paschal sacrifice is a sacrifice of the whole world, taking in all the sacrifices of the world, with all human beings and God mutually disclosing themselves in a common self-communication through Jesus Christ.

4.7.4.5 THE SACRAMENT OF CONFIRMATION AND ECUMENISM

Cardinal J.-M. Lustiger, in his article "Juifs et Chrétiens, demain?" (1998), remarked how difficult it was for Judaism and Christianity to accept with mind and heart the truth that both, Jews and Christians, are "chosen people." We may find a similar difficulty in Islam. Saadia Khawar Khan Chishti shrewdly observed in her article "Female Spirituality in Islam": "In Islam, union with the Divine is contingent upon love for the Prophet, who is the last of the spiritual monarchs ruling over the earth. In this respect, the Qumranic mandate is as follows: Say – if ye love God, follow me: God will love you and forgive you your sins" (Khawar, 1997, 199). There is a similar pattern in the Christian theology of Jesus Christ as divine legate. Yet Islam, Judaism, and Christianity find it difficult to accept with mind and heart the truth that Jews, Moslems, and Christians, and by the same token the whole human race, can all be "chosen people." Ecumenism is more than a dialogue. It is a fundamental human love for every human being and so a task of every human being.

The event of Pentecost extends the notion of "chosen people" to all people on earth, and "The Universal Call to Holiness in the Church" of the

Second Vatican Council (*LG*, nos. 39–42; Tanner, 1990, 880–4) should be advanced to all people of the world (Horvath, 1993, 146–8). This is all the more the case since the last paragraph of the "Universal Call" presents a universal program that each human being is expected to strive for (Tanner, 884).

The message of Pentecost and the program of the sacrament of confirmation for ecumenism is a task for every confirmed Christian faithful person. Consolation, peace, the ability to persuade, love, authenticity, and solidarity, being a person for others – these are the effects of the sacrament of confirmation and the gifts of the Holy Spirit. Wisdom, intelligence, science, fear and counsel, and fortitude and piety are all welcome qualities for each confirmed Christian in order to successfully promote ecumenism (Jn 17, 23) by listening to what God has to tell us in the language of the non-Catholic religions and the secular world. It is not Christ who is the dividing wall between Christians and non-Christians but we all who do not let God get close to us human beings here on the earth.

4.7.5 *The Sacrament of Confirmation and Systematic Theology*

4.7.5.1 THE SACRAMENT OF CONFIRMATION IS A SYMBOL FOR THE WORLD: LANGUAGE IS A WAY TO UNITY IN ACTION

Language is communication and communication is life. In contrast, death is the end of any communication with others, with the world, and with life. Language is the key to success in the world because it is universal. It is science, art, gift, and grace, and by the same token it is the key to theology, the science of faith, and love for God. Evidently, language is more than just words. Being is by its own being sayable, *sagbar, dicible*, because any language is a language of love. Even the language of hatred is the language of a distorted, zealous love. Language is saying and therefore doing, creating, or destroying.

Within the many different languages, syntaxes, and philosophies there is the universal human ability to speak, the ability to be able to understand everyone else. This ability is the ability of self-communication in which the listener finds an affirmation of his or her own being. This basic nature of language was affirmed on the day of Pentecost. The apostles expressed in their language what they had discovered as their own fulfillment. And their listeners found in it their own language, their own self-affirmation, fulfillment, perfection. When they heard Peter, "they were [κατενύγησαν] cut to the heart, and said to Peter and the rest of the apostles, 'Brethren, what shall we do?'" (Acts 2, 37). The words moved them to action. They were ready to do what Peter and the rest had already done. They were set for a common action and for a commonly desired purpose and end. At that time, language reached its end: unity in action for one's own betterment and for that of the whole world. Language is the key to success in the world. The conditions may be analyzed and studied, but the criterion of a right language seems to be clear.

4.7.5.2 THE SACRAMENT OF CONFIRMATION IS A SYMBOL FOR HUMAN EXISTENCE: A CHALLENGE TO CREATE CLARITY IN CONFUSION

Change, progress, the new, the unexpected, good or bad, may cause confusion. On the day of Pentecost, "all were amazed and perplexed, saying to one other, 'What does this mean?' But others mocking said, 'They are filled with new wine'" (Acts 2, 12–13). Confusion is a concomitant of human existence. Each human being finds him or herself thrown into this world, the centre of going and coming, within which each "poor soul" has to find a place for herself or himself. More often we are carried away by decisions rather than making them. Each one of us attempts to rationalize just at a time when we detect that today's rationality has turned out to be tomorrow's irrationality. Agnosticism, existentialism, nihilism, and deconstructionism are different kinds of rationalization of the irrational. Can there be any light or clarity in the confusion?

The answer of Pentecost is simple and clear. It is Jesus Christ who was crucified, died, and is now risen. He is redemption, salvation, eternal life, and above all, love. He is the Saviour who loves and may be loved. To the question "Brethren, what shall we do?" the challenging invitation is "Come join us and see for yourselves that faith in this man is salvation, which means light, love, joy, peace, patience, kindness, goodness, faithfulness, gentleness, self-control, and so on" (cf. Gal 5, 25). The Christian existence is a challenge to human existence. It is a call for conversion to Christ, who is the light in confusion. With him the converted one is able to find light in agnosticism, existentialism, nihilism, and destructionism and in natural disasters.

4.7.5.3 THE SACRAMENT OF CONFIRMATION IS A SYMBOL FOR THE CHURCH AS THE UNITY OF ALL HUMANITY

The Church is a people, institution, community, service, mission, and sacrament, and yet the contribution that Pentecost and with it the sacrament of confirmation can make to ecclesiology is to recall again and again what the Church is: "the sacrament or instrumental sign of ... the unity of all humanity" (*LG*, no. 1; Tanner, 1990, 849). It is the life function of the Church to help all human beings, all peoples and nations, to remain faithful to their origin and to all that made possible who and what they are. That they are and that they are the way they are today and tomorrow is due to their vocation to make a contribution by sharing their light and unique human values with the rest of the world. It is the function of the Church to invite everyone to serve the unity of all humanity.

Since the day of Pentecost the Church's concern for the unity of the world seems to have been constant. From the time of Augustine to the global village of our days there have been many metamorphoses of this City of God (Horvath, 1993, 142–4; Gilson, 1952). All were inspired by Christian concern for the unity of all peoples of the world. In the time of the great hostilities of the early twentieth century, theologians such as Gaston Fessard (1936) and popes such as Pius XII (Arès, 1949) and John Paul II were the apostles of the Church as the sacrament for the unity of all humanity.

Since there is one creator and one saviour for the whole world made one by the unity of the Holy Spirit, the sanctifier, the Church has cultivated a Christian love for one's own country as the foundation and the condition of universal love for the world. Christ, who lived and died for the whole world, could love his own people and cry over Jerusalem (Lk 19, 41). Love for one's own people is a guarantee for the love one may have for any other people of the world. Each country is the country of one of our brothers and sisters.

The real and lasting unity of the countries of the world does not fundamentally come from a unity of languages, from a unity of ideological doctrine, or from culture or technology. The unity of doctrine, the unity of organization, and the unity of culture or liturgy have their foundation in the unity of each one's ability to cultivate a love and understanding of every other human person. All could be inspired by the love for one human being who carried his *own* cross to his crucifixion and through death to his resurrection. He brought his hope, mercy, tolerance, and freedom into this world, and he invites all human beings, nations, and countries of the world to bring their hope, mercy, tolerance, and human freedom into the world and make them a common good. It is this love that inspired the Church's international apostolate, its mission, and its love for each country and language. The call of Jesus Christ has to be the call of the Church: "Come, to me all who labor and are heavy laden, and I will give you rest. Take my yoke upon you, and learn from me; for I am gentle and humble in heart, and you will find rest for you. For my yoke is easy, and my cross in light" (Mt 11, 28–30). Happy are the confirmed Christians who are able to offer rest for those who labour, are in trouble, and find their cross unbearable.

4.7.5.4 THE SACRAMENT OF CONFIRMATION IS A SYMBOL FOR CHRISTOLOGY: CHRIST IS OUR PEACE

Šālôm, peace, is more than an absence of war. Rather, it is an inventive, ingenious ongoing task of making peace in the world of hostilities and competition by solving daily problems caused by the confronting movements and forces of life. Christ is our peace, *Pax nostra* (Eph 2, 22), because he brings near those who are far off and makes one the divided by breaking down the dividing walls of hostility. He joins together the structure of the Church and unites societies together so that God may reconcile all to God " in the Spirit."

Spirit means not only a communion with God but also wisdom, an inventive mind illuminating, teaching (Jn 14, 26), and guiding all into all the truth (16, 13). Spirit is the real Paraclete defending the poor in the court against false accusations (Mt 10, 19–20). Thus the sacrament of confirmation challenges Christology to present Christ as a paradigm for solving social, moral, and ecological problems of the coming age through the wisdom of the Spirit.

Peoples are different because their love, expressed in their ethos, world views, and aspirations, is different. The early Christians found the foundation of all these different loves in Jesus Christ, the redeeming, saving God for every nation. Through him and in him everything was created and redeemed out of the love of God. He is the ἀρχηγός and τελεωτής, the originator and fulfiller, the founder and perfecter of love. Thus the many implicit loves, world views, and theologies that each people and each person have formulated are created and redeemed by his love. All loves have their origin and their end, their "eschaton," in that "*ur*-love," the foundation of being, of existing. So any love can be summed up in Christology and the whole Christology in the love a person or people has for Jesus Christ. And such a love for Jesus Christ (see Mt 25, 40) is the unifying force of peoples and of any system.

The reality and truth of the unifying power of Jesus dying on the cross was tangibly experienced and deeply felt on the day of Pentecost. "They were cut to the heart," and so are the confirmed faithful when they experience the Eucharistic God's love joining peoples in sacrifice, suffering, and death. There was not and seemingly there is not and will not be Pentecost without Good Friday (Jn 16, 7). The crucified Christ dying for others was the author of the Pentecostal unity. So are human beings by their death. In spite of its sad and terrifying reality, death seems to facilitate progress, unity, and peace. Death is the realization of the inevitability of unselfish love (Horvath, 1989b, 2329). Christ dying on the cross made his death the heart of the unity of the human race.

The 150,000–300,000 victims killed by the tsunami of 26 December 2004 and broadcast by television to all the nations of the world "cut to the heart" of the whole world, and people on the earth asked, "What should we do?" (Acts 3, 37c). And they began to give and to love, united as never before. It is to be hoped that the world will not forget. The victims of the tsunami of 2004 are the martyrs of the unity of the human race, evoked by the hostile forces of nature waiting to be disarmed and humanized by a humanity defending, supporting, and loving one other.

4.7.5.5 THE SACRAMENT OF CONFIRMATION IS A SYMBOL FOR THE REVELATION OF THE TRIUNE GOD: COMMUNICATING GOD'S TRINITARIAN LIFE IN THE CHURCH, THE COMMUNITY OF FAITH, CHARITY, AND HOPE

The sacrament of confirmation joins the revelation of the Trinitarian God to the revelation of the Trinitarian church as the community of faith, charity, and hope. It closely relates the "immanent" trinity to the "economic" trinity, God *in se* and God *ad extra,* as well as academic and pastoral theology. The one-sided separation of either would turn the immanent trinity into philosophy and the economic trinity into human enterprise. On the day of Pentecost the early church learned both that there is a Holy Spirit and that there is a mission to the whole world without limitation to any one people.

The revelation of God by the sacrament of confirmation is the same as the revelation of God by the sacrament of baptism, but it more fully expresses its power in our life. It is through the love of Jesus Christ that we enter into the Trinitarian love of God and are able to love our enemies, who in reality are only their own enemies. By loving them, we actually let them learn to appreciate and really love themselves, so that by loving themselves, they may love us and God. The Trinitarian God is almighty but cannot do one thing. The Trinitarian God cannot not love. Love is rational, and the one who cannot love is irrational. And God cannot be irrational.

4.7.5.6 THE SACRAMENT OF CONFIRMATION IS A SYMBOL FOR ESCHATOLOGY: THE UNITY OF ALL LANGUAGES; CHRIST THE LANGUAGE OF LANGUAGES

Language is conditioned by love. We speak because we love. Love is the foundation of all languages. Since Jesus Christ is the source of any love, he is the source of the unity of all languages. Since language is the vehicle as well as the realization of any culture or social community, Christ as the language of languages means that he is to be the fulfillment of cultures, that is, the fulfillment of the progressive development of the intellectual and moral talents to secure human existence, not just in time but in eternity. He is the language of all languages since in him any communication between heaven and earth, between "I" and "you," has been made possible. Communication with any human being is basically and fundamentally a communication with the Trinitarian God (Horvath, 1993, 79–80, 142–3). It is in this sense that one can say that the mission of the holy Spirit is the mission of Jesus of Christ (Jn 16, 15).

4.7.5.7 THE SACRAMENT OF CONFIRMATION IS A SYMBOL FOR PNEUMATOLOGY: A NEW NOTION OF TIME

Pentecost was the revelation of Christ as the unity of languages. Pneumatology, the theology of the Holy Spirit, means the universalization and "contemporalization" or, more precisely, the eternization of all languages. The same Holy Spirit – who made possible that the word of human beings became the word of God, and that the conception of a human being was "the conception" of God, and that the bread and wine becomes the Eucharistic body and blood of Christ, and that a love of a human being may reveal the love of God and the love of God for a human being – also makes it possible that the "then" and "there" of Jesus Christ may reach the "here" and "now" of every human being of any space and time. His historical time reached and vanquished the human past and the future by becoming the redeeming standard for both (Horvath, 1993, 65–80).

A notion of time is operative in geology, cosmology, physics, biology, psychology, sociology, history, philosophy, and theology. Summarizing them, we could say that "time is a balance in a multiplicity of sub-times characterized by an irreversibility measured through uniformly reversible changes pointing to a self-sublating singularity event. Thus in a hermeneutic language event time can be interpreted as way-making for eternity " (Horvath, 1993, 60). Christ understood as the eschatological union of time and eternity is the "Lord" of times and eternity and, as such, a key for both (ibid., 65–80). He is the unity of times and eternity in the Spirit.

4.7.5.8 THE SACRAMENT OF CONFIRMATION IS A SYMBOL FOR MARIOLOGY: MARY IS THE SOURCE OF UNITY OF ALL WHO ARE WAITING BOTH KNOWING AND NOT KNOWING FOR WHAT

The sacrament of confirmation illustrates Mary's role in the salvation of the world. She was the source of unity for one hundred and twenty people waiting in the Cenacle as well as for the three thousand who did not know at first what they were waiting for but then joined Christ's followers on the day of Pentecost. So she is the source of unity for the Church's knowing that the Lord will be adding to its number day by day from that day on (Zielinsky, 1999; Group des Dombes, 1997–98) and for all those who are waiting without yet knowing for what.

The reason is that Mary can unite all loves for her son. Loving her son, she was loving God, and her loving God could become the love of a human child. And loving her own child could become her loving every human child who entered this world. Mary is the image of unity in multiplicity and thus an image for every human being.

5

Finale and Overture

We have raised a number of questions and tried to answer them. The questions we have asked were the questions of love, and we have looked for the answers that love would give. The love that raised the questions and gave the answers is not the love many think of. Yet it is also a love, a real love, the foundation and aspiration of any love a human mind and heart ever recognized as such. It is the love that is the innermost reality of any being and makes such a being to be. It is the ur-being which transcends and comprehends every being and which each human being tries to reach out to and to express in his or her faith and hope. This is the love that is not the end of questions. It is the one that is also the beginning of many new questions. It is simply a love that is a love for any and for all human beings, with no exceptions, a love that finds every human being beautiful and lovable.

In our Overture we recommended these pages to all those who have questions and who raise that questions we have failed to raise. The love that was active in asking and answering these questions is the same love that is willing to appropriate any question the readers ask and any answer they propose as its own, and it invites the questioners to walk along in search of the answer. And so this book begins to live.

Following our motto and hermeneutic principle, announced on the first page, that "we love so that we may believe and understand; we love so that we may understand and believe," we have tried to love all those whose texts we have interpreted in this book. In dealing with the history of theology in the second part of our *Summa,* we shall interpret theologians, philosophers, and thinkers, such as Theodore of Mopsuestia, Descartes, Kant with the same love, so that we may understand their search for love and understand and believe what they say. The interpretation may turn out to be different from the one we are used to, yet it is understandable and believable. Our *Summa* is planned to be a *Summa of love, faith, and hope.* May this initial *Summa* be an inspiration, challenge, and invitation to non-Catholic, non-Christian believers, to any secular philosopher and thinker, to attempt to present their denomination, religion, or philosophical or scientific system under the headings of love, faith, and hope, our unifying triad in the present and common aspiration for the future.

APPENDIX

Sacramental Theology's Contribution to Systematic Theology: A Summary

1 World / Creation/ Theological Epistemology: Sacraments Are Symbols for the World

1.1 Presence: Eucharist
1.2 Pattern of difference: Marriage
1.3 Call: Order
1.4 Forgiveness
1.5 The World is more than we know about it: Anointing of the sick
1.6 The Name is real: Baptism
1.7 Language is for unity in action: Confirmation

2 Christian Anthropology, a New Life in Christ: A Challenge to Human Existence

2.1 To love and trust: Eucharist
2.2 To cooperate with the other as other: Marriage
2.3 To initiative: Order
2.4 Forgiveness requires strength and courage: Forgiveness
2.5 To never give up: Anointing of the sick
2.6 To transcendence: Baptism
2.7 To clarity in confusion: Confirmation

3 Ecclesiology: Life Functions of the Church

3.1 Being with people in the world: Eucharist
3.2 Self-giving to the human race: Marriage

3.3 Constant dependence on the historical Jesus as its Creator: Order
3.4 Forgiveness as a mission: Forgiveness
3.5 Love of the poor, the sick, and Marginal: Anointing of the sick
3.6 Growth: Baptism
3.7 Unity of all humanity: Confirmation

4 Christology: Features

4.1 Christ is in the world: Eucharist
4.2 Christ has feelings and desires to be loved: Marriage
4.3 Christ's call is once for all: Order
4.4 Forgiveness is God's prerogative of love and justice: Forgiveness
4.5 Love for the sick: Anointing of the sick
4.6 Filiation within the Trinity: Baptism
4.7 Christ is our peace: Confirmation

5 Trinity: Revelation of the Triune God

5.1 A God pleased to be with human beings: Eucharist
5.2 God's unrestricted self-giving in the fallible love of a woman and a man chosen by God's infallible word: Marriage
5.3 Wherever this person is Christ will be there as a saviour: Order
5.4 Forgiving freely and independently of the worthiness of the sinner: Forgiveness
5.5 God is incomprehensible: Anointing of the sick
5.6 God the Father, generosity; the Son, integrity; and the Holy Spirit, authenticity: Baptism
5.7 God's Trinitarian life in the Church: Confirmation

6 Eschatology: Kerygma

6.1 The reality of eternal life in the kerygma: Eucharist
6.2 Love has a future; hate does not. The future is stronger than the present and the past: Marriage
6.3 Actions in the present have a decisive impact on the future: Order
6.4 The merciful, they shall obtain mercy: Forgiveness
6.5 Time is the revelation of eternity: Anointing of the sick
6.6 Trinitarian life is eternity: Baptism
6.7 The unity of all languages; Christ the language of languages: Confirmation

7 Pneumatology: The Spirit Has an Incarnational Mission

7.1 Building the Church: Eucharist
7.2 Sanctification of one in the community of "others": Marriage
7.3 Christological pneumatology; the revelation of sin: Order
7.4 There is no forgiveness without the Holy Spirit: Forgiveness
7.5 The sick, the poor, and the marginal as a test case for the authenticity of a theology of the Holy Spirit: Anointing of the sick
7.6 The Spirit is a person with a real name: Baptism
7.7 A new notion of time: Confirmation

8 Mariology: Pre-eminent Model of the Redeemed Person

8.1 Eucharistic grace is universal; Mary is the mediatrix of all graces: Eucharist
8.2 Mary is the pre-eminent model of marital and celibate love: Marriage
8.3 Mary is the co-redemptrix: Order
8.4 Mary is the *refugium peccatorum,* the refuge of sinners: Forgiveness
8.5 Bodily assumption into heaven: Anointing of the sick
8.6 Immaculate conception: Baptism
8.7 Source of unity: Confirmation

References

AA: *Apostolicam Actuositatem.* Vatican II, 1962–65. *Decree on the Apostolate of the Laity.* In *Decrees of the Ecumenical Councils,* edited by N.P. Tanner, 981–1001. Washington, DC: Georgetown University Press, 1990.

Abulides or Hippolytus. 1869. "Heads of Canons." *Ante-Nicene Christian Library,* 9, 2: 135–7. Edinburgh: T. and T. Clark.

Acta Synodalia Sacrosancti Concilii Documenti Vaticani II. 1970–80. Vatican City.

AG: *Ad Gentes.* Vatican II, 1962–65. *Decree on the Missionary Activity of the Church.* In *Decrees of the Ecumenical Councils,* edited by N.P. Tanner, 1011–42. Washington, DC: Georgetown University Press, 1990.

Alexander III. 1963. "Letters to the Archbishop of Salermo." In *Enchiridion Symbolorum. Definitiones et Declarationes de Rebus Fidei et Morum,* edited by H. Denzinger and A. Schönmetzer, 240–1. New York: Herder.

Alivastos, H.S. 1960. "Les conciles oecuméniques VE, VIE, VIIE et VIIIE." In *Le Concile et les conciles,* 111–23. Paris: Editions du Cerf.

Alszeghy, Z. 1983. "Gyónás (Sacrament of Forgiveness)." In *Theológia Vázlatok* V. (*Theological Essays*), edited by Z. Alszeghy et al., 259–62. Budapest: St. Stephen's Press.

Altaner, B. 1960. *Patrology.* Translated by H.C. Graf. New York: Herder and Herder.

Amand, S. 1984. "The Trinity as God in History." *Vidyajyoti* 48: 166–77.

Amann, É. 1927. "Maldonat." In *Dictionnaire de théologie catholic,* 9: 1772–6.

Ambrose of Milan. 1962. *Explanatio Psalmorum.* Edited by M. Petschenig. Corpus Scriptorum Ecclesiasticorum Latinorum. New York: Johnson Reprint Corp.

Appleton, G., ed. 1985. *The Oxford Book of Prayer.* New York: Oxford University Press.

Ardrey, R. 1966. *The Territorial Imperative.* New York: Dell Publishing Co.

Arès, R. 1949. *L'Église catholique et l'organisation de la Société internationale contempo-*

raine, 1939–1949. Montréal: Les Facultés de philosophie et de théologie de la Compagnie de Jésus.

Armstrong, C.B. 1969. *Creeds and Credibility*. London: Mowbray.

Athenagoras. 1953. *A Plea Regarding Christians*. In *Early Christian Fathers*, edited by C.C. Richardson, 1: 300–40. Philadelphia: The Westminster Press.

Aubert, R. 1967. *Vatican I. Histoire des conciles oecuméniques*. Paris: Éditions de l'Orante.

Augustine of Hippo. 1956. *Enarrationes in Psalmos*. 1–2. Corpus Christanorum S.L., vol. 38. Turnhoult: Brepolis.

– 1988. *Tractates on the Gospel of John*. In *The Fathers of the Church*, vol. 78. Washington, DC: Catholic University of America Press.

– 1993. *Confessions*. Translated by F.J. Sheed. Indianapolis, IN: Hackett Publishing.

– 1995. *Tractates on the First Epistle of John*. In *The Fathers of the Church*, vol. 92, 95–277. Washington, DC: Catholic University of America Press.

Babos, I. 1983a. "A Betegek Kenete [Anointing of the Sick]." In *Theológia Vázlatok* V. [*Theological Essays*], edited by Z. Alszeghy et al., 299–397. Budapest: St. Stephen's Press.

– 1983b. "A Keresztség és Bérmálás [Baptism and Confirmation]." In *Theológia Vázlatok* V. [*Theological Essays]*, edited by Z. Alszeghy et al., 164–76). Budapest: St. Stephen's Press.

Barber, M. 1978. *The Trial of the Temples*. Cambridge: Harvard University Press.

Barrosse, T. 1957. "The Relationship of Love to Faith in St. John." *Theological Studies* 18: 538–59.

Barth, K. 1969. In "The Doctrine of Reconciliation." *Church Dogmatics*, 4, part 4. Edinburgh: T. Clark.

Batiffol, P. 1928. "Theologia, Theologi." *Ephemerides Theologicae Lovanienses* 5: 205–20.

Baus, K. 1965. "From the Apostolic Community to Constantine." In *Handbook of Church History*, edited by H. Jedin and J. Dolan, vol 1. Freiburg: Herder.

Bayes, N.H. 1951. "The Icons before Iconoclasm." *Harvard Theological Review*. 44: 93–106.

Behm, J. 1985. "καινος." In *Biblical Dictionary of the New Testament*, edited by G. Kittel, 3: 447–54. Grand Rapids: Eerdmans Publishing Co.

Berggren, E. 1975. *The Psychology of Confession*. Leiden: Brill.

Berkhof, H. 1964. *The Doctrine of the Holy Spirit*. Atlanta: John Knox Press.

Bernard, L.W. 1967. *Justin Martyr, His Life and Thought*. New York: Cambridge University Press.

Bettenson, H. 1967. *Documents of the Christian Church*. Oxford: Oxford University Press.

Bilaniuk, P. 1973. *The Fifth Lateran Council and the Eastern Churches*. Toronto: The Central Committee for the Defence of Rite.

Billot, L. 1896. *De ecclesiae sacramentis*. Vol. 1. Rome: Aedes Universitatis Gregorianae.

Blumberg, A., and L.G. Panos. 1990. *Edward Teller, Giant of the Golden Age of Physics: A Biography.* New York: Charles Scribner's Sons.

Boff, L. 1985. *Church: Charism and Power.* New York: Crossroad.

Boularand, É. 1964. "Les débuts d'Arius." *Bulletin de littérature ecclésiastique* 64: 175–203.

Bowden, H.W. 1991. *Church History in an Age of Uncertainty: Historiographical Patterns in the United States, 1906–1990.* Carbondale: Southern Illinois University Press.

Bowker, J. 1970. *Problems of Suffering in Religions of the World.* Cambridge: Cambridge University Press.

Bracken, J.A. 1974. "The Holy Trinity as a Community of Divine Persons." *Heythrop Journal* 15: 166–82; 257–70.

Breisach, E. 1983. *Historiography.* Chicago: University of Chicago Press.

Bright, W. 1882. *Notes on the Canons of the First Four General Councils.* Oxford: Clarendon Press.

Bulletin. 1998. "Interreligious Prayer." *Pro Dialogo* (Città del Vaticano: Pontificium Consilium pro Dialogo inter Religiones) 98: 230–6.

Bultmann, R. 1953. "New Testament and Mythology." In *Kerygma and Myth,* edited by H.W. Bartsch, 1–44. London: Hodder.

– 1961. "The Concept of Revelation in the New Testament." In *Existence and Faith,* 58–91. London: Hodder.

– 1964. "δικαιοσύνη Θεοῦ." *Journal of Biblical Literature* 83: 12–16.

– 1970. "ἀφίημι, αφεσις, παρίημι, πάρεσις." In *Theological Dictionary of the New Testament,* edited by G. Kittel; translated by G.W. Bromiley, 509–12. Grand Rapids: Eerdmans Publishing Co.

Burn, A.E. 1925. *The Council of Nicaea.* London: S.P.C.K.

Burtchaell, J.T. 1992. *From Synagogue to Church: Public Services and Offices in the Earliest Christian Communities.* New York: Cambridge University Press.

Buttersworth, G.W. 1936. *Origen on First Principles.* London: Society for Promoting Christian Knowledge.

Calderone, M., ed. 1974. *Sexuality and Human Values.* New York: Association Press.

Camelot, P. 1962. *Ephèse et Chalcédone.* Histoire des conciles oecuméniques. Paris: Éditions de l'Orante.

Canons of the Church of Alexandria. 1883. In *Ante-Nicene Christian Library,* 9, 2: 138–40. Edinburgh: T. and T. Clark.

Catechism of the Catholic Church. 1994. Ottawa: Canadian Conference of Catholic Bishops.

CCSL: Corpus Christianorum. 1971– . *Series Latina.* Turnhout: Brepolis.

CD, Christus Dominus. Vatican II, 1962–65. *Decree on the Pastoral Office of Bishops in the Church.* In *Decrees of the Ecumenical Councils,* edited by N.P. Tanner, 921–39. Washington, DC: Georgetown University Press, 1990.

Chadwick, H. 1953. *Origen: Contra Celsum.* New York, Cambridge: At the University Press.

Chapelle, A. 1996. "La chasteté conjugale et la célébration du sacrament du pénitence." *Nouvelle revue théologique* 118: 852–61.

Cheney, C.R. 1906. "The Numbering of the Lateran Councils of 1179 and 1212." In *Medieval Texts and Studies*, 203–9. Oxford: Clarendon Press.

Clark, F. 1962. *The Catholic Church and Anglican Orders.* London: Catholic Truth Society.

Clement of Rome. 1953. *First Letter.* In *Early Christian Fathers*, 1. Philadelphia: The Westminster Press.

Codrington, R.H. 1891. *Melanesian Studies in Anthropology and Folklore.* Oxford: Clarendon Press.

Concilium Tridentinum Nova Collectio. Freiburg: Görresgesellschaft, 1901–38.

Congar, M.-J. 1983. *I Believe in the Holy Spirit.* Vol. 1–3. New York: The Seabury Press.

Connolly, R.H. 1929. *Didascalia Apostoloum: The Syriac Version.* Oxford: Clarendon Press.

Conzelmann, H 1969. *Der erste Brief an die Korinthers.* Göttingen: Vandenhoek & Ruprecht.

Crowder, C.M.D. 1977. *Unity, Heresy and Reform, 1378–1460.* London: Edward Arnold.

CSEL: *Corpus Scriptorum Eccleasticorum Latinorum.* Vienna: C. Geroldi filium, 1866–1939.

CT: 1965. *Concilium TridentinumI Diariorum, Actorum, Epistularum, Tractatuum.* Nova ed., Cura Stephanus Ehses; 2nd ed, edited by Societas Goerresiana. Freiburg: Herder, 1965.

Cuervo, M. 1948. "Los teólgos de la Escuela salmantina en los discussiones del concilio de Trento sobre el sacrificio de la Cena." *Ciencia Tomistica* 75: 177–216.

Cyprian, Thasci Caecilii. 1871. *Opera Omnia: Epistulae.* Edited by G. Hartel. Vienna: Geralt.

Daniélou, J. 1955. *Origen.* Translated by W. Mitchell. New York: Sheed and Ward.

"Découverte d'un text sur l'Extrème Onction." 1963. *Ami du clergé* 73: 490.

de la Taille, M. 1921. *Mysterium Fidei de Augustissimo Corporis et Sanguinis Christi Sacrificio atque Sacramento.* Paris: Beauchesne. Translated as *The Mystery of Faith* (London: Sheed and Ward, 1950).

De Sales, T. 1963. "Hindu Marriage." *Path Margah* 2: 42–75.

de Vaux, R. 1961. *Ancient Israel: Its Life and Institutions.* Translated by J. McHugh. New York: McGraw-Hill.

DH: *Dignitatis Humanae.* Vatican II, 1962–65. *Declaration on Religious Freedom.* In *Decrees of the Ecumenical Councils*, edited by N.P. Tanner, 1001–11. Washington, DC: Georgetown University Press, 1990.

Diognetus, Epistle to. 1947. In *The Fathers of the Church*, edited by L. Schopp, 351–67. New York: Cima Publishing Co.

Dix, G. 1937. *Hippolytus: The Treatise of the Apostolic Tradition.* London: SPCK.

Doronzo, E. 1962. *De Ordine.* 3 vols. Milwaukee: Bruce.

DS: *Enchiridion Symbolorum Definitionum et Declarationum de Rebus Fidei et Morum.* Edited by H. Denzinger and A. Schönmetzer. New York: Herder, 1963.

Dudon, P. 1939. "Sur un text inédit de Salmeron." *Gregorianum.* 11: 410–17.

Dumège, J. 1976. *Nicée II*. Histoire des conciles oecuméniques. Paris: Éditions de l'Orante.

DV: *Dei Verbum*. Vatican II, 1962–65. *Dogmatic Constitution on Divine Revelation*. In *Decrees of the Ecumenical Councils*, edited by N.P. Tanner, 971–81. Washington, DC: Georgetown University Press, 1990.

Elster, J. 1979. *Ullysses and the Sirens*. New York: Cambridge University Press.

Emery, R.W. 1966. "The Second Council of Lyons and the Mendicant Orders." *Catholic Historical Review* 39: 257–72.

Falls, T.B. 1948. *Writings of Saint Justin Martyr*. In *The Fathers of the Church*, vol. 6. New York: Christian Heritage.

Feltoe, C. 1918. *Dionysius of Alexandria, Letters and Treatises*. London: SPCK.

Fessard, G. 1936. *"Pax nostra": Examen de conscience international*. Paris: Granet.

Flick, M. 1962. *De Gratia Christi*. Roma: Gregorian University Press.

Ford, L. 1975. "Process Trinitarianism." *Journal of the American Academy of Religion* 43: 207.

Forde, D. 1964. *Yakö Studies*. Oxford: Oxford University Press.

Foreville, R. 1965. *Latran I, II, III, et Latran IV*. Histoire des conciles oecuméniques. Paris: Editions de l'Orante.

Fransen, P. 1975. "Confirmation." In *Encyclopedia of Theology: The Concise Sacramentum Mundi*, edited by K. Rahner, 276–83. New York: The Seabury Press.

Frazer, J.G. 1910. *Totemism and Exogamy*. London: Macmillan.

Freud, S. 1935. *General Introduction to Psychoanalysis*. New York: Perma Books.

Funk, F.X., ed. 1901. *Patres Apostolici*. Vol. I. Tübingen: Libraria H. Laupp.

– 1905. *Didascalia et Constitutiones Apostolicae*. Paderborn: Schoeningh.

Gaechter, P. 1952. "Die Sieben, Apg. 6, 1–6." *Zeitschrift für Katholische Theologie* 74: 129–66.

Gaines, D.P. 1966. *The World Council of Churches*. Peterborough, NH: The Richard R. Smith Co.

Gassman, G. 1964. *Das historische Bischofsamt and die Einheit der Kirche in der neueren Anglikanischen Theologie*. Göttingen: Vanderhoeck & Ruprecht.

GE: *Gravissimum Educationis*. Vatican II, 1962–1965. *Declaration on Christian Education*. In *Decrees of the Ecumenical Councils*, edited by N.P. Tanner, 959–68. Washington, DC: Georgetown University Press, 1990.

Geanakoplos, D.J. 1959. *Emperor Michael Paleologus and the West, 1258–1282*. Cambridge: Harvard University Press.

Gill, J. 1953. *Concilium Florentinum: Acta Graeca*. Rome: Pontificium Orientalium Studiorum.

– 1959. *The Council of Florence*. Cambridge: Harvard University Press.

– 1964. *Personalities of the Council of Florence*. London: Oxford University Press.

– 1965. *Constance et Bale-Florence*. Histoire des conciles oecuméniques. Paris: Éditions de l'Orante.

Gill, J. H., ed. 1968. *Philosophy and Religion: Some Contemporary Perspectives*. Minneapolis: Burgess Publishing Co.

Gilson, É. 1952. *Les métamorphoses de la cité de Dieu.* Louvain: Publications universitaires.

– 1960. *The Christian Philosophy of St. Augustine.* New York: Random.

Goertz, G. 1994. *Contexts of International Politics.* Translated by L.E.M. Lynch. New York: Cambridge University Press.

Goetz, J. 1956. "Priester." In *Religionswissenschaftliches Wörterbuch.* Edited by F. König. Freiburg: Herder.

Grant, R.M. 1956. "Aristotle and the Conversion of Justin." *Journal of Theological Studies* 57: 248.

Grillmeier, A. 1962. *Das Konzil von Chalkedon.* Würzburg: Echter Verlag.

– 1989. *Jesus Christus in Glauben der Kirche.* Band 2/2, 451–620. Freiburg: Herder.

Groupe des Dombes. 1997–98. *Marie dans le dessein de Dieu et la communion des saints.* Vol. 1, *Dans l'historie et l'Écriture*; Vol. 2, *Controverse et conversion.* Paris: Bayard Éd. Centurion.

GS: *Gaudium et Spes.* Vatican II, 1962–65. *Pastoral Constitution on the Church in the World of Today.* In *Decrees of the Ecumenical Councils,* edited by N.P. Tanner, 1069–135. Washington, DC: Georgetown University Press, 1990.

Gwatkin, H.M. 1990. *Studies of Arianism.* New York: University of Cambridge Press.

Haddan, A.W. 1869–78. *Councils and Ecclesial Documents Related to Great Britain and Ireland.* 3 vols. in 4. Oxford: Clarendon Press.

Haekel, J. 1963. " Priester. Religionsgeschichtlich." In *Lexikon für Theologie und Kirche.* 8: 735–41. Freiburg: Herder.

Hanson, R.P.C. 1983. "The Holy Spirit in Creeds and Confessions of Faith in the Early Church." In *Credo in Spiritum Sanctum,* 291–302. Vatican City: Libreria Editrice Vaticana.

Hardwick, C. 1881. *A History of the Articles of Religion: to Which is Added a Series of Comments from A.D. 1536–1615.* London: George Bell & Sons.

Hartshorne, C. 1978. "Panpsychism: Mind as Sole Reality." *Ultimate Reality and Meaning* 1: 115–29.

Hasler, A.B. 1981. *How the Pope Became Infallible.* New York: Doubleday.

Hayen, A. 1957. *La communication de l'être d'après Saint Thomas d'Aquin.* Paris: Desclée Brower.

Hayes, J.H., and J.H. Hanscom. 1983. *Ancient Civilizations: Prehistory to the Fall of Rome.* New York: Macmillan.

Hefele, P., and H. Leclerq. 1907–38. *Histoire des conciles d'après les documents originaux.* Paris: Letouzey et Ané.

Heidegger, M. 1968. "The Problem of a Non-objectifying Thinking and Speaking in Contemporay Theology." *Philosophy and Religion: Some Contemporary Perspect* edited by J.H. Gill, 59–65 Minneapolis: Burgess Publishing Co.

Hill, W.J. 1982. *The Three-Personed God.* Washington, DC: Catholic University Press.

Hoffmann, G., ed. 1959. *Concilium Florentinum: Acta Graeca, Acta Latina.* Rome: Pontificium Orientalium Studiorum.

Holmes, D.S. 1984. "Defence Mechanism." In *Encyclopedia of Psychology*, edited by R.J. Corsini, 1: 347–50. New York: J. Wiley and Sons.

Honigmann, E. 1936. "Recherches sur les listes des pères de Nicée et de Constantinople." *Byzantion* 11: 429–49.

Horvath, T. 1966. *Caritas est in Ratione: Die Lehre des hl. Thomas über die Einheit der intellectiven und affektiven Begnadung des Menschen*. Beiträge zur Geschichte der Philosophie und Theologie des Mittelalters, XLI, 3. Münster: Verlag Aschendorff.

– 1968. "Theology of a New Diaconate." *Revue de l'Université d'Ottawa* 38: 248–76, 495–523.

– 1969. "Why Was Jesus Brought to Pilate." *Novum Testamentum* 51: 174–84.

– 1970. "The Sacrament of Marriage as Revelation of God." *Heythrop Journal* 11: 388–407.

– 1971a. "Sacrament of Ordination as Revelation of God." *Heythrop Journal* 12: 44–52.

– 1971b. "Is hēmôn in Mk 9, 40 Authentic?" *Journal of Ecumenical Studies* 8: 385–6.

– 1972. "Germanus of Constantinople and the Cult of the Virgin Mary, Mother of God, Mediatrix of All Human Beings." In *De Cultu Mariano Saeculis VI-XI: Acta Congressus Mariologici-Mariani Internationalis in Croatia Anno 1971 Celebrati*, 4: 285–99. Rome: Pontificia Academia Mariana Internationalis.

– 1974. "3 Jn 11b: An Early Ecumenical Creed?" *Expository Times* 85: 339–40.

– 1975a. *Faith under Scrutiny*. Notre Dame: Fides Publishers.

– 1975b. "Prelegomenon to a Theology of Sacrifice." In *Word and Spirit*, edited by J. Plevnik, 349–70. Toronto: Regis College Press.

– 1976. "Revelation, Combat of Culture-Types, Thermodynamics. A Fundamental Theological Analysis of Crisis Event." In *Traditio-Krisis-Renovatio aus theologischer Sicht: Festschrift Winfried Zeller zum 65. Geburtstag*, edited by B. Jaspert and R. Mohr, 445–53. Marburg: N.G. Elvert Verlag.

– 1977. "A Structural Understanding of the Magisterium of the Church." *Science et esprit* 29: 283–311.

– 1978. "Forward." *Ultimate Reality and Meaning* 1: 1–8.

– 1979a. "Marriage: Contract? Covenant? Community? Sacraments of Sacraments? Fallible Symbol of Infallible Love. Revelation of Sin ad Love." In *Sacraments: God's Love and Mercy Actualized*. Proceedings of the Theology Institute of Villanova University, edited by F.E. Eigo, 143–81.Villanova: Villanova University.

– 1979b. *The Sacrificial Interpretation of Jesus' Achievement in the New Testament*. New York: Philosophical Library.

– 1980a."The Structure of Scientific Discovery and Man's Ultimate Reality and Meaning." *Ultimate Reality and Meaning* 3: 144–63.

– 1980b. "Tod." In *Lexikon für Psychologie*, edited by W. Arnold, 3: 2329. Freiburg.in Br.: Herder.

– 1981. "Theologies of Non-Christian Religions." *Science et esprit* 33: 299–322.

– 1983. "Can a Roman Catholic Be a Historian? A Response and a Proposal for Research." *Journal of Ecumenical Studies* 20: 657–8.

– 1984. "Needed: A Solemn Feast Day for the Sacrament of Marriage." *Homiletic and Pastoral Review* 84, no. 9: 62–7.

– 1985a. "L'apologetica nella Chiesa occidentale dal periodo classico della scholastica all'inizio della Riforma (sec XIII–XV)." In *Enciclopedia de teologia fondamentale*, edited by G. Ruggieri, 1: 249–74. Torino: Marietti.

– 1985b. "Who Presided at Eucharist? A Comment on BEM." *Journal of Ecumenical Studies* 22: 604–7.

– 1988. "The Sacrament of Penance as Revelation of God." *Asia Journal of Theology* 2: 496–9.

– 1989. "The Sacrament of the Anointing of the Sick as Revelation of God." *Asia Journal of Theology* 3: 532–9.

– 1993. *Eternity and Eternal Life: Speculative Theology and Science in Discourse.* Waterloo, Ont: Wilfrid Laurier University Press.

– 1994. *Jesus Christ as Ultimate Reality and Meaning: A Contribution to the Hermeneutics of Counciliar Theology.* Toronto: URAM, Regis College.

– 1997. "Theodore Karman, Paul Wigner, John Neumann, Leo Szilard, Eward Teller and Their Ideas of Ultimate Reality and Meaning." *Ultimate Reality and Meaning* 20: 123–46.

Hostiensis, H. 1963. *Summa Aurea. 4, De Secundis Nuptiis.* Torino: Bottega d'Erasmo.

Hugh of Armiens. 1855. *De Ecclesia ejusque ministris. Contra haereticos.* In *PL*, 192: 1255–90.

Hughes, J.J. 1968. *Absolutely Null and Utterly Void.* Washington, DC: Corpus Books.

Hussey, J. 1986. *The Orthodox Church in the Byzantine Empire.* Oxford: Oxford University Press

Ignatius of Loyola. 1973. *The Spiritual Exercises.* Translated by T. Corbishley. Tenbury Wells, Worcs.: Fowler Wright Books.

IM: *Inter Mirifica*, Vatican II, 1962–65. *Decree on the Mass Media.* In *Decrees of the Ecumenical Councils*, edited by N.P. Tanner, 843–9. Washington, DC: Georgetown University Press, 1990.

Irenaeus. 1867. *Adversus Haereses.* In *Ante-Nicene Christian Library*, vol 5. Edited by A. Roberts and J. Donatson. Edinburgh: T.& T. Clark.

Jacob, E.F. 1943. *Essays on the Conciliar Epoch.* Historical Series 80. Manchester: Publications of the University.

Jarvis, E.A. 1980. "Josiah Royce's Idea of Ultimate Reality and Meaning." *Ultimate Reality and Meaning* 3: 168–86.

Jedin, H. 1951. *A History of the Council of Trent.* St. Louis: Herder.

– 1960. *Ecumenical Councils of the Catholic Church.* New York: Herder and Herder.

– 1967. *Crisis and Closure of the Council of Trent: A Retrospective View from the Second Vatican Council.* London: Sheed and Ward.

Jedin, H., and J. Dolan. 1980. *History of the Church.* London: Burns and Oates.

John Paul II. 1979. *Redemptor Hominis: Encyclical.* Ottawa: Canadian Conference of Catholic Bishops.

– 1983. "Christians on the Eve of Third Millennium: Papal Bull on the Holy Year." *Origins* 12: 564–8.

– 1984. "Apostolic Exhortation on Reconciliation and Penance." *Origins* 14: 432–58.

– 1988. "Dies Domini." *Acta Apostolici Sedis* 90: 713–66. Città del Vaticano: Libraria Vaticana.

– 1998. *Encyclical on Faith and Reason.* New Hope, Ky: Inside the Vatican.

Joyce, G.H. 1948. *Christian Marriage: A Historical and Doctrinal Study.* London: Sheed and Ward.

Jüngel, E. 1976. *The Doctrine of the Trinity: God's Being Is in Becoming.* Grand Rapids: Eerdmans Pubishing Co.

– 1983. *God as the Mystery of the World; or, The Foundation of the Theology of the Crucified One in the Dispute between Theism and Atheism.* Edinburgh: T. and T. Clark.

Jungmann, J.A. 1932. *Die Lateinische Busszeremonie in ihrer geschictlichen Entwicklung.* Innsbruck: Felizian Rauch.

– 1956. *Das Eucharistische Hochgebet, Grundgedanken des Canon Missae.* Würzburg: Werkbund.

– 1968. "Eucharist II: Liturgical." In *Sacramenum Mundi,* 2: 267–73, edited by K. Rahner, Basel; Montreal: Palm Publishers.

Junod, H.A. 1962. *The Life of a Son of an African Tribe.* 2 vols. New Hyde Park: University Books.

Kannengisser, C. 1981. "Athanasius of Alexandria and the Holy Spirit between Nicaea I and Constantinople I." *Irish Theological Quarterly* 48: 166–80.

Kelly, J.N.D. 1958. *Early Christian Doctrines.* London: Adam and Charles Black.

Khawar, Saadia Khan Chisti. 1997. "Female Spirituality in Islam." In *Islam Spprituality Foundations,* edited by Seyyed Hossein Nasr, 199–219. New York: Crossroad.

King, N.Q. 1957. "The 150 Holy Fathers of the Council of Constantinople 381 A.D.: Some Notes on the Bishops-lists." *Studia Patristica* 1: 635–41.

Knauber, A. 1975. *Pastoral Theology of the Anointing of the Sick.* Collegeville, Minn.: The Liturgical Press.

Kohler, K. 1923. *Jewish Theology.* New York: The Macmillan Co.

Kremnitz, F.M. 1971. *Examination of the Council of Trent.* St. Louis: Concordia.

Kroll, J. 1968. *Die christliche Hymnodik bis zum Klemens von Alexandria.* Darmstadt: Wissenschaftliche Buchgesellschaft.

Kuhn, T.S. 1970. *The Structure of Scientific Revolutions.* Chicago: University of Chicago Press.

Kuttner, S. 1957. "Brief Note Concerning the Canons of the Third Lateran Council." *Traditio* 13: 505–6.

Kuttner, S., and A. Garcia y Garcia. 1964. "A New Eyewitness Account of the Fourth Lateran Council." *Traditio* 20: 115–78.

Lafonte, G. 1969. *Peut-on connaître Dieu en Jesus-Christ? Problématique.* Paris: du Cerf.

Lane, M. 1970. *Introduction to Structuralism.* New York: Basic Books.

Langkammer, P.H. 1970–71. "Literarische und Theologische Einzelstücke in 1 Kor VIII, 6." *New Testament Studies* 17: 193–7.

Le Bras, G. 1927. " La doctrine du marriage chez le théologians et les canonists depuis l'an mille." In *Dictionnaire de théologie catholique,* edited by A.Vacant, 9: 2123–31. Paris: Letouzey et Ané.

Lecler, J. 1964. *Vienne.* Histoire des conciles oecuméniques. Paris: Editions de l'Orante.

Lecler, J., et al. 1981. *Trente.* Histoire des conciles oecuméniques. Paris: Editions de l'Orante.

Lécuyer, J. 1953. " Episcopat et presbyterat dans les écrit de Hippolyte de Rome." *Recherches de science religieuse* 41: 30–50.

– 1962. *Le sacrifice de la Nouvelle Alliance.* Le Puy: Mappus.

Leo XXXI. 1879–80. "Arcanum Divinae Sapientiae." *Acta Apostolicae Sedis* 12: 385–402.

Lepin, M. 1926. *L'idée du sacrficie de la messe d'après les théologiens depuis l'origine jusqu'à nos jours.* Paris: Beauchesne.

Lercher, L. 1950. *Institutiones Theologiae Dogmaticae.* Vol. 4.2. Innsbruck: Felician Verlag.

Léry, L.C. de. 1960. "Deux nouveaux cas de dissolution du mariage en faveur de la foi." *Sciences ecclésiastiques* 12: 266–7.

LG: *Lumen Gentium.* Vatican II, 1962–65. *Dogmatic Constitution on the Church.* In *Decrees of the Ecumenical Councils,* edited by N.P. Tanner, 849–98. Washington, DC: Georgetown University Press, 1990.

Lightfoot, J.B. 1970. *The Apostolic Fathers.* Grand Rapids: Baker Book House.

Loisy, A.F. 1971. *Les évangiles synoptiques.* Vol. 1. Frankfurt a. M.: Minerva.

Lonergan, B.F.J. 1942. "Finality, Love, Marriage." *Theological Studies* 4: 477–510.

– 1976. *The Way to Nicea: The Dialectical Development of Trinitarian Theology.* London: Darton, Longman, Todd.

Longère, J. 1982. *Le troisième concile du Latran (1179): Sa place dans l'histoire.* Paris: Études augustiniennes.

Loomis, L.R. 1961. *The Council of Constance.* New York: Columbia University Press.

Luchaire, A. 1980. "Innocent III et le quatrième concile du Latran." *Revue historique* 97: 166–72.

Lunt, W. 1918. "The Sources for the First Council of Lyons. 1245." *English Historical Review* 33: 72–8.

Lustiger, J.-M. 1998. "Juifs et Chrétiens, demain?" *Nouvelle revue théologique* 120: 529–43.

Luther, M. 1883–1928. *Werke. Kritische Gesamtausgabe.* Weimar: Hermann Böhlaus Nachfolger.

Lyonnet, S. 1957–60. *De Peccato et Redemptione.* Vol. 1, *De Notione Peccati.* Vol. 2, *De Vocabulario Redemptionis.* Romae: Pontificium Institutum Biblicum.

MacDonald, M.Y. 1996. *Early Christian Women and Pagan Opinion.* New York: Oxford University Press.

McEnerey, J.I. 1987. *St. Cyril of Alexandria: Letters 1–50.* Washington, DC: Catholic University of America Press.

Mansi. J.D. 1889–1927. *Sacrorum Conciliorum Nova et Amplissima Collectio.* Paris: H. Welter.

Martin, E.J. 1978. *A History of the Iconoclastic Controversy.* New York: Macmillan.

Mayer, J., ed. 1938. *Monumenta de Viduis, Diaconissis Virginibusque Tractantia.* Bonn: Hanstein.

Mbiti, J.S. 1975. *African Religions and Philosophy.* London: Heinemann.

Meyendorf, J. 1970. *Marriage: An Orthodox Perspective.* Washington, DC: Corpus Books.

Michel, A. 1928. "La messe chez les théologians postérieux au concile de Trent: Essence et efficacité." In *Dictionnaire de théologie catholique,* 12: col. 1143–315. Paris: Libraire Letouzey et Ané.

Middleton, J. 1960. *Lugbara Religion: Ritual and Authority among an East African People.* Oxford: Oxford University Press.

Minnich, N. 1982. "Paride de Gravi's Diary of the Fifth Lateran Council." *Annuarium Historiae Conciliorum* 14: 370–460.

Moeller, C. 1951. "Le cinquième concile et le magistère ordinaire du 6ième siècle." *Revue des sciences philosophiques et théologiques* 35: 413–23.

Mohr, J.P. 1980. "Ultimate Reality and Symbols." *Ultimate Reality and Meaning* 3: 316–29

Moingt, J. 1968. "Le divorce pour motif d'impudicité: Matt 5, 32:19, 6." *Recherches de science religieuse* 56: 337–84.

Mollat, M., and P. Tombeur. 1974a. *Les conciles Latran I à Latran IV: Concordance, index, listes de fréquences, tables comparatives.* Conciles oecuméniques médiévaux. 1. Louvain: Université Catholique de Louvain.

– 1974b. *Les conciles Lyon I et Lyon II: Concordance, index, listes de fréquences, tables comparatives.* Conciles oecuméniques. Louvain: Université catholique de Louvain.

Moltmann, J. 1974. *The Crucified God.* London: SCM Press.

– 1981. *The Trinity of the Kingdom.* San Francisco: Harper and Row.

Montagnes, B. 1963. *La doctrine de l'analogie de l'être d'après S. Thomas.* Louvain: Publications Universitaires

Monumenta. 1929. *Monumenta Germaniae Historica. Scriptores* 2. Hannover: Impensis Bibliopoli Hahniani.

Morris, D. 1976. *The Naked Ape.* New York: McGraw Hill.

Morrison, K.F. 1978. *The Investiture Controversy: Issues, Ideals, and Results.* Huntington, NY: R.E. Krieger Pub. Co.

Mühlen, H. 1963. *Der Heilige Geist als Person: In der Trinität, bei der Inkarnation und im Gnadenbund.* Münster: Aschendorf.

– 1969. *Die Veränderlichkeit Gottes als Horizont einer zuküngftigen Christologie.* Münster: Aschendorf.

Muller, E. 1987. *Trinity and Marriage in Paul: Theological Shape as Ground for a Scrip-*

tural Warrant for a Communitarian Analogy of the Trinity. Ann Arbor, Mich.: University Microfilms International.

Murphy, F.X. 1974. *Constantinople II et Constantinople III.* Histoire des conciles oecuméniques. Paris: Editions de l'Orante.

NA: *Nostra Aetate,* Vatican II, 1962–64. *Declaration on the Church's Relation to Non-Christian Religions.* In *Decrees of the Ecumenical Councils,* edited by N.P. Tanner, 968–71. Washington, DC: Georgetown University Press, 1990.

Nasalli-Rocca, E. 1966. "Hospitals: History of Christian Hospital to 1500." In *New Catholic Encyclopedia,* 7, 159–63. New York: McGraw-Hill Book Company.

Nemeshegyi, P. 1960. *La paternité de Dieu chez Origène.* Paris: Desclée.

Neubauer, J. 1920. *Beiträge zur Geschichte der biblich-talmudischen Eheschliessungsrechtes.* Leipzig: Mitteilungen der Vorderasiatischen Gesellschaft.

Newman, J.H. 1833. *The Arians of the Fourth Century.* London: Pickering.

Nicholas I. 1963. "Responsa. 'Ad consulta vestra' ad Bulgaros, 13 Nov. 866." In *Enchiridion Symbolorum Definitionum et Declarationum de Rebus Fidei et Morum,* edited by H. Denzinger and A. Schönmetzer. New York: Herder.

OE: *Orientalium Ecclesiarum.* Vatican II, 1962–65. *Decree on the Eastern Catholic Churches.* In *Decrees of the Ecumenical Councils,* edited by N.P. Tanner, 900–7. Washington, DC: Georgetown University Press, 1990.

Ontario Status of Women Council. 1977. *About Face: Towards a Positive Image of Housewives.* Researched by Marianne Pringle. Toronto.

Origins: Catholic News Documentary. Washington, DC.

Orsy, L. 1978. *The Evolving Church and the Sacrament of Penance.* Denville, NJ: Dimension Books.

Ortiz de Urbina, I. 1963. *Nicée et Constantinople.* Histoire des conciles oecuméniques. Paris: Éditions de l'Orante.

Osborn, E.F. 1957. *The Philosophy of Clement of Alexandria.* New York; Cambridge: University Press.

– 1973. *Justin Martyr.* Tübingen: J.C.B. Mohr.

OT: *Optatam Totius.* Vatican II, 1962–65. *Decree on Priestly Formation.* In *Decrees of the Ecumenical Councils,* edited by N.P. Tanner, 947–59. Washington, DC: Georgetown University Press, 1990.

Ouspensky, L. 1976. *Theology of Icon.* Crestwood, NY: St. Vladimir's Seminary Press.

Pannenberg, W. 1969. *Theology and the Kingdom of God.* Philadelphia: The Westminster Press.

Paschen, W. 1970. *Rein und Unrein: Untersuchung zur biblischn Wortgeschichte.* München: Kösel.

Paul VI. 1967a. "Enchiridion Indulgentiarum."*Acta Apostolicae Sedis* 59: 5–24.

– 1967b. "Motu Proprio: Generales Normae de Diaconatu Permanente in Ecclesia Latina Restituendo Feruntur." *Acta Apostolicae Sedis* 59: 697–704.

– 1968. "Humanae Vitae." *Acta Apostolicae Sedis* 60: 481–503.

PC: *Perfectae Caritatis.* Vatican II, 1962–65. *Decree on the Sensitive Renewal of Religious Life.* In *Decrees of the Ecumenical Councils,* edited by N.P. Tanner, 939–68. Washington, DC: Georgetown University Press, 1990.

Pelikan, J. 1959. *The Riddle of Roman Catholicism: Its History, Its Beliefs, Its Future.* New York: Abingdon Press.

– 1965. *The Finality of Jesus Christ in an Age of Universal History: A Dilemma of the Third Century.* London: Lutterworth Press.

– 1971. *The Church Tradition.* Vol. 1, *The Emergence of the Catholic Tradition (100–600).* Chicago: University of Chicago Press.

– 1987. *Jesus through the Centuries: His Place in the History of Culture.* New York: Harper & Row.

Percival, H.R., ed. 1974. "The Third Council of Constantinople." In *The Seven Ecumenical Councils of the Undivided Church: Nicene and Post Nicene Fathers,* 14: 325–52. Grand Rapids: Eerdmans.

PG: *Patrologia Graeca.* Edited by J.P. Migne. Paris: Migne, 1857–66.

Physics Survey Committee, National Research Council. 1986. *Physics through the 1990s: An Overview.* Washington, DC: National Academy Press.

Pius XII. 1947. "Encyclical: Mediator Dei." *Acta Apostolicae Sedis* 39: 528–80.

– 1948. "Sacramentum Odinis: Constitutio Apostolica." *Acta Apostolicae Sedis* 40: 5–7.

PL: *Patrologia Latina.* Edited by J.P. Migne. Paris: Migne, 1878–90.

PO: *Presbyterorum Ordinis.* Vatican II, 1962–65. *Decree on the Ministry and Life of Priests.* In *Decrees of the Ecumenical Councils,* edited by N.P. Tanner, 1042–69. Washington, DC: Georgetown University Press, 1990.

Polanyi, M. 1958. *Personal Knowledge: Towards a Post-critical Philosophy.* Chicago: University of Chicago Press.

Polkinghorne, John P. 1996. *Scientists as Theologians: A Comparison of the Writings of Ian Barbour, Arthur Peacocke and John Polkinghorne.* London: SPCK.

– 2001. *Faith, Science, and Understanding.* New Haven: Yale University Press.

Pollard, T.E. 1958. "The Origin of Arius." *Journal of Theological Studies* 9. 103–11.

Polle, R.L. 1923. "The English Bishops at the Lateran Concil of 1139." *English Historical Review* 3: 61–3.

Poschmann, B. 1948. *Der Ablass im Licht der Bussgeschichte.* Bonn: Hanstein.

– 1964. *Penance and the Anointing of the Sick.* Translated by F. Courteny. New York: Herder and Herder.

Pottmeyer, H.J. 1968. *Der Glaube vor dem Anspruch der Wissenschaft: Die Konstitution "Dei Filius" des I Vatikanisches Konzils.* Freiburg: Herder.

Powers, J.M. 1967. *Eucharistic Theology.* New York: Herder.

Pseudo-Dionysius. 1987. *The Complete Works.* Translated by Colm Luibheid. The Classics of Western Spirituality. New York: Paulist Press.

Quell, G. 1985. "ἀγαπάω." In *Biblical Dictionary of the New Testament,* edited by G. Kittel, 1: 21–35. Grand Rapids: Eerdmans Publishing Co.

Rahner, K. 1962. "The Episcopate and the Primacy." In *The Episcopate and Primacy,* edited by K. Rahner and J. Ratzinger, 20–30. New York: Herder.

– 1963. *The Church and the Sacraments.* New York: Herder.

– 1966a. *Spiritual Exercises.* New York: Herder and Herder.

– 1966b."Theology of Symbols." *Theological Investigations* 4: 221–52.

– 1969. "Beatific Vision." In *Sacramentum Mundi,* 1: 151–3. Montreal: Palm Publishers.

– 1970. *Trinity.* New York: Herder,

– 1975. "Sacrament of Penance." In *Encyclopedia of Theology: The Concise Sacramentum Mundi,* edited by K. Rahner, 1189–204. New York: The Seabury Press.

Raynal, W. 1871. *The Ordinal of King Edward VI: Its History, Theology and Liturgy.* London: T. Richardson and Son.

Rengstorf, K.H. 1985. "ἀπόστολος." In *Biblical Dictionary of the New Testament.* Edited by G. Kittel, 1: 424–45. Grand Rapids: Eerdmans Publishing Company.

Ritter, A.M. 1965. *Das Konzil von Konstantinopel und sein Symbol.* Göttigen: Vandenhoeck & Ruprecht.

Royce, J. 1913. *The Problem of Christianity.* New York: Macmillian Co.

Sabourin, L. 1961. *Redemption sacrificielle.* Paris: Desclée.

– 1973. *Priesthood: A Comparative Study.* Leiden: Brill.

Sanders, J. 1971. *The New Testament Christological Hymns.* Cambridge: Cambridge University Press.

SC: *Sacrosanctum Concilium,* Vatican II, 1962–65. *Constitution on the Sacred Liturgy.* In *Decrees of the Ecumenical Councils,* edited by N.P. Tanner, 820–43. Washington, DC: Georgetown University Press, 1990.

Schaff, P. 1974. *A Select Library of the Nicene and Post-Nicene Fathers of the Christian Church.* 14 vols. Grand Rapids: Eerdmans Publishing Co.

Scheeben, M. 1946. *The Mysteries of Christianity.* St Louis: Herder and Herder.

Schepens, P. 1924. "Sententia Suarezii de esentia Sacrifici Missae." *Gregorianum* 5: 94–102.

Schermann, T. 1910. "Das 'Brotbrechen' im Urchristentum." *Biblische Zeitschrift* 8: 33–52, 162–83.

Schillebeeckx, E. 1963. *Christ the Sacrament of Encounter with God.* New York: Paulist Press.

– 1982. "Transsubstantiation, Transfiguration, Transsignification." In *Living Bread, Saving Cup: Readings in the Eucharist,* edited by R.K. Seasoltz, 131–93. Collegeville: Liturgical Press.

Schlitt, D.M. 1984. *Hegel's Trinitarian Claim: A Critical Reflection.* Leiden: Brill.

Schmidt, W. 1922. "Ethnologische Bemerkungen zu theologischen Opfertheorien." *Jahrbuch des Missionshauses St. Gabriel* 1: 2–57.

Schneider, G. 1982. *Die Apostelgeschichte.* Freiburg: Herder.

– 1992. *Jesusübelieferung und Christologie: Neutestamentliche Aufsätze, 1970–1990.* Leiden: Brill.

Schoeck, R. 1981. "The Fifth Lateran Council: Its Partial Successes and Its Larger Failures." In *Reform and Authority in the Medieval and Reformation Church,* edited by G. Little, 99–116. Washington, DC: Catholic University Press.

Schönborn, C. von. 1976. *L'icône du Christ: Fondements théologiques élaborés entre Ier et le IIe Concile de Nicée (325–387).* Fribourg: Éditions universitaires.

Schroeder, H.J. 1937. *Disciplinary Decrees of the General Councils.* St Louis: Herder.

– 1967. *Canons and Decrees of the Council of Trent.* New York: Herder and Herder.

Schwartz, E. 1922–40. *Acta Conciliorum Oecumenicorum.* Berlin: W. de Gruyter.

Schweid, E. 1991. "The Holocaust as a Challenge to Jewish Thoughts on Ultimate Reality and Meaning." *Ultimate Reality and Meaning.* 14: 185–209.

Scipioni, L.I. 1974. *Nestorio e il concilio de Epheso.* Milan: Vita e Pensiero.

Sellers, R.V. 1953. *The Council of Chalcedon: A Historical and Doctrinal Survey.* London: SPCK.

Sendler, E. 1981. *L'icône, image de l'Invisible: Élements de théologie, esthétique et techniques.* Paris: Desclée.

Shea, J. 1923. "How Is the Mass a True Sacrifice?" *Ecclesiastical Review* 69: 633–6.

Sieben, H.J. 1979. *Die Konzilidee der Alten Kirche.* Paderborn: F. Schöningh.

Smith, W.R. (1889) 1959. *The Religion of the Semites.* New York: Meridian Library.

– 1962. "Sacrifice." In *Encyclopaedia Britannica,* 14th ed., 19: 802–5.

Sola, F.A. 1962. "De Sacramento Ordinis et Marimonii." In *Sacrae Theologiae Summa,* 4: 571–824. Madrid: Biblioteca de Autores Cristianos.

Solano, J. 1952. *Textos Eucharisticos primitivos.* Madrid: BAC.

Spencer, H. 1885. *Principles of Sociology.* Westport, Conn.: Greenwood.

Spinka, M. 1965. *John Hus at the Council of Constance.* New York: Columbia University Press.

Splett, J., and L.B. Puntel, 1968. "Analogy of Being." In *Sacramentum Mundi* 1: 21–5. Montreal: Palm Publishers.

Stanley, D.M. 1958. "The Divinity of Christ in Hymns of the New Testament." In *Proceeding of the Fourth Annual Convention of the Catholic College Teachers of Sacred Doctrine,* 4: 12–29.

– 1961. *Christ's Resurrection in Pauline Soteriology.* Rome: Gregorian University Press.

Stauffer, E. 1969. "*ἀγαπάω.*" In *Biblical Dictionary of the New Testament,* edited by G. Kittel, 1: 21–55. Grand Rapids: Eerdmans Publishing Co.

Stead, G.S. 1964. "The Platonism of Arius."*Journal of Theological Studies* 15: 16–31.

Stiernon, D. 1967. *Constantinople IV.* Histoire des conciles oecuméniques. Paris: Éditions de l'Orante.

Stiglmayr, J. 1919. "Mannigfache Bedeuting in 'Theologie' und 'Theologen.'" *Theologie und Glaube* 1: 296–309.

Story, C.I.K. 1981. "Ultimate Reality and 'The Gospel of Truth.'" *Ultimate Reality and Meaning* 4: 279–96.

Strack, H.L., and P. Billerbeck. 1926. *Kommentar zum neuen Testament aus Talmud und Midrasch.* München: O. Beck.

Tanner, N.P., ed. 1990. *Decrees of the Ecumenical Councils.* Washington, DC: Georgetown University Press.

Teller, E. 1969. "Niels Bohr and the Idea of Complementarity." In *Great Men of Physics,* edited by E. Teller et al., 78–97. Los Angeles: Timon-Brown.

– 1980. *The Pursuit of Simplicity.* Malibu, Calif.: Pepperdine University.

Teller, E., Teller, W. and W. Talley, 1991. *Conversations on the Dark Secrets of Physics.* New York: Plenum Press.

Teresa of Avila.1971. *Selected Writings.* Arranged by J. Pons. New York: Vantage Press.

Tertullian. 1954. *Corpus Scriptorum Ecclesisticorum Latinorum.* Edited by J.G.Ph. Borleffs and A. Kroymann. Turnholt: Brepolis.

Theodore of Mopsuestia. 1933. *Commentary on the Lord's Prayer and on the Sacraments of Baptism and Eucharist.* Edited by A. Mingana. Woodsbrooke Studies, vol. 6. Cambridge: W. Heffer and Sons.

Thomas Aquinas. 1929. *Scriptum super Libros Sententiarum.* Paris: Lethielleux.

– 1948. *Summa theologiae.* Torino: Marietti.

– 1934. *Summa contra gentiles.* Roma: Apud sedem commissionis Leoninae.

Thomson, R.J. 1963. *Penitence and Sacrifice in Early Israel Outside the Levitical Law: An Examination of the Fellowship Theory of Early Israelite Sacrifice.* Leiden: Brill.

Tillard, J.M. R. 1967. *The Eucharist, Pasch of God's People.* New York: Alba House.

Toman, W. 1979. "Defense, Defense-Mechanism." In *Encyclopedia of Psychology*, edited by J.J. Eyseneck, W. Arnold, and R. Meili, 252. New York: Seabury Press.

Tylor, E.B. 1958. I. *The Origins of Culture.* Vol. 2, *Religion in Primitive Culture.* New York: Peter Smith.

URAM: *Ultimate Reality and Meaning: Interdisciplinary Studies in the Philosophy of Understanding.* Toronto: University of Toronto Press, 1978–.

UR: *Unitatis Redintegratio.* Vatican II, 1962–65. *Decree on Ecumenism.* In *Decrees of the Ecumenical Councils*, edited by N.P.Tanner, 908–20. Washington, DC: Georgetown University Press, 1990.

van der Leeuw, G. 1920–21. " Die *do-ut-des* Formel in der Opfertheorie." *Archiv für Religionswissenschaft* 20–1: 241–53.

Van Iersel, B.M.F. 1961. *"Der Sohn" in den synoptischn Jesusworten.* Leiden: Brill.

Van Roo, G. 1957. *De Sacramentis in Genere.* Roma: Gregorian University Press.

Veder, H. (1928) 1966. "The Herero." In *The Native Tribes of South West Africa*, edited by C.H.L. Hahn, H. Veder, and L.Tourie, 153–208. New York: Barnes and Noble.

Vernet, F. 1925. "Latran III." In *Dictionnaire de théologie catholique*, vol. 8, pt. 2, col. 2649. Paris: Letouzey et Ané.

Vorgrimler, H.E. 1967. *Commentary with the Documents of Vatican II.* New York: Herder and Herder.

– 1978. *Busse und Krankensalbung.* Handbuch der Dogmengeschichte, Bd. 4, Fasz 3. Freiburg: Herder.

– 1992. *Sacramental Theology.* Collegeville: Liturgical Press.

Wanamaker, C.A. 1999. "The Conversion of Jesus' Disciples and the Emergence of Christianity." *Journal of Theology for Southern Africa* 104: 16–31.

Wasserman, D. 1966. *Man of La Mancha: A Musical Play.* New York: Random House.

Wengst, K. 1972. *Christologische Formeln und Lieder des Urchristentums.* Gütterloch: Güterlocher Verlagshaus.

Whitehead, A.N. 1929. *Process and Reality: An Essay in Cosmology.* Cambridge: Cambridge University Press.

Wiles, M. 1962. "In Defense of Arius." *Journal of Theological Studies* 13: 339–47.

Wolter, H., and H. Holstein. 1966. *Lyon I et Lyon II*. Histoire des conciles oecuméniques. Paris: Éditions de l'Orante.

Young, F. 1983. *From Nicaea to Chalcedon*. Philadelphia: Fortress Press.

Ziegenaus, A. 1975. "Ausdehnung der Spendevollmacht der Krankensalbung?" *Münchener Theologische Zeitschrift* 26: 345–63.

Zielinsky, V. 1999. "Le mystère de Marie, source d'unité." *Nouvelle revue théologique* 121: 72–91.

Zizioulas, J.D. 1983. "The Teaching of the 2nd Ecumenical Council on the Holy Spirit in Historical and Ecumenical Perspective." In *Credo in Spiritum Sanctum*, 29–54. Vatican City: Libreria Editrice Vaticana.

Žužek, I. 1989. "The *Ecclesiae Sui Iuris* in the Revision of Canon Law." In *Vatican II: Assessment and Perspectives*, edited by R. Latourelle, 3: 288–304. Mahwah, NJ: Paulist Press.

Index